O-Parts Hunter

SEISHI KISHIMOTO

11

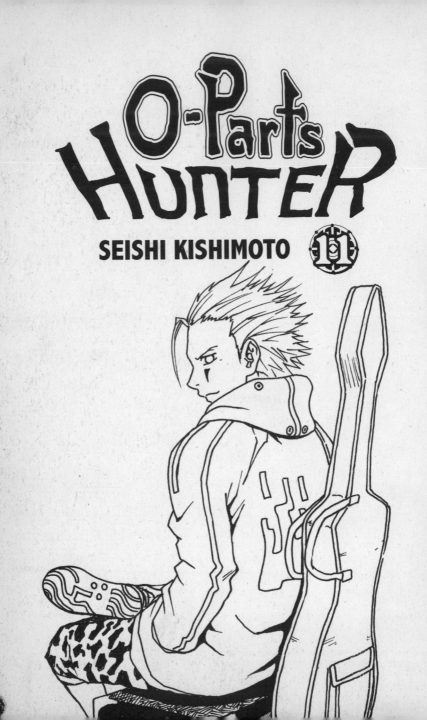

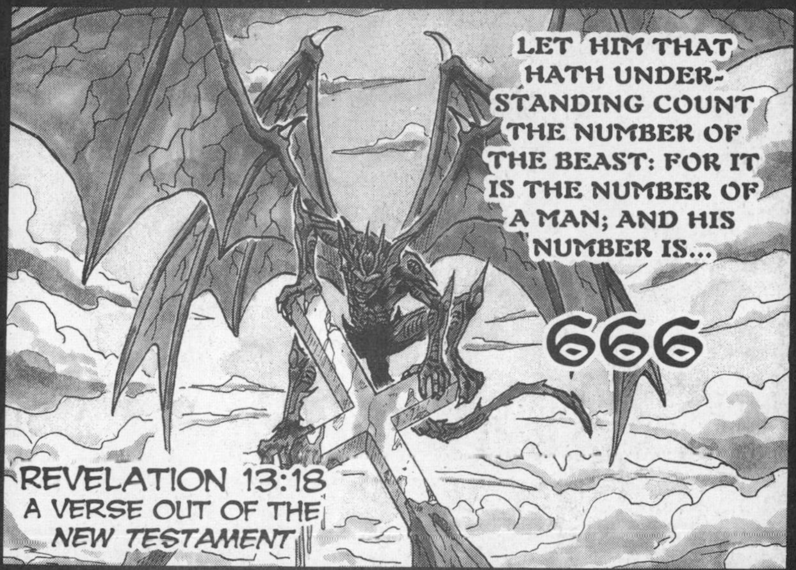
LET HIM THAT HATH UNDER-STANDING COUNT THE NUMBER OF THE BEAST: FOR IT IS THE NUMBER OF A MAN; AND HIS NUMBER IS...
666
REVELATION 13:18
A VERSE OUT OF THE *NEW TESTAMENT*

O-Parts Hunter

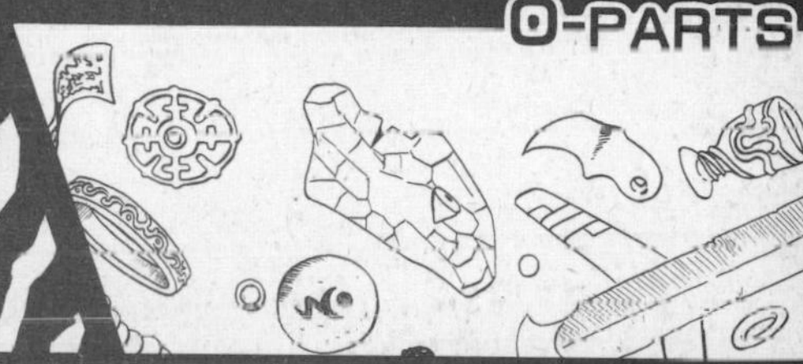
O-PARTS

O-Parts: Amazing artifacts with mystical powers left from an ancient civilization. They have been excavated from various ruins around the world. Depending on their Effects, O-Parts are given a rank from E to SS within a seven-tiered system.

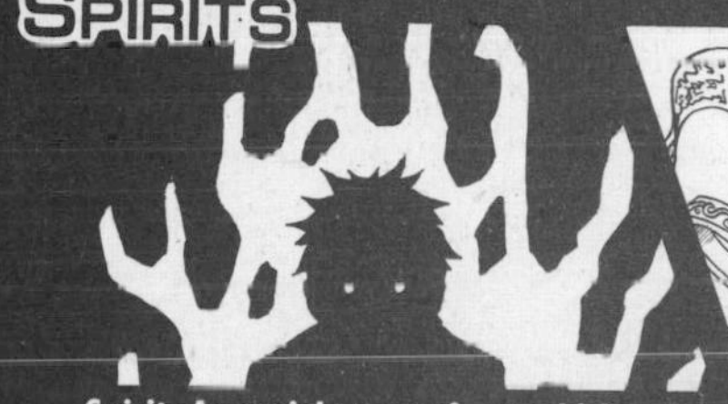
SPIRITS

Spirit: A special energy force which only the O.P.T.s have. The amount of Spirit they have within them determines how strong of an O.P.T. they are.

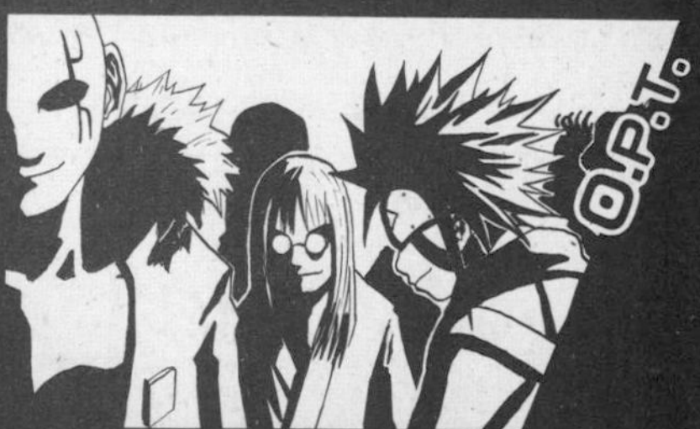
O.P.T.

O.P.T.: One who has the ability to release and use the powers of the O-Parts. The name O.P.T. is an abbreviated form of O-Part Tactician.

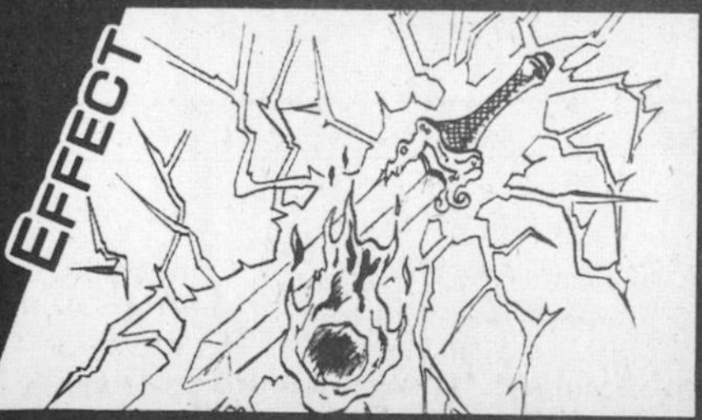
EFFECT

Effect: The special energy (power) the O-Parts possess. It can only be used when an O.P.T. sends his Spirit into an O-Part.

CHARACTERS

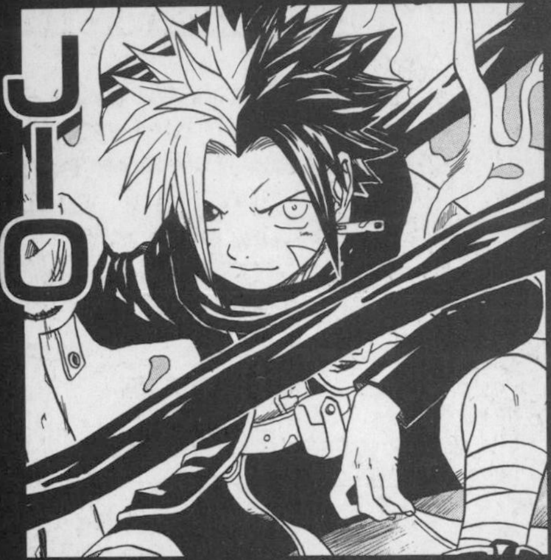
JIO

Jio Freed
A wild O.P.T. boy whose dream is world domination! He has been emotionally damaged by his experiences in the past, but is still gung-ho about his new adventures! O-Part: New Zero-shiki (Rank B)
Effect: Triple (Increasing power by a factor of three)

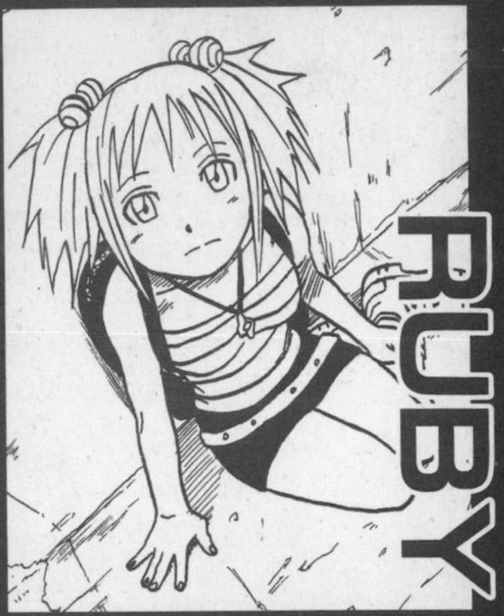
RUBY

Ruby
A treasure hunter who can decipher ancient texts. She meets Jio during her search for a legendary O-Part.

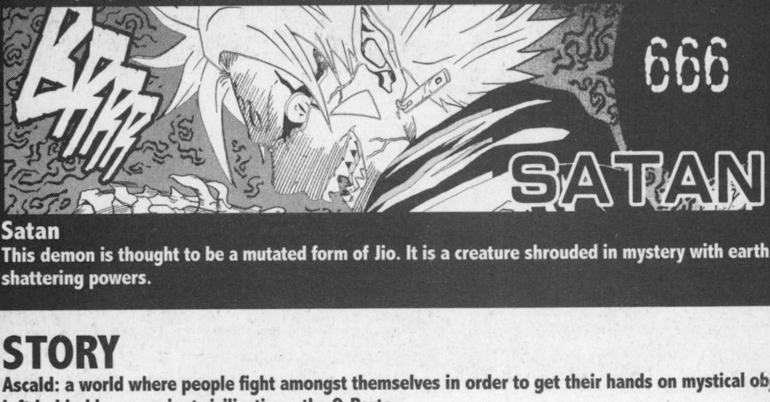
666
SATAN

Satan
This demon is thought to be a mutated form of Jio. It is a creature shrouded in mystery with earth-shattering powers.

STORY

Ascald: a world where people fight amongst themselves in order to get their hands on mystical objects left behind by an ancient civilization...the O-Parts.

In that world, a monster that strikes fear into the hearts of the strongest of men is rumored to exist. Those who have seen the monster all tell of the same thing–that the number of the beast, 666, is engraved on its forehead.

***

Jio, an O.P.T. boy who wants to rule the world, travels the globe with Ball, a novice O.P.T., and Ruby, a girl searching for a legendary O-Part and her missing father. On a quest to find the Kabbalah before the Stea Government can use it to dominate the world, Jio's team stumbles onto the city of Rock Bird, where Olympia, a deadly world tournament for O.P.T.s, is being held. There Jio encounters some very interesting contestants: Michael, an angel of the Kabbalah; Yuria, a young girl whose O-Part turns out to be Lucifuge, a demon of the Reverse Kabbalah; and Jin, a long-lost childhood friend of Jio's...who, in the tournament's latest round, just got stabbed through the chest.

O-Parts HUNTER

11

Table of Contents

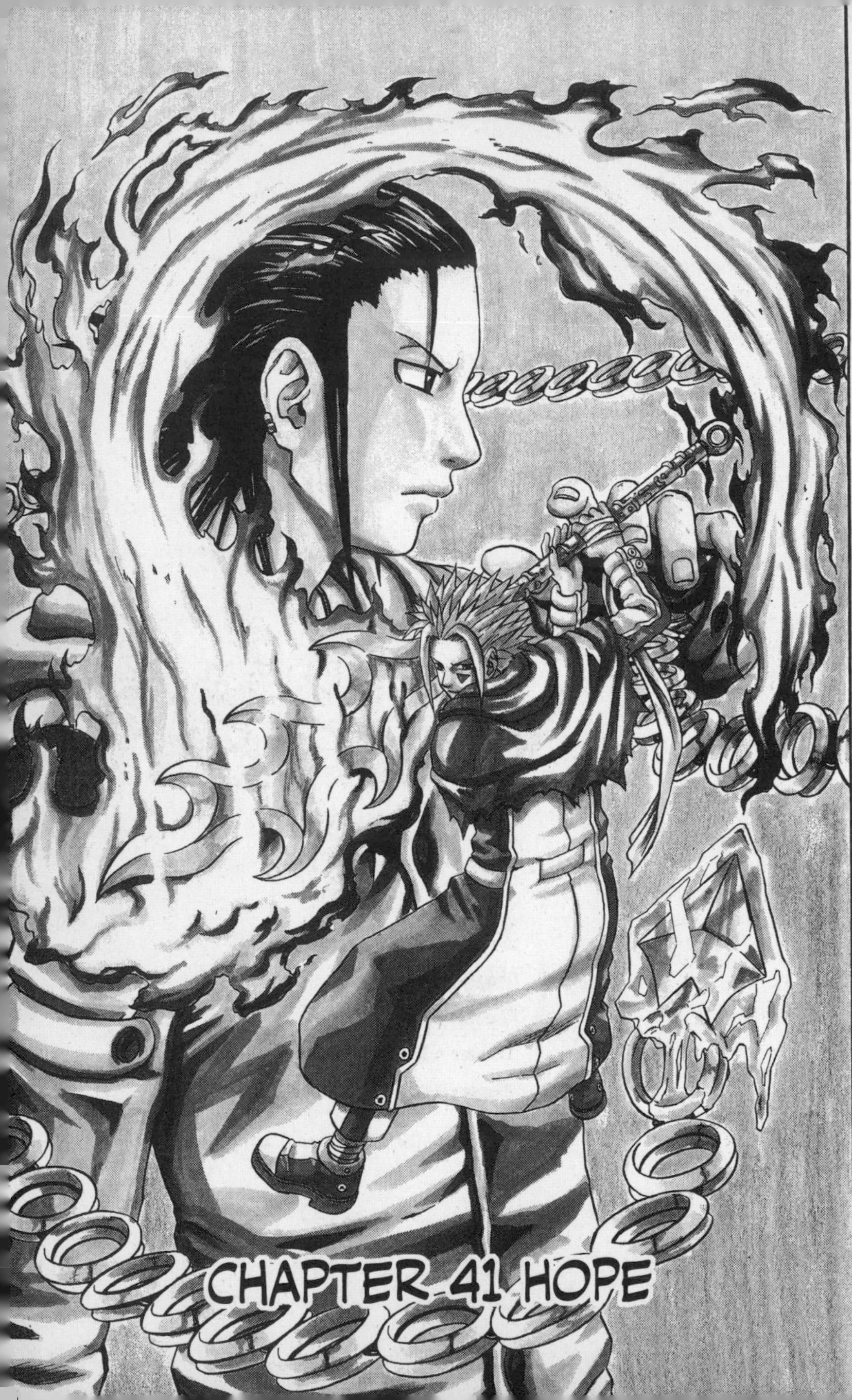
CHAPTER 41 HOPE

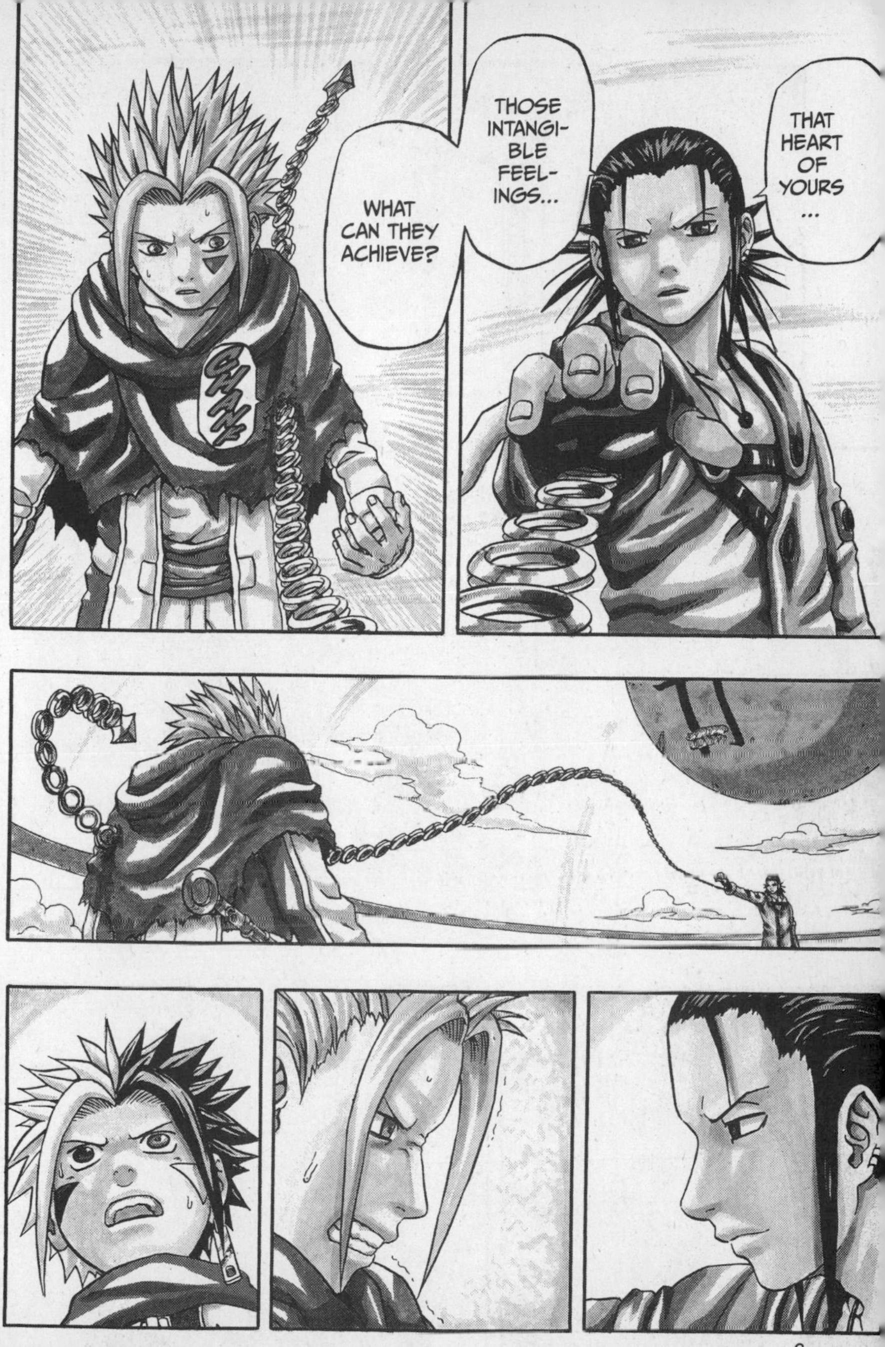
THAT HEART OF YOURS ...
THOSE INTANGI-BLE FEEL-INGS...
WHAT CAN THEY ACHIEVE?
CHAK

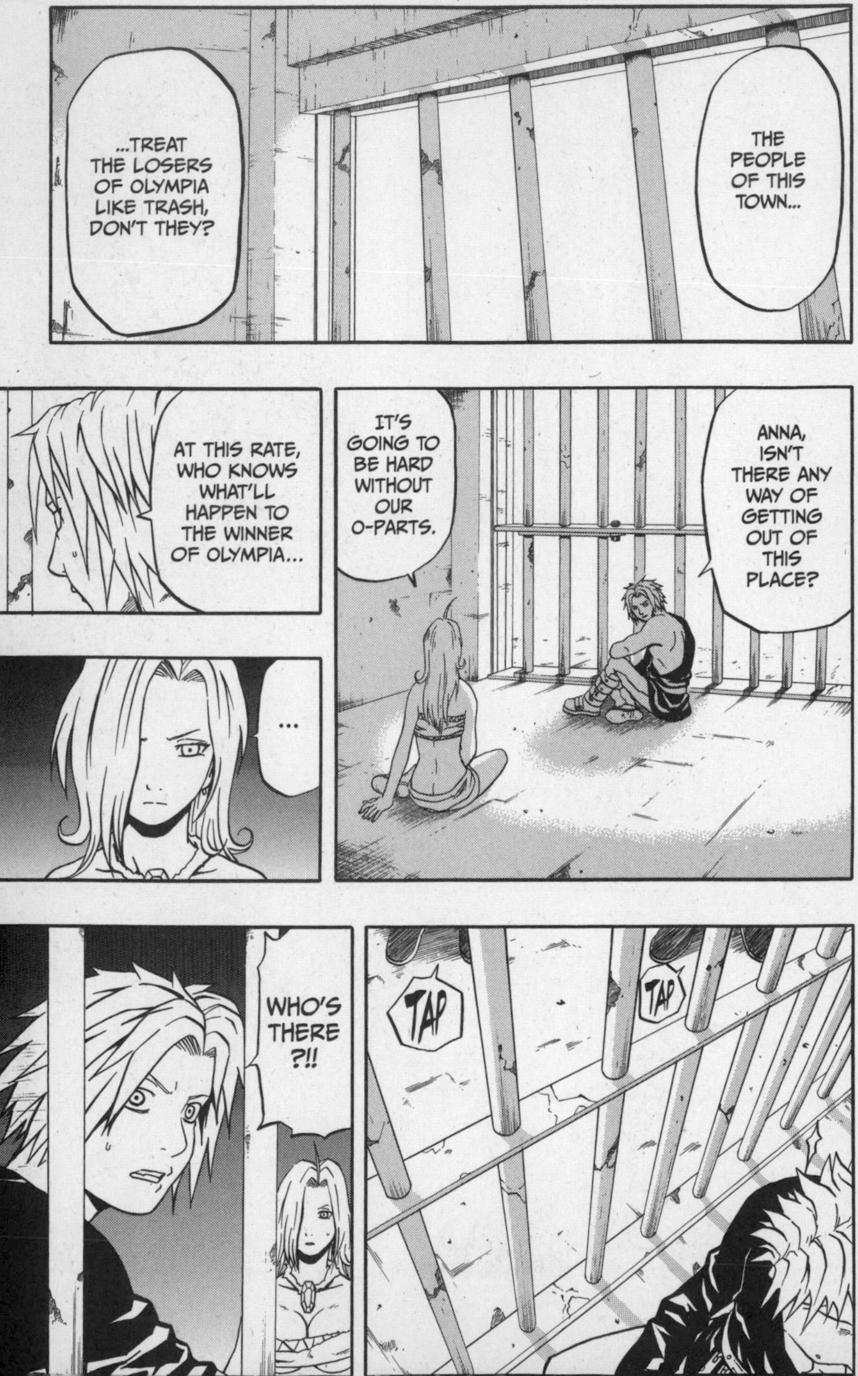
THE PEOPLE OF THIS TOWN...
...TREAT THE LOSERS OF OLYMPIA LIKE TRASH, DON'T THEY?
ANNA, ISN'T THERE ANY WAY OF GETTING OUT OF THIS PLACE?
IT'S GOING TO BE HARD WITHOUT OUR O-PARTS.
AT THIS RATE, WHO KNOWS WHAT'LL HAPPEN TO THE WINNER OF OLYMPIA...
...
TAP
TAP
WHO'S THERE ?!!

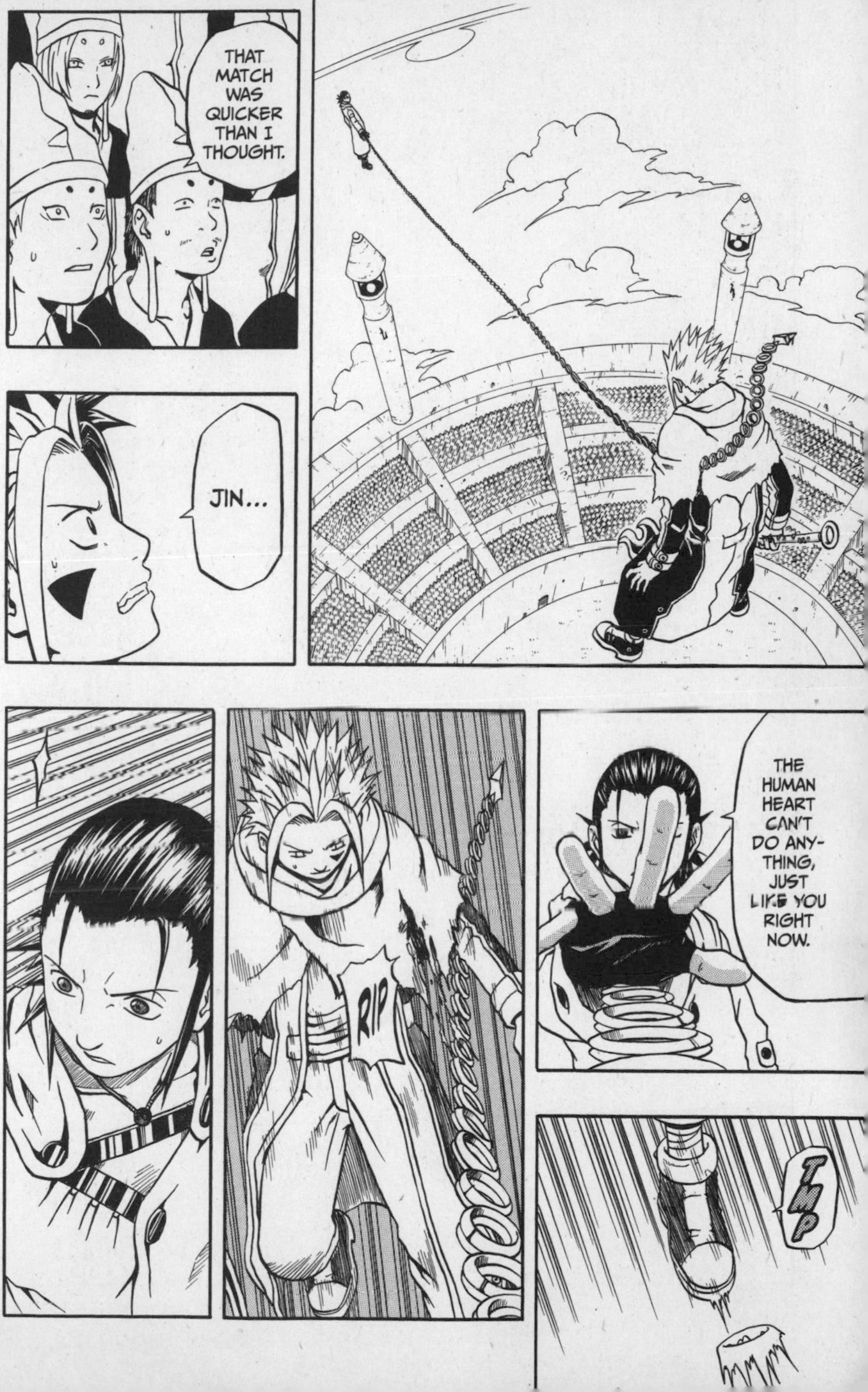
THAT MATCH WAS QUICKER THAN I THOUGHT.
JIN...
THE HUMAN HEART CAN'T DO ANY-THING, JUST LIKE YOU RIGHT NOW.
TMP

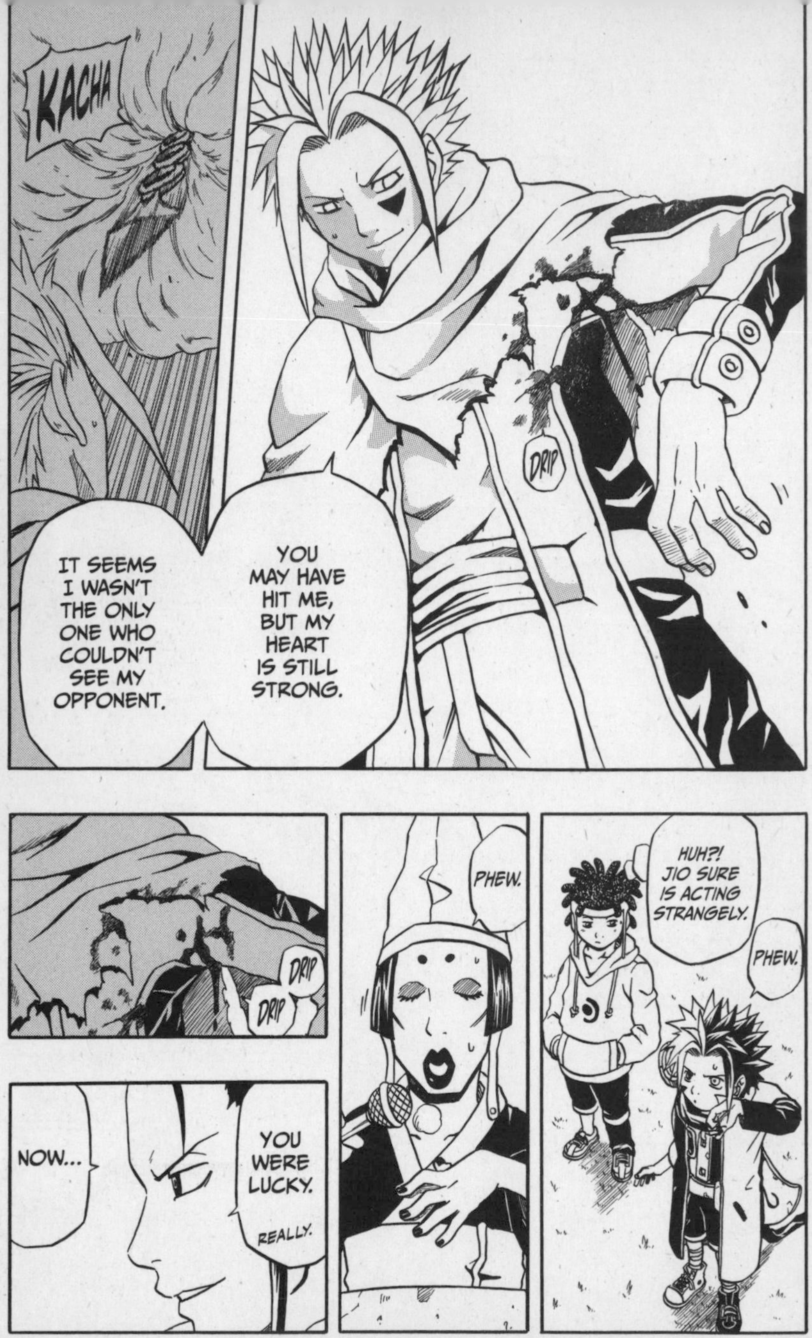
KACHA
DRIP
YOU MAY HAVE HIT ME, BUT MY HEART IS STILL STRONG.
IT SEEMS I WASN'T THE ONLY ONE WHO COULDN'T SEE MY OPPONENT.
HUH?! JIO SURE IS ACTING STRANGELY.
PHEW.
PHEW.
DRIP
DRIP
YOU WERE LUCKY.
REALLY.
NOW...

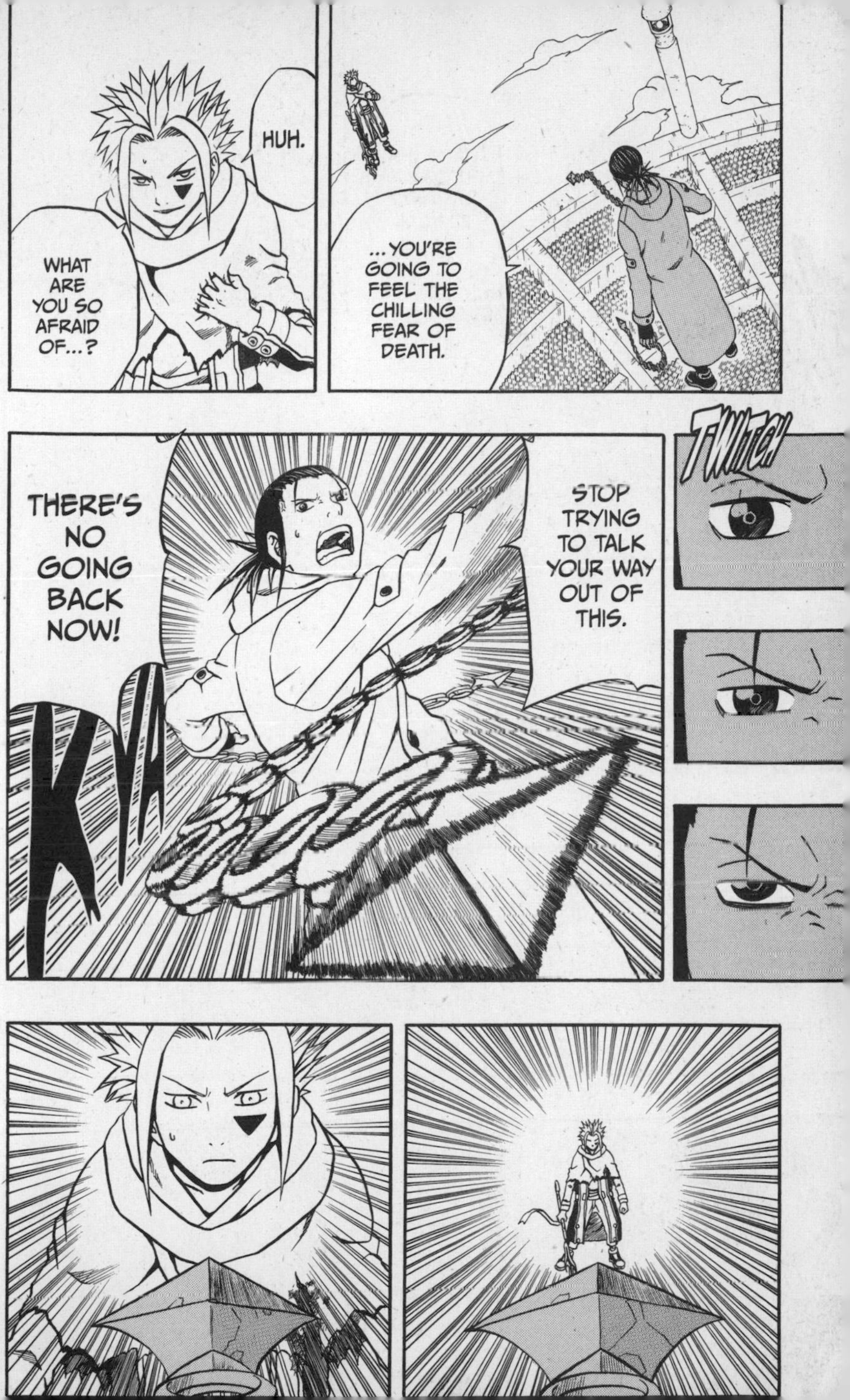
...YOU'RE GOING TO FEEL THE CHILLING FEAR OF DEATH.
HUH.
WHAT ARE YOU SO AFRAID OF...?
TWITCH
STOP TRYING TO TALK YOUR WAY OUT OF THIS.
THERE'S NO GOING BACK NOW!
KYA

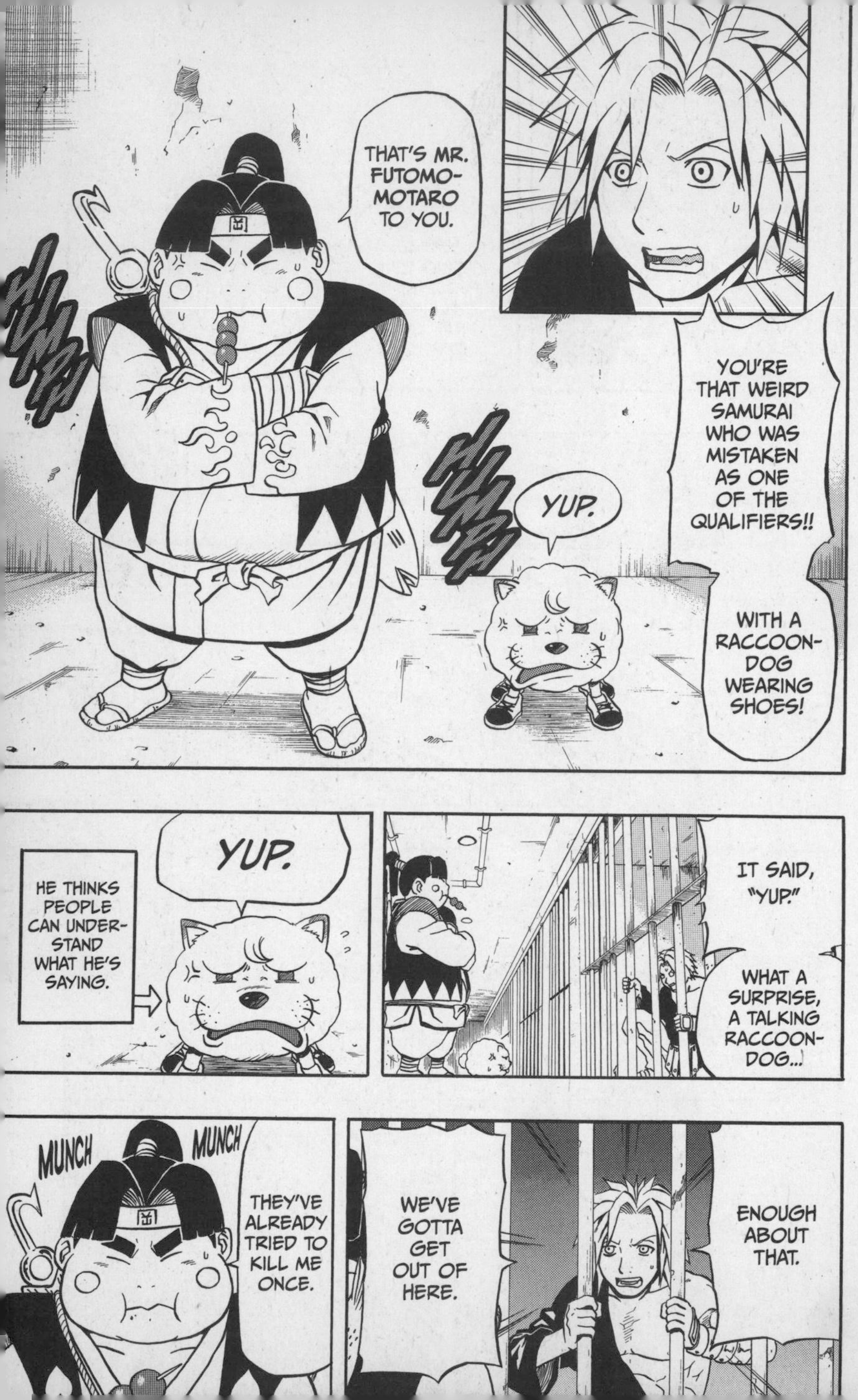
YOU'RE THAT WEIRD SAMURAI WHO WAS MISTAKEN AS ONE OF THE QUALIFIERS!!
WITH A RACCOON-DOG WEARING SHOES!
THAT'S MR. FUTOMO-MOTARO TO YOU.
YUP.
IT SAID, "YUP."
WHAT A SURPRISE, A TALKING RACCOON-DOG...
YUP.
HE THINKS PEOPLE CAN UNDER-STAND WHAT HE'S SAYING.
ENOUGH ABOUT THAT.
WE'VE GOTTA GET OUT OF HERE.
THEY'VE ALREADY TRIED TO KILL ME ONCE.
MUNCH
MUNCH

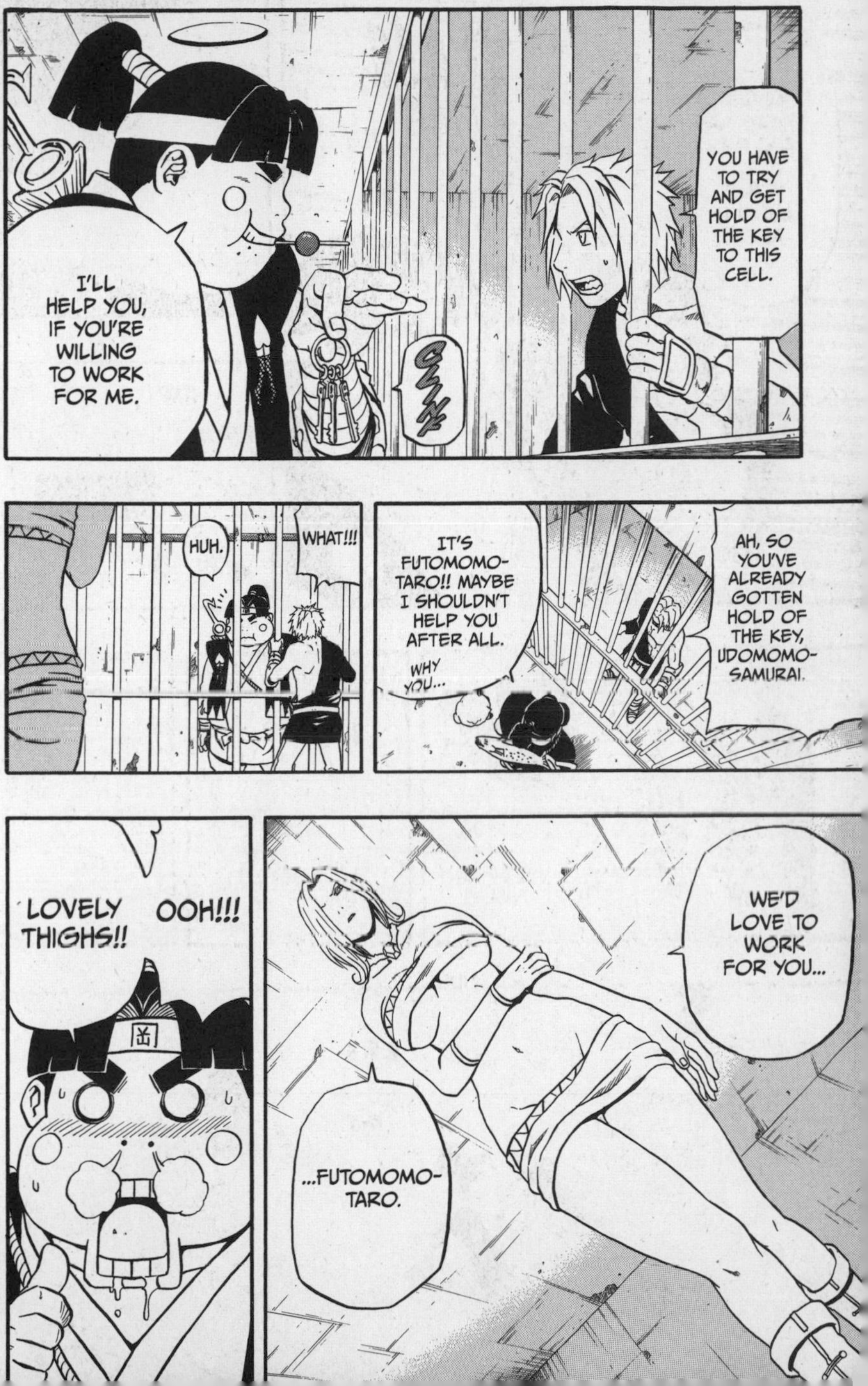
YOU HAVE TO TRY AND GET HOLD OF THE KEY TO THIS CELL.
I'LL HELP YOU, IF YOU'RE WILLING TO WORK FOR ME.
AH, SO YOU'VE ALREADY GOTTEN HOLD OF THE KEY, UDOMOMO-SAMURAI.
IT'S FUTOMOMO-TARO!! MAYBE I SHOULDN'T HELP YOU AFTER ALL.
WHY YOU...
WHAT!!!
HUH.
WE'D LOVE TO WORK FOR YOU...
...FUTOMOMO-TARO.
OOH!!!
LOVELY THIGHS!!

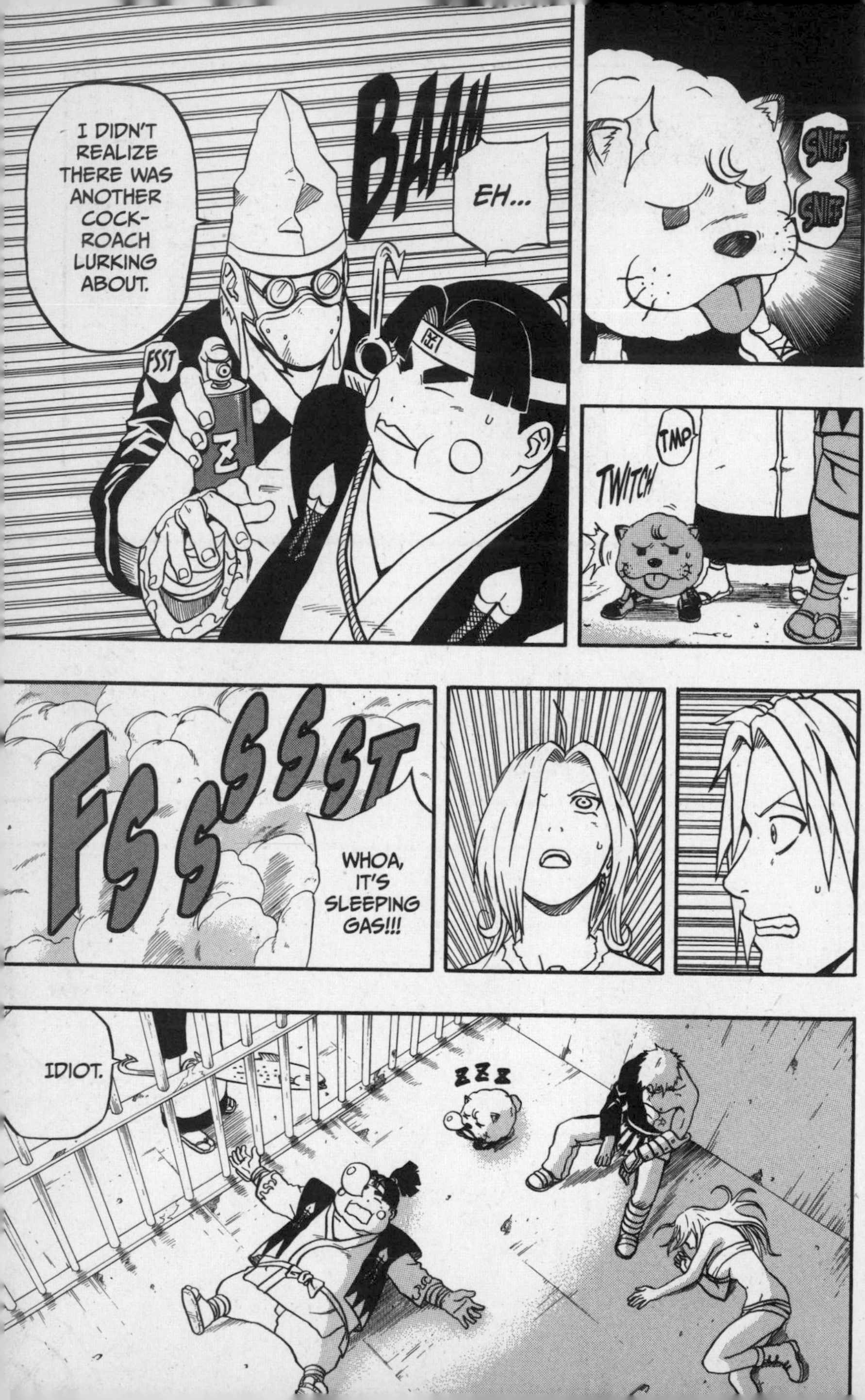
SNIFF
SNIFF
TMP
TWITCH
BAAM
EH...
I DIDN'T REALIZE THERE WAS ANOTHER COCK-ROACH LURKING ABOUT.
FSST
FSSSSST
WHOA, IT'S SLEEPING GAS!!!
IDIOT.
Z Z Z

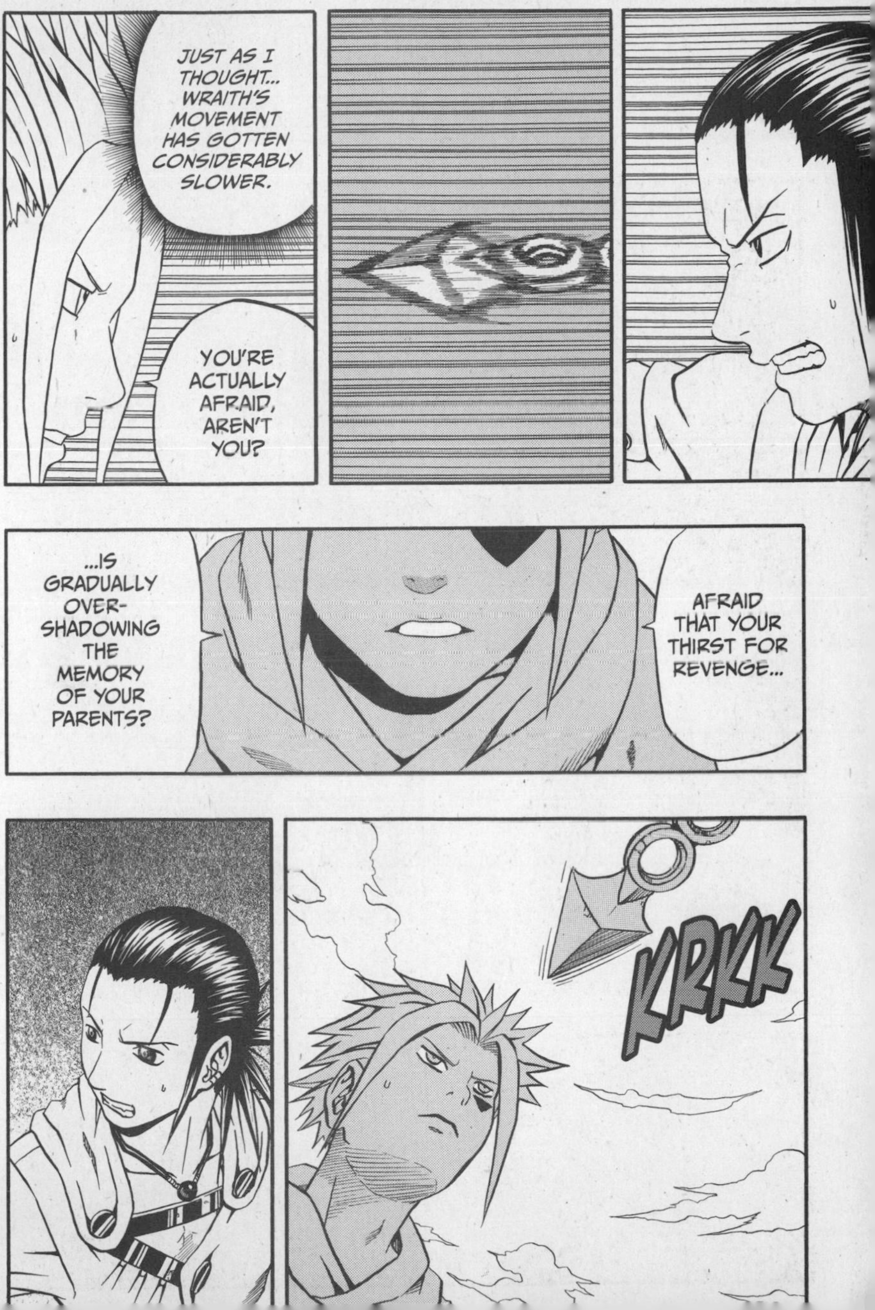
JUST AS I THOUGHT... WRAITH'S MOVEMENT HAS GOTTEN CONSIDERABLY SLOWER.
YOU'RE ACTUALLY AFRAID, AREN'T YOU?
AFRAID THAT YOUR THIRST FOR REVENGE...
...IS GRADUALLY OVER-SHADOWING THE MEMORY OF YOUR PARENTS?
KRKK

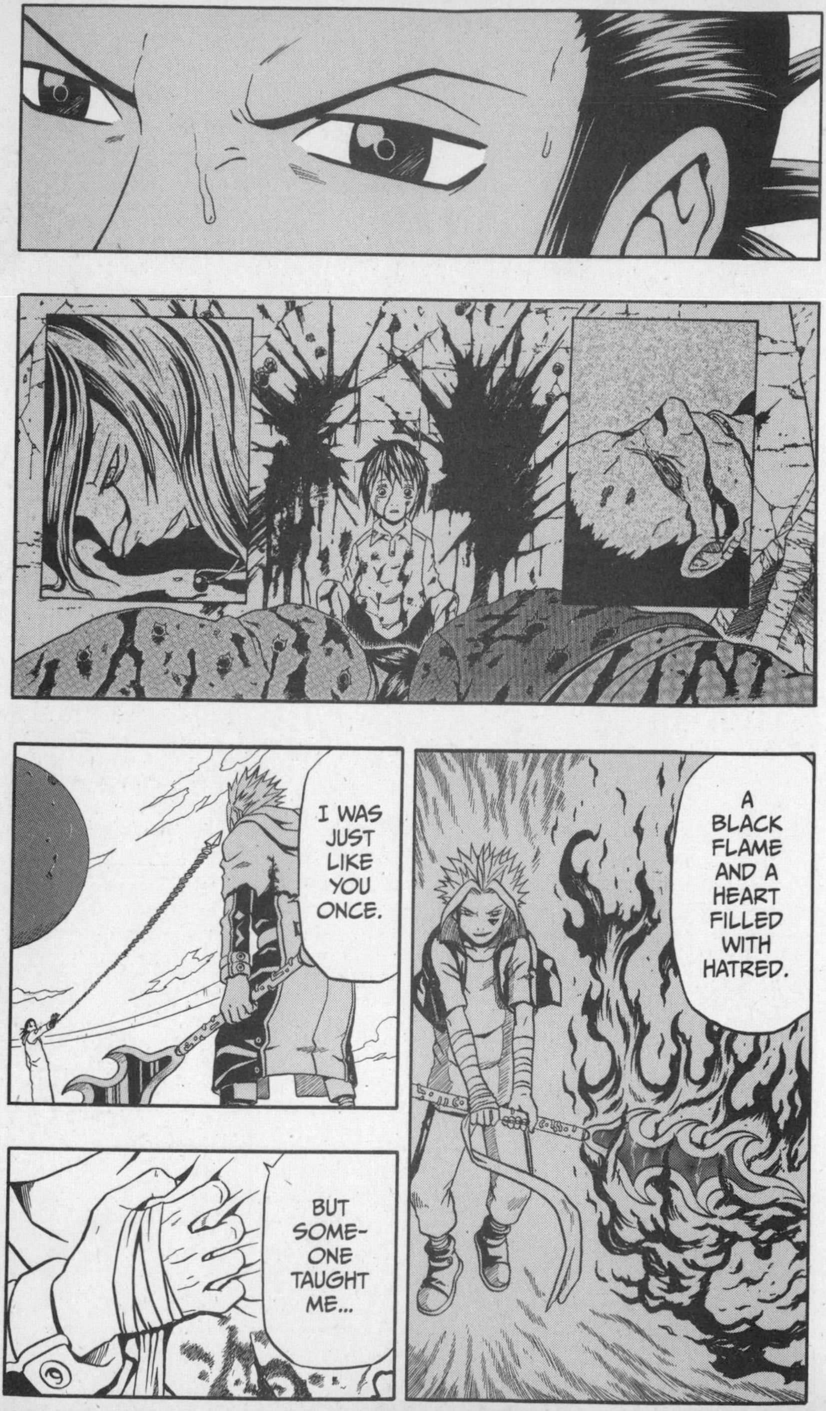
A BLACK FLAME AND A HEART FILLED WITH HATRED.
I WAS JUST LIKE YOU ONCE.
BUT SOME-ONE TAUGHT ME...

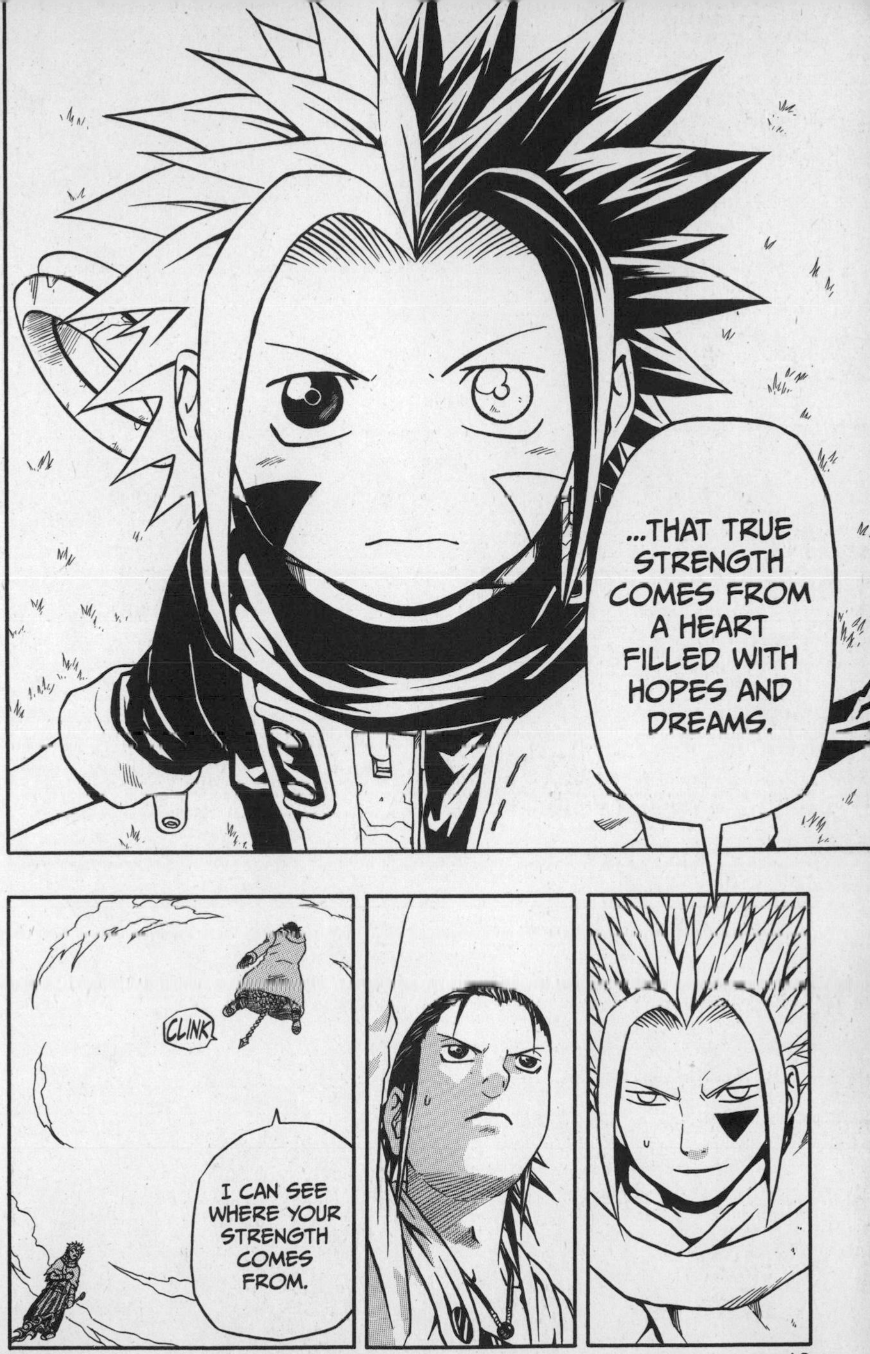
...THAT TRUE STRENGTH COMES FROM A HEART FILLED WITH HOPES AND DREAMS.
CLINK
I CAN SEE WHERE YOUR STRENGTH COMES FROM.

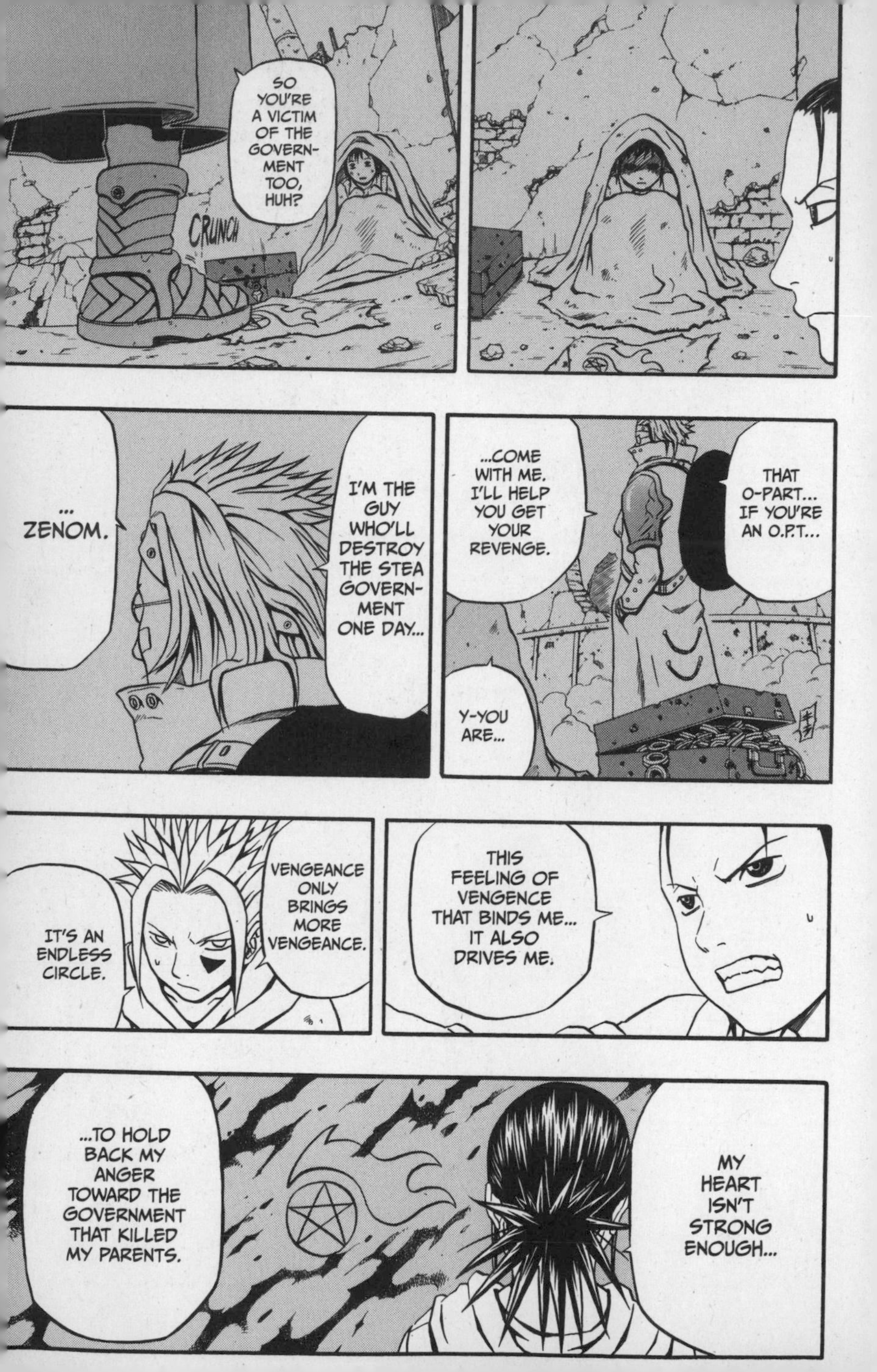
SO YOU'RE A VICTIM OF THE GOVERNMENT TOO, HUH?
CRUNCH
THAT O-PART... IF YOU'RE AN O.P.T...
...COME WITH ME. I'LL HELP YOU GET YOUR REVENGE.
Y-YOU ARE...
I'M THE GUY WHO'LL DESTROY THE STEA GOVERNMENT ONE DAY...
... ZENOM.
THIS FEELING OF VENGENCE THAT BINDS ME... IT ALSO DRIVES ME.
VENGEANCE ONLY BRINGS MORE VENGEANCE.
IT'S AN ENDLESS CIRCLE.
MY HEART ISN'T STRONG ENOUGH...
...TO HOLD BACK MY ANGER TOWARD THE GOVERNMENT THAT KILLED MY PARENTS.

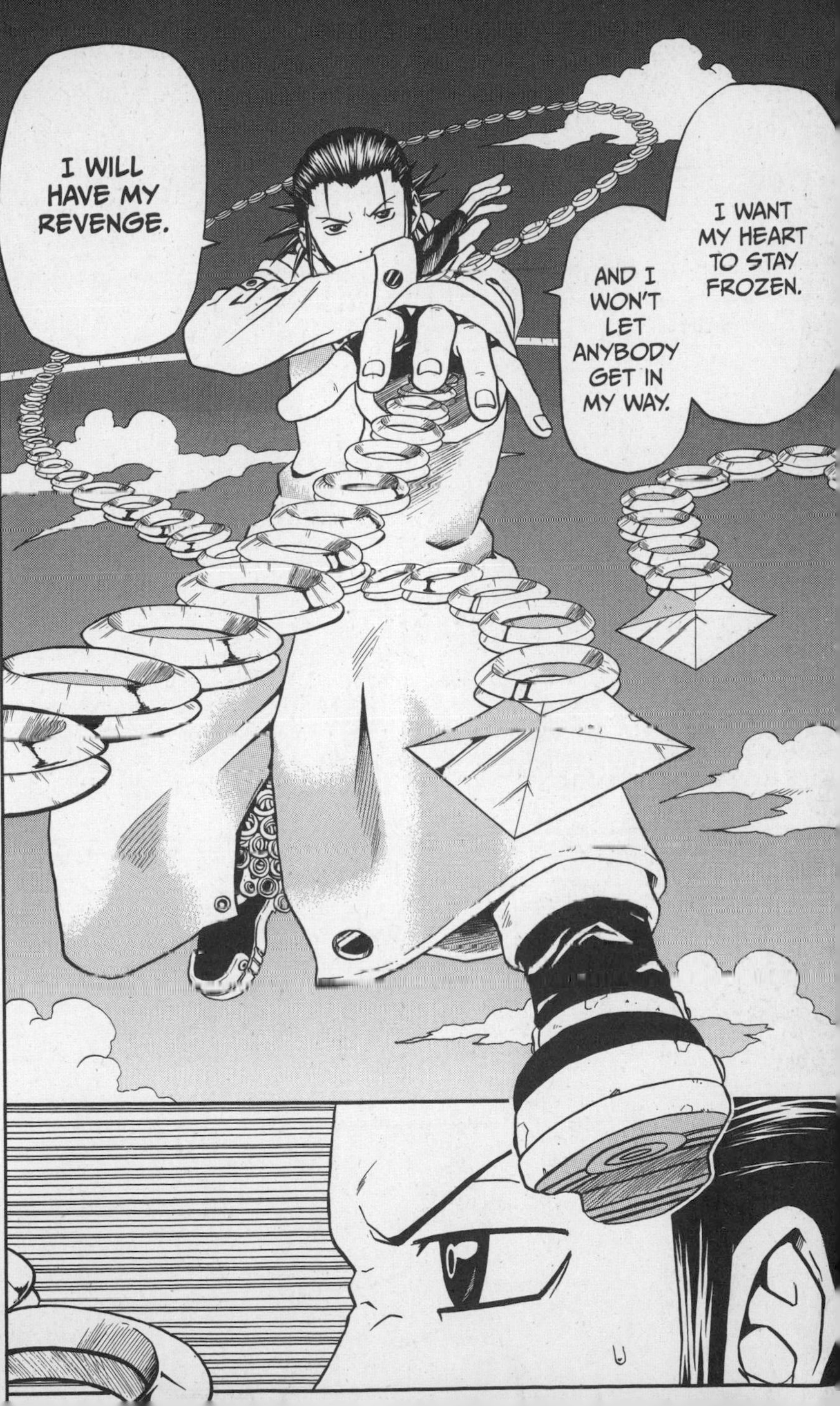
I WANT MY HEART TO STAY FROZEN.
AND I WON'T LET ANYBODY GET IN MY WAY.
I WILL HAVE MY REVENGE.

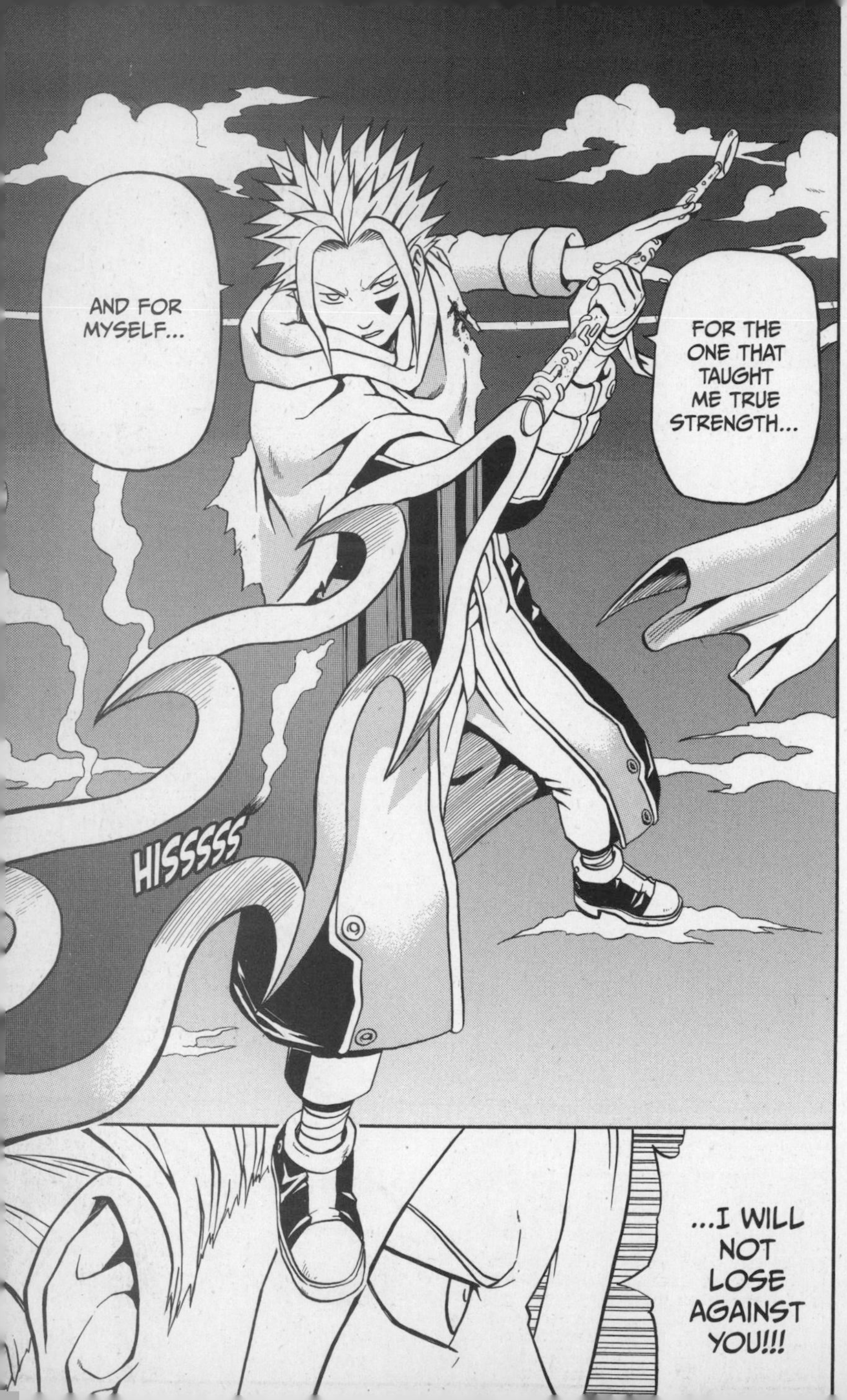
FOR THE ONE THAT TAUGHT ME TRUE STRENGTH...
AND FOR MYSELF...
HISSSSS
...I WILL NOT LOSE AGAINST YOU!!!

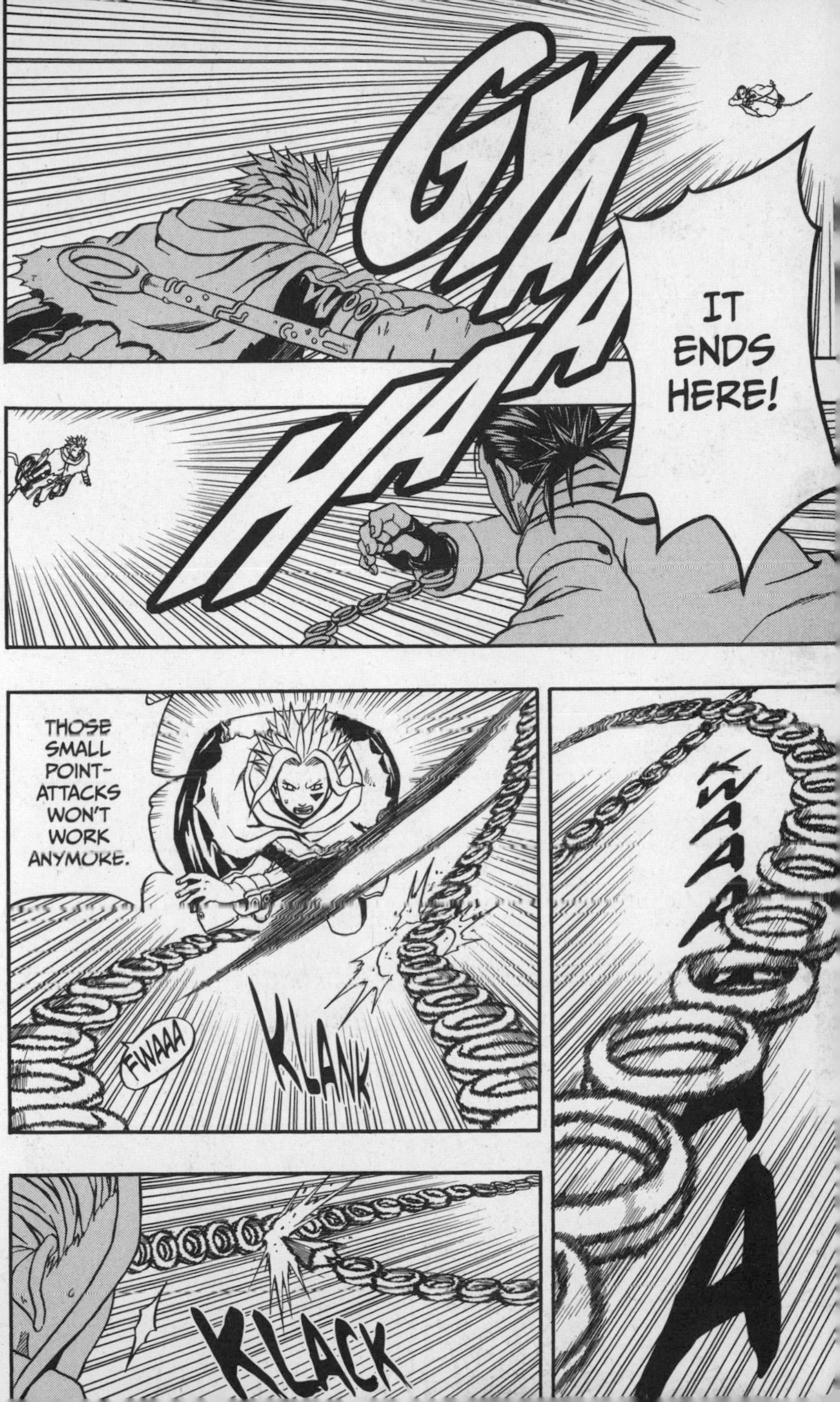
GYAAAH
IT ENDS HERE!
FWAAAA
THOSE SMALL POINT-ATTACKS WON'T WORK ANYMORE.
FWAAA
KLANK
KLACK

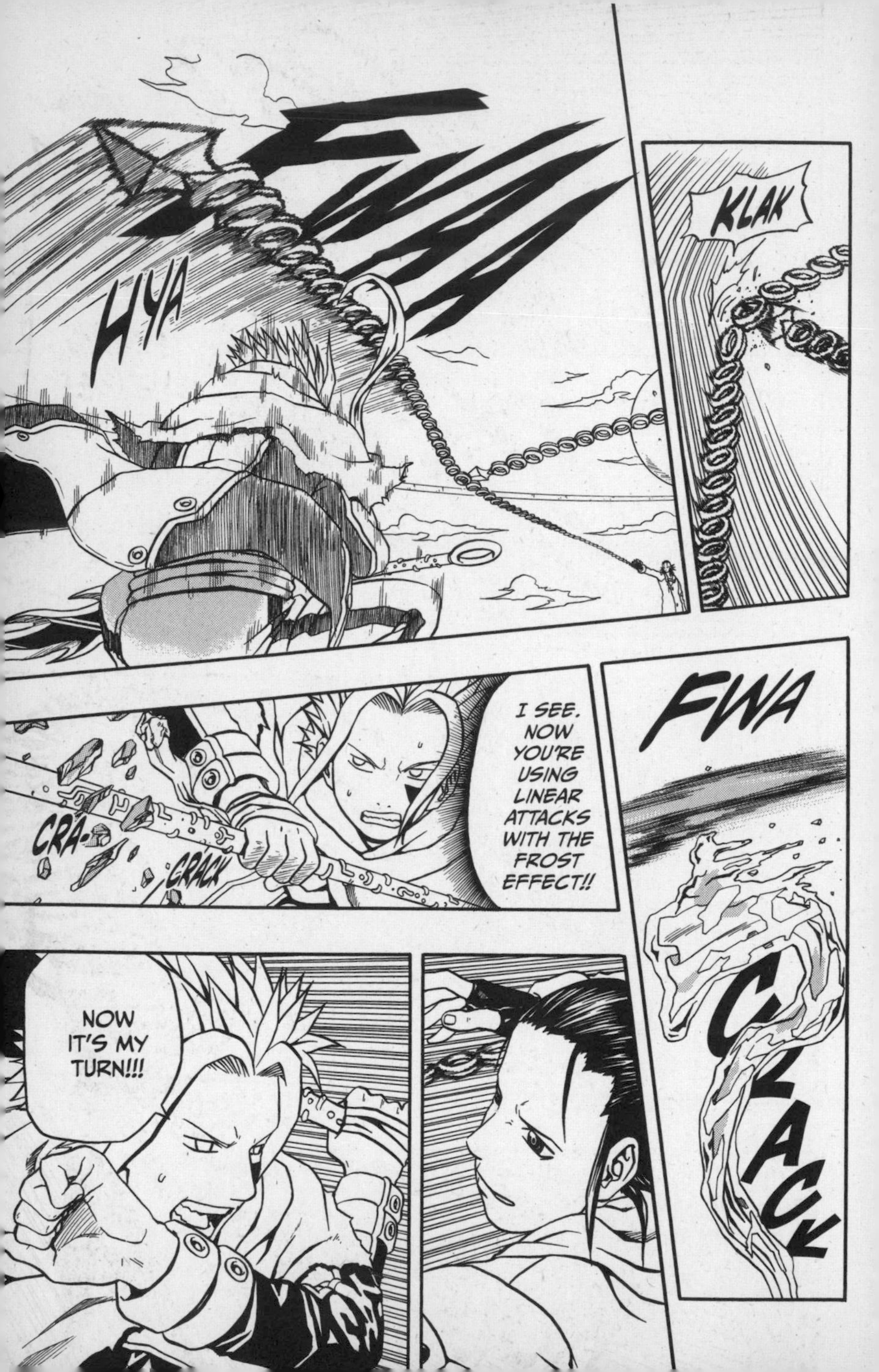
KLAK
HYA
FWA
CLACK
I SEE. NOW YOU'RE USING LINEAR ATTACKS WITH THE FROST EFFECT!!
CRA-
CRACK
NOW IT'S MY TURN!!!

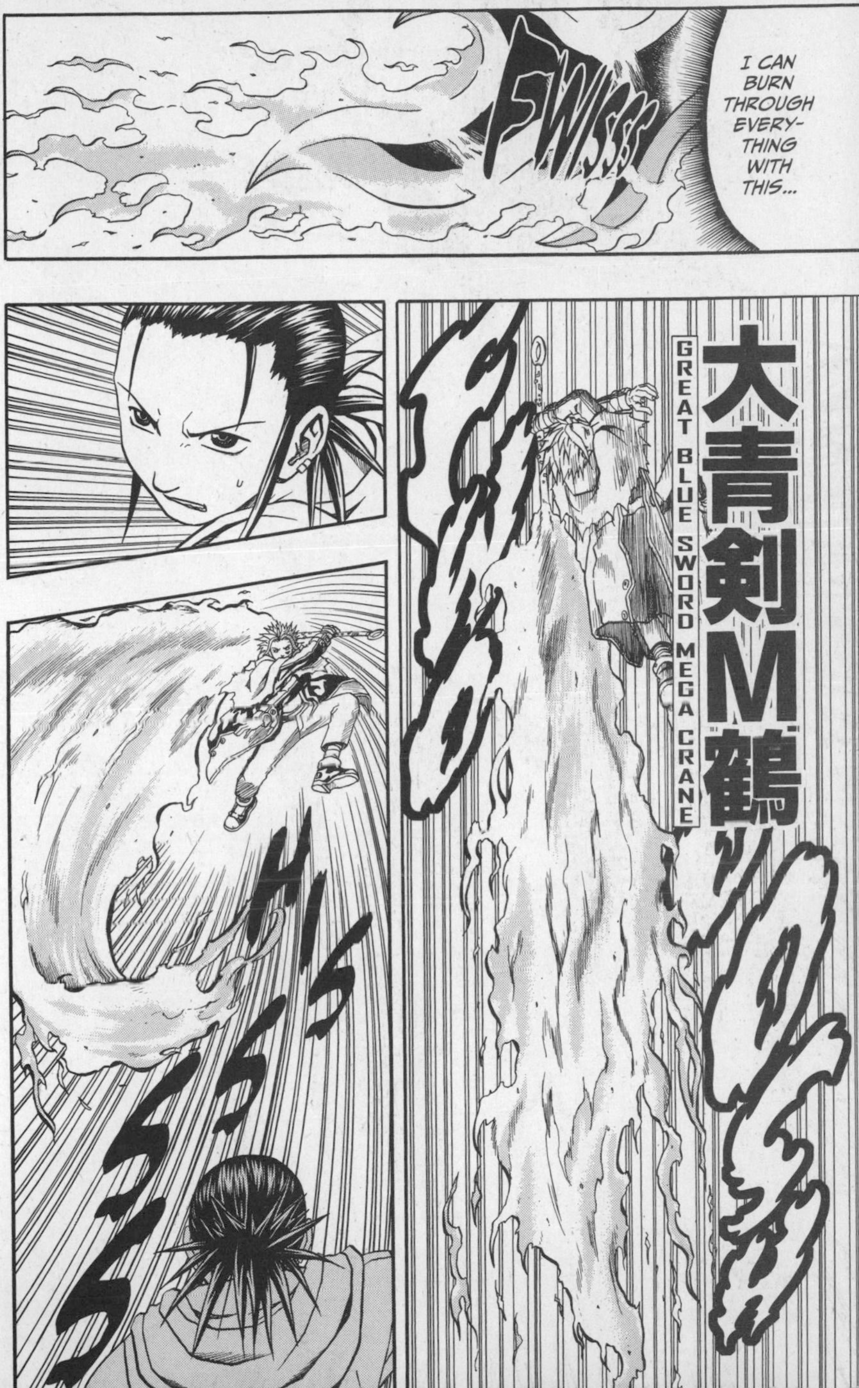
FWISSS
I CAN BURN THROUGH EVERYTHING WITH THIS...
大青剣M鶴
GREAT BLUE SWORD MEGA CRANE
HISSSSS

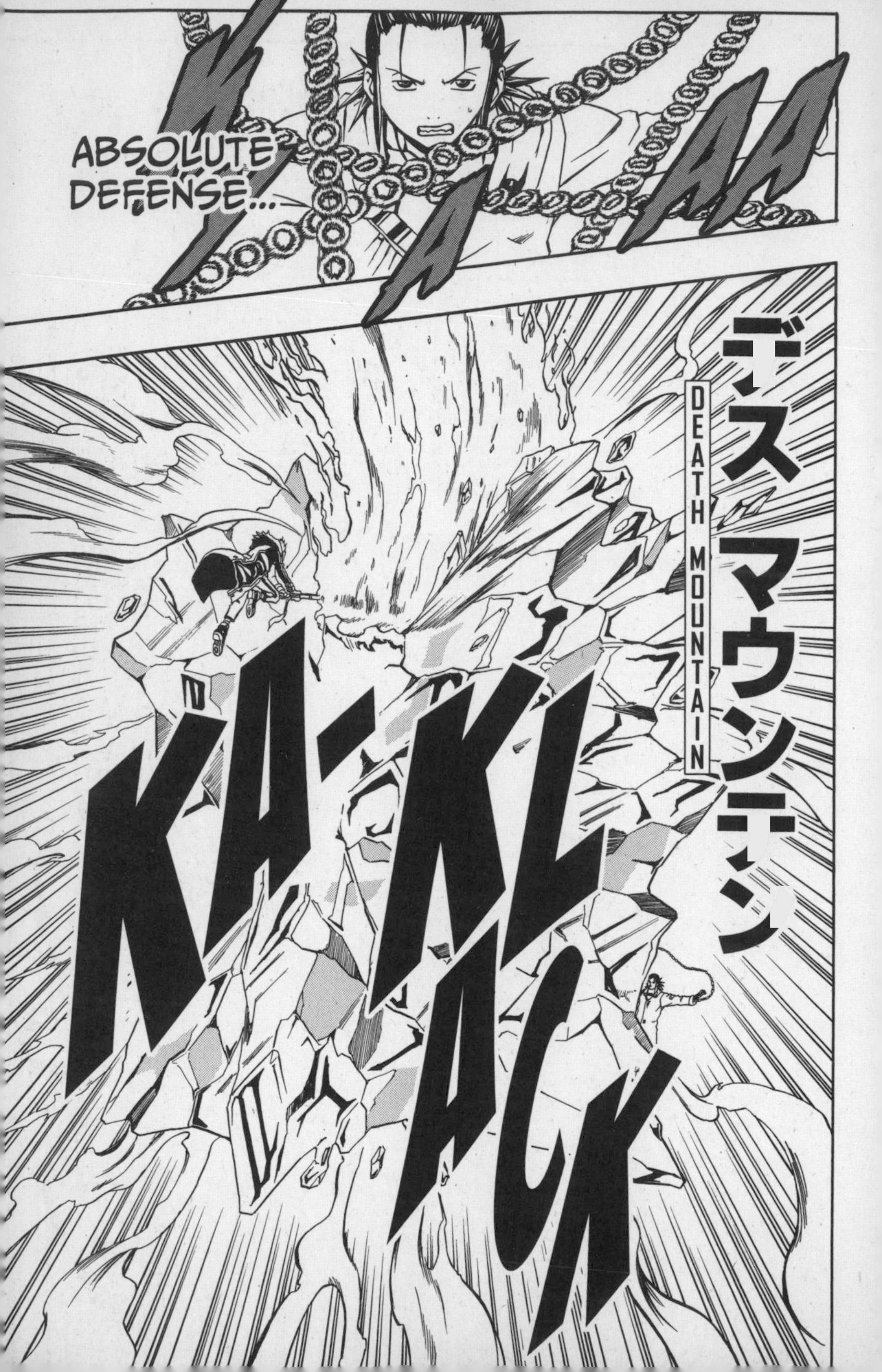
ABSOLUTE DEFENSE...
デスマウンテン
DEATH MOUNTAIN
KA-KL-ACK

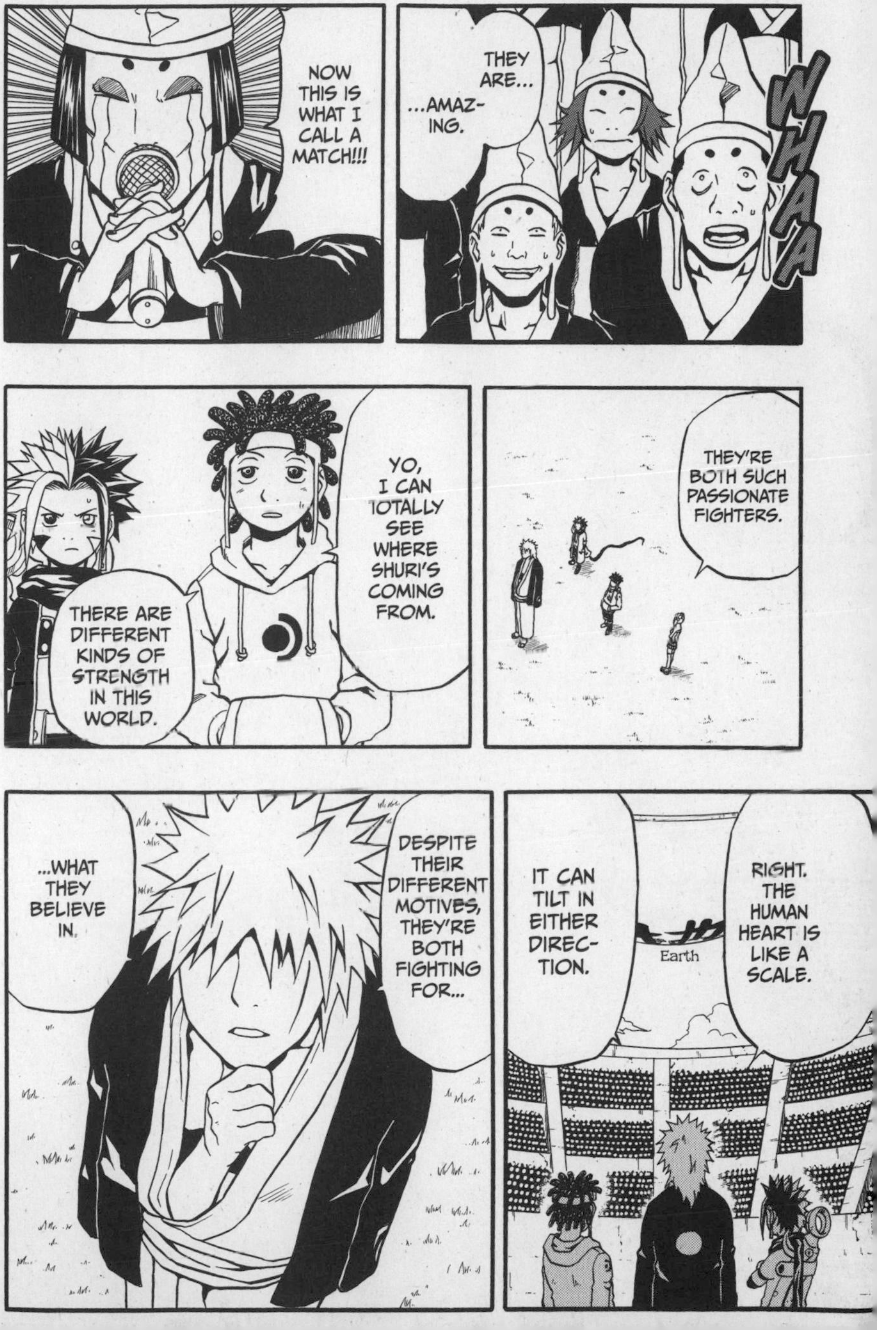
THEY ARE...
...AMAZ-ING.
WHHAA
NOW THIS IS WHAT I CALL A MATCH!!!
THEY'RE BOTH SUCH PASSIONATE FIGHTERS.
YO, I CAN TOTALLY SEE WHERE SHURI'S COMING FROM.
THERE ARE DIFFERENT KINDS OF STRENGTH IN THIS WORLD.
RIGHT. THE HUMAN HEART IS LIKE A SCALE.
Earth
IT CAN TILT IN EITHER DIREC-TION.
DESPITE THEIR DIFFERENT MOTIVES, THEY'RE BOTH FIGHTING FOR...
...WHAT THEY BELIEVE IN.

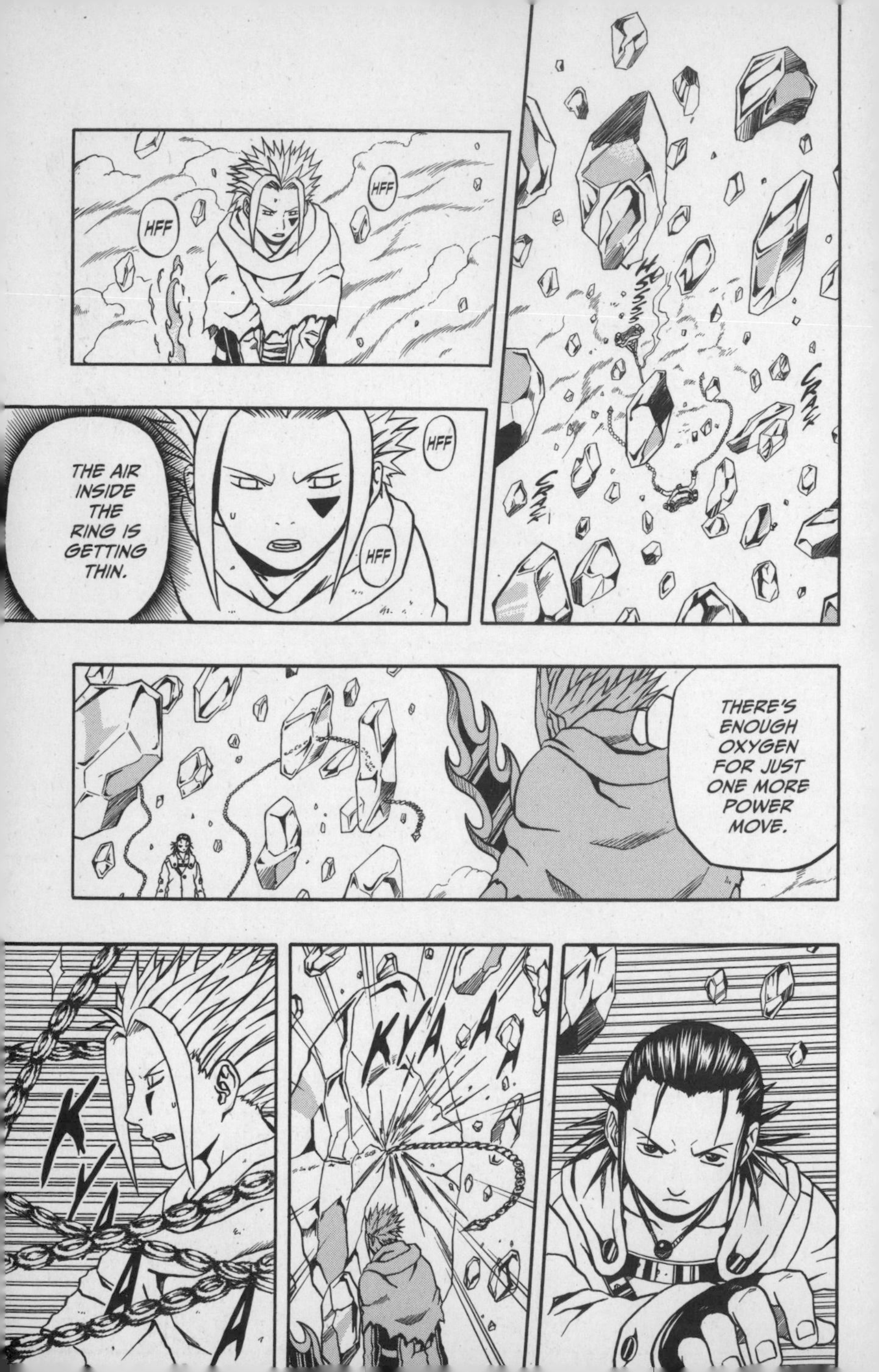
CRAK
CRAK
HFF
HFF
HFF
HFF
THE AIR INSIDE THE RING IS GETTING THIN.
THERE'S ENOUGH OXYGEN FOR JUST ONE MORE POWER MOVE.
KYAA
KYAAA

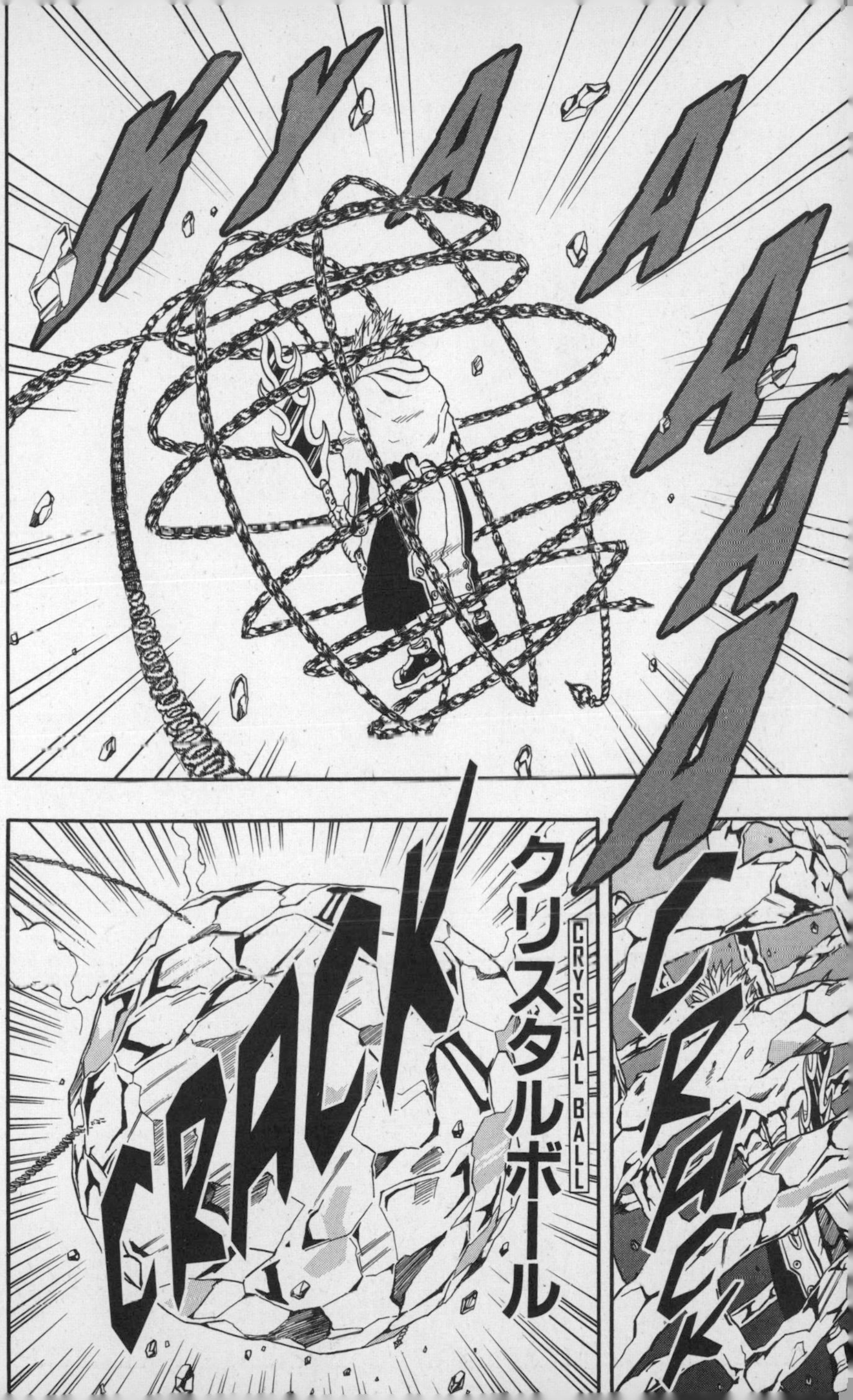
HYAAAAAAAA
CRACK
CRACK
クリスタルボール
CRYSTAL BALL

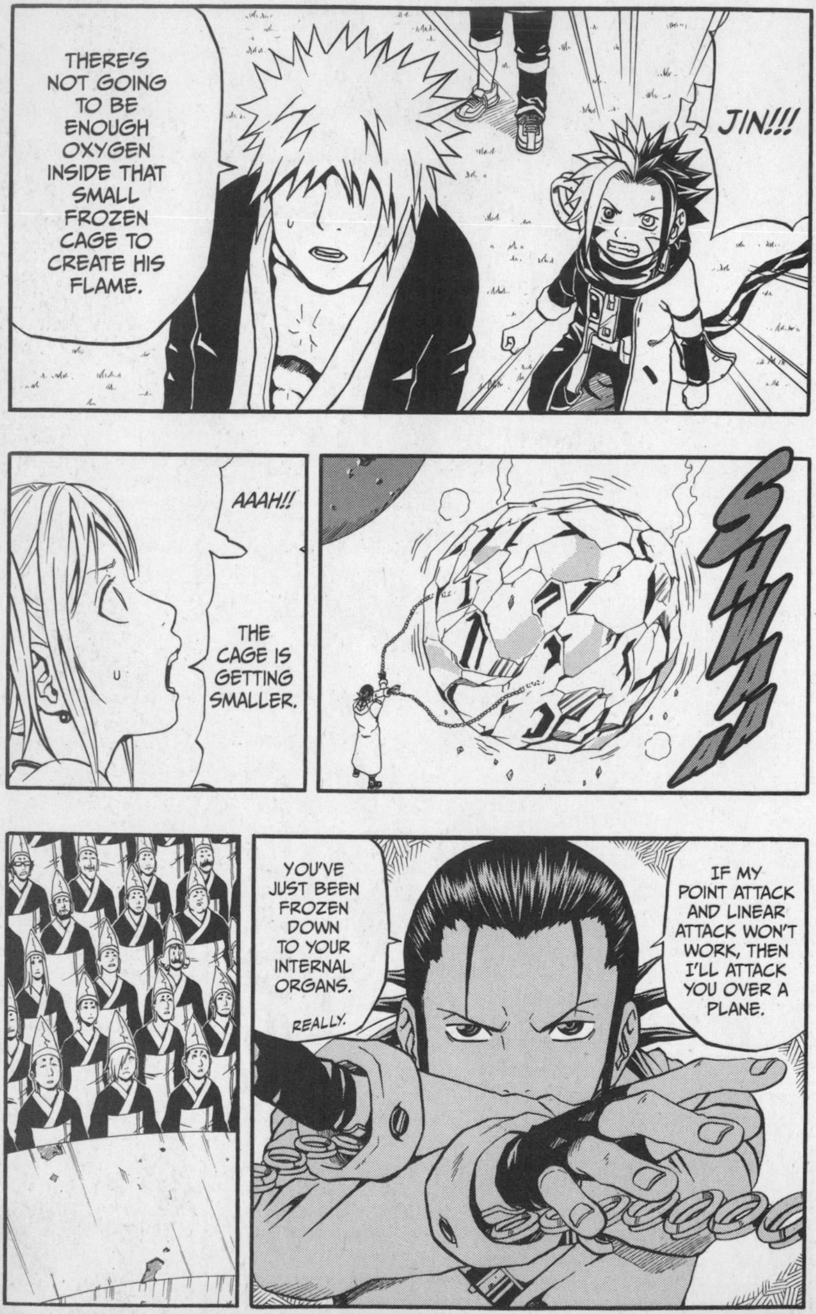
JIN!!!
THERE'S NOT GOING TO BE ENOUGH OXYGEN INSIDE THAT SMALL FROZEN CAGE TO CREATE HIS FLAME.
SHAAAA
AAAH!!
THE CAGE IS GETTING SMALLER.
IF MY POINT ATTACK AND LINEAR ATTACK WON'T WORK, THEN I'LL ATTACK YOU OVER A PLANE.
YOU'VE JUST BEEN FROZEN DOWN TO YOUR INTERNAL ORGANS.
REALLY.

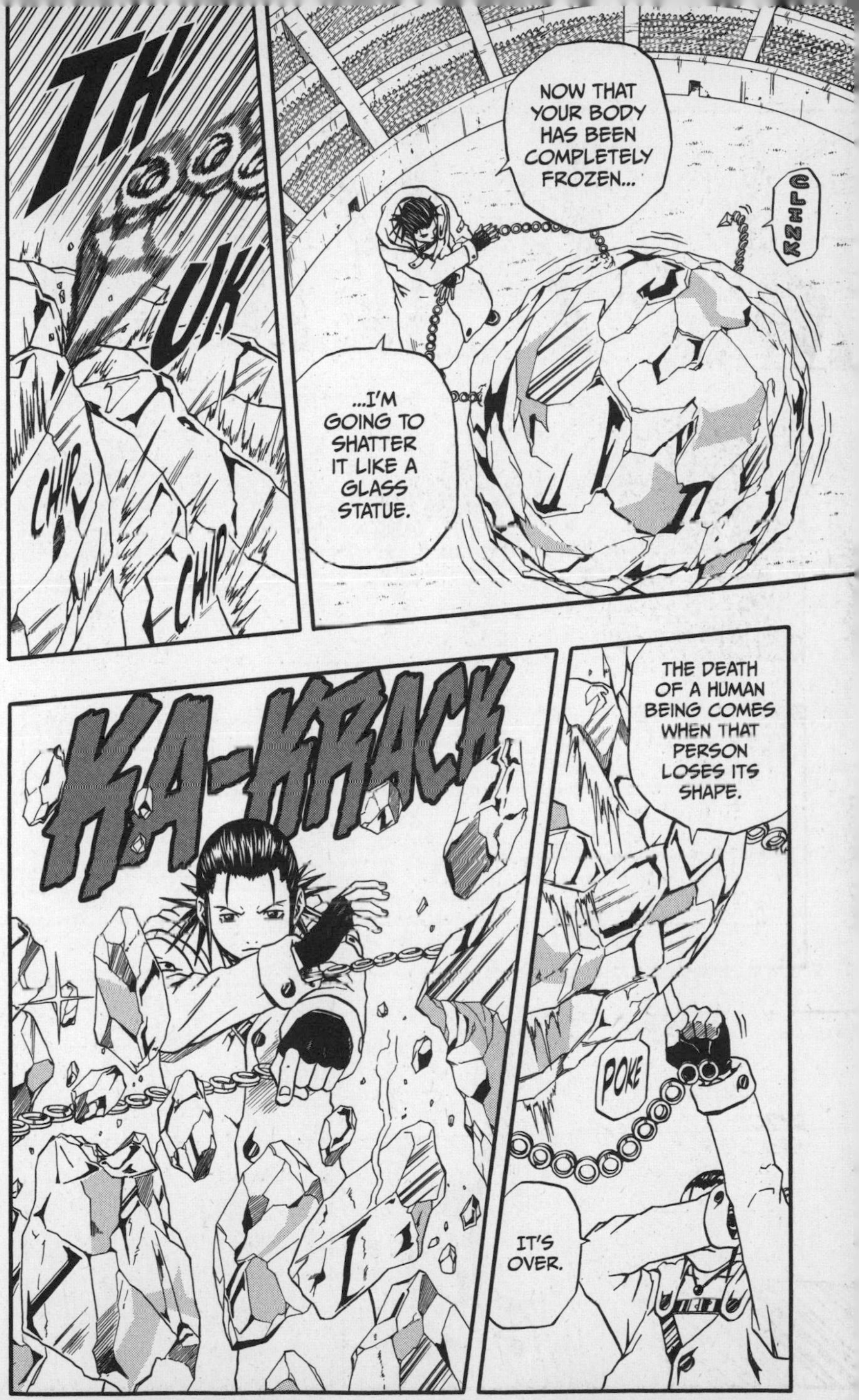
NOW THAT YOUR BODY HAS BEEN COMPLETELY FROZEN...
CLINK
...I'M GOING TO SHATTER IT LIKE A GLASS STATUE.
THUK
CHIP
CHIP
THE DEATH OF A HUMAN BEING COMES WHEN THAT PERSON LOSES ITS SHAPE.
POKE
IT'S OVER.
KA-KRACK

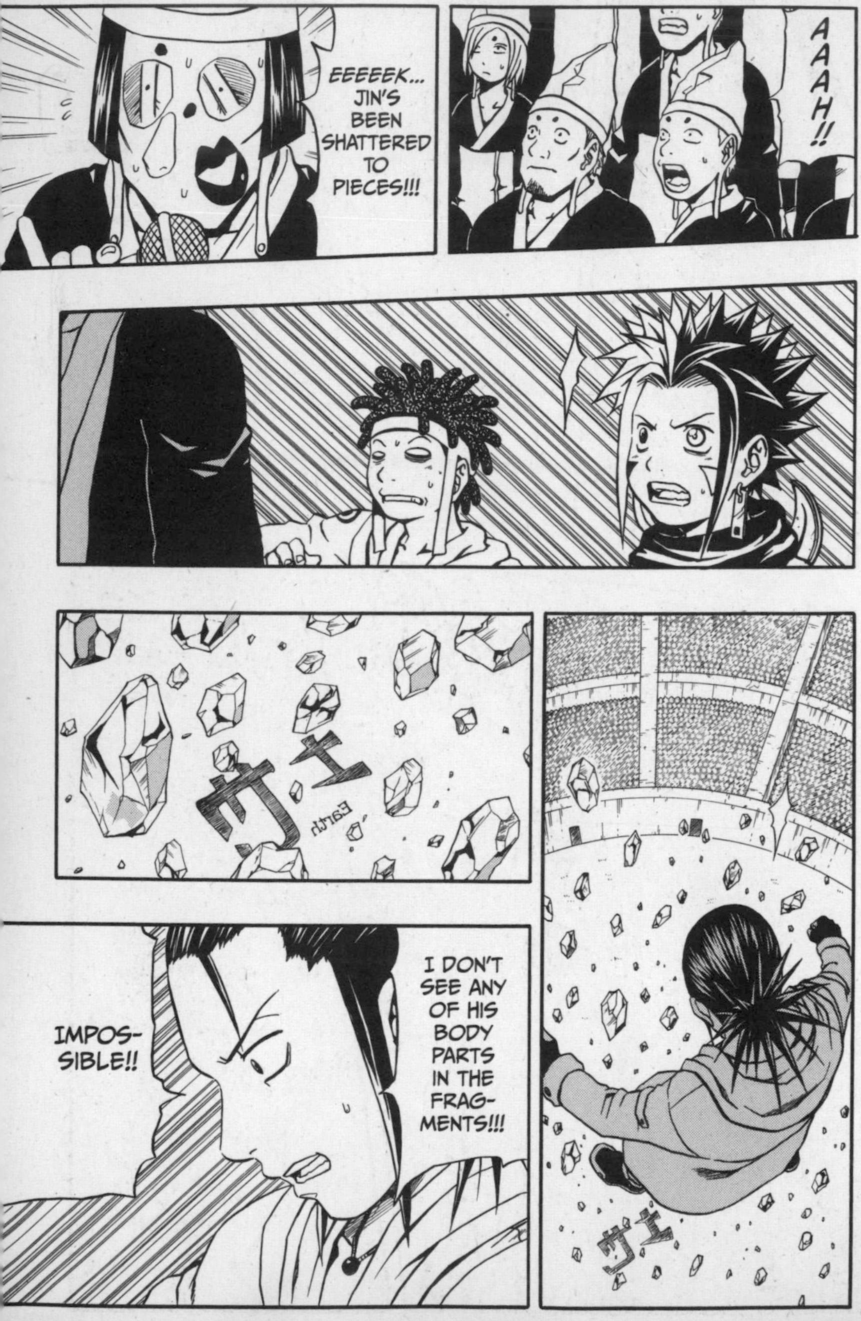
AAAH!!
EEEEEK... JIN'S BEEN SHATTERED TO PIECES!!!
Earth
I DON'T SEE ANY OF HIS BODY PARTS IN THE FRAG- MENTS!!!
IMPOS- SIBLE!!

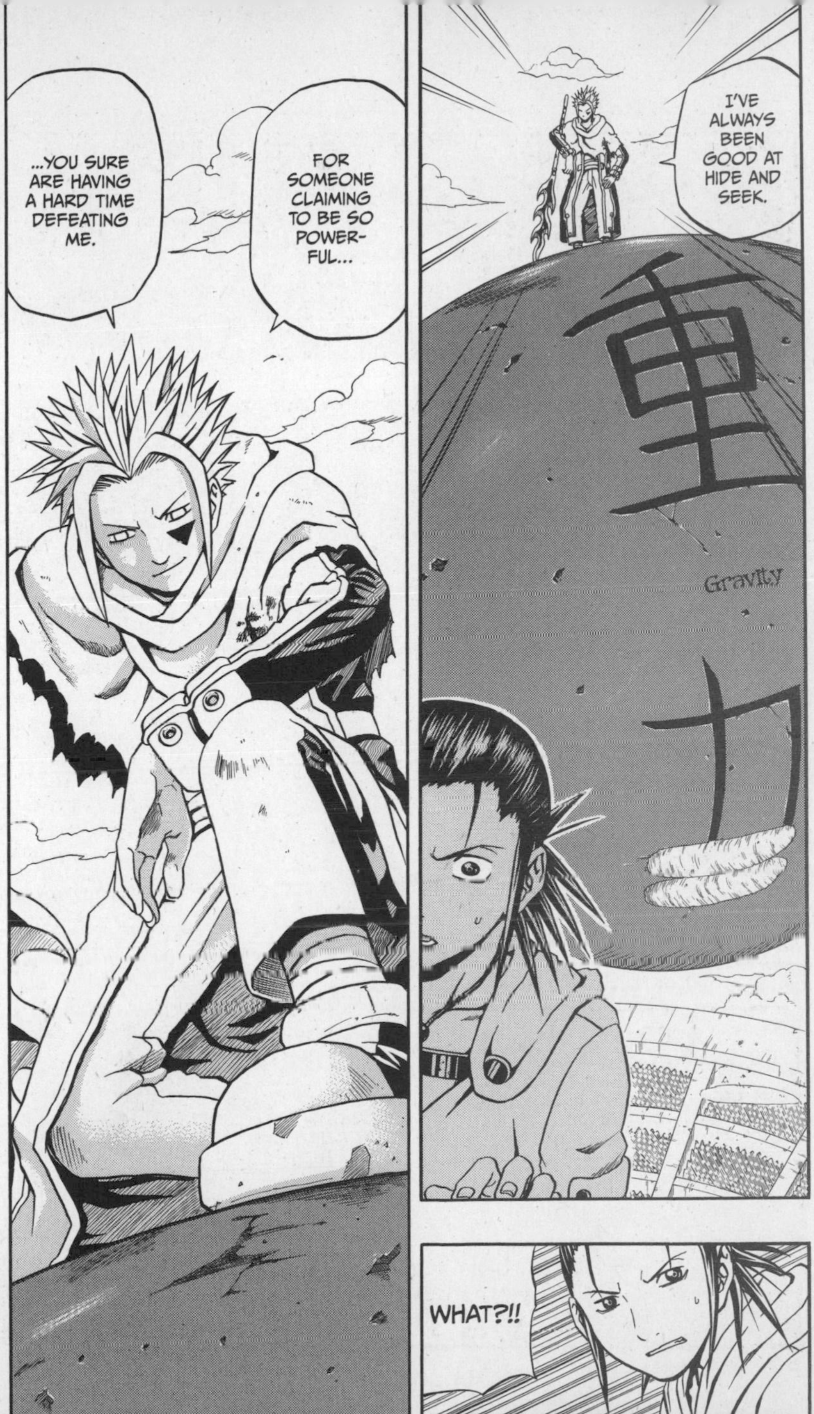
I'VE ALWAYS BEEN GOOD AT HIDE AND SEEK.
重力
Gravity
WHAT?!!
FOR SOMEONE CLAIMING TO BE SO POWER-FUL...
...YOU SURE ARE HAVING A HARD TIME DEFEATING ME.

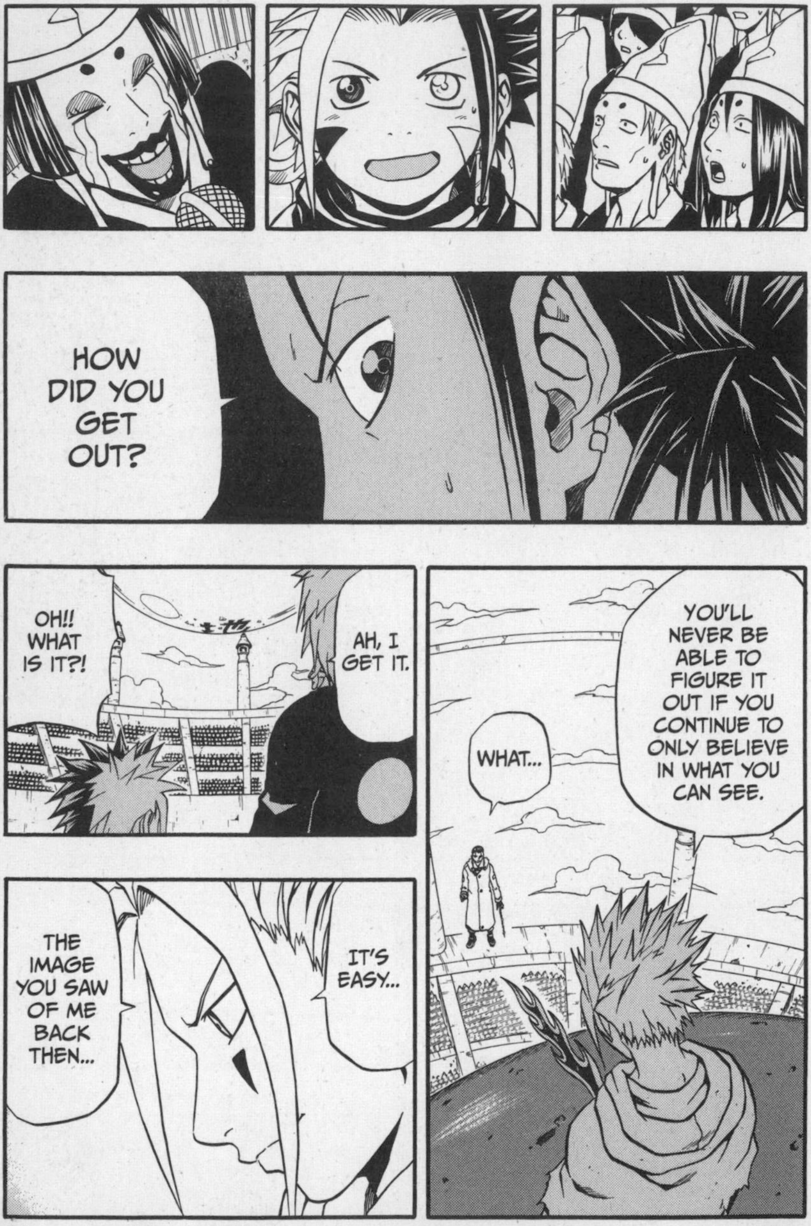
HOW DID YOU GET OUT?
YOU'LL NEVER BE ABLE TO FIGURE IT OUT IF YOU CONTINUE TO ONLY BELIEVE IN WHAT YOU CAN SEE.
WHAT...
AH, I GET IT.
OH!! WHAT IS IT?!
IT'S EASY...
THE IMAGE YOU SAW OF ME BACK THEN...

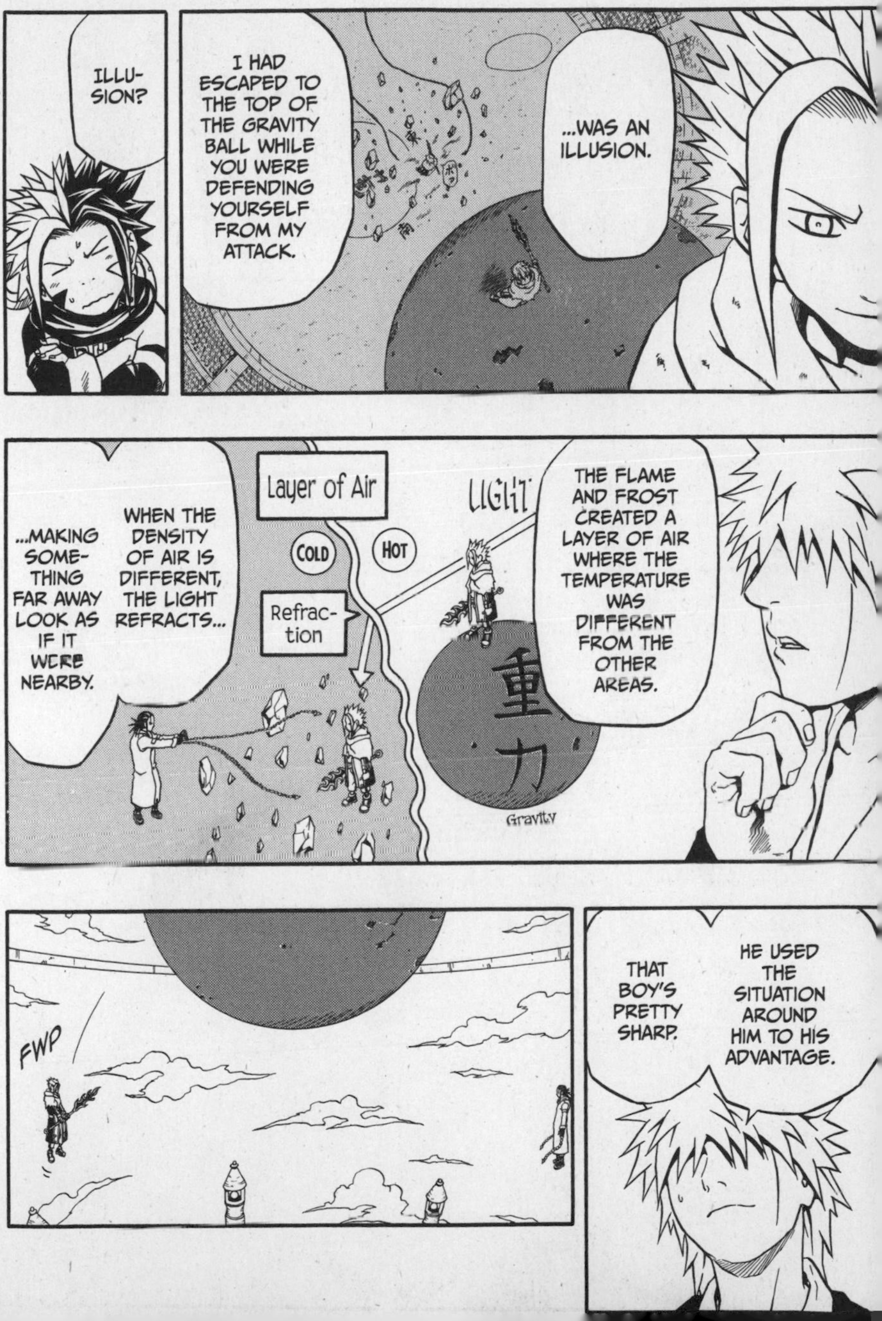
...WAS AN ILLUSION.
I HAD ESCAPED TO THE TOP OF THE GRAVITY BALL WHILE YOU WERE DEFENDING YOURSELF FROM MY ATTACK.
ILLUSION?
THE FLAME AND FROST CREATED A LAYER OF AIR WHERE THE TEMPERATURE WAS DIFFERENT FROM THE OTHER AREAS.
LIGHT
Layer of Air
HOT
COLD
Refraction
重力
Gravity
WHEN THE DENSITY OF AIR IS DIFFERENT, THE LIGHT REFRACTS...
...MAKING SOMETHING FAR AWAY LOOK AS IF IT WERE NEARBY.
HE USED THE SITUATION AROUND HIM TO HIS ADVANTAGE.
THAT BOY'S PRETTY SHARP.
FWP

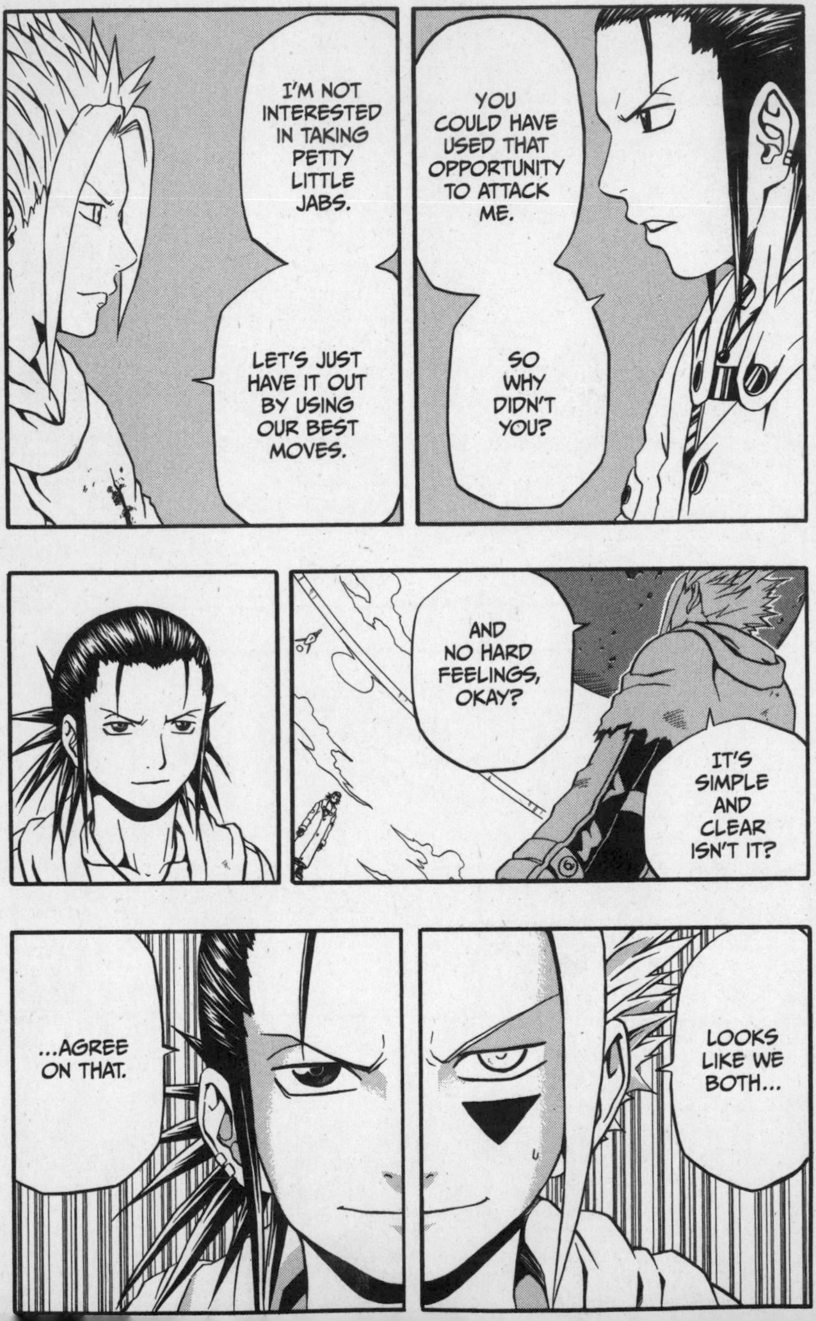
YOU COULD HAVE USED THAT OPPORTUNITY TO ATTACK ME.
SO WHY DIDN'T YOU?
I'M NOT INTERESTED IN TAKING PETTY LITTLE JABS.
LET'S JUST HAVE IT OUT BY USING OUR BEST MOVES.
AND NO HARD FEELINGS, OKAY?
IT'S SIMPLE AND CLEAR ISN'T IT?
LOOKS LIKE WE BOTH...
...AGREE ON THAT.

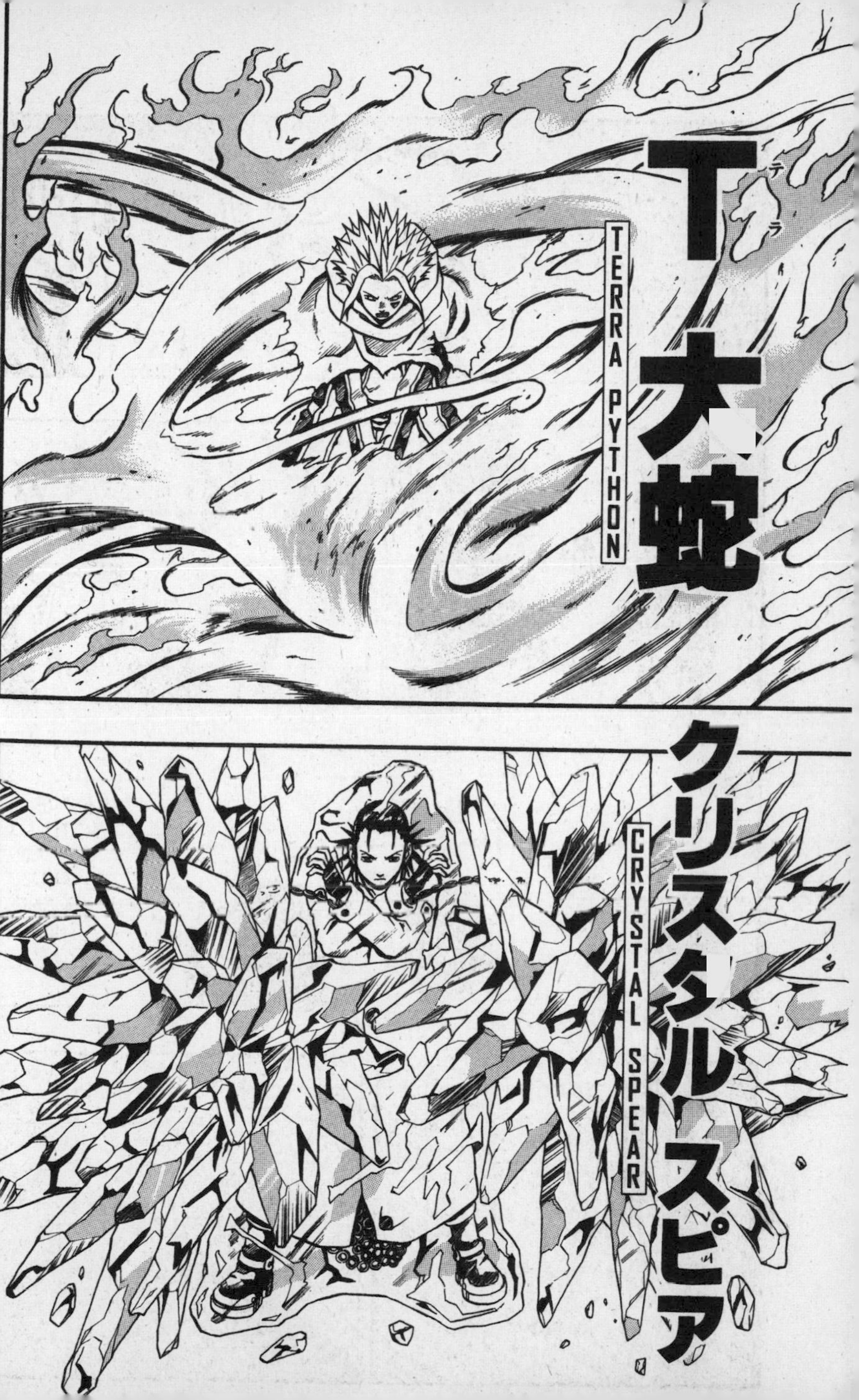
テラ
土大蛇
TERRA PYTHON
クリスタルスピア
CRYSTAL SPEAR

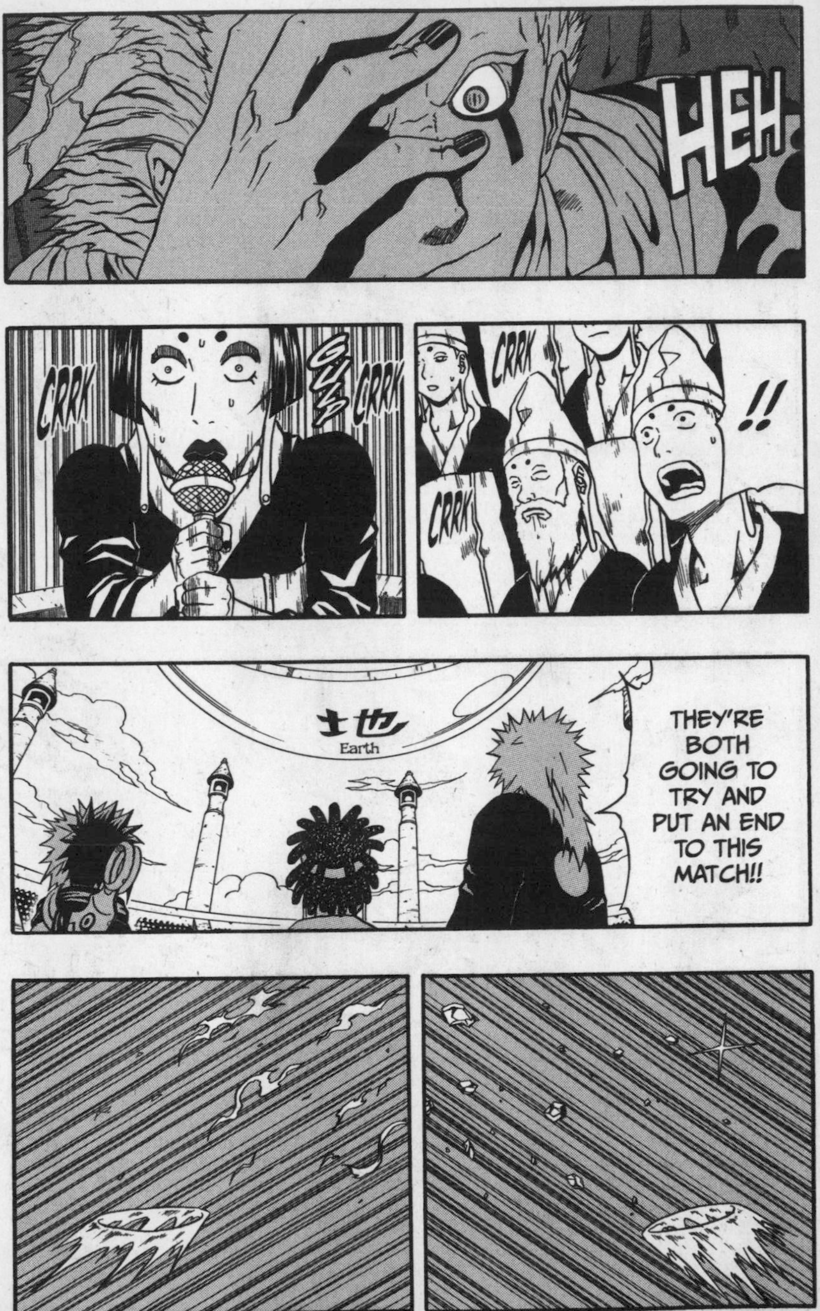
HEH
CRRK
!!
CRRK
CRRK
GULP
CRRK
土也
Earth
THEY'RE BOTH GOING TO TRY AND PUT AN END TO THIS MATCH!!

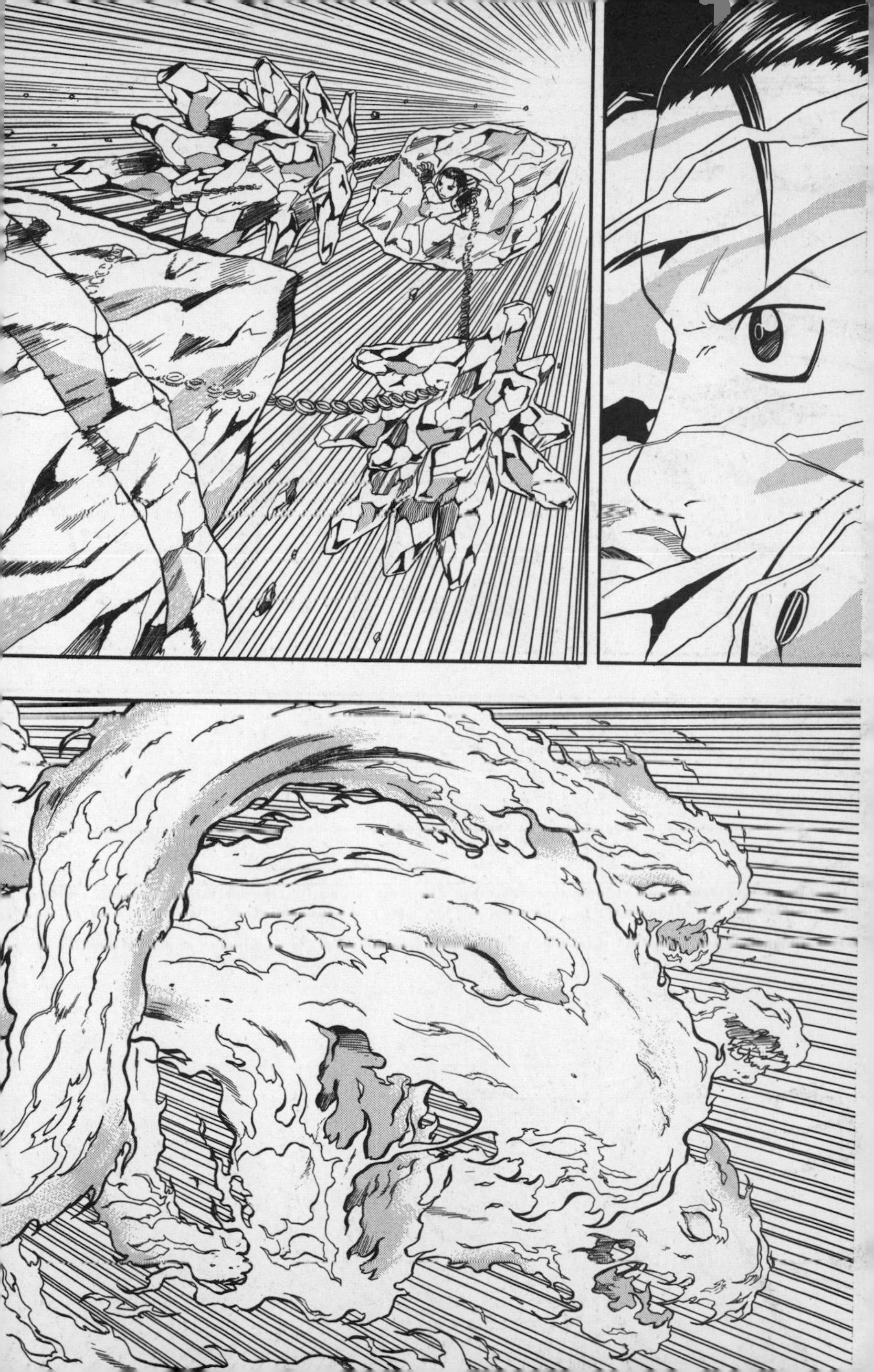

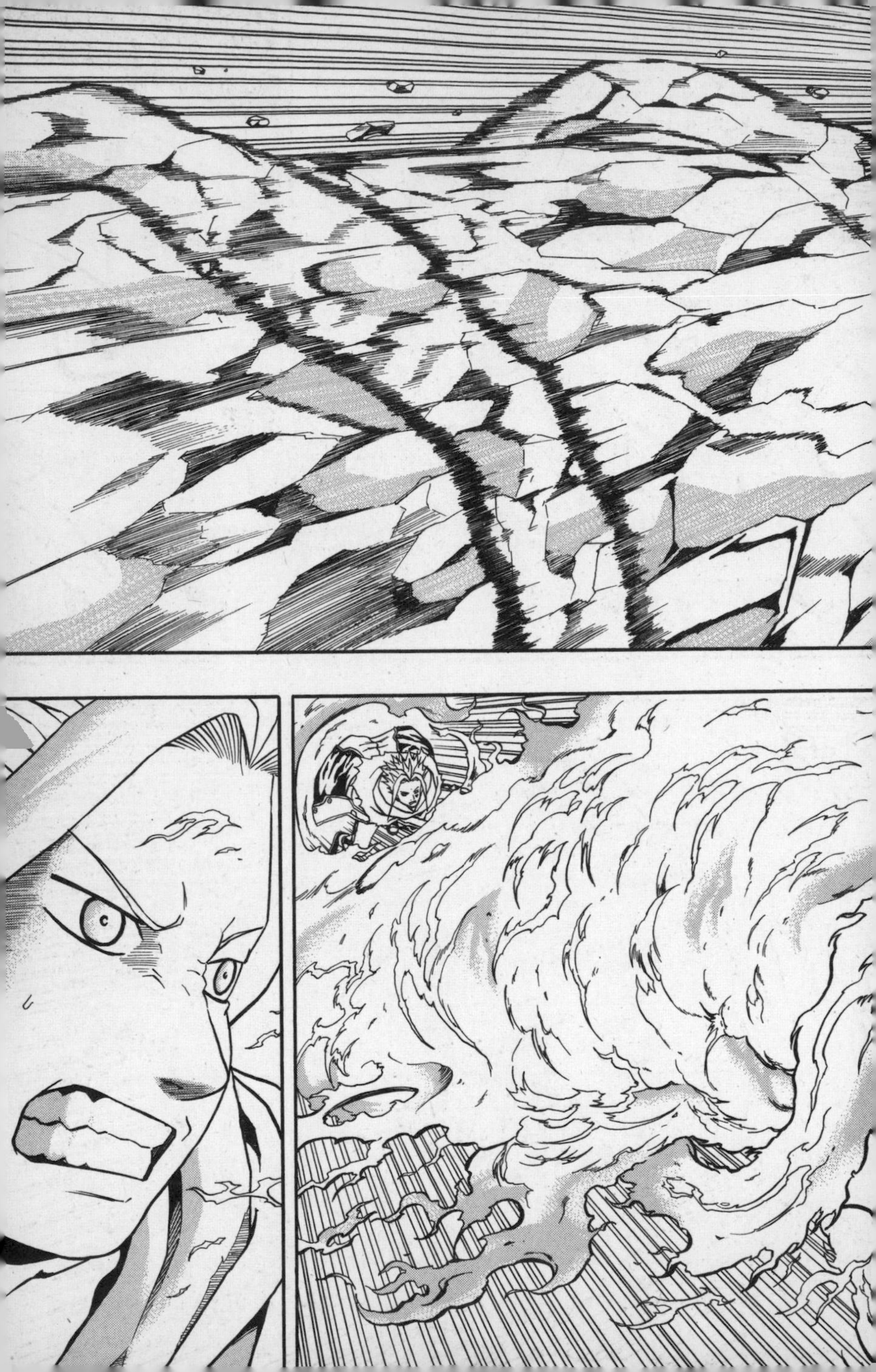

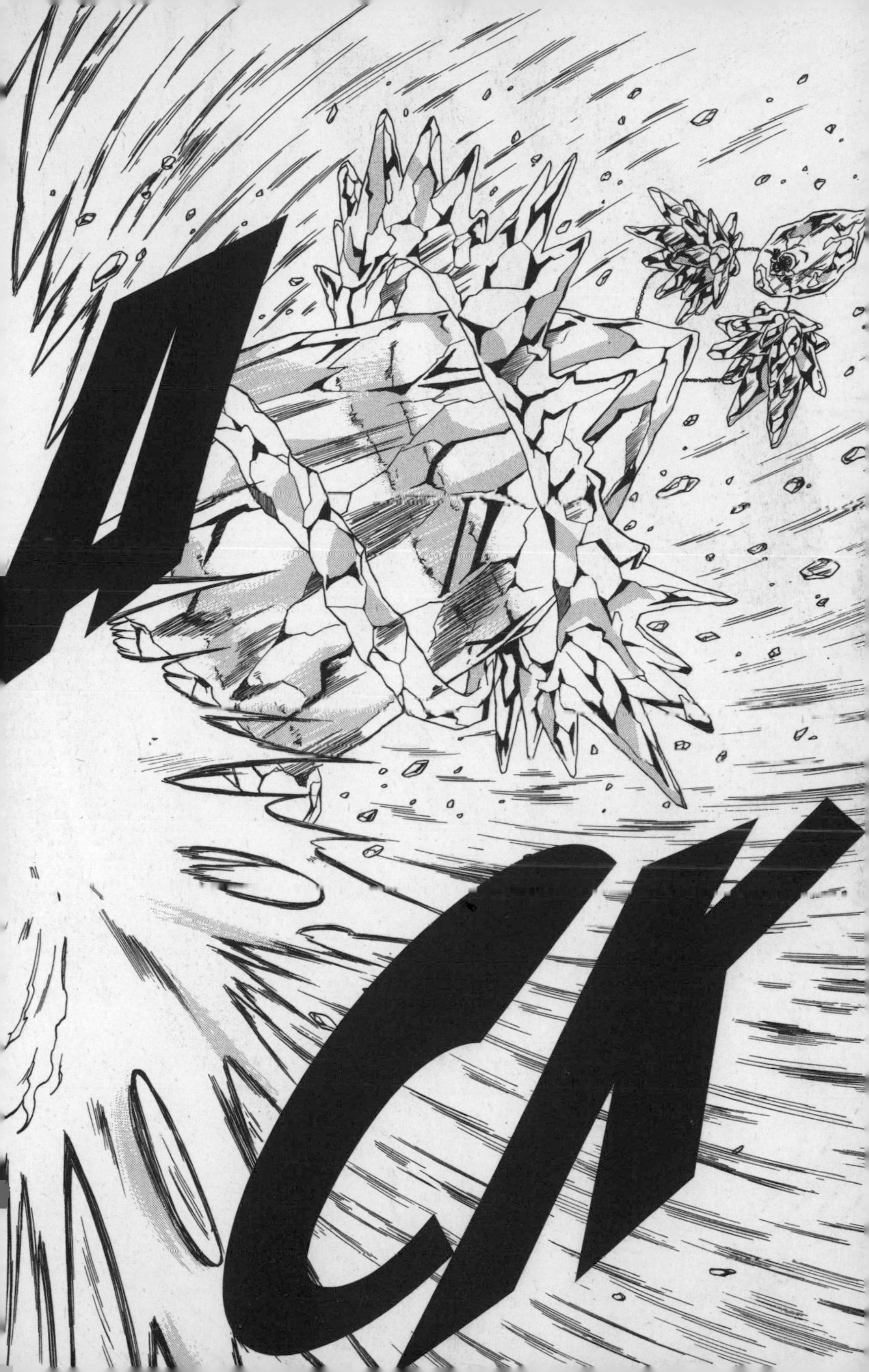

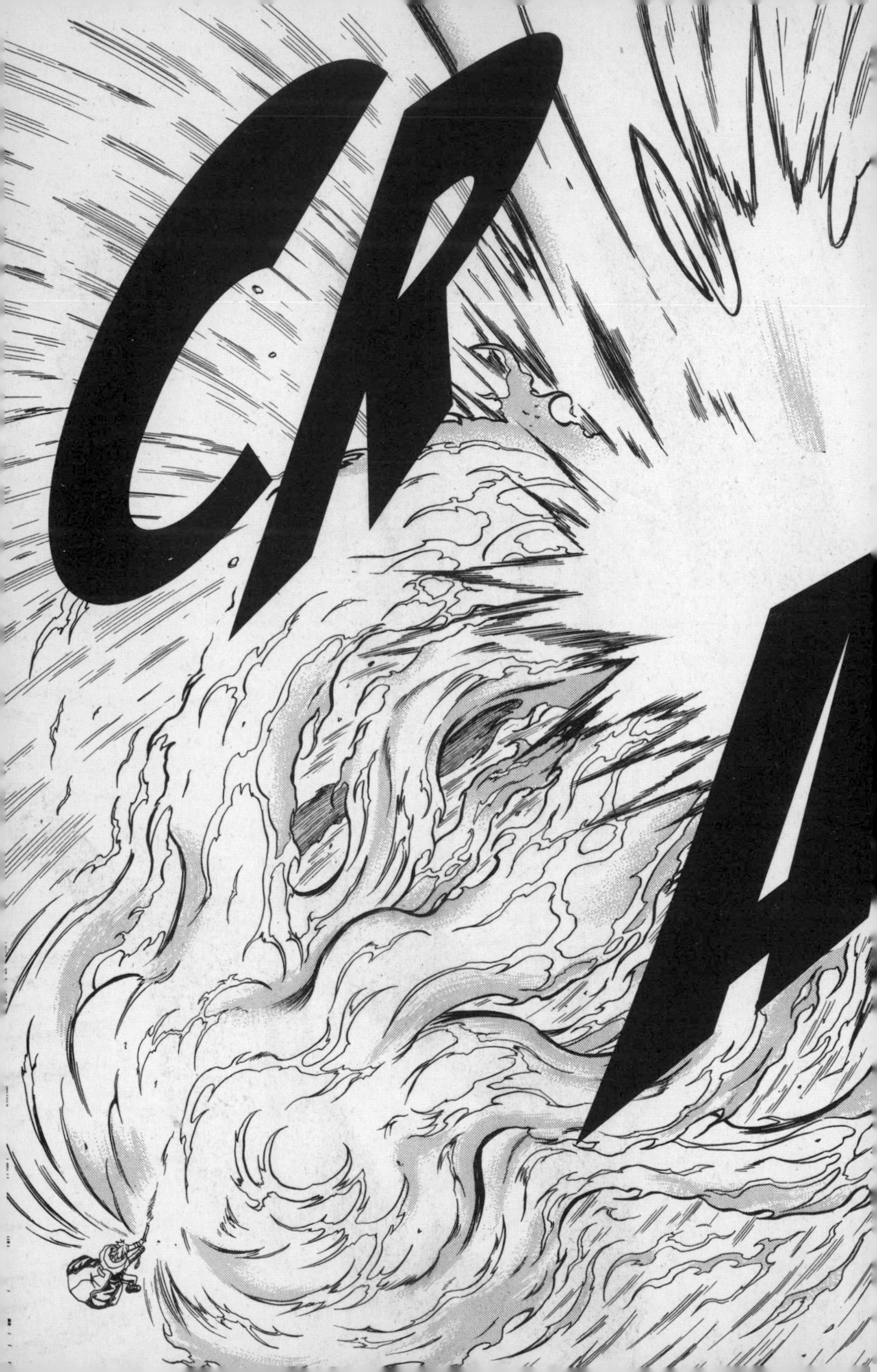
CRA

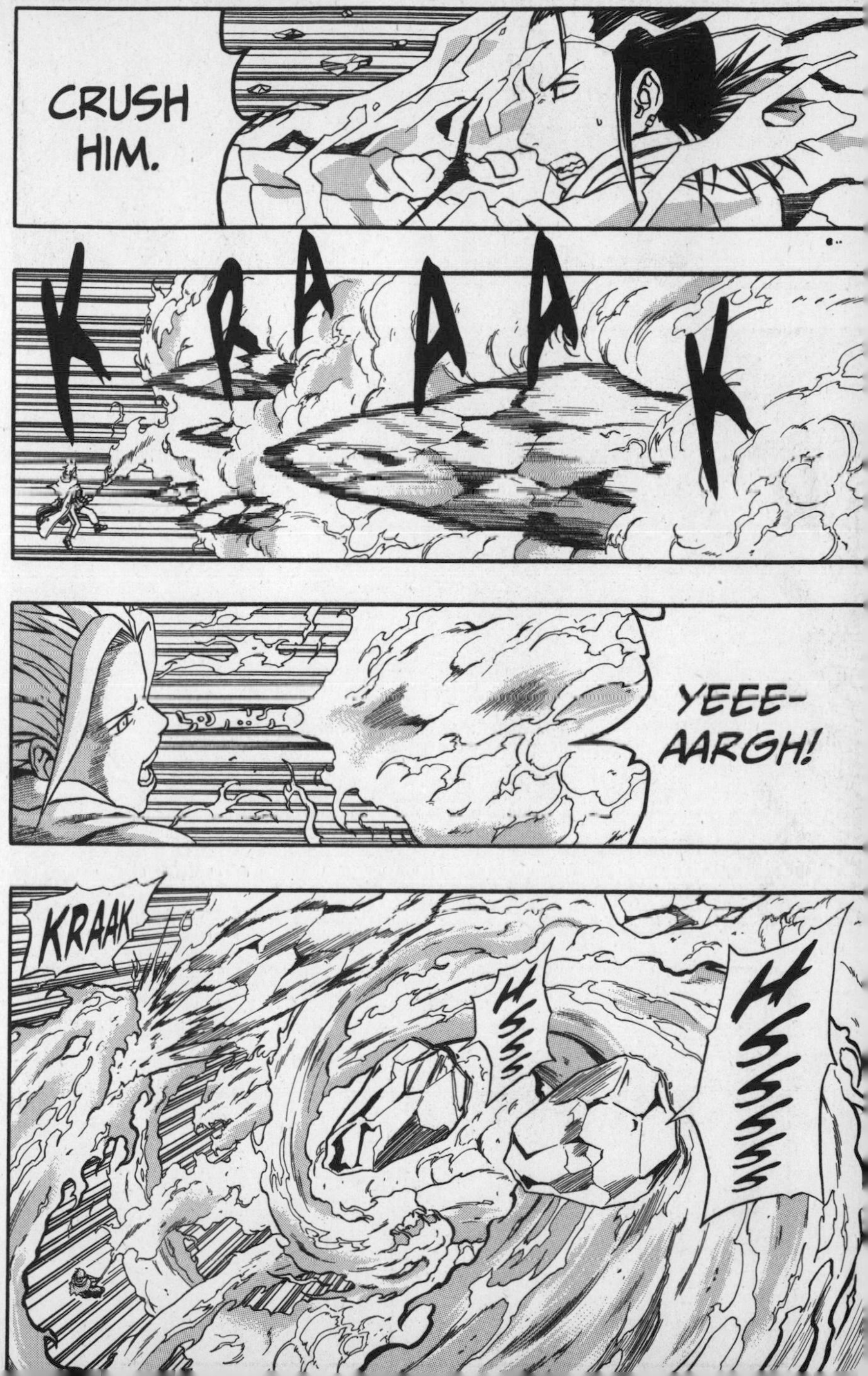
CRUSH HIM.
KRAAAK
YEEE-AARGH!
KRAAK

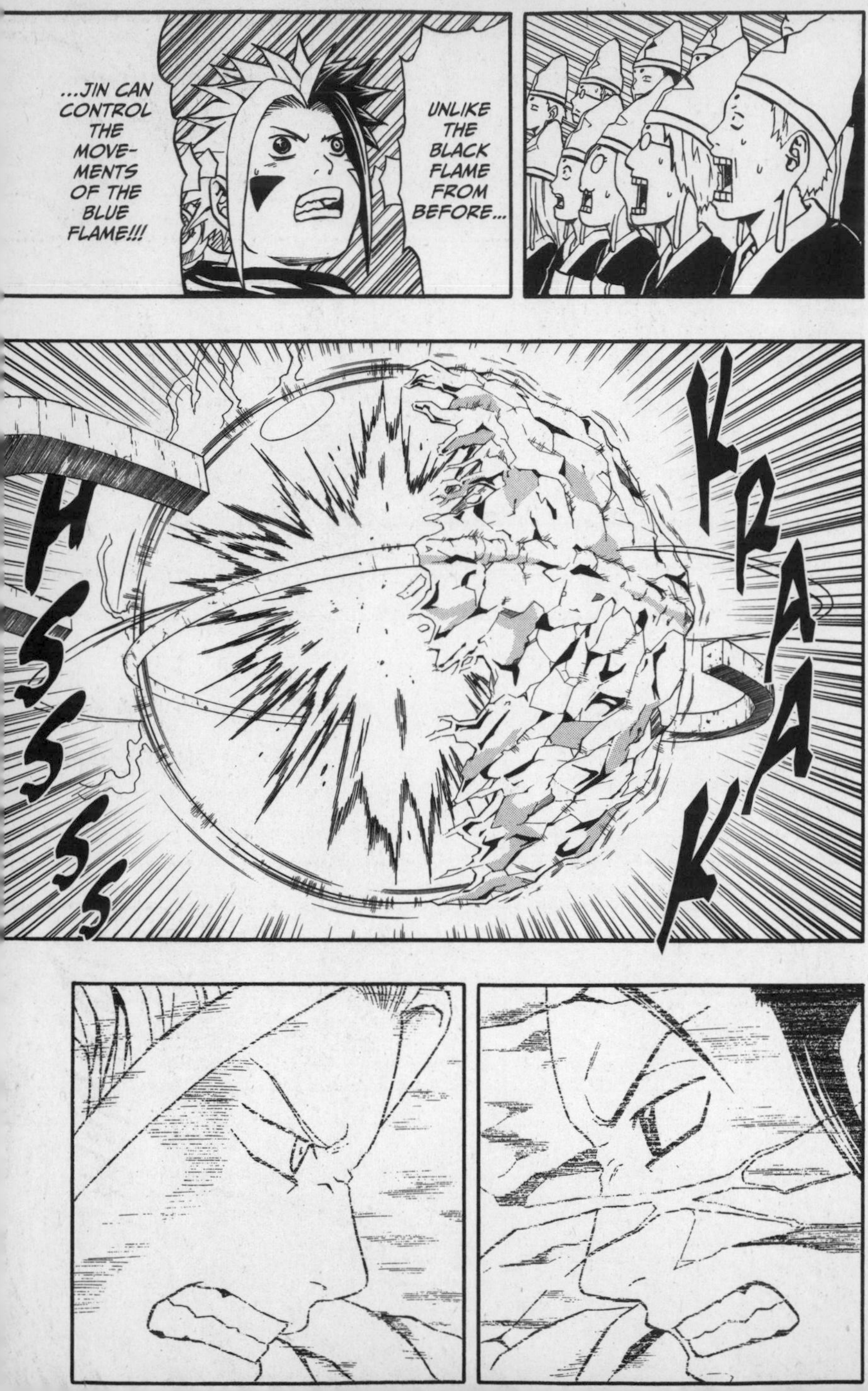
UNLIKE THE BLACK FLAME FROM BEFORE...
...JIN CAN CONTROL THE MOVEMENTS OF THE BLUE FLAME!!!
KRAAK
HSSSSS

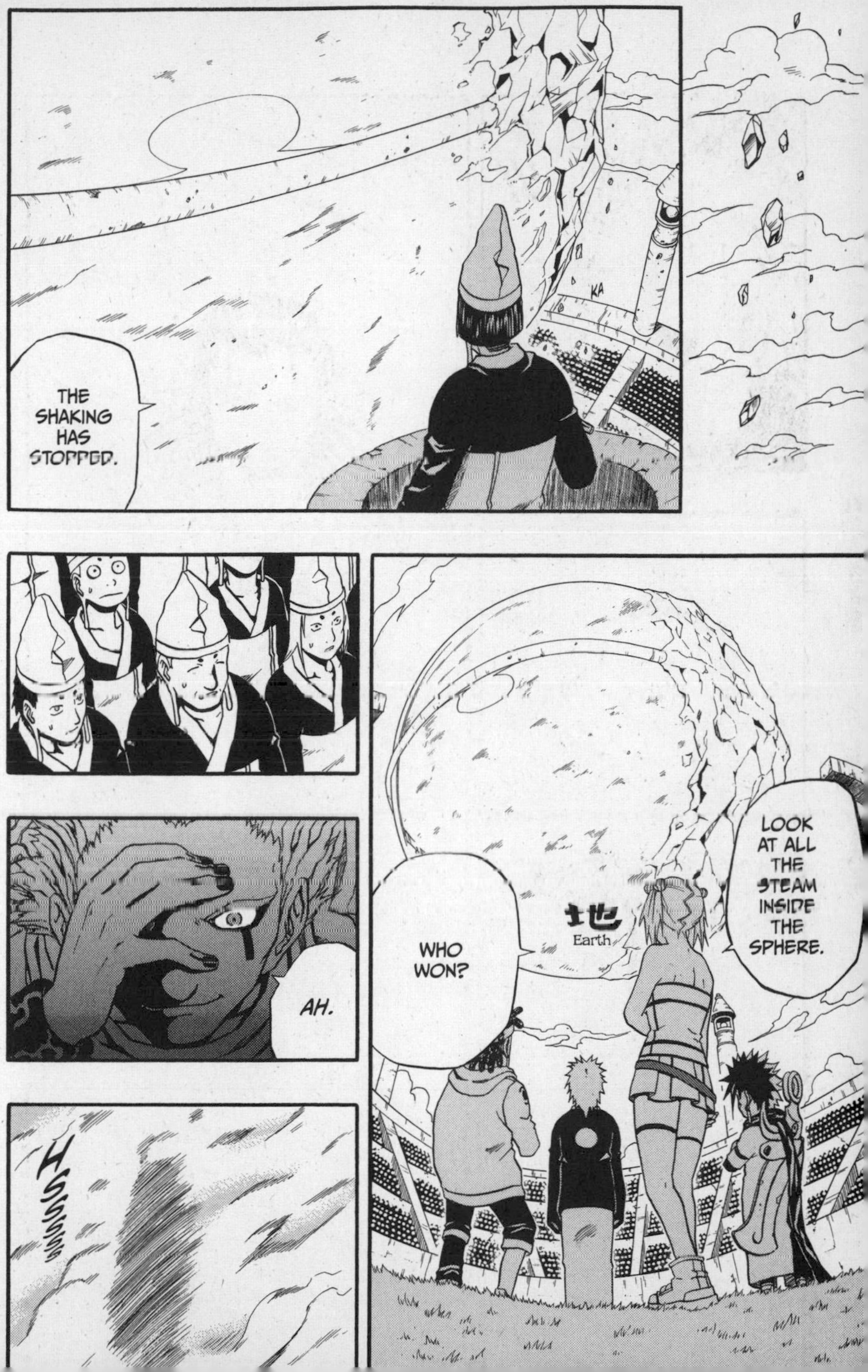
KA
THE SHAKING HAS STOPPED.
LOOK AT ALL THE STEAM INSIDE THE SPHERE.
地
Earth
WHO WON?
AH.
HSSSSSS

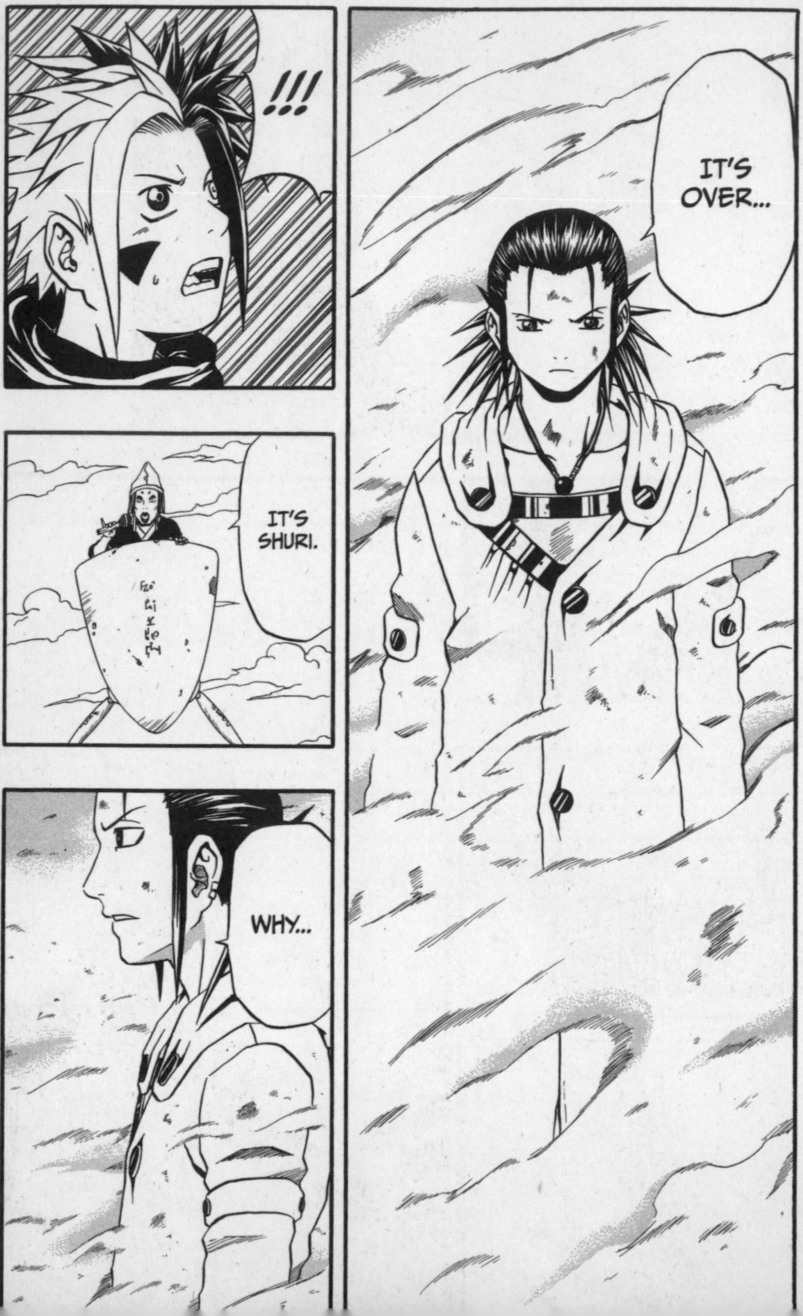
IT'S OVER...
!!!
IT'S SHURI.
WHY...

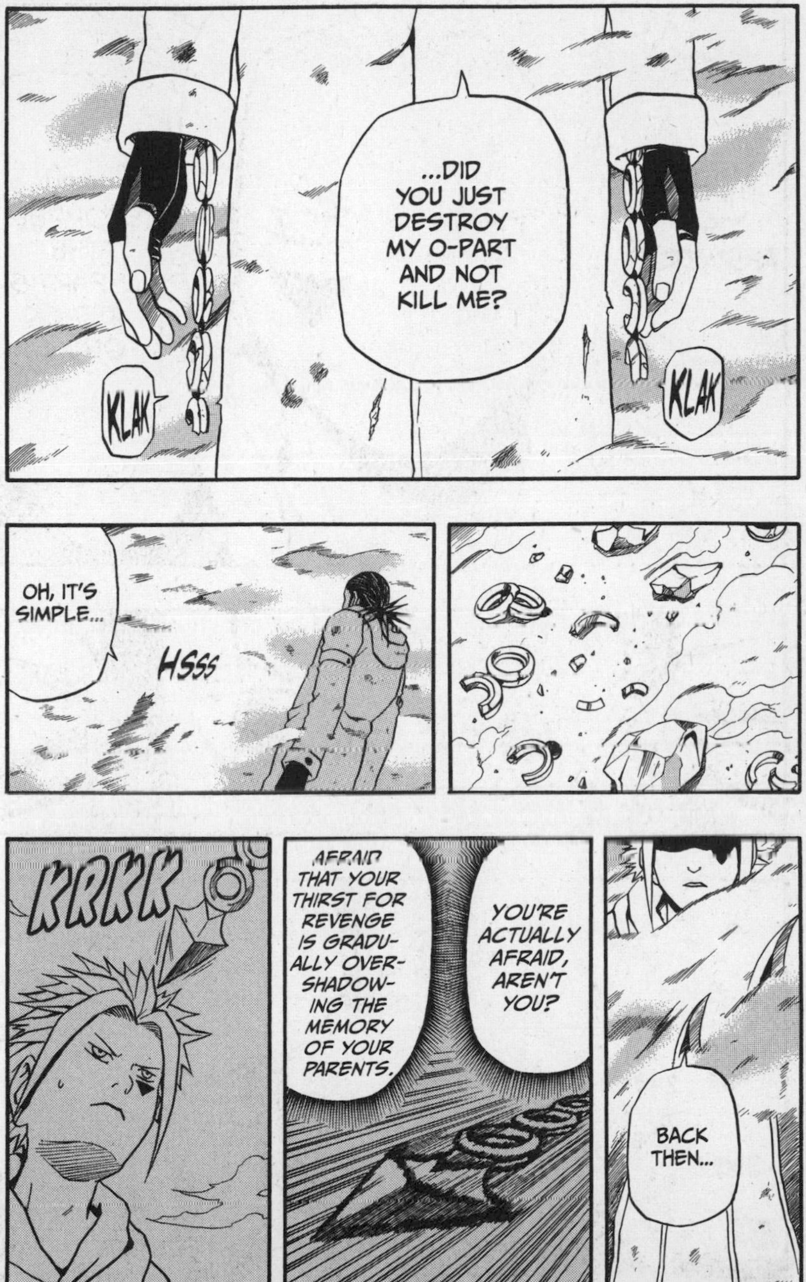
KLAK
...DID YOU JUST DESTROY MY O-PART AND NOT KILL ME?
KLAK
OH, IT'S SIMPLE...
HSSS
BACK THEN...
YOU'RE ACTUALLY AFRAID, AREN'T YOU?
AFRAID THAT YOUR THIRST FOR REVENGE IS GRADUALLY OVER-SHADOWING THE MEMORY OF YOUR PARENTS.
KRKK

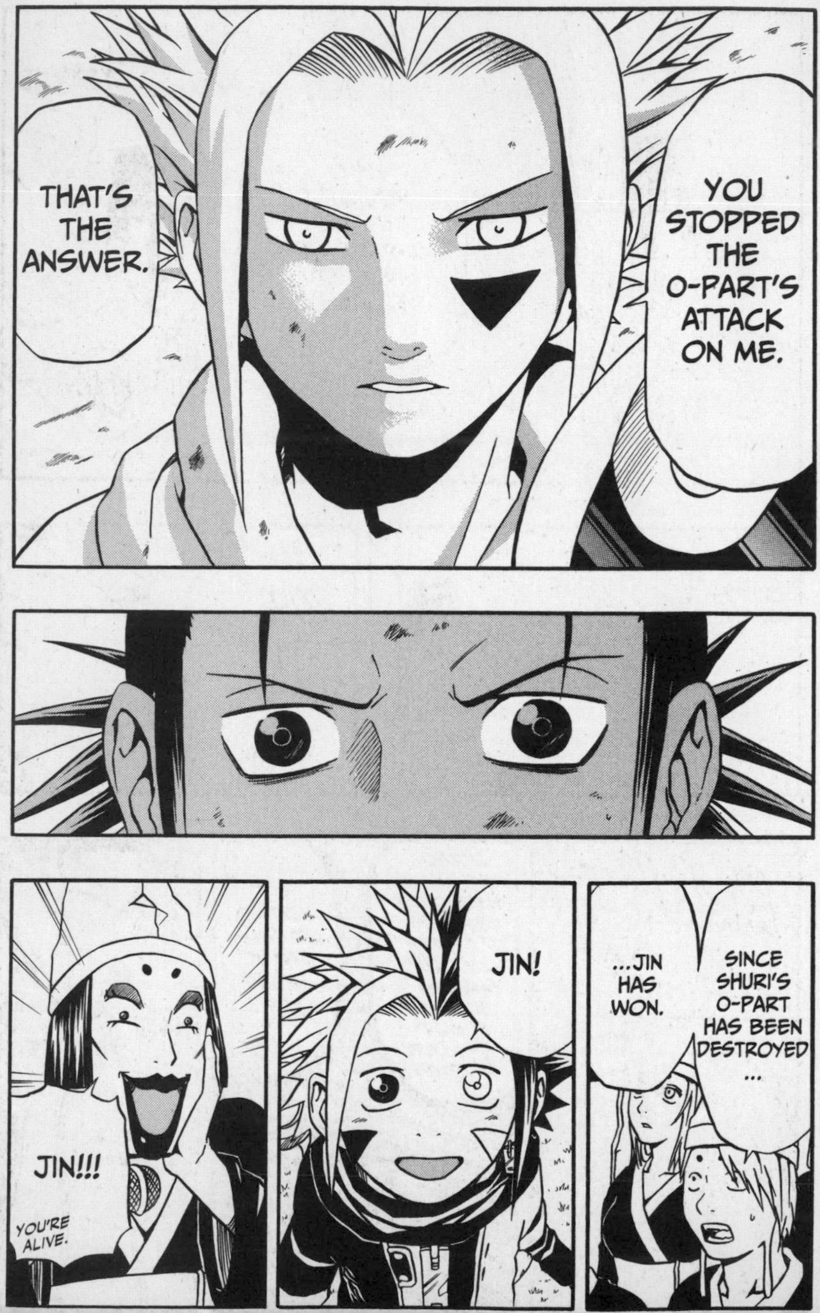
YOU STOPPED THE O-PART'S ATTACK ON ME.
THAT'S THE ANSWER.
SINCE SHURI'S O-PART HAS BEEN DESTROYED ...
...JIN HAS WON.
JIN!
JIN!!!
YOU'RE ALIVE.

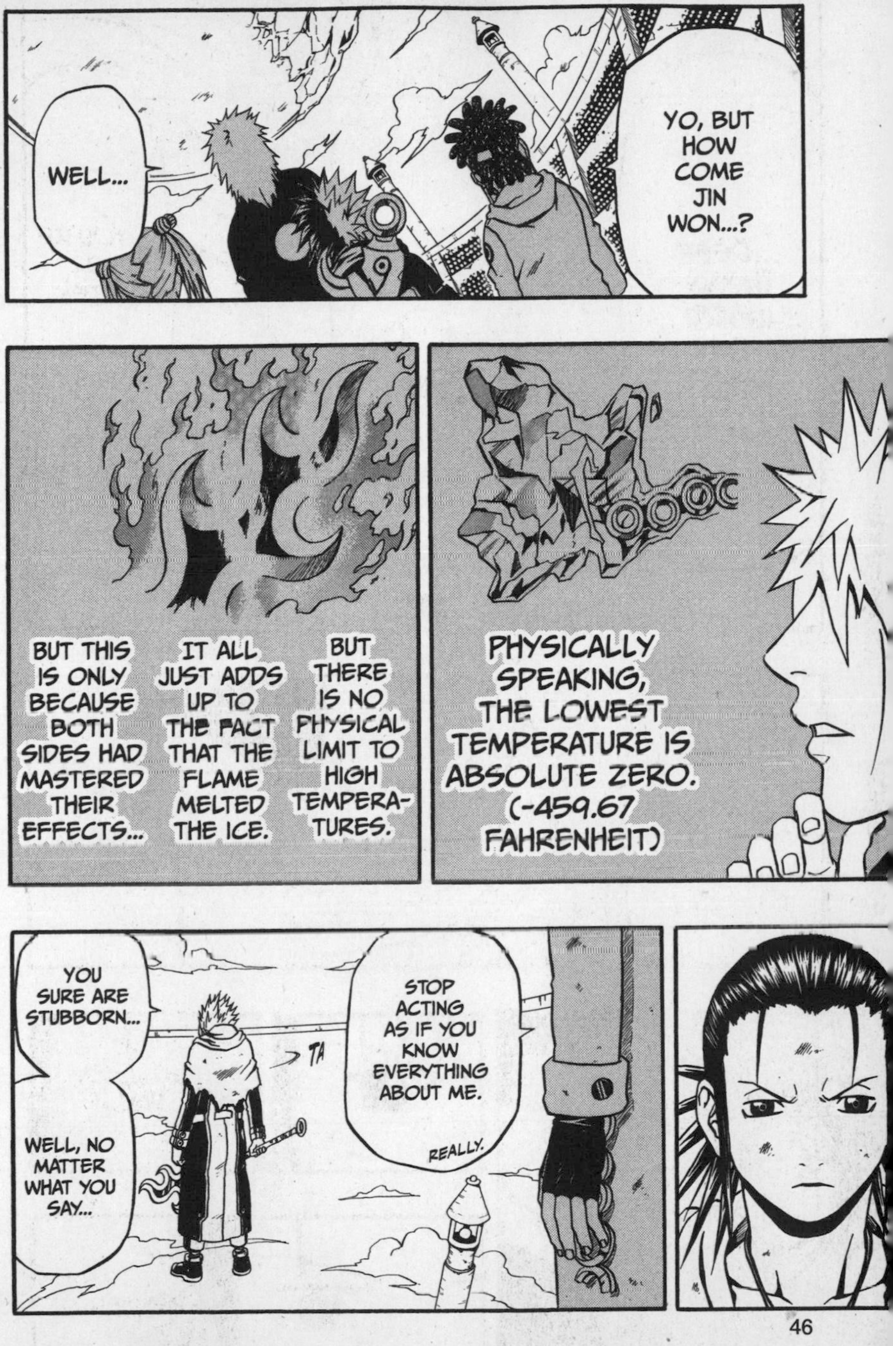
YO, BUT HOW COME JIN WON...?
WELL...
PHYSICALLY SPEAKING, THE LOWEST TEMPERATURE IS ABSOLUTE ZERO. (-459.67 FAHRENHEIT)
BUT THERE IS NO PHYSICAL LIMIT TO HIGH TEMPERA-TURES.
IT ALL JUST ADDS UP TO THE FACT THAT THE FLAME MELTED THE ICE.
BUT THIS IS ONLY BECAUSE BOTH SIDES HAD MASTERED THEIR EFFECTS...
STOP ACTING AS IF YOU KNOW EVERYTHING ABOUT ME.
REALLY.
TA
YOU SURE ARE STUBBORN...
WELL, NO MATTER WHAT YOU SAY...

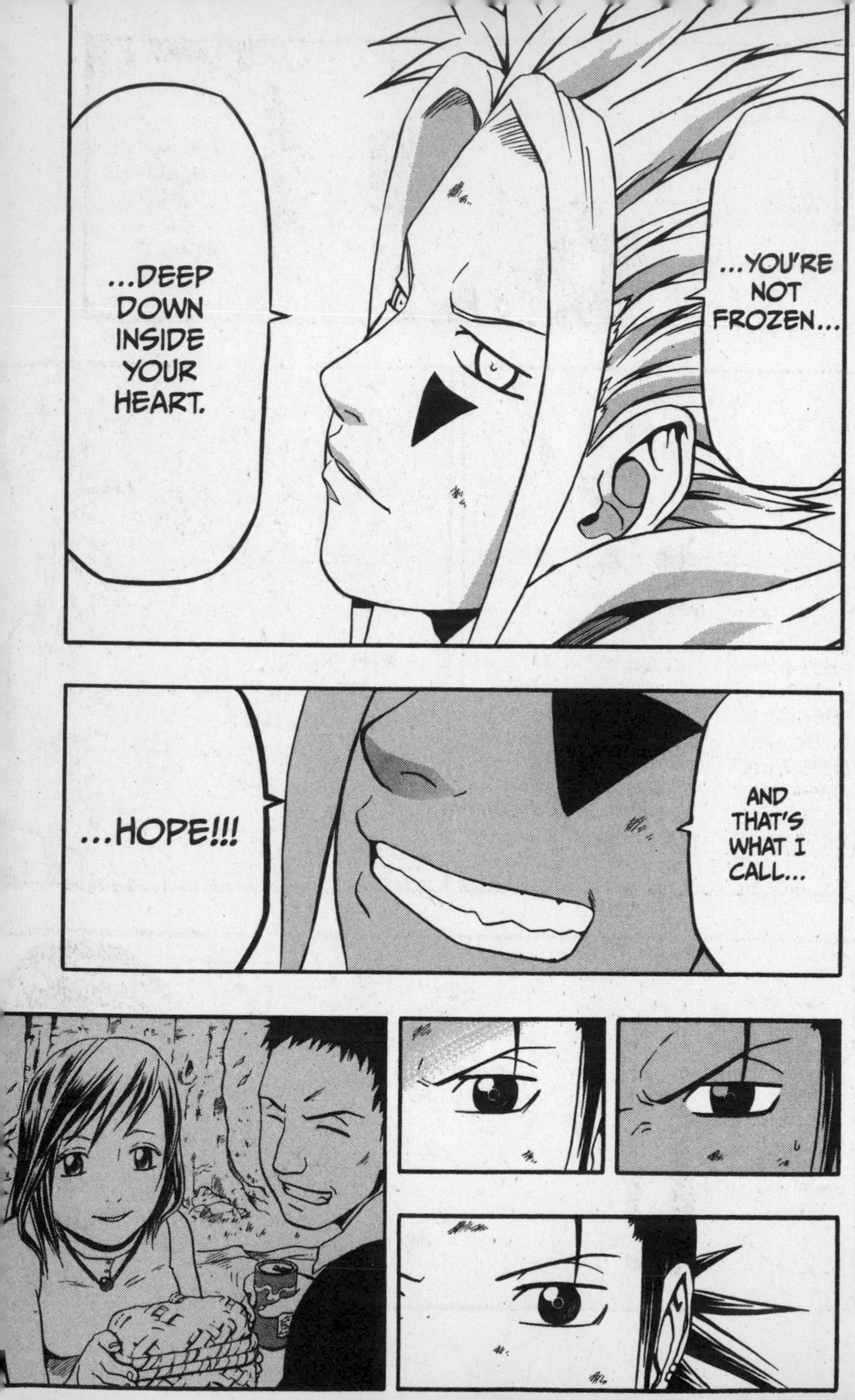
...YOU'RE NOT FROZEN...
...DEEP DOWN INSIDE YOUR HEART.
AND THAT'S WHAT I CALL...
...HOPE!!!

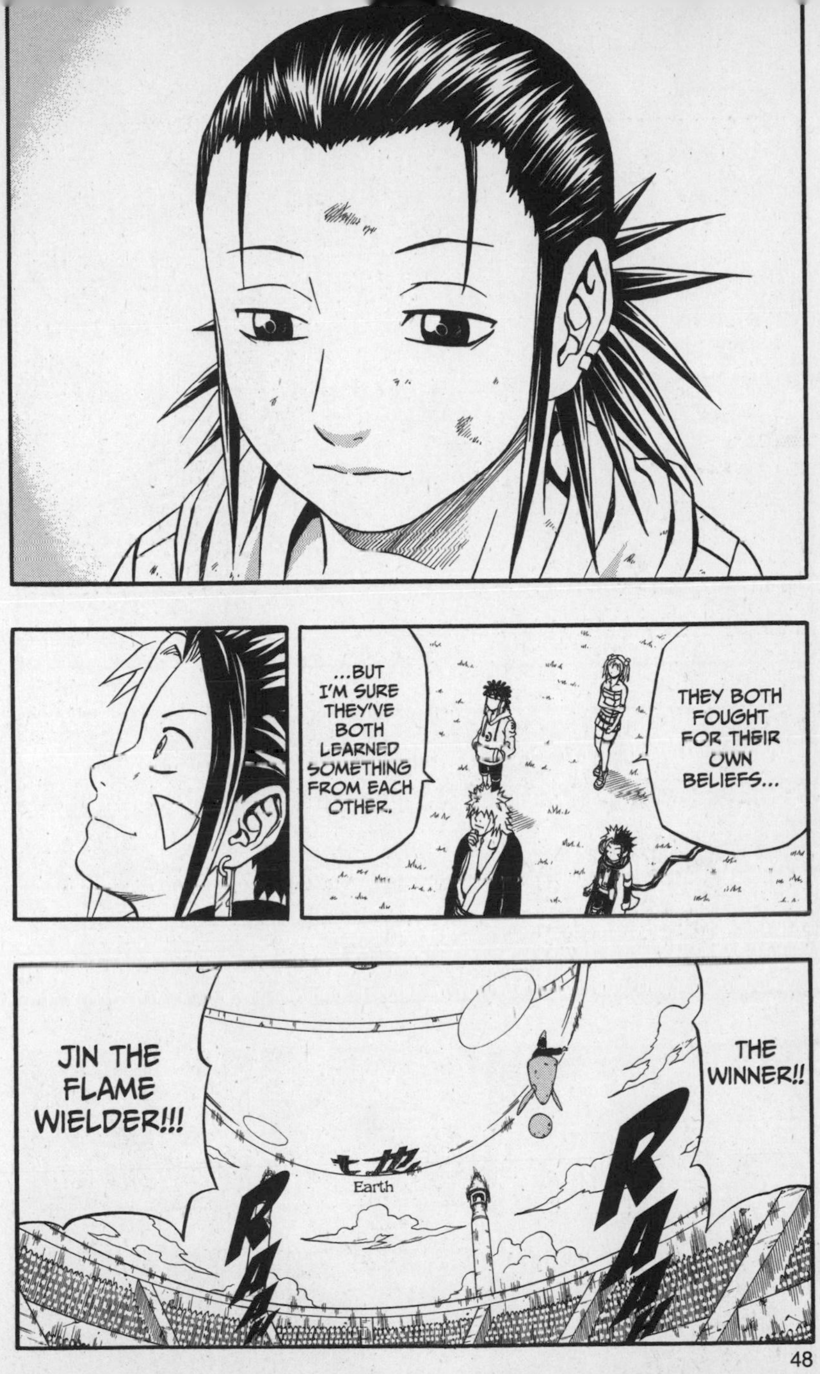
THEY BOTH FOUGHT FOR THEIR OWN BELIEFS...
...BUT I'M SURE THEY'VE BOTH LEARNED SOMETHING FROM EACH OTHER.
THE WINNER!!
JIN THE FLAME WIELDER!!!
Earth

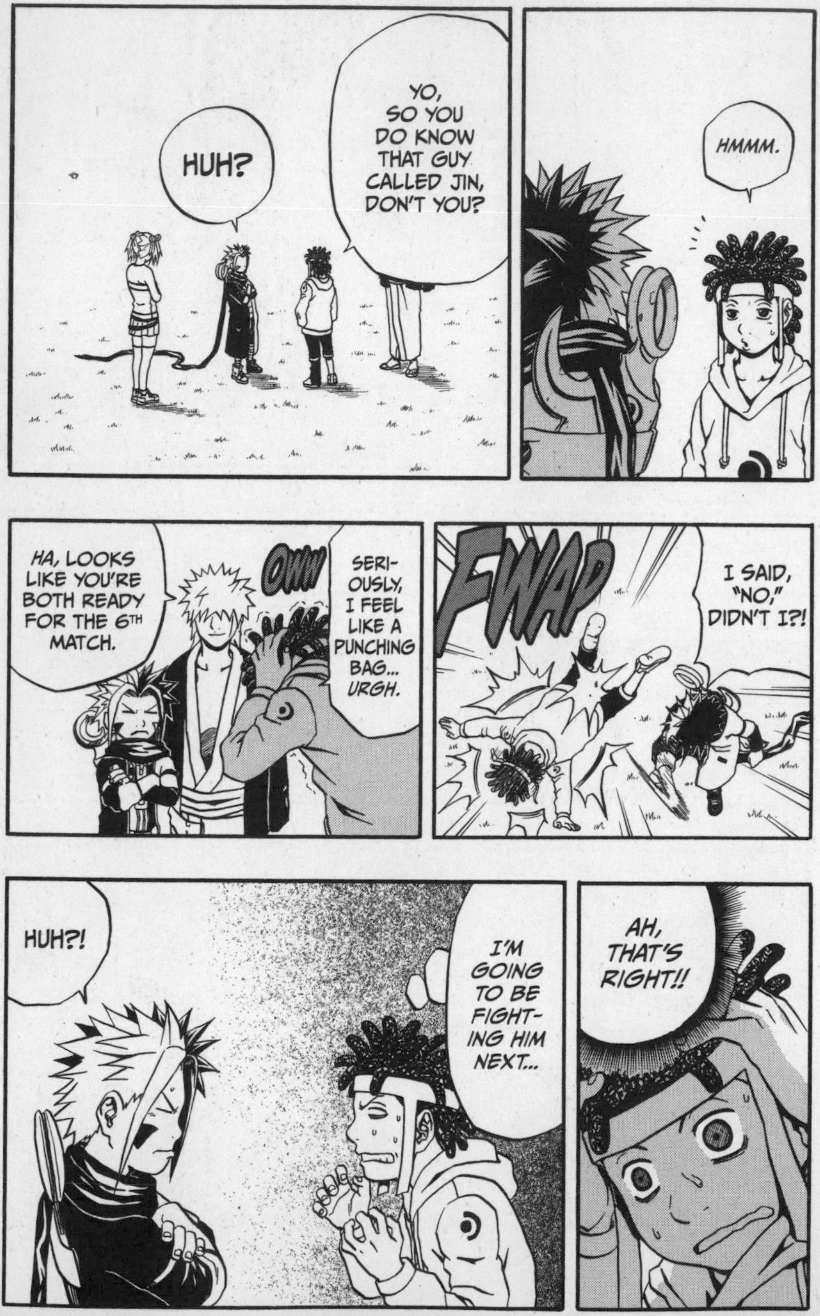
HMMM.
YO, SO YOU DO KNOW THAT GUY CALLED JIN, DON'T YOU?
HUH?
I SAID, "NO," DIDN'T I?!
FWAP
SERI-OUSLY, I FEEL LIKE A PUNCHING BAG... URGH.
OWW
HA, LOOKS LIKE YOU'RE BOTH READY FOR THE 6TH MATCH.
AH, THAT'S RIGHT!!
I'M GOING TO BE FIGHT-ING HIM NEXT...
HUH?!

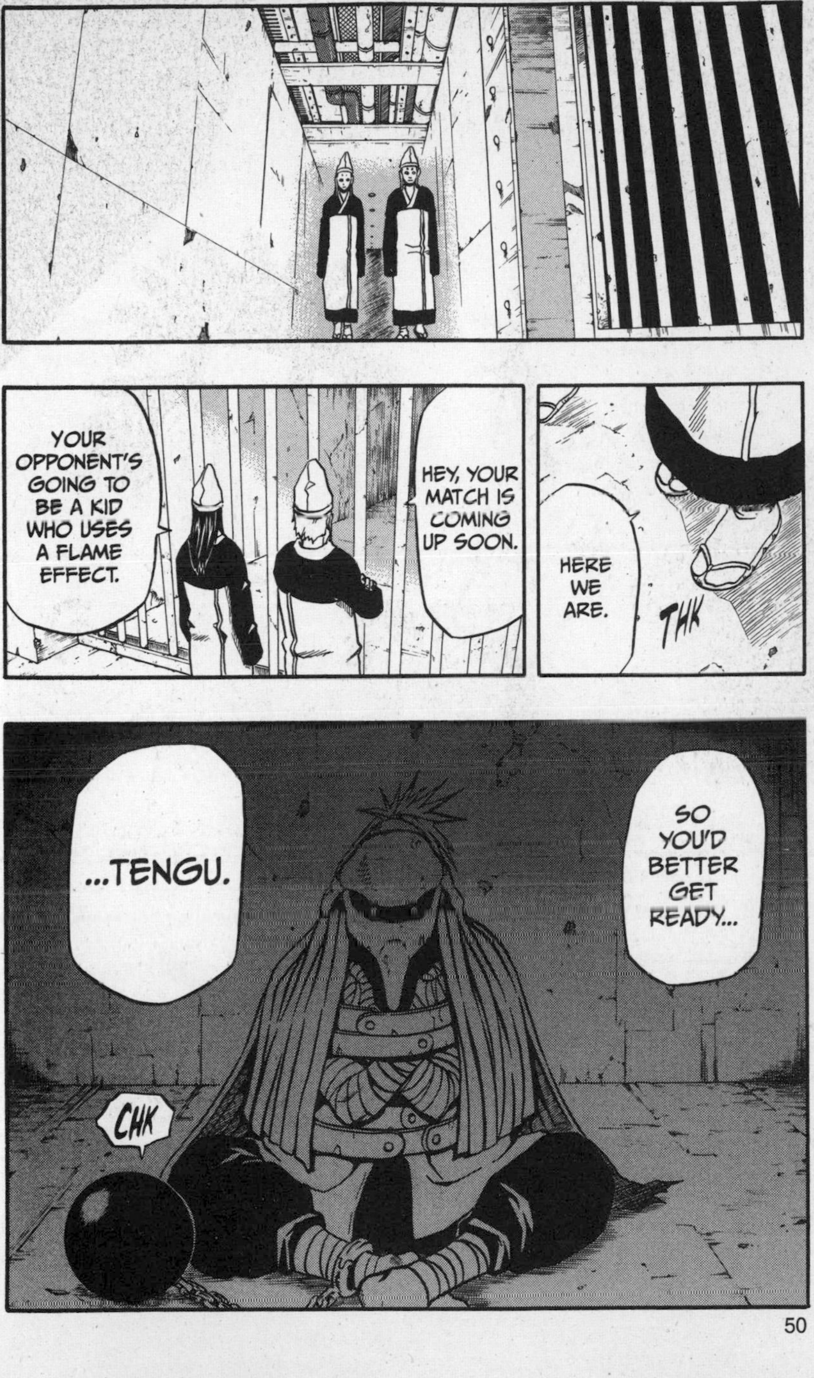
HERE WE ARE.
THK
HEY, YOUR MATCH IS COMING UP SOON.
YOUR OPPONENT'S GOING TO BE A KID WHO USES A FLAME EFFECT.
SO YOU'D BETTER GET READY...
...TENGU.
CHK

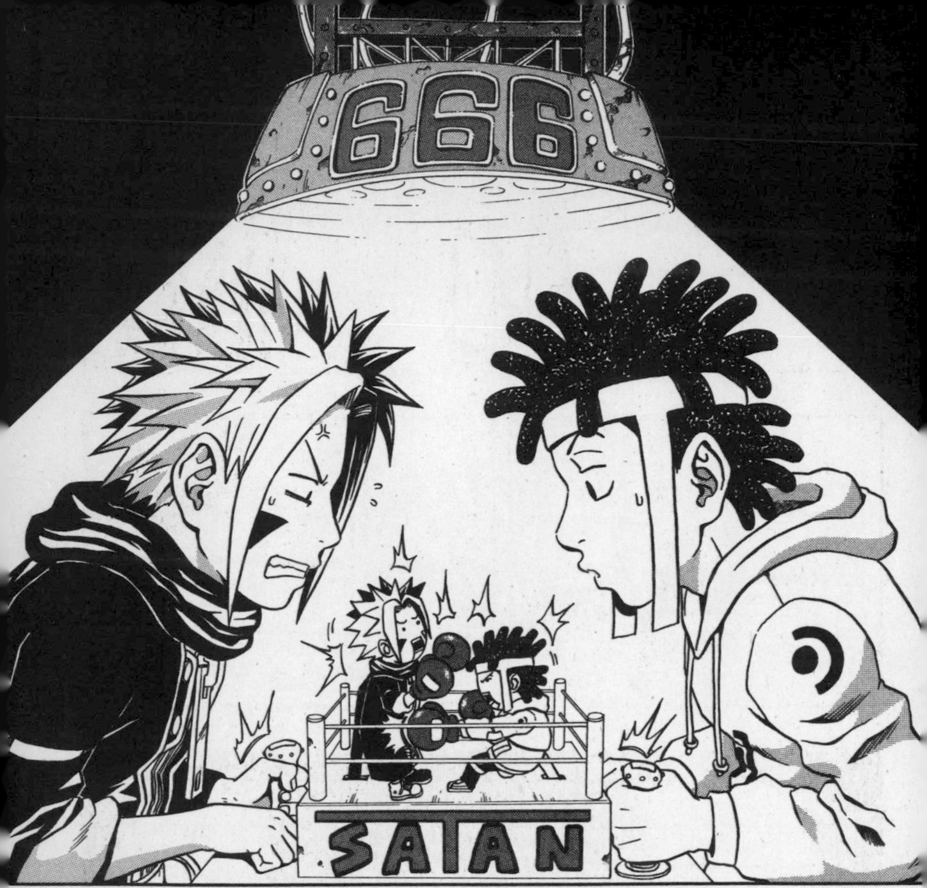
666
SATAN

CHAPTER 42
A RIVAL

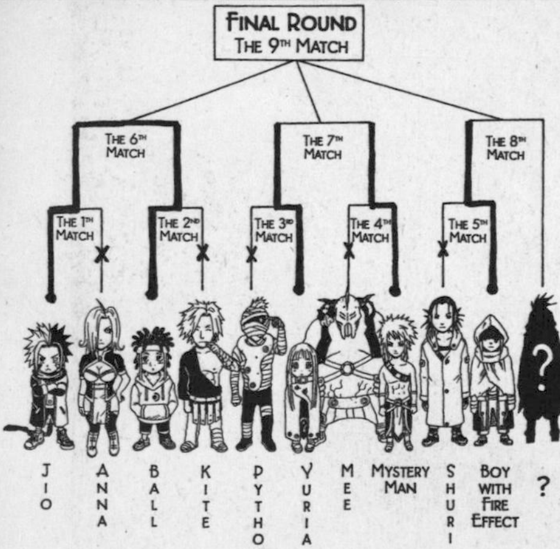
FINAL ROUND
THE 9TH MATCH
THE 6TH MATCH
THE 7TH MATCH
THE 8TH MATCH
THE 1ST MATCH
THE 2ND MATCH
THE 3RD MATCH
THE 4TH MATCH
THE 5TH MATCH
JIO
ANNA
BALL
KITE
PYTHON
YURIA
MEE
MYSTERY MAN
SHURI
BOY WITH FIRE EFFECT
?

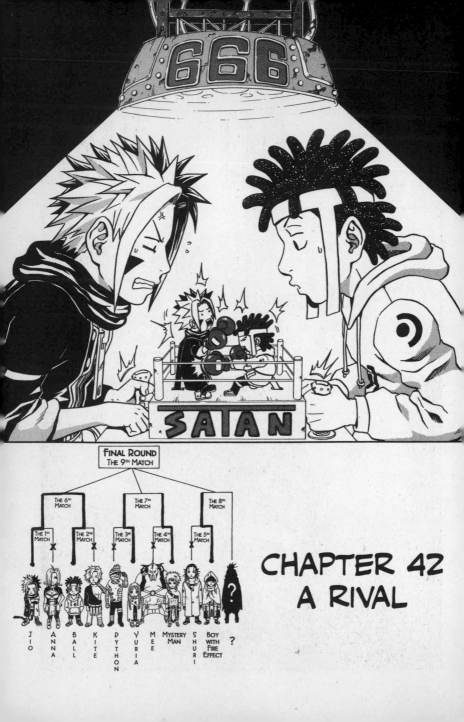

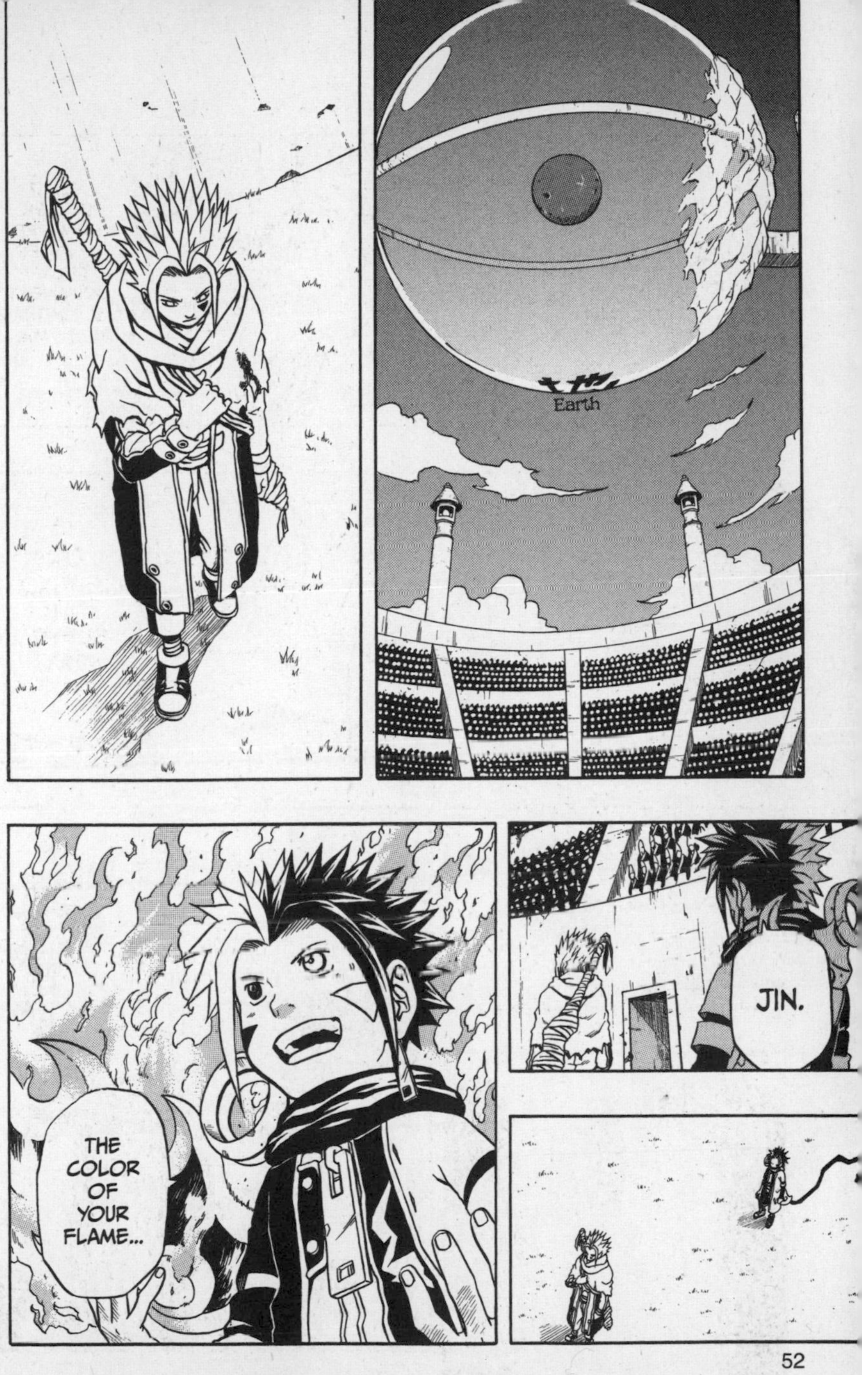
Earth
JIN.
THE COLOR OF YOUR FLAME...

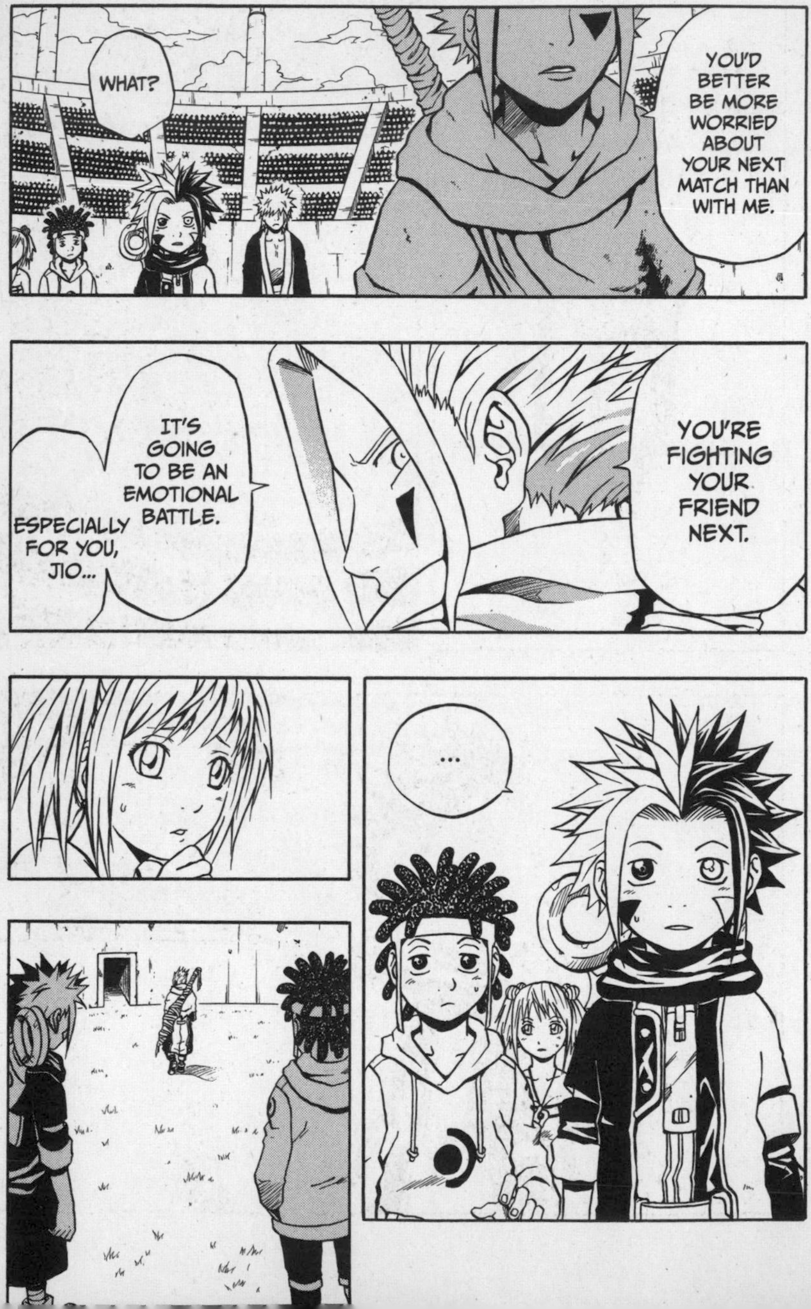
YOU'D BETTER BE MORE WORRIED ABOUT YOUR NEXT MATCH THAN WITH ME.
WHAT?
YOU'RE FIGHTING YOUR FRIEND NEXT.
IT'S GOING TO BE AN EMOTIONAL BATTLE.
ESPECIALLY FOR YOU, JIO...
...

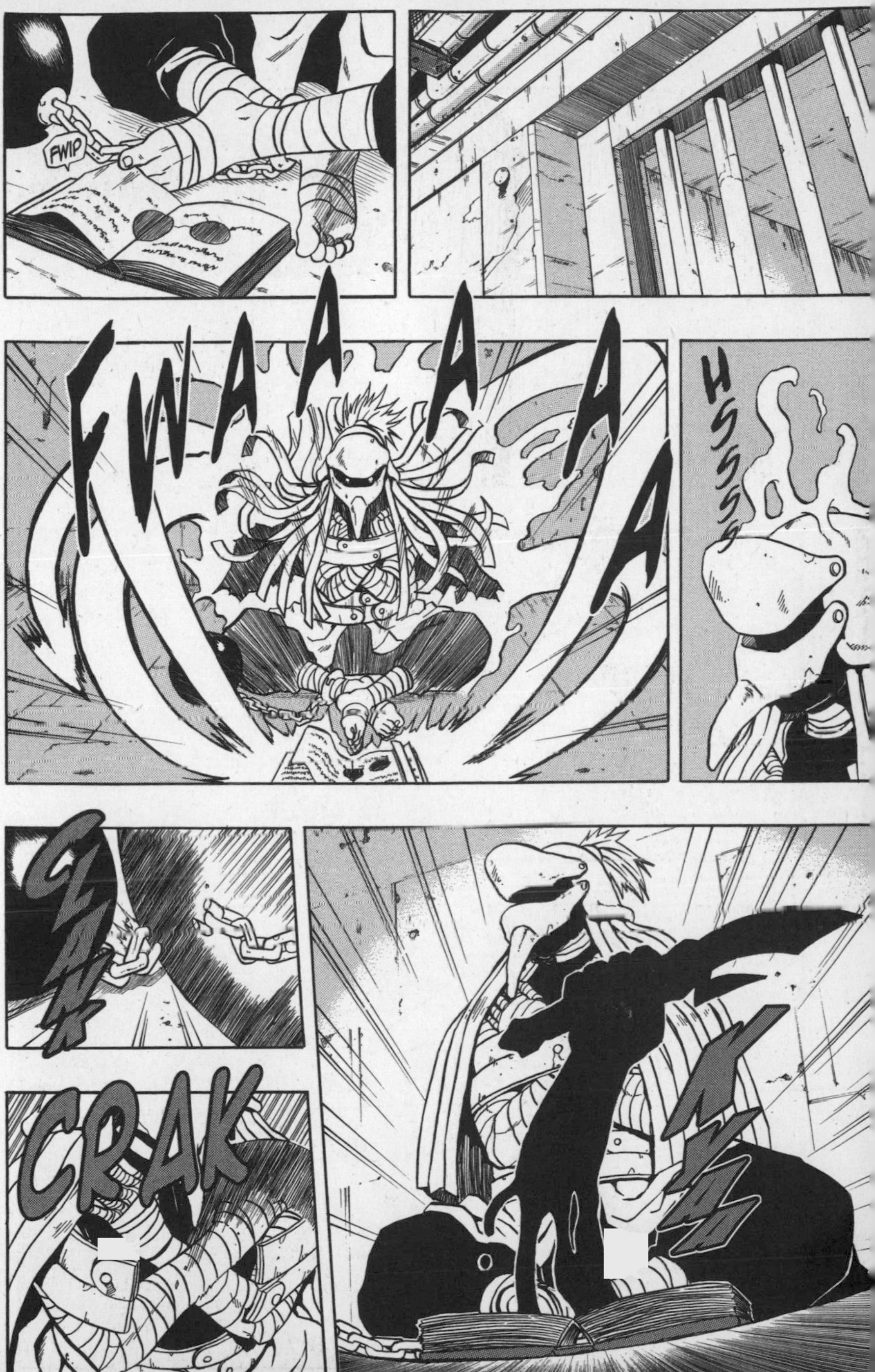
FWIP
HSSSS
FWAAAAA
CRAK

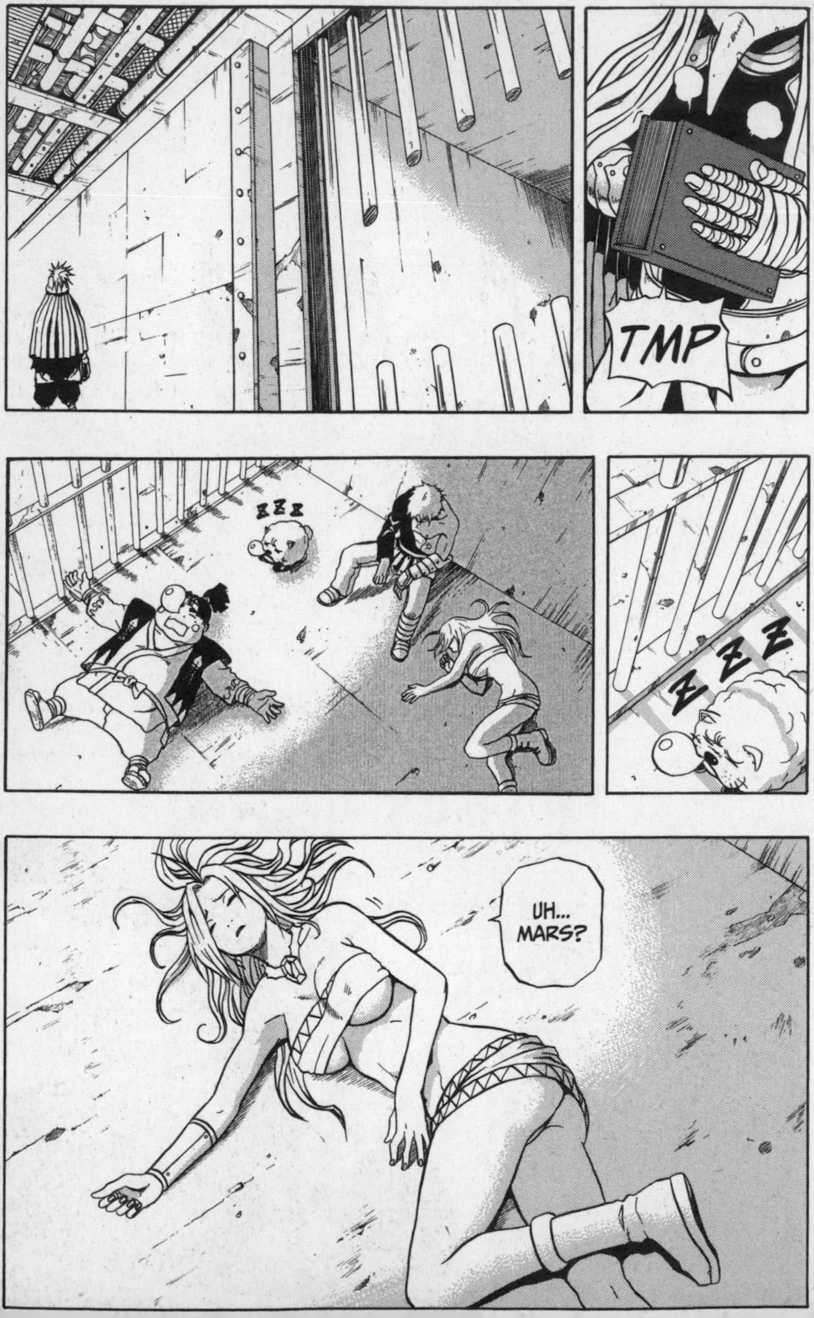
TMP
ZZZ
ZZZ
UH... MARS?

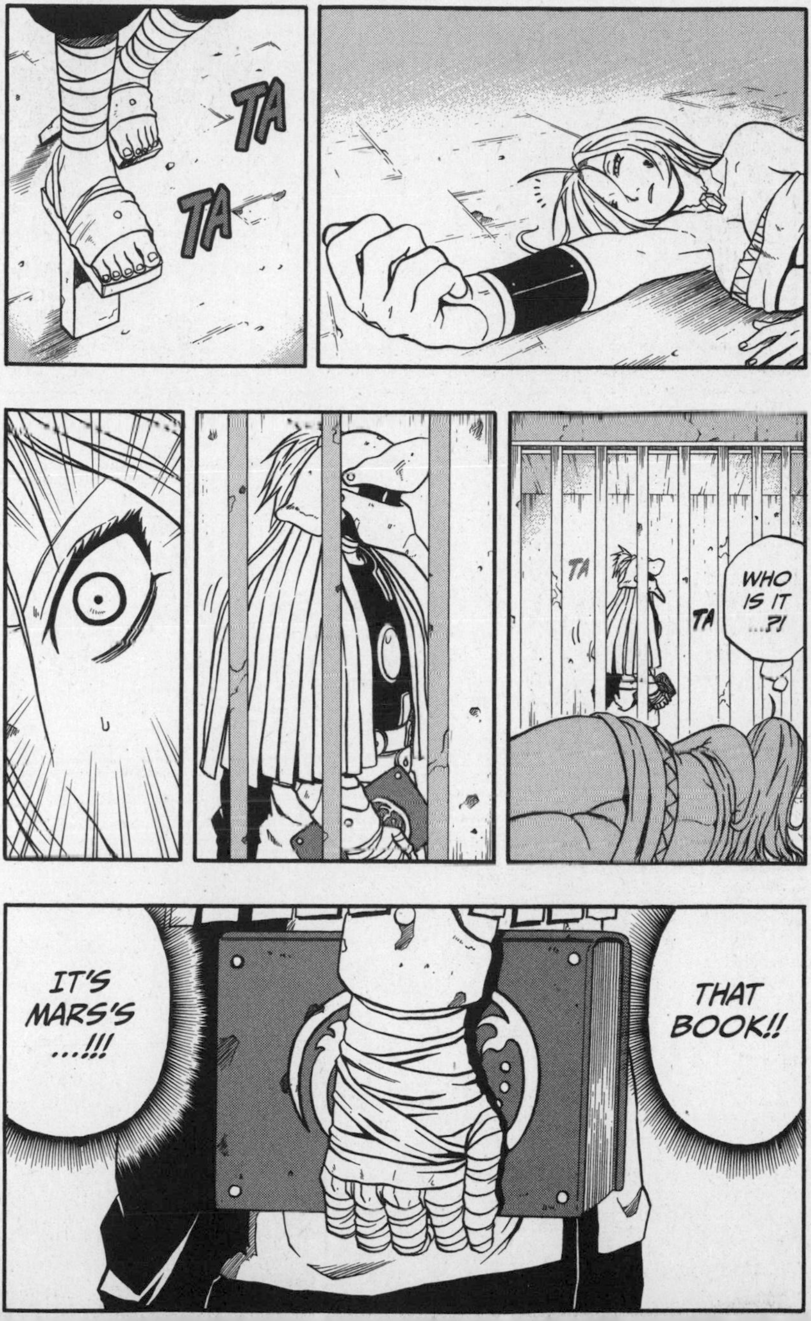
TA
TA
TA
TA
WHO IS IT ...?!
THAT BOOK!!
IT'S MARS'S ...!!!

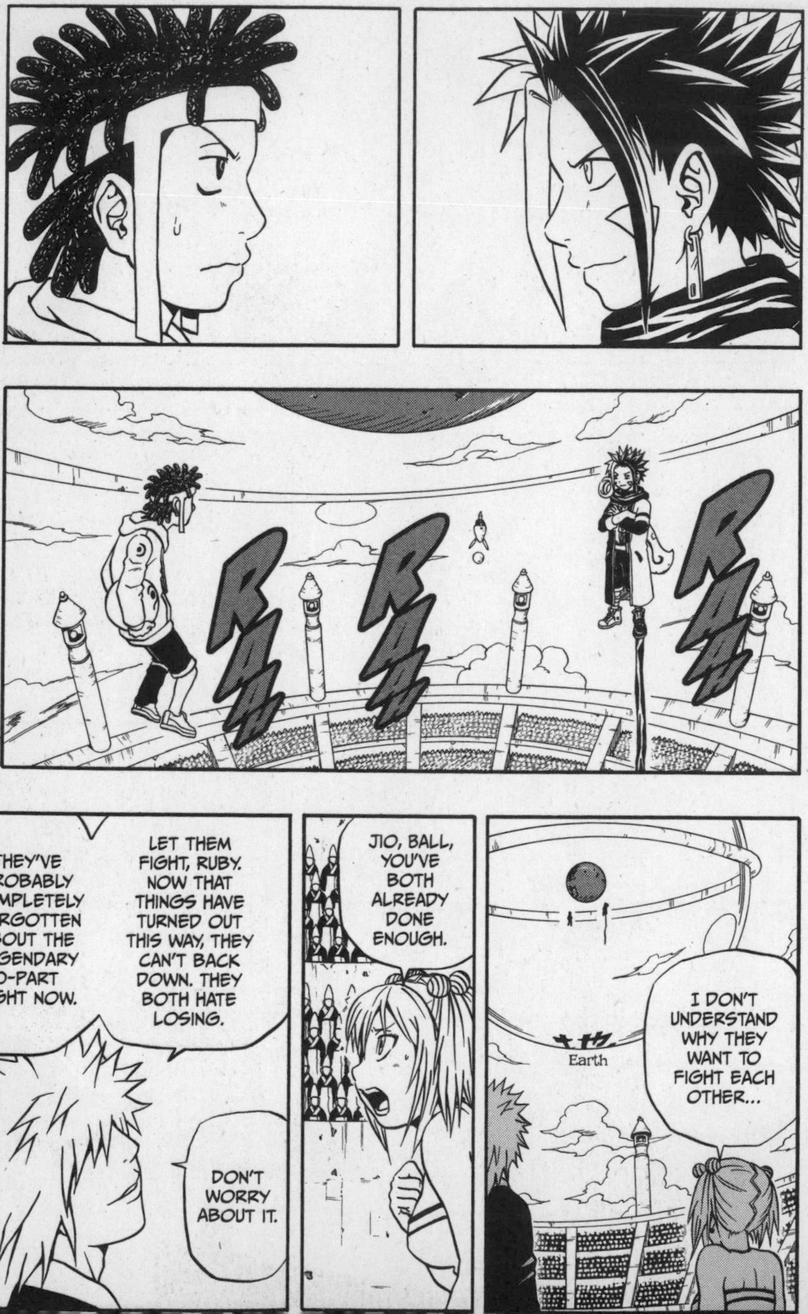
Earth
I DON'T UNDERSTAND WHY THEY WANT TO FIGHT EACH OTHER...
JIO, BALL, YOU'VE BOTH ALREADY DONE ENOUGH.
LET THEM FIGHT, RUBY. NOW THAT THINGS HAVE TURNED OUT THIS WAY, THEY CAN'T BACK DOWN. THEY BOTH HATE LOSING.
THEY'VE PROBABLY COMPLETELY FORGOTTEN ABOUT THE LEGENDARY O-PART RIGHT NOW.
DON'T WORRY ABOUT IT.

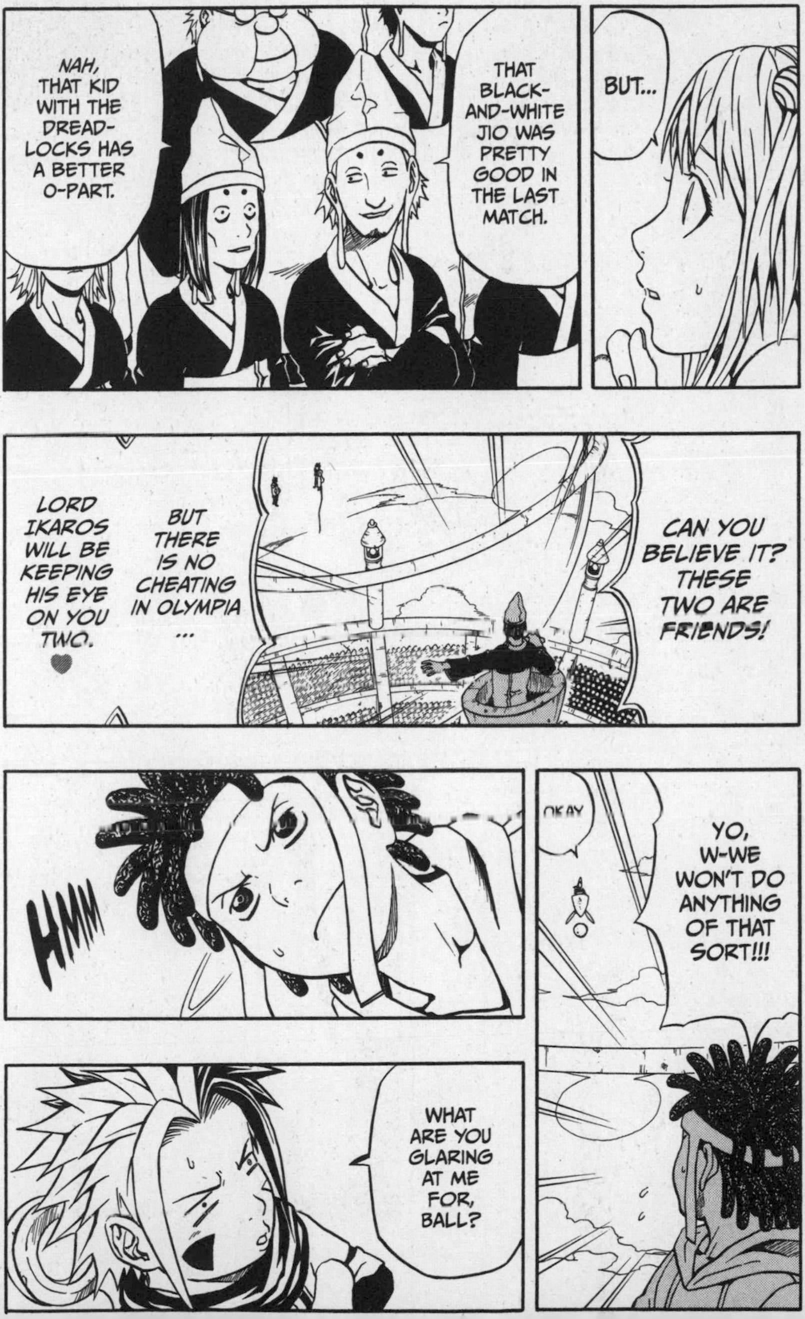
BUT...
THAT BLACK-AND-WHITE JIO WAS PRETTY GOOD IN THE LAST MATCH.
NAH, THAT KID WITH THE DREAD-LOCKS HAS A BETTER O-PART.
CAN YOU BELIEVE IT? THESE TWO ARE FRIENDS!
BUT THERE IS NO CHEATING IN OLYMPIA ...
LORD IKAROS WILL BE KEEPING HIS EYE ON YOU TWO. ♥
YO, W-WE WON'T DO ANYTHING OF THAT SORT!!!
OKAY
HMM
WHAT ARE YOU GLARING AT ME FOR, BALL?

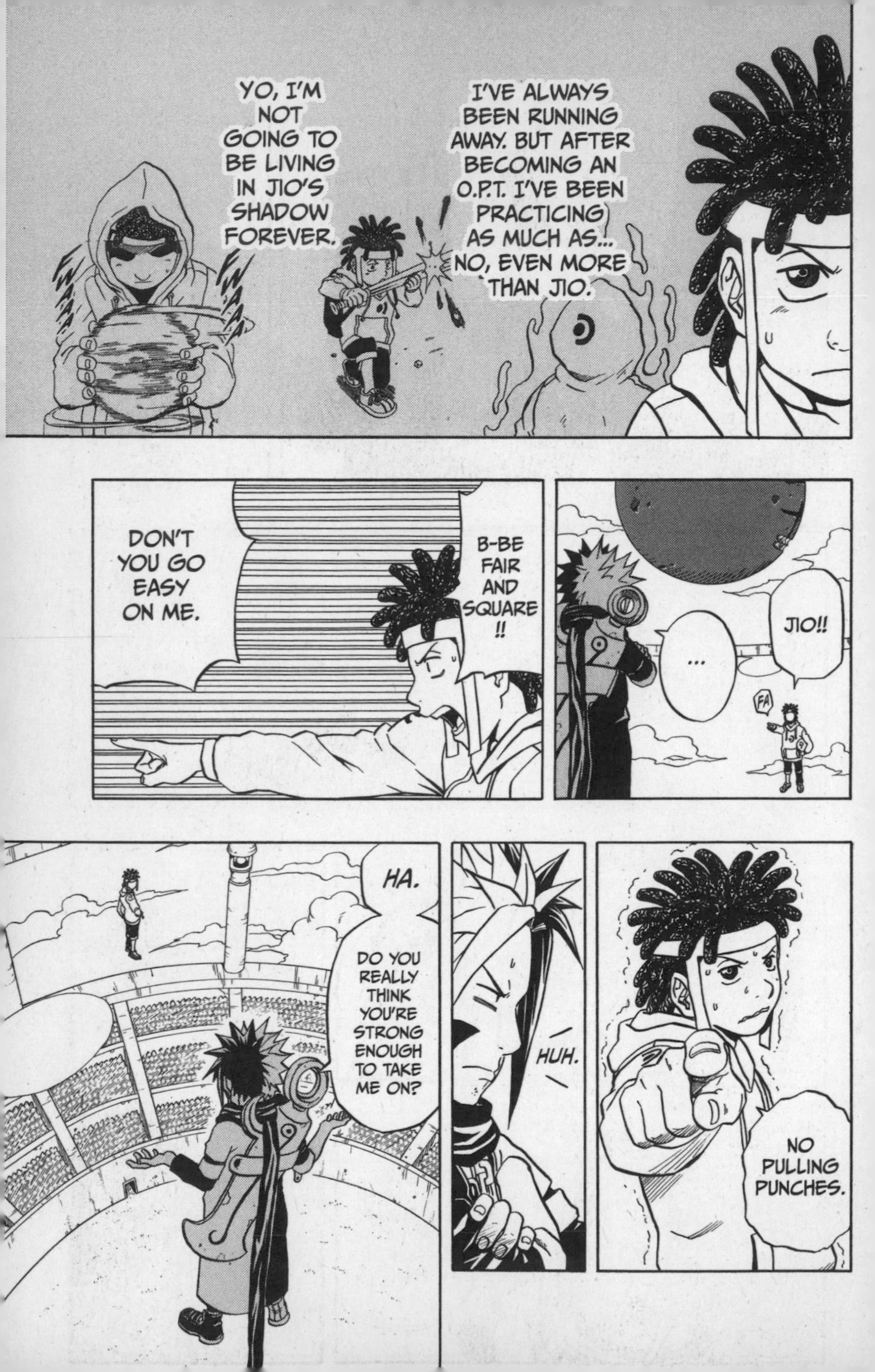
I'VE ALWAYS BEEN RUNNING AWAY. BUT AFTER BECOMING AN O.P.T. I'VE BEEN PRACTICING AS MUCH AS... NO, EVEN MORE THAN JIO.
YO, I'M NOT GOING TO BE LIVING IN JIO'S SHADOW FOREVER.
JIO!!
...
FA
B-BE FAIR AND SQUARE!!
DON'T YOU GO EASY ON ME.
NO PULLING PUNCHES.
HUH.
HA.
DO YOU REALLY THINK YOU'RE STRONG ENOUGH TO TAKE ME ON?

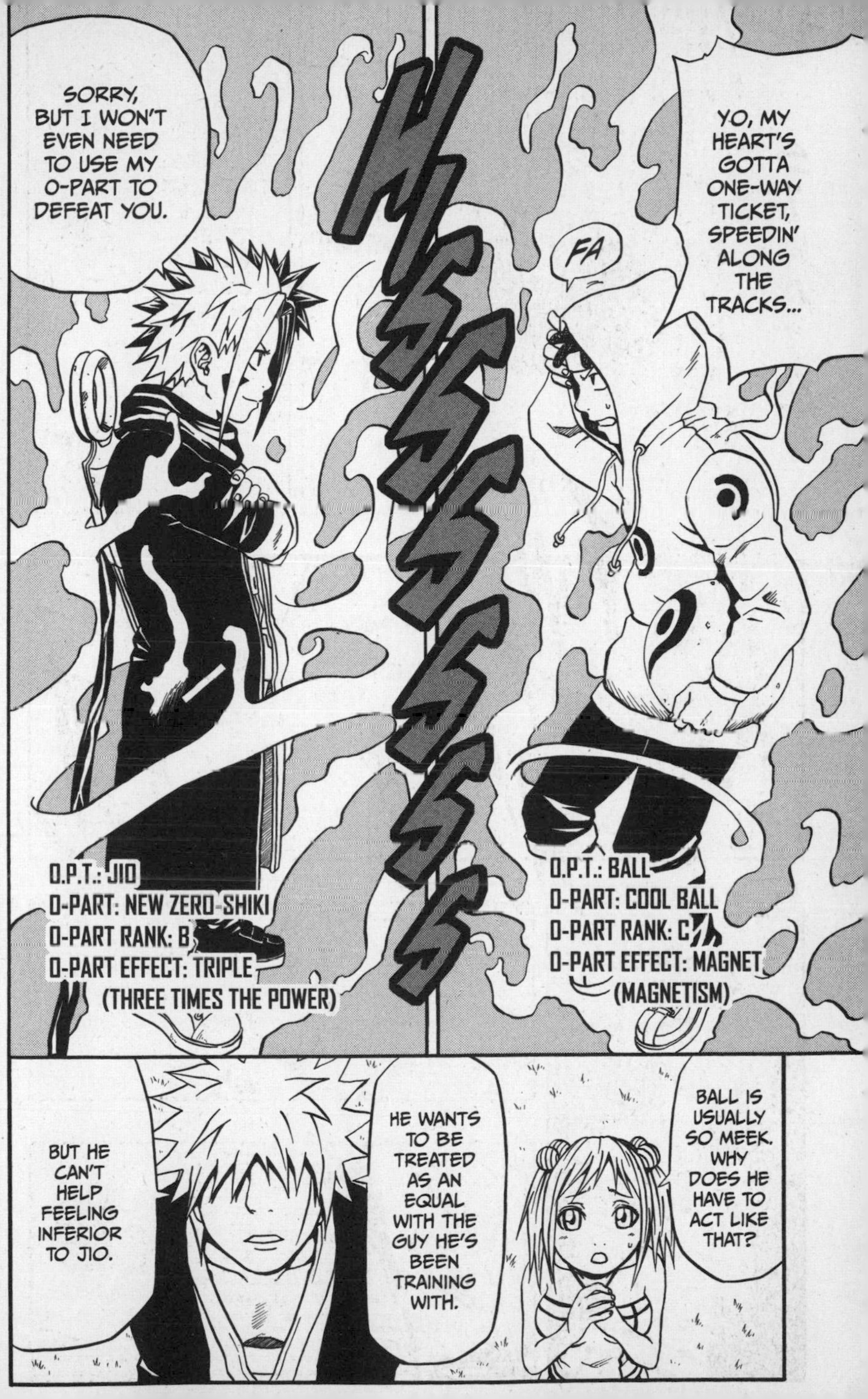

YO, MY HEART'S GOTTA ONE-WAY TICKET, SPEEDIN' ALONG THE TRACKS...
FA
SORRY, BUT I WON'T EVEN NEED TO USE MY O-PART TO DEFEAT YOU.
O.P.T.: BALL
O-PART: COOL BALL
O-PART RANK: C
O-PART EFFECT: MAGNET (MAGNETISM)
O.P.T.: JIO
O-PART: NEW ZERO-SHIKI
O-PART RANK: B
O-PART EFFECT: TRIPLE (THREE TIMES THE POWER)
BALL IS USUALLY SO MEEK. WHY DOES HE HAVE TO ACT LIKE THAT?
HE WANTS TO BE TREATED AS AN EQUAL WITH THE GUY HE'S BEEN TRAINING WITH.
BUT HE CAN'T HELP FEELING INFERIOR TO JIO.

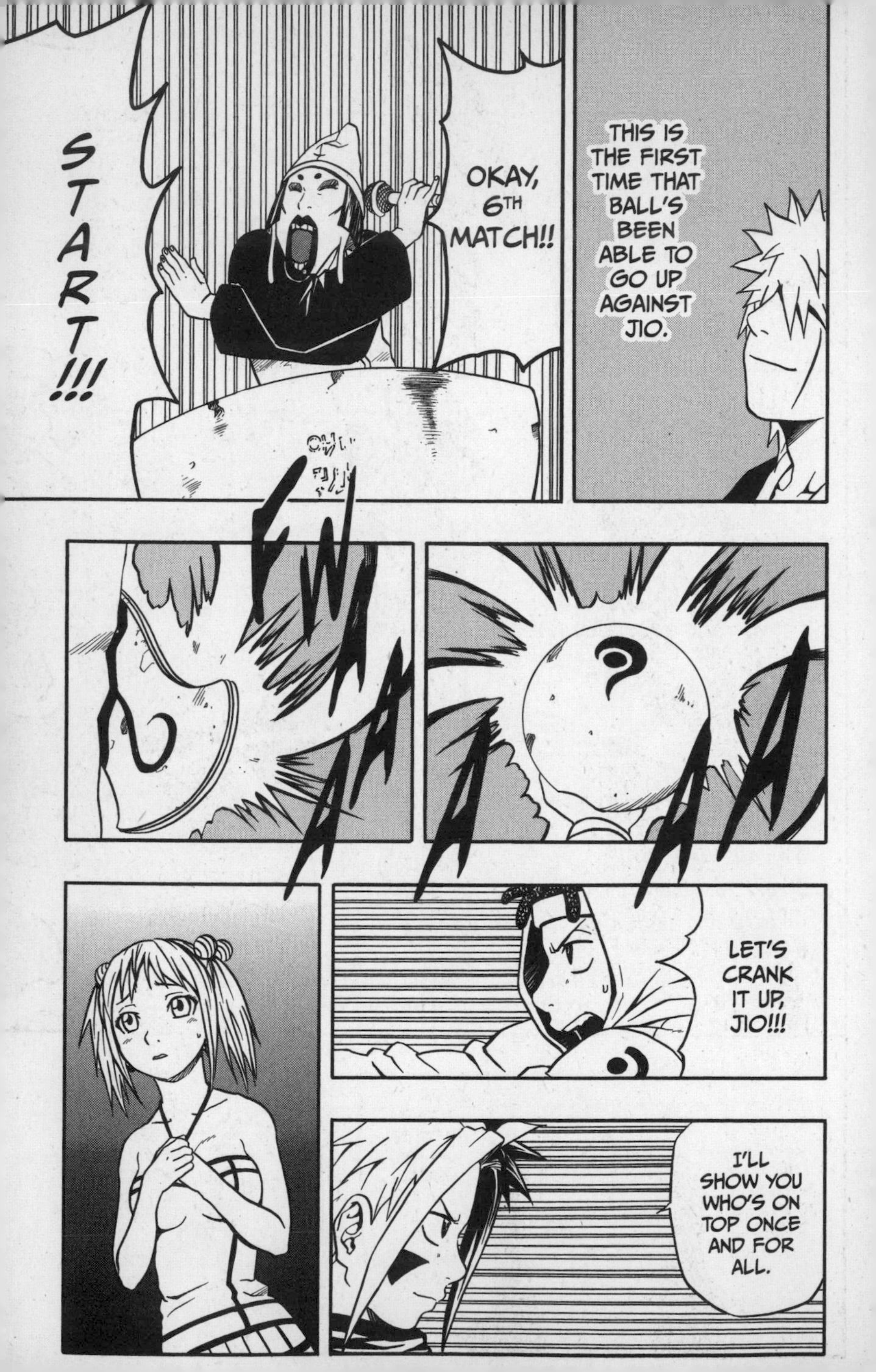
THIS IS THE FIRST TIME THAT BALL'S BEEN ABLE TO GO UP AGAINST JIO.
OKAY, 6TH MATCH!!
START!!!
LET'S CRANK IT UP, JIO!!!
I'LL SHOW YOU WHO'S ON TOP ONCE AND FOR ALL.

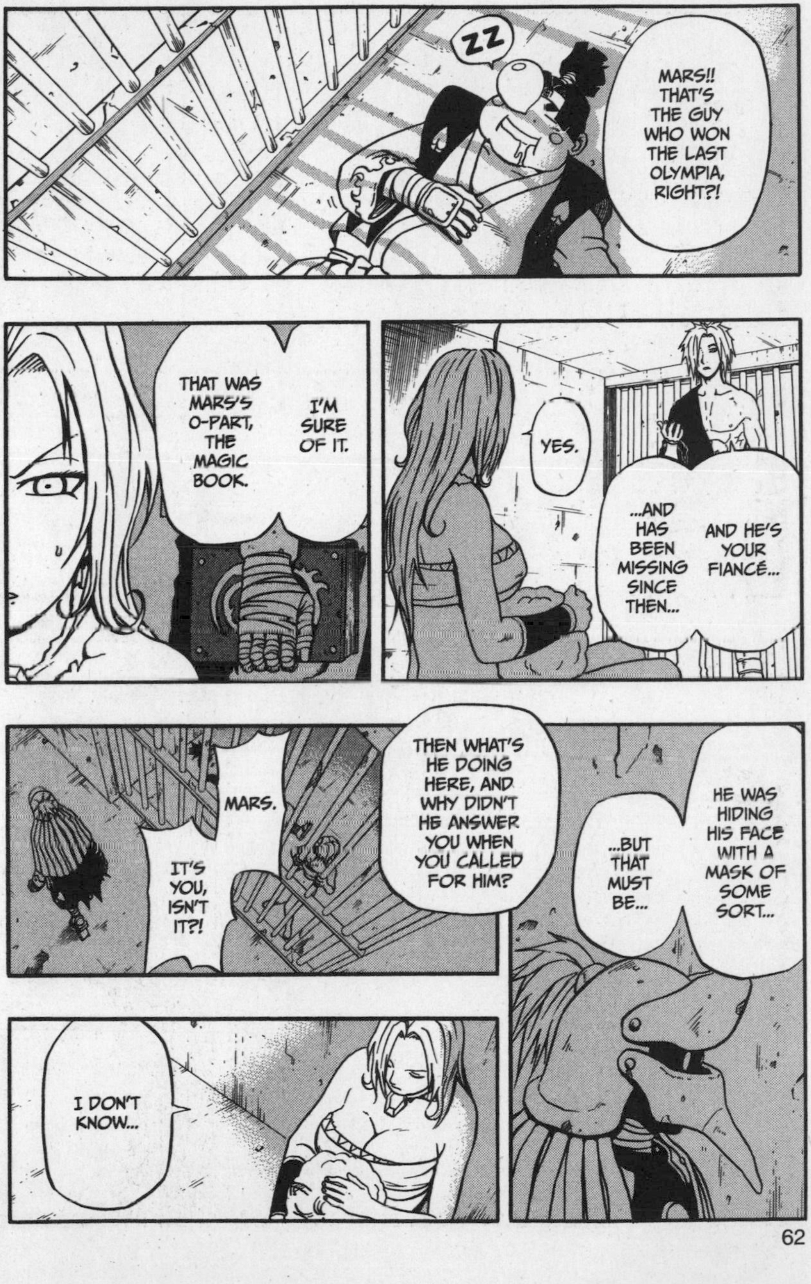

MARS!! THAT'S THE GUY WHO WON THE LAST OLYMPIA, RIGHT?!
ZZ
YES.
AND HE'S YOUR FIANCÉ...
...AND HAS BEEN MISSING SINCE THEN...
I'M SURE OF IT.
THAT WAS MARS'S O-PART, THE MAGIC BOOK.
HE WAS HIDING HIS FACE WITH A MASK OF SOME SORT...
...BUT THAT MUST BE...
THEN WHAT'S HE DOING HERE, AND WHY DIDN'T HE ANSWER YOU WHEN YOU CALLED FOR HIM?
MARS.
IT'S YOU, ISN'T IT?!
I DON'T KNOW...

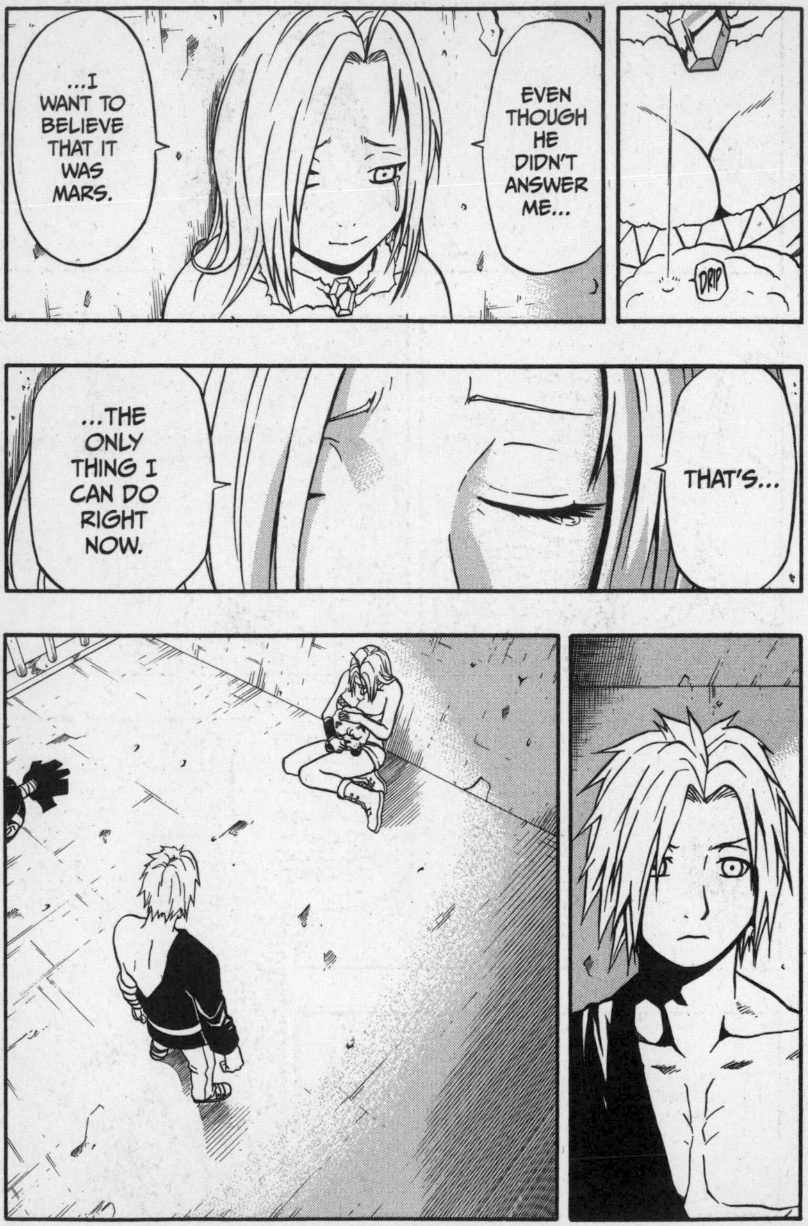
DRIP
EVEN THOUGH HE DIDN'T ANSWER ME...
...I WANT TO BELIEVE THAT IT WAS MARS.
THAT'S...
...THE ONLY THING I CAN DO RIGHT NOW.

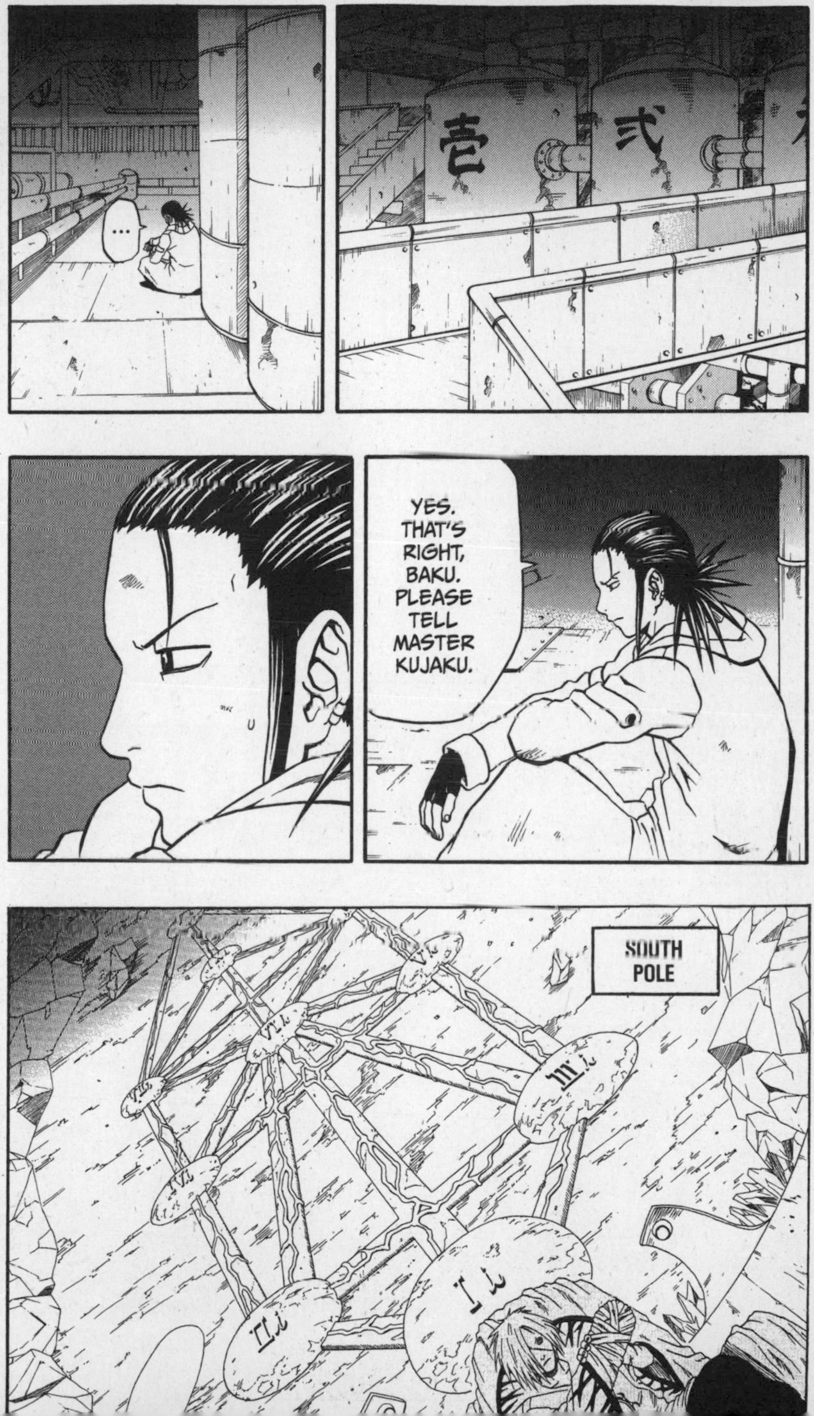
壱
弐
...
YES. THAT'S RIGHT, BAKU. PLEASE TELL MASTER KUJAKU.
SOUTH POLE

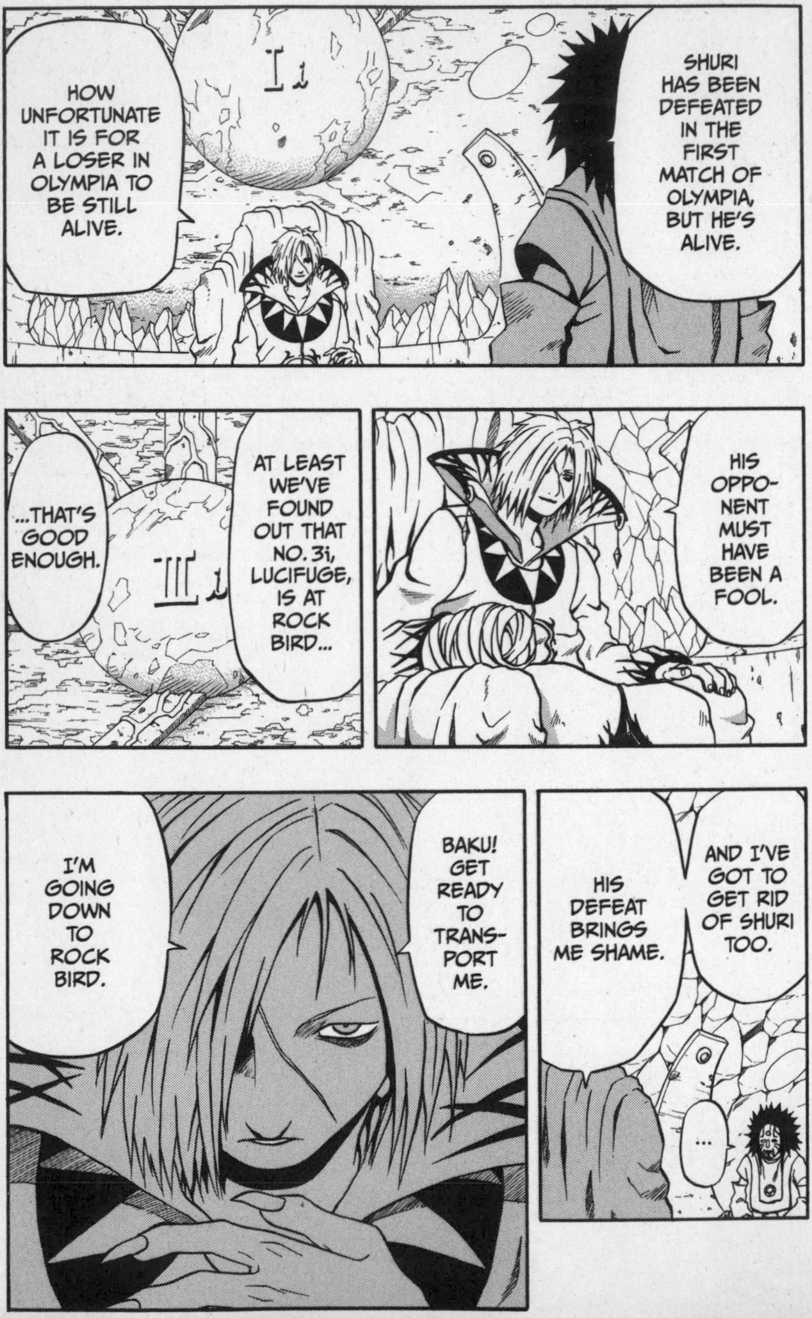
SHURI HAS BEEN DEFEATED IN THE FIRST MATCH OF OLYMPIA, BUT HE'S ALIVE.
HOW UNFORTUNATE IT IS FOR A LOSER IN OLYMPIA TO BE STILL ALIVE.
HIS OPPONENT MUST HAVE BEEN A FOOL.
AT LEAST WE'VE FOUND OUT THAT NO. 3i, LUCIFUGE, IS AT ROCK BIRD...
...THAT'S GOOD ENOUGH.
AND I'VE GOT TO GET RID OF SHURI TOO.
HIS DEFEAT BRINGS ME SHAME.
...
BAKU! GET READY TO TRANSPORT ME.
I'M GOING DOWN TO ROCK BIRD.

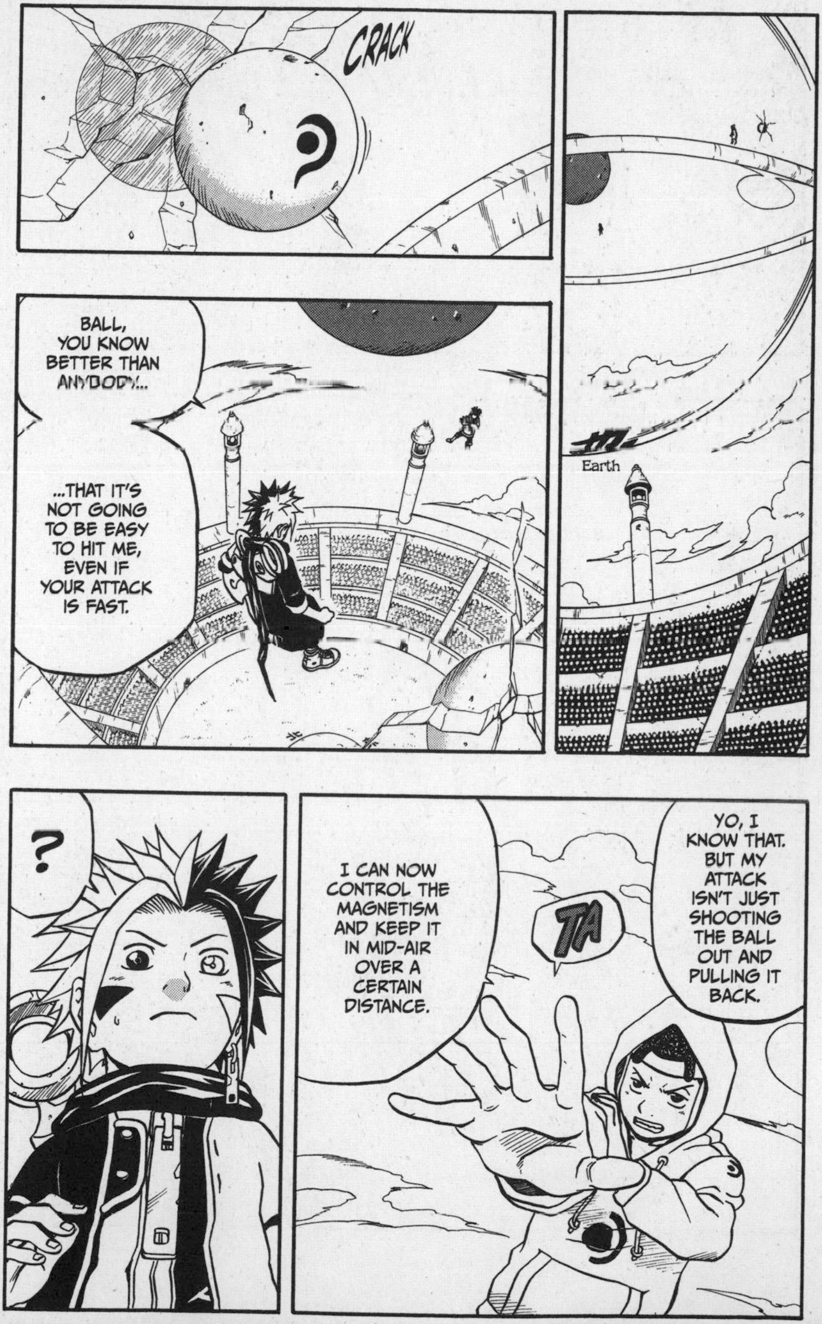
Earth
CRACK
BALL, YOU KNOW BETTER THAN ANYBODY...
...THAT IT'S NOT GOING TO BE EASY TO HIT ME, EVEN IF YOUR ATTACK IS FAST.
YO, I KNOW THAT. BUT MY ATTACK ISN'T JUST SHOOTING THE BALL OUT AND PULLING IT BACK.
TA
I CAN NOW CONTROL THE MAGNETISM AND KEEP IT IN MID-AIR OVER A CERTAIN DISTANCE.
?

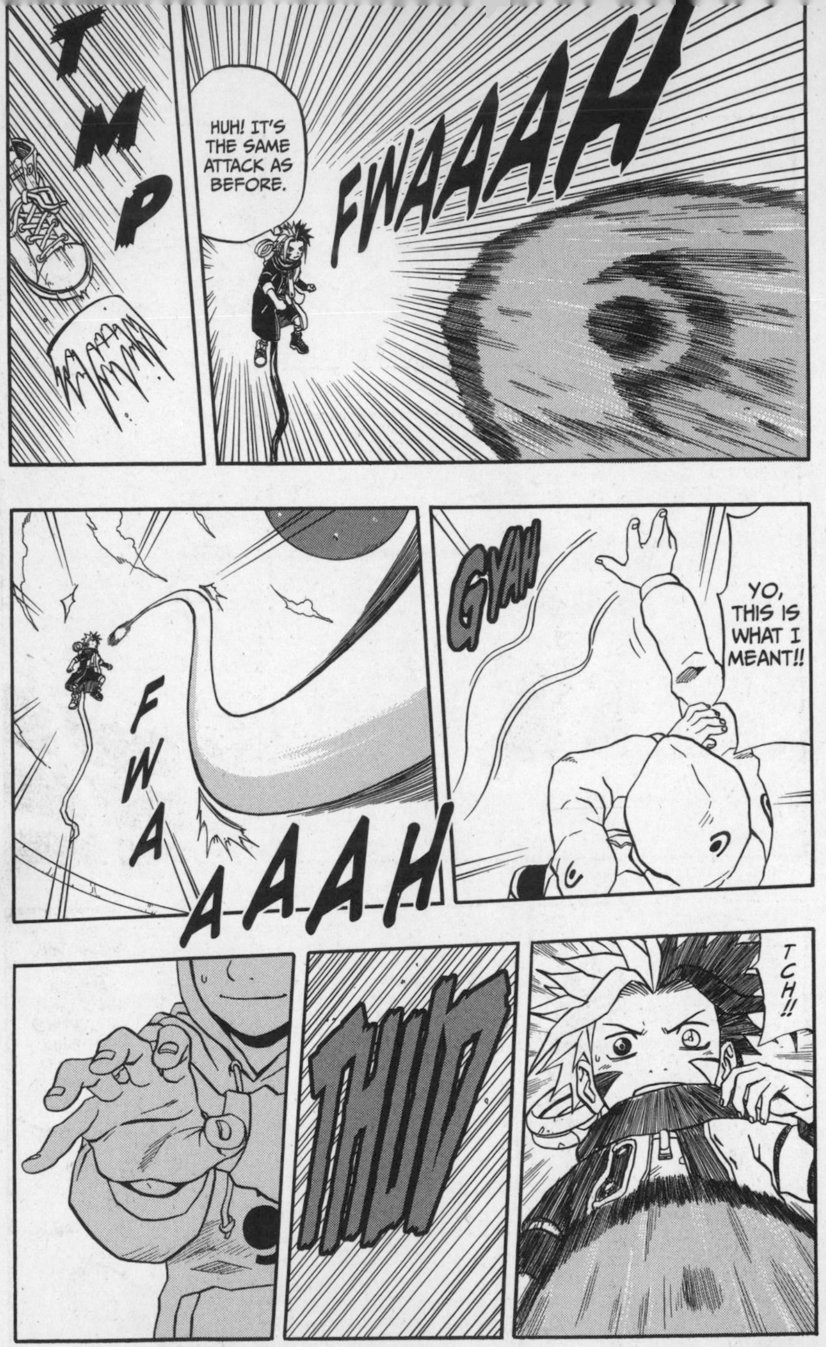
FWAAAH
HUH! IT'S THE SAME ATTACK AS BEFORE.
TMP
GYAH
YO, THIS IS WHAT I MEANT!!
FWA AAAH
TCH!!
THUD

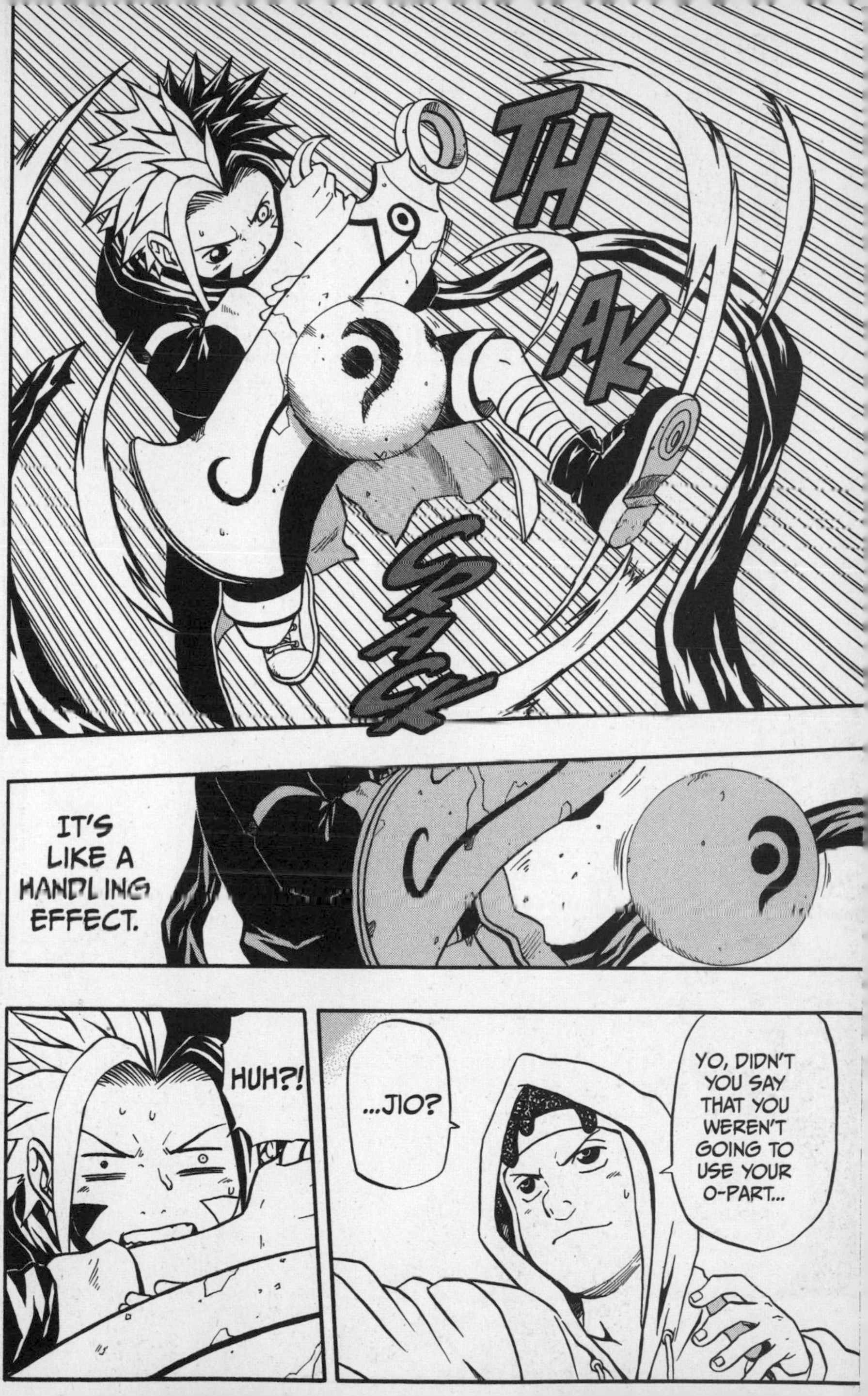
TH
AK
CRACK
IT'S LIKE A HANDLING EFFECT.
YO, DIDN'T YOU SAY THAT YOU WEREN'T GOING TO USE YOUR O-PART...
...JIO?
HUH?!

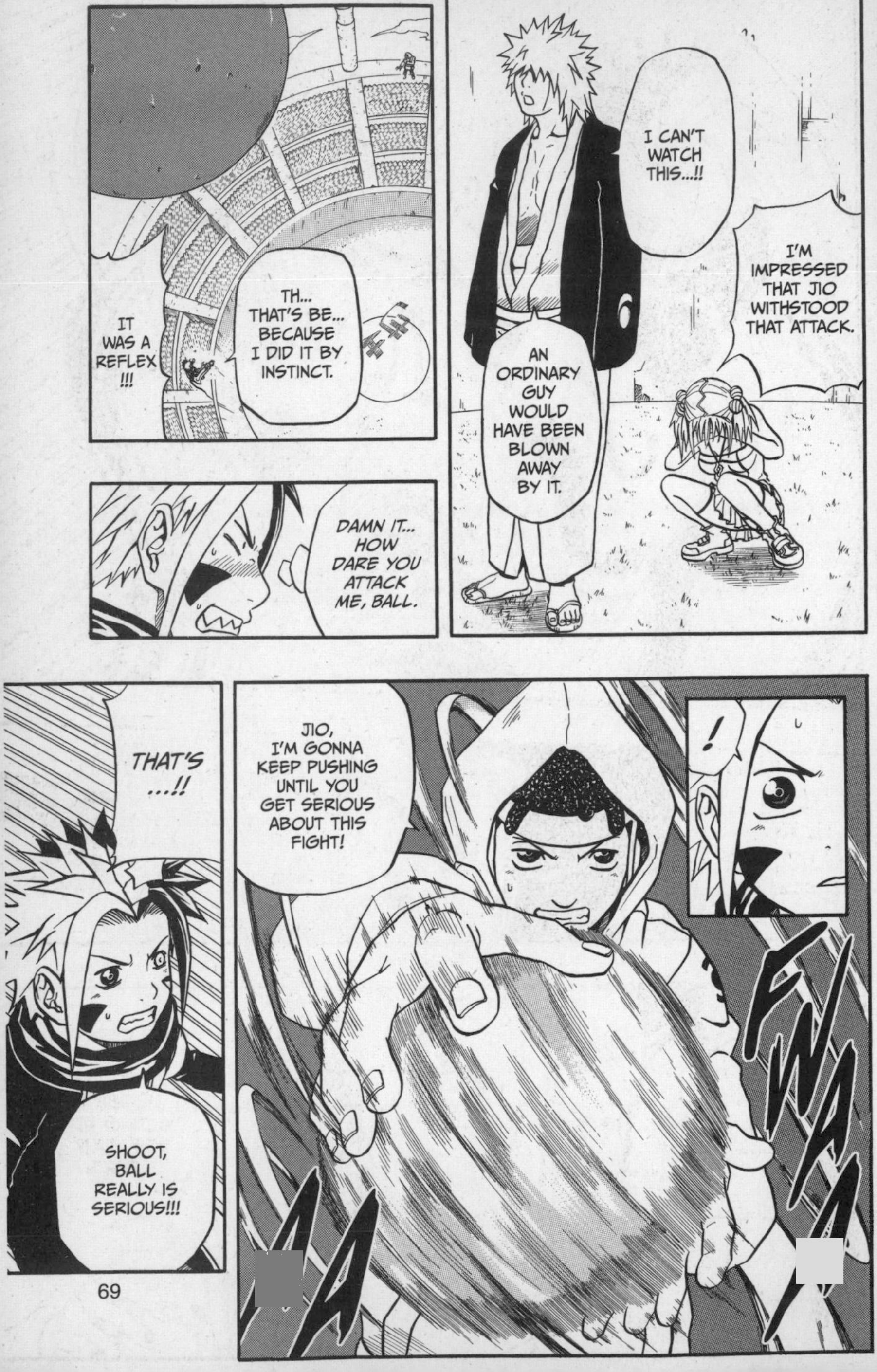
I CAN'T WATCH THIS...!!
I'M IMPRESSED THAT JIO WITHSTOOD THAT ATTACK.
AN ORDINARY GUY WOULD HAVE BEEN BLOWN AWAY BY IT.
TH... THAT'S BE... BECAUSE I DID IT BY INSTINCT.
IT WAS A REFLEX!!!
DAMN IT... HOW DARE YOU ATTACK ME, BALL.
!
JIO, I'M GONNA KEEP PUSHING UNTIL YOU GET SERIOUS ABOUT THIS FIGHT!
THAT'S ...!!
SHOOT, BALL REALLY IS SERIOUS!!!

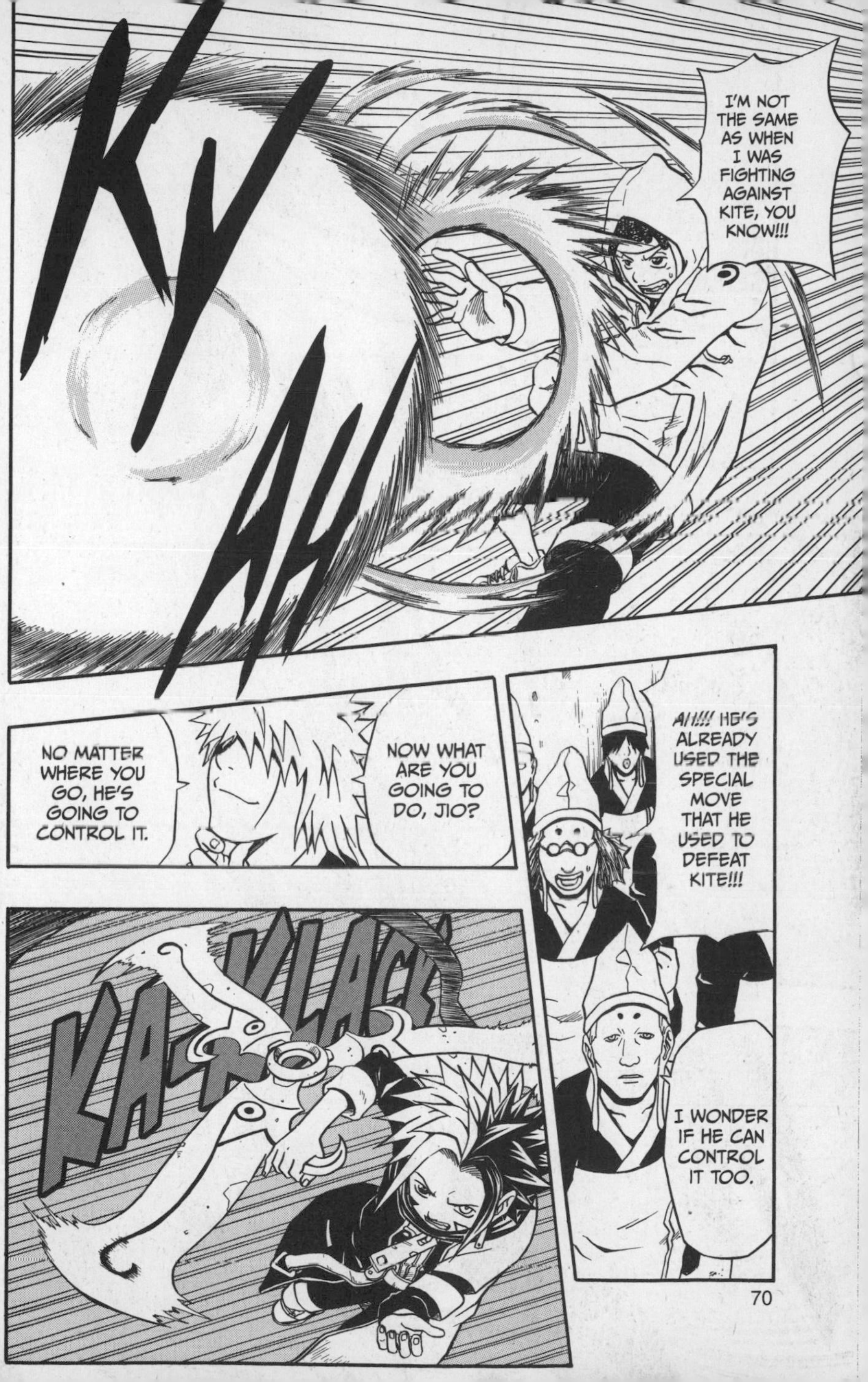
I'M NOT THE SAME AS WHEN I WAS FIGHTING AGAINST KITE, YOU KNOW!!!
KYAH
AH!!!! HE'S ALREADY USED THE SPECIAL MOVE THAT HE USED TO DEFEAT KITE!!!
I WONDER IF HE CAN CONTROL IT TOO.
NOW WHAT ARE YOU GOING TO DO, JIO?
NO MATTER WHERE YOU GO, HE'S GOING TO CONTROL IT.
KA-KLACK

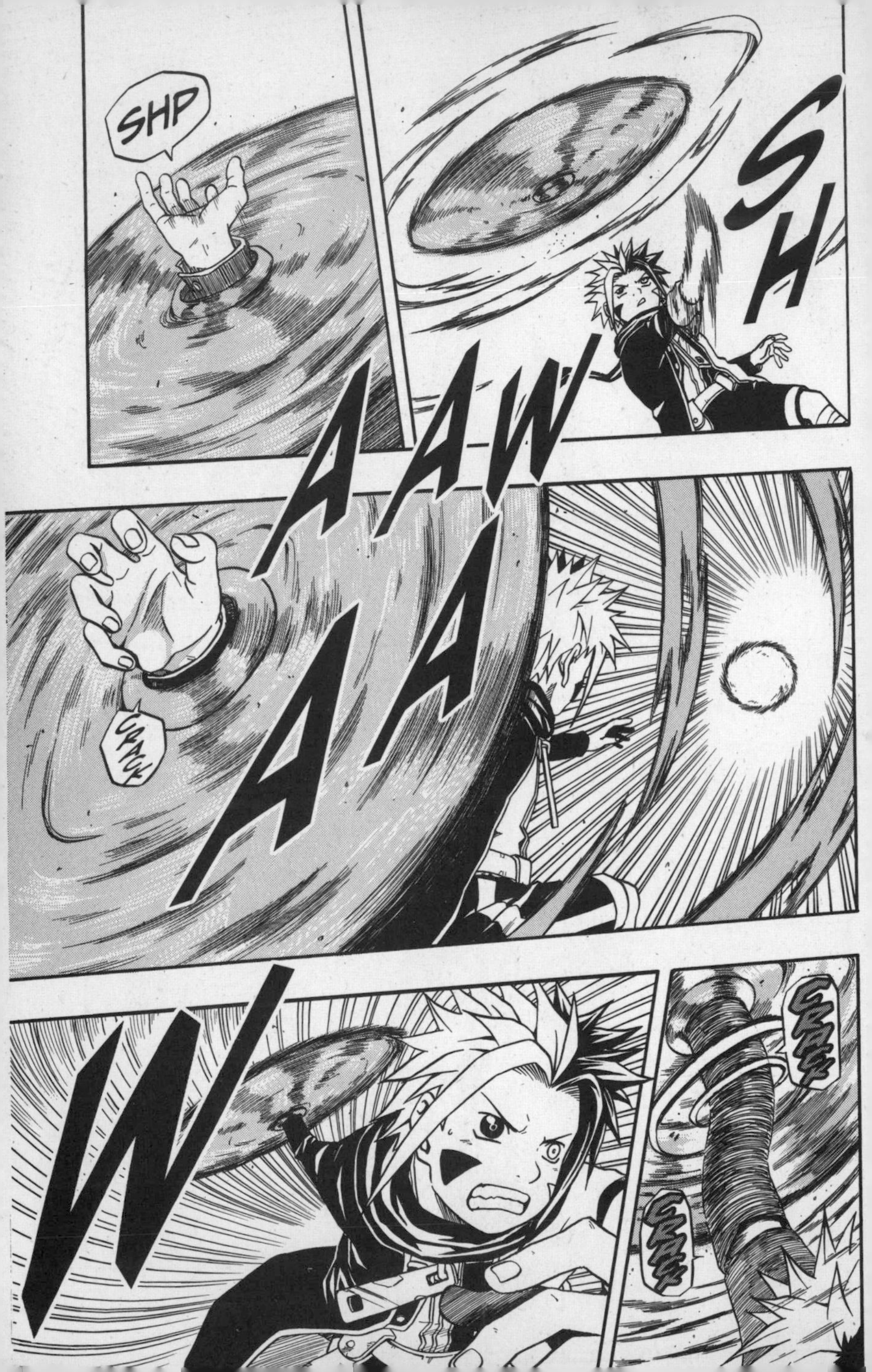
SH
SHP
AAW
AA
CRACK
W

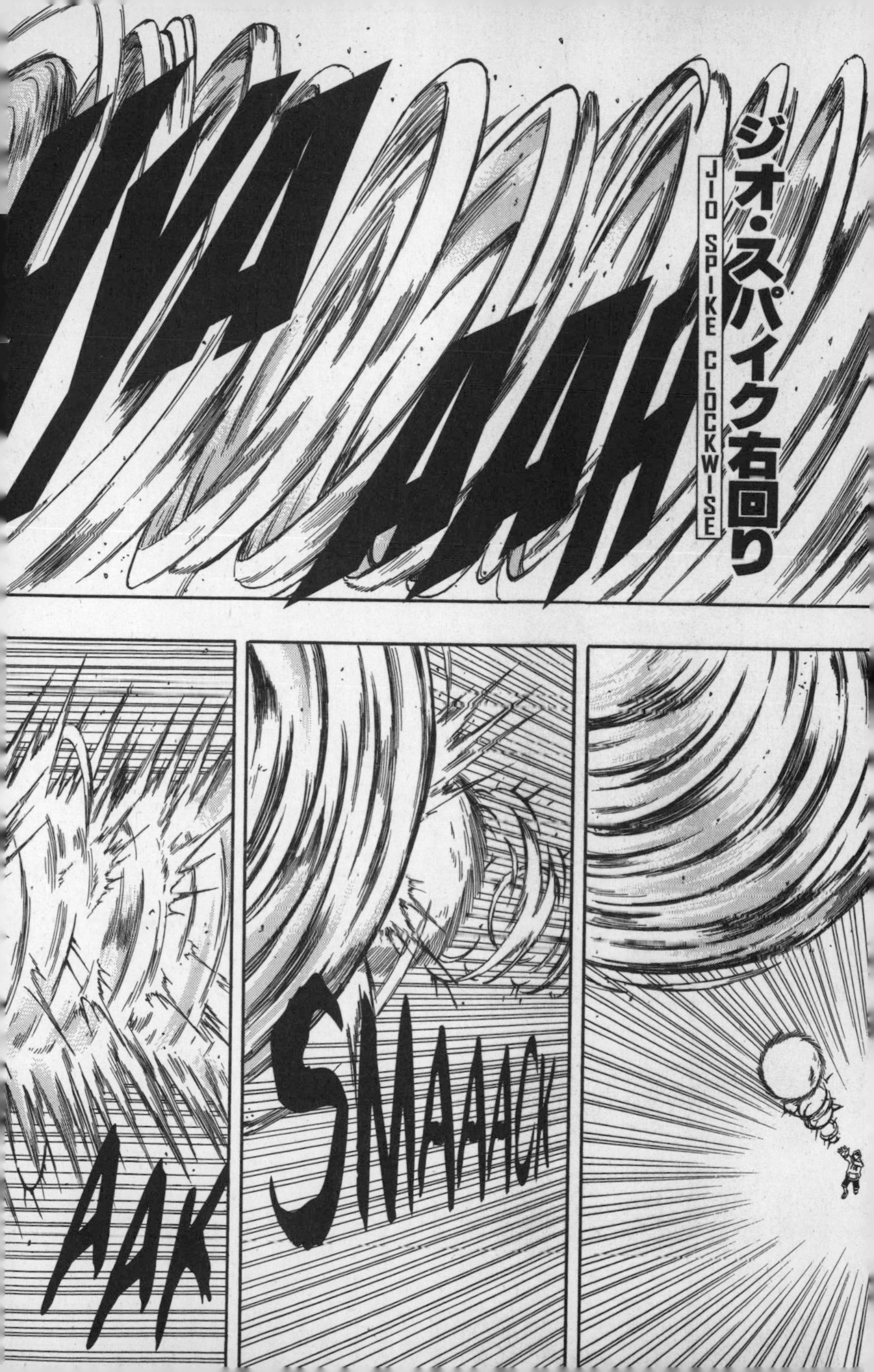
ジオ・スパイク右回り
JIO SPIKE CLOCKWISE
SMAAACK
AAK

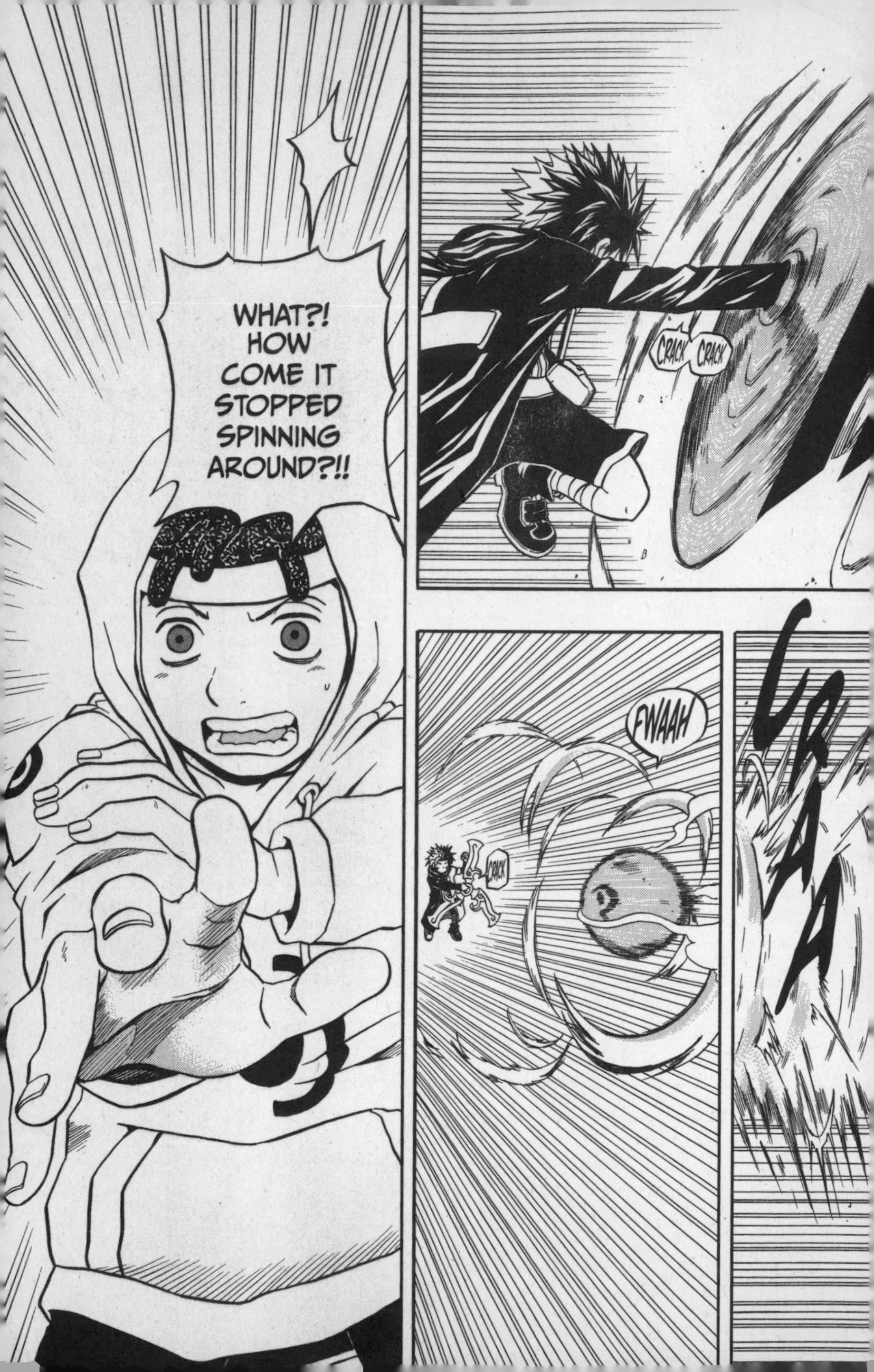
CRACK
CRACK
CRAAA
FWAAH
CRACK
WHAT?! HOW COME IT STOPPED SPINNING AROUND?!!

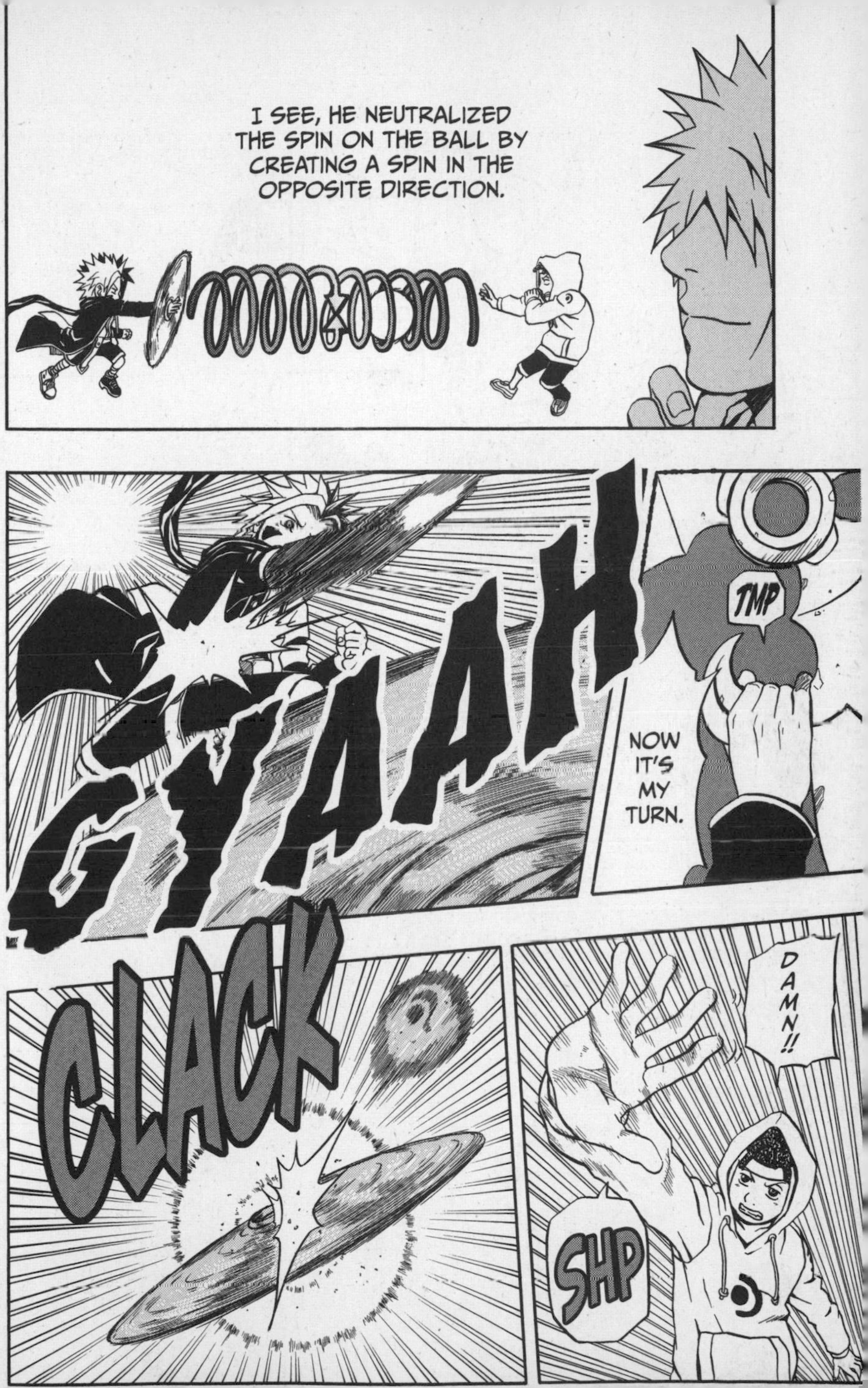
I SEE, HE NEUTRALIZED THE SPIN ON THE BALL BY CREATING A SPIN IN THE OPPOSITE DIRECTION.
TMP
NOW IT'S MY TURN.
GYAAH
DAMN!!
SHP
CLACK

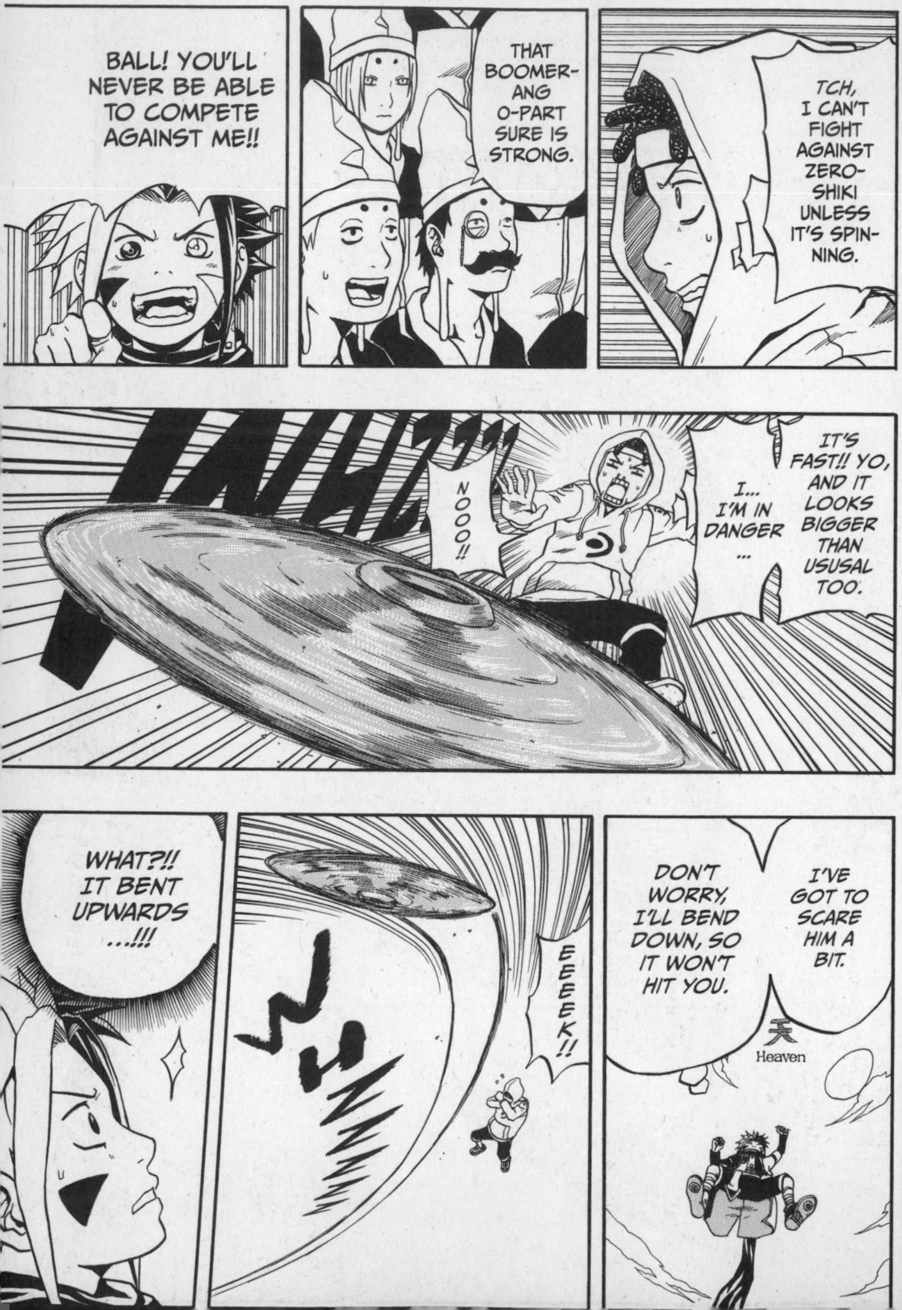
TCH, I CAN'T FIGHT AGAINST ZERO-SHIKI UNLESS IT'S SPINNING.
THAT BOOMERANG O-PART SURE IS STRONG.
BALL! YOU'LL NEVER BE ABLE TO COMPETE AGAINST ME!!
IT'S FAST!! YO, AND IT LOOKS BIGGER THAN USUSAL TOO.
I... I'M IN DANGER ...
NOOO!!
I'VE GOT TO SCARE HIM A BIT.
DON'T WORRY, I'LL BEND DOWN, SO IT WON'T HIT YOU.
天
Heaven
EEEEEK!!
WHAT?!! IT BENT UPWARDS ...!!!

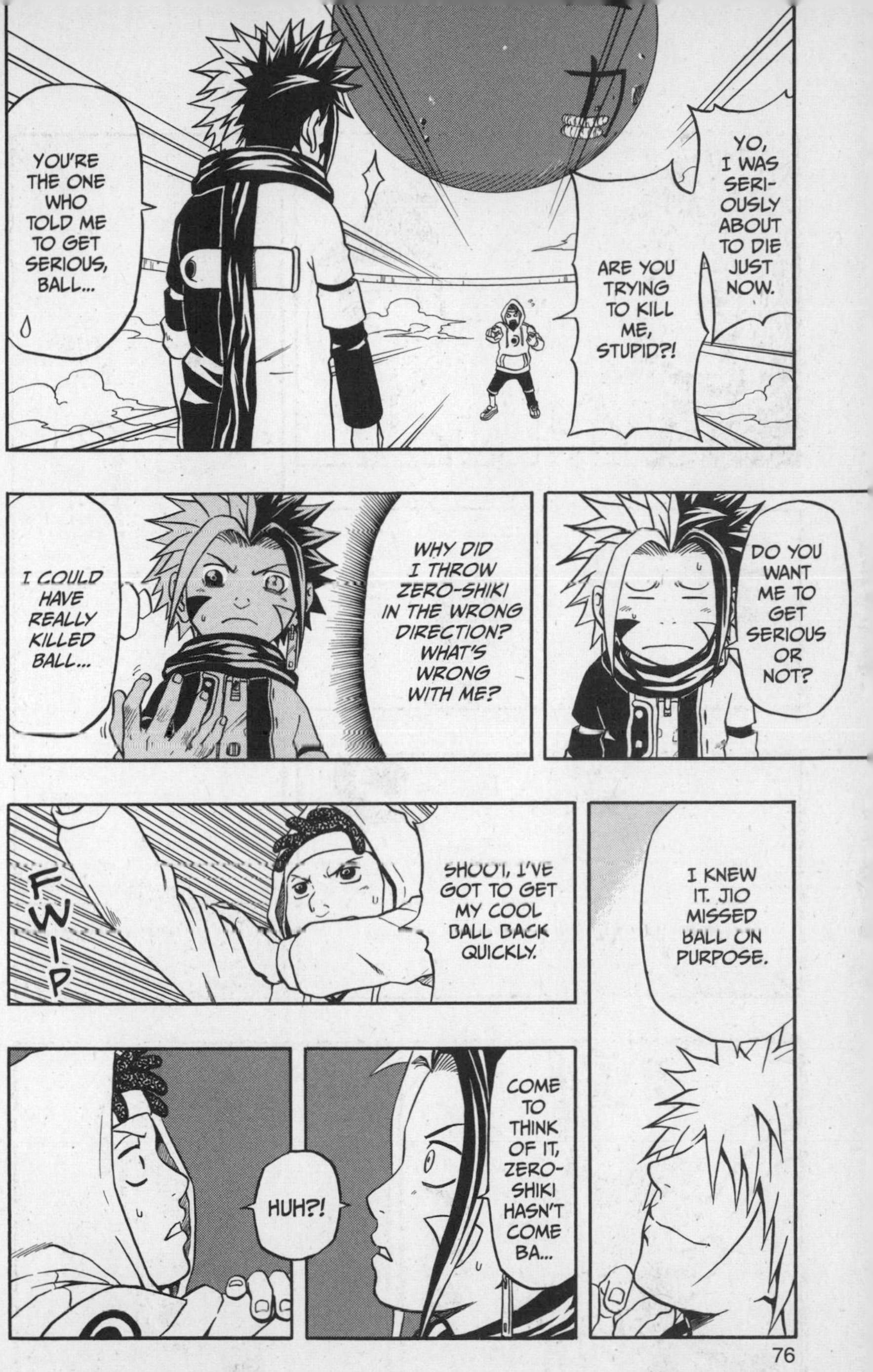
YO, I WAS SERIOUSLY ABOUT TO DIE JUST NOW.
ARE YOU TRYING TO KILL ME, STUPID?!
YOU'RE THE ONE WHO TOLD ME TO GET SERIOUS, BALL...
DO YOU WANT ME TO GET SERIOUS OR NOT?
WHY DID I THROW ZERO-SHIKI IN THE WRONG DIRECTION? WHAT'S WRONG WITH ME?
I COULD HAVE REALLY KILLED BALL...
I KNEW IT. JIO MISSED BALL ON PURPOSE.
SHOOT, I'VE GOT TO GET MY COOL BALL BACK QUICKLY.
FWIP
COME TO THINK OF IT, ZERO-SHIKI HASN'T COME BA...
HUH?!

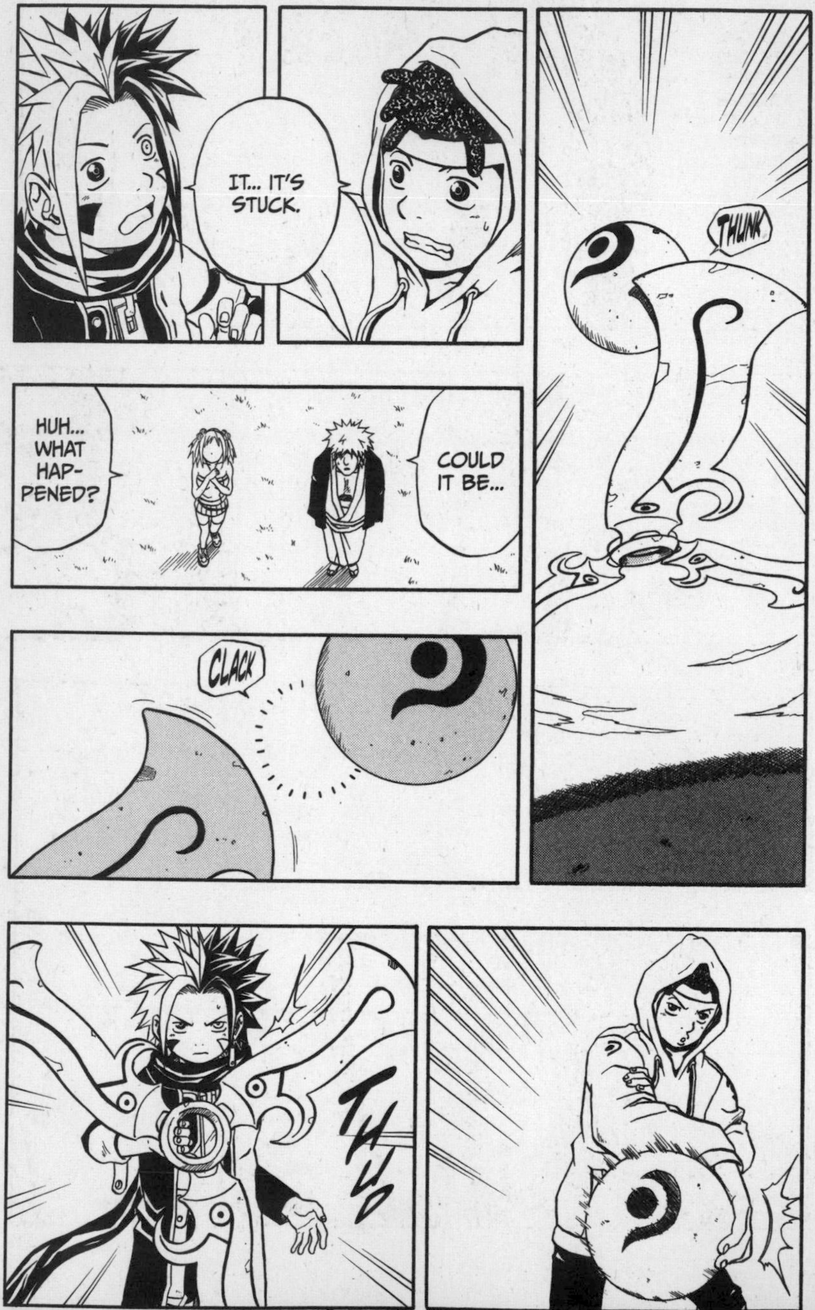
THUNK
IT... IT'S STUCK.
COULD IT BE...
HUH... WHAT HAP-PENED?
CLACK
THUD

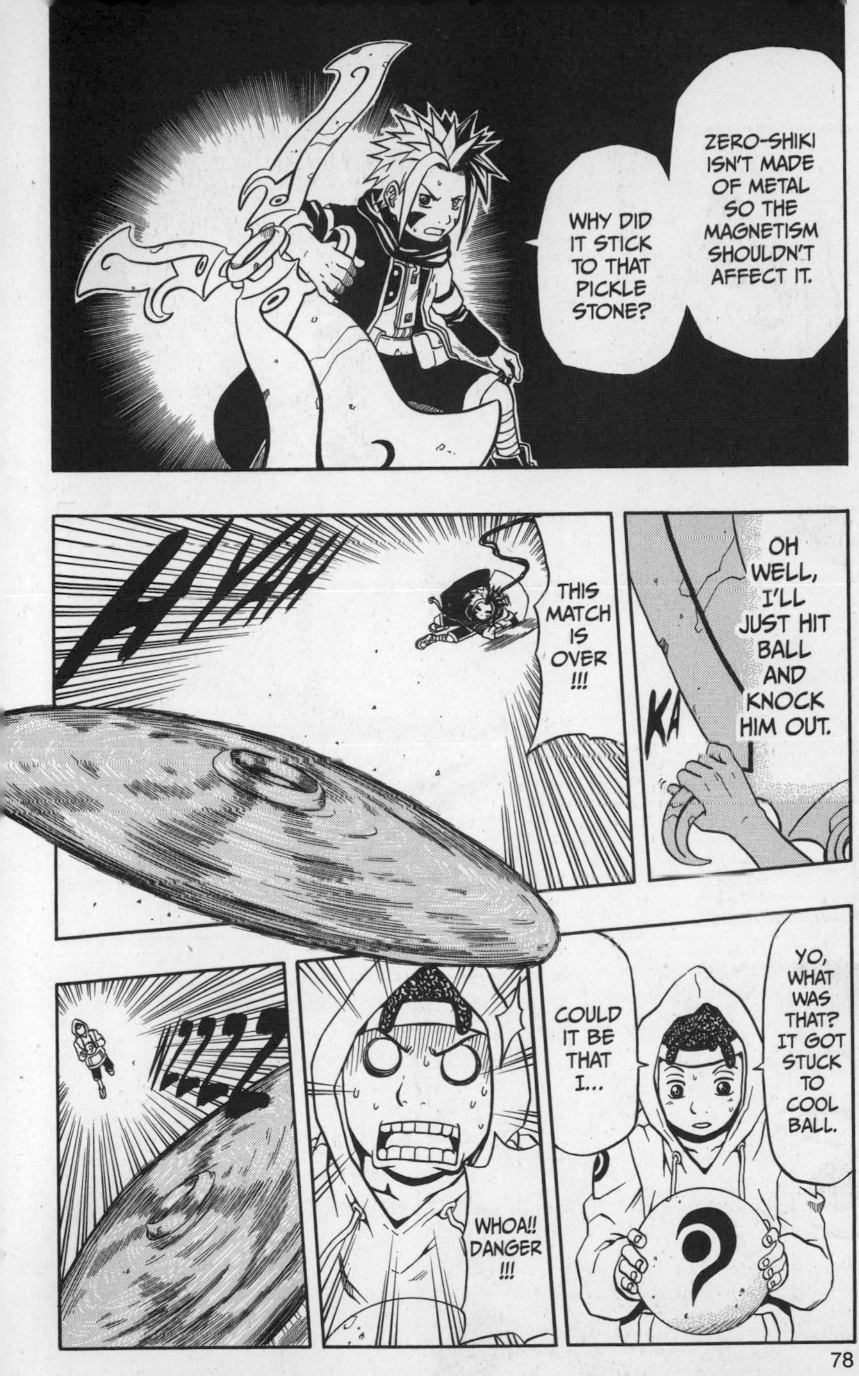
ZERO-SHIKI ISN'T MADE OF METAL SO THE MAGNETISM SHOULDN'T AFFECT IT.
WHY DID IT STICK TO THAT PICKLE STONE?
KA
OH WELL, I'LL JUST HIT BALL AND KNOCK HIM OUT.
HIYAH
THIS MATCH IS OVER!!!
YO, WHAT WAS THAT? IT GOT STUCK TO COOL BALL.
COULD IT BE THAT I...
WHOA!! DANGER!!!

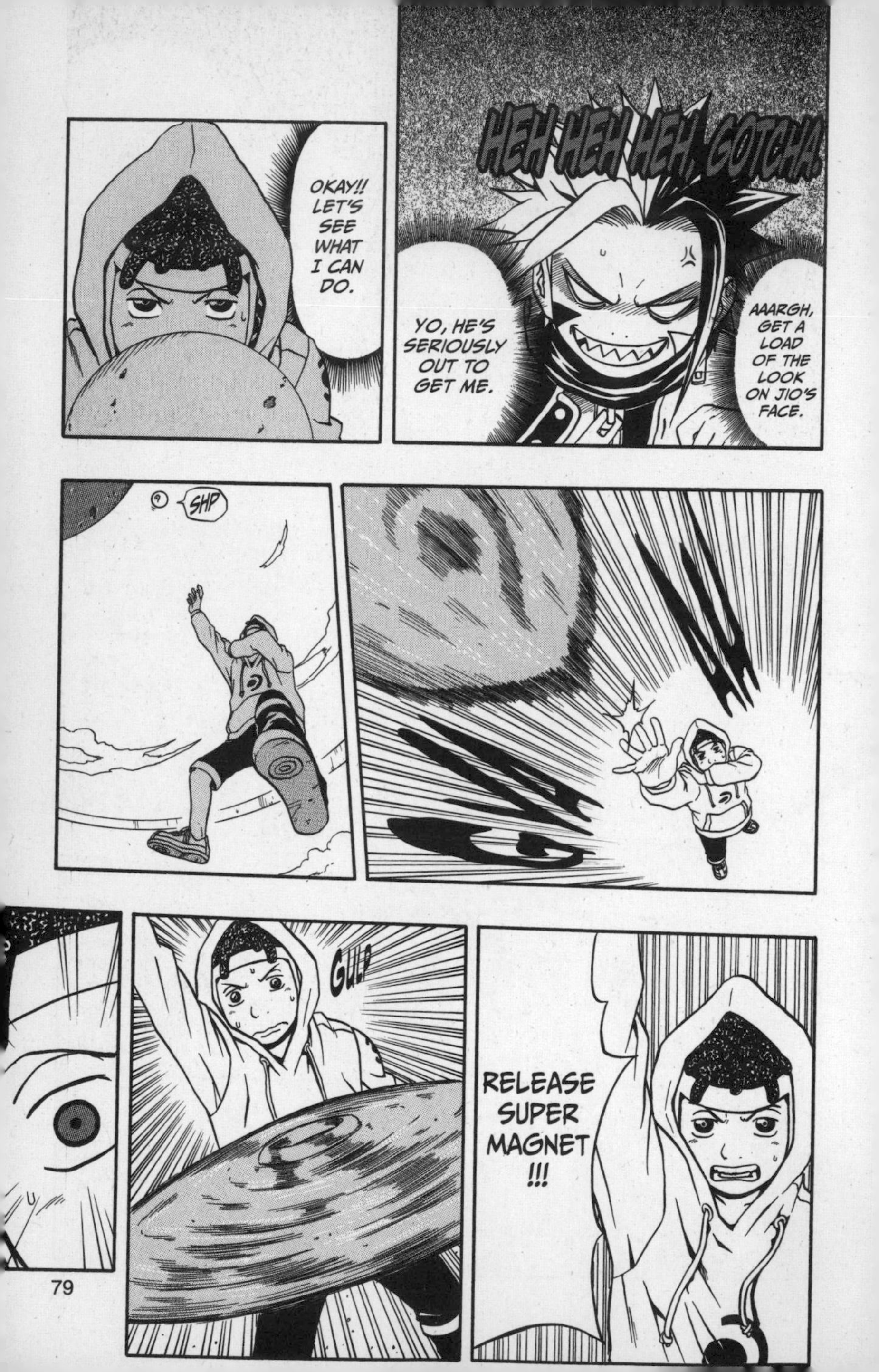
HEH HEH HEH, GOTCHA!
AAARGH, GET A LOAD OF THE LOOK ON JIO'S FACE.
YO, HE'S SERIOUSLY OUT TO GET ME.
OKAY!! LET'S SEE WHAT I CAN DO.
SHP
RELEASE SUPER MAGNET!!!
GULP

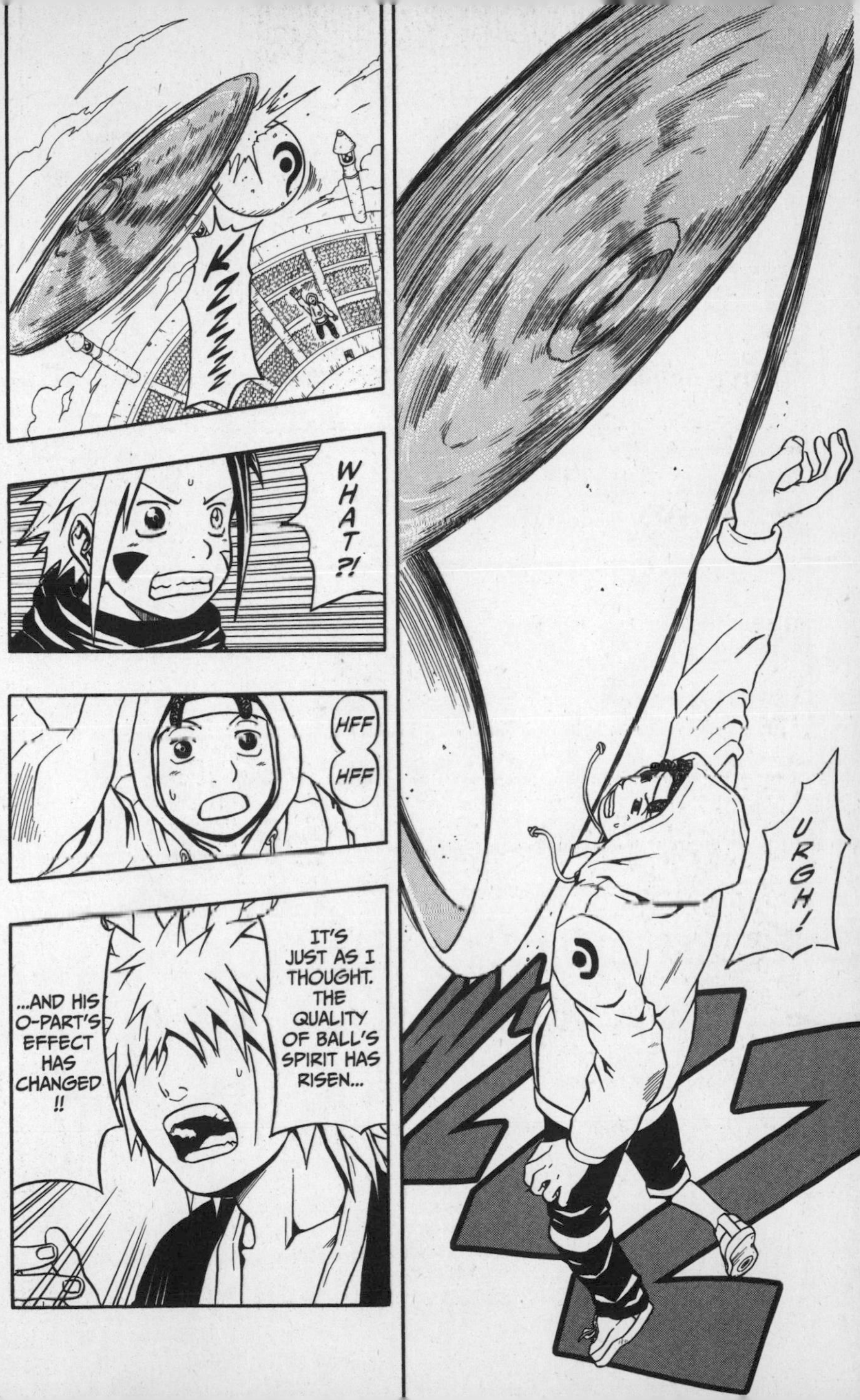
URGH!
WHAT?!
HFF
HFF
IT'S JUST AS I THOUGHT. THE QUALITY OF BALL'S SPIRIT HAS RISEN...
...AND HIS O-PART'S EFFECT HAS CHANGED!!

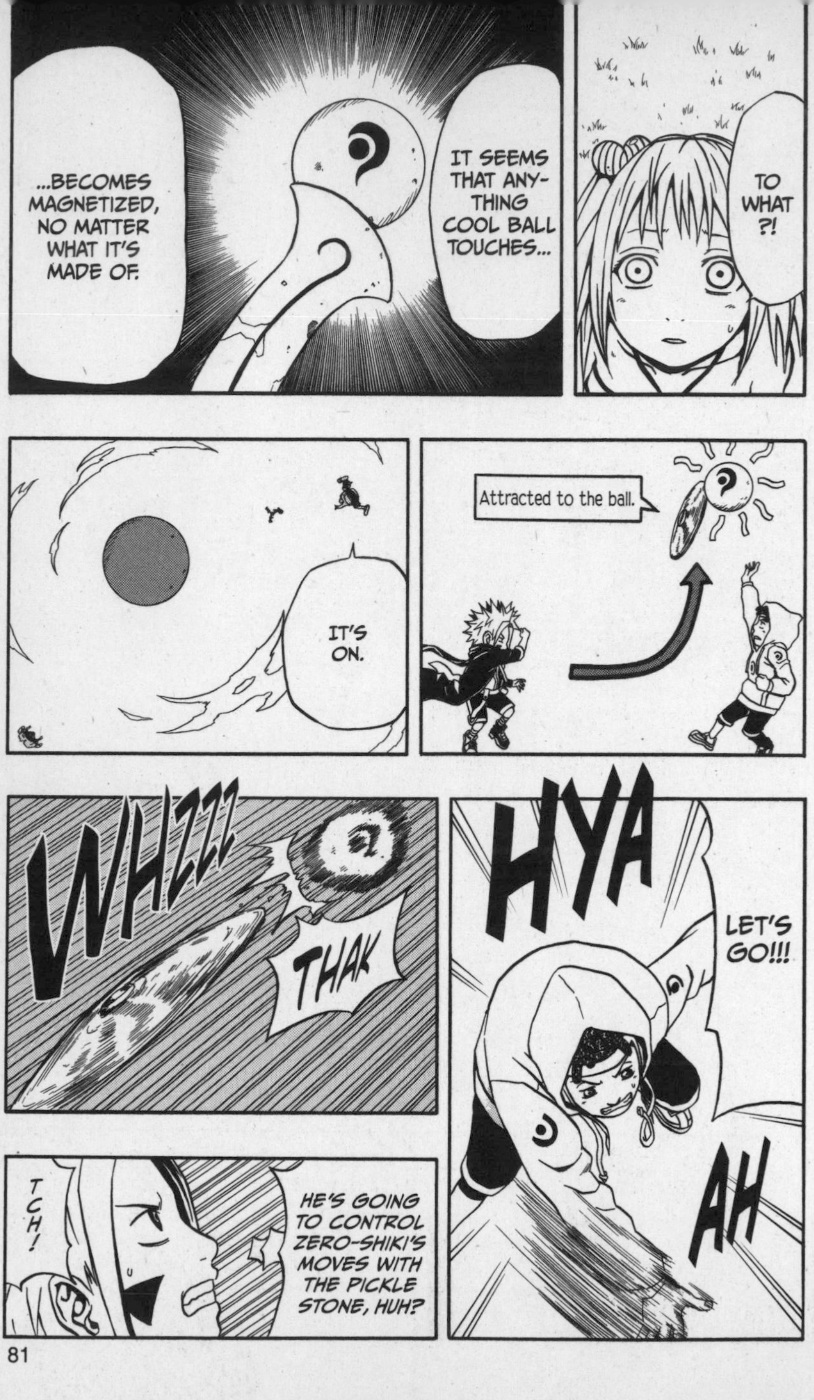
TO WHAT ?!
IT SEEMS THAT ANYTHING COOL BALL TOUCHES...
...BECOMES MAGNETIZED, NO MATTER WHAT IT'S MADE OF.
Attracted to the ball.
IT'S ON.
HYA
LET'S GO!!!
AH
WHZZZ
THAK
TCH!
HE'S GOING TO CONTROL ZERO-SHIKI'S MOVES WITH THE PICKLE STONE, HUH?

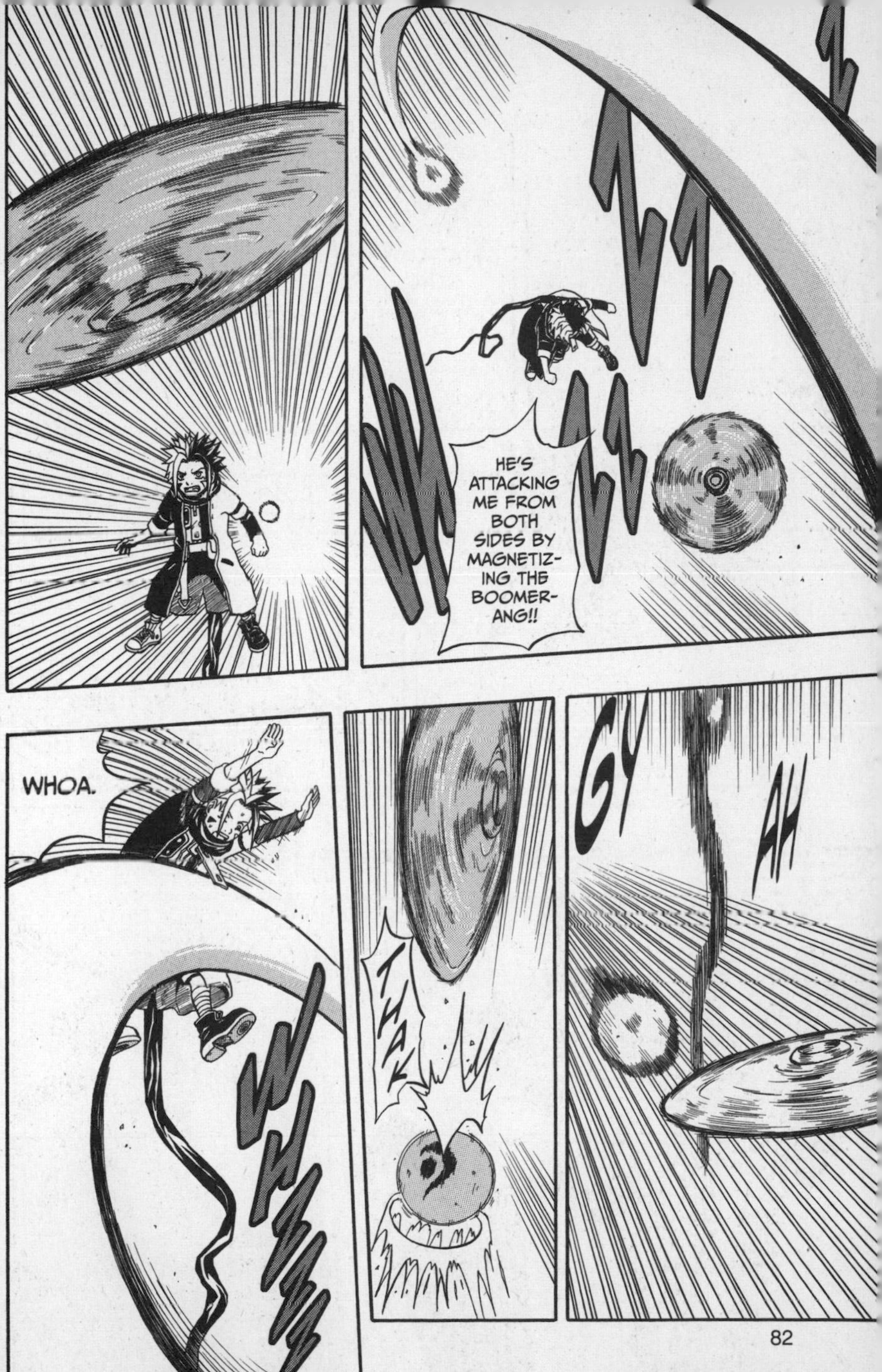
HE'S ATTACKING ME FROM BOTH SIDES BY MAGNETIZ-ING THE BOOMER-ANG!!
GY AH
THWAK
WHOA.

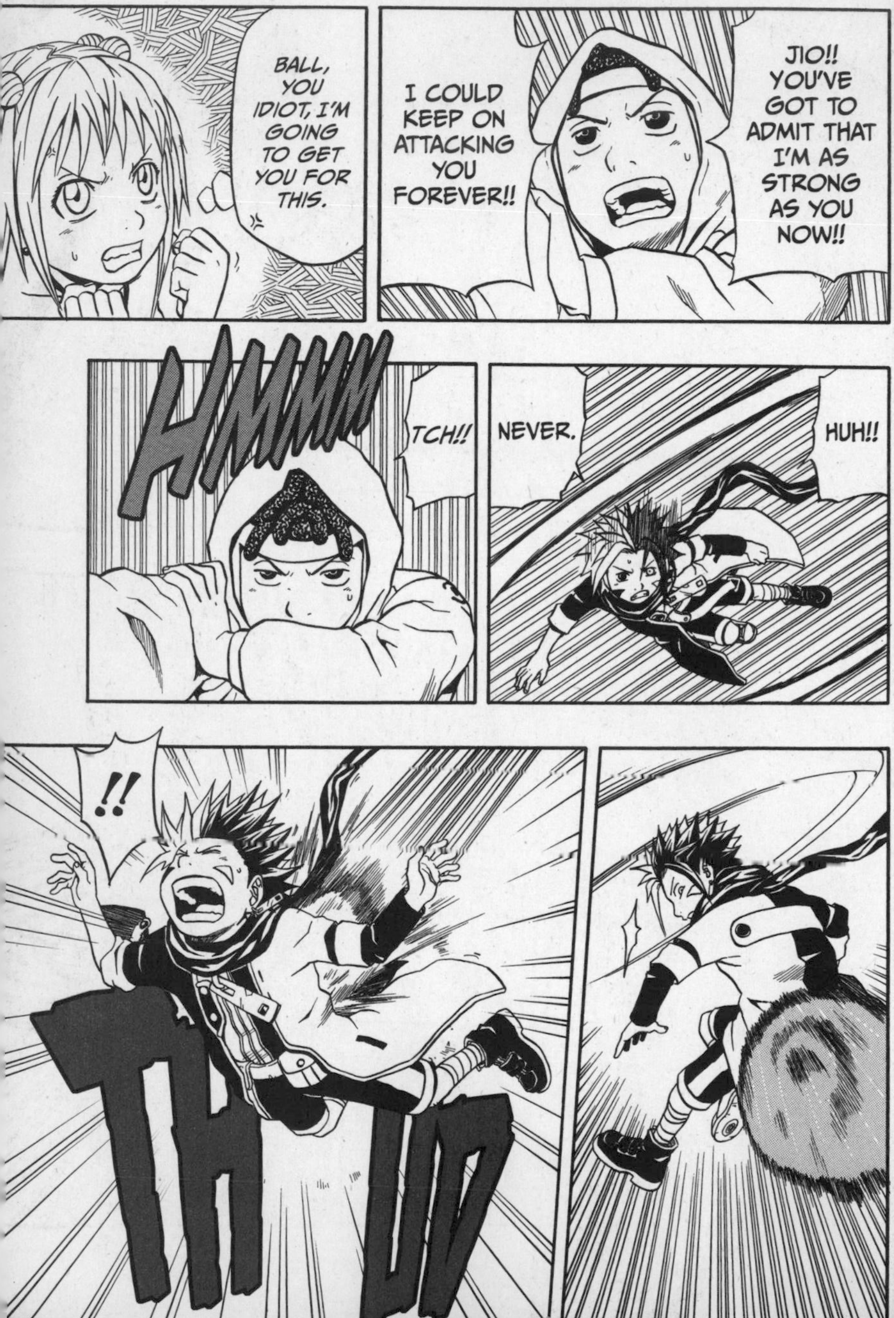
JIO!! YOU'VE GOT TO ADMIT THAT I'M AS STRONG AS YOU NOW!!
I COULD KEEP ON ATTACKING YOU FOREVER!!
BALL, YOU IDIOT, I'M GOING TO GET YOU FOR THIS.
HUH!!
NEVER.
TCH!!
HMMMM
!!
THUD

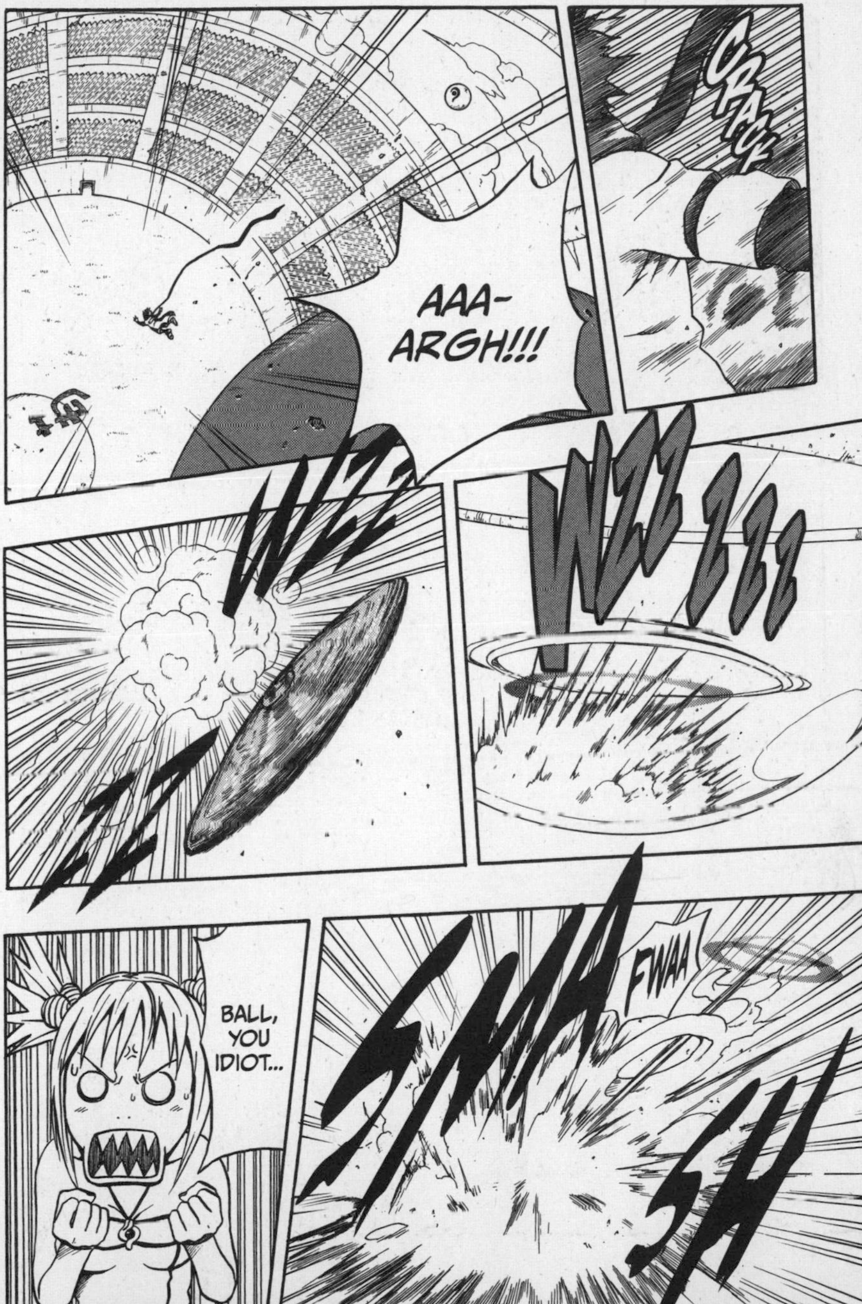
CRACK
AAA-
ARGH!!!
WZZZZZ
WZZ
ZZ
SMAA
FWAA
SHA
BALL,
YOU
IDIOT...

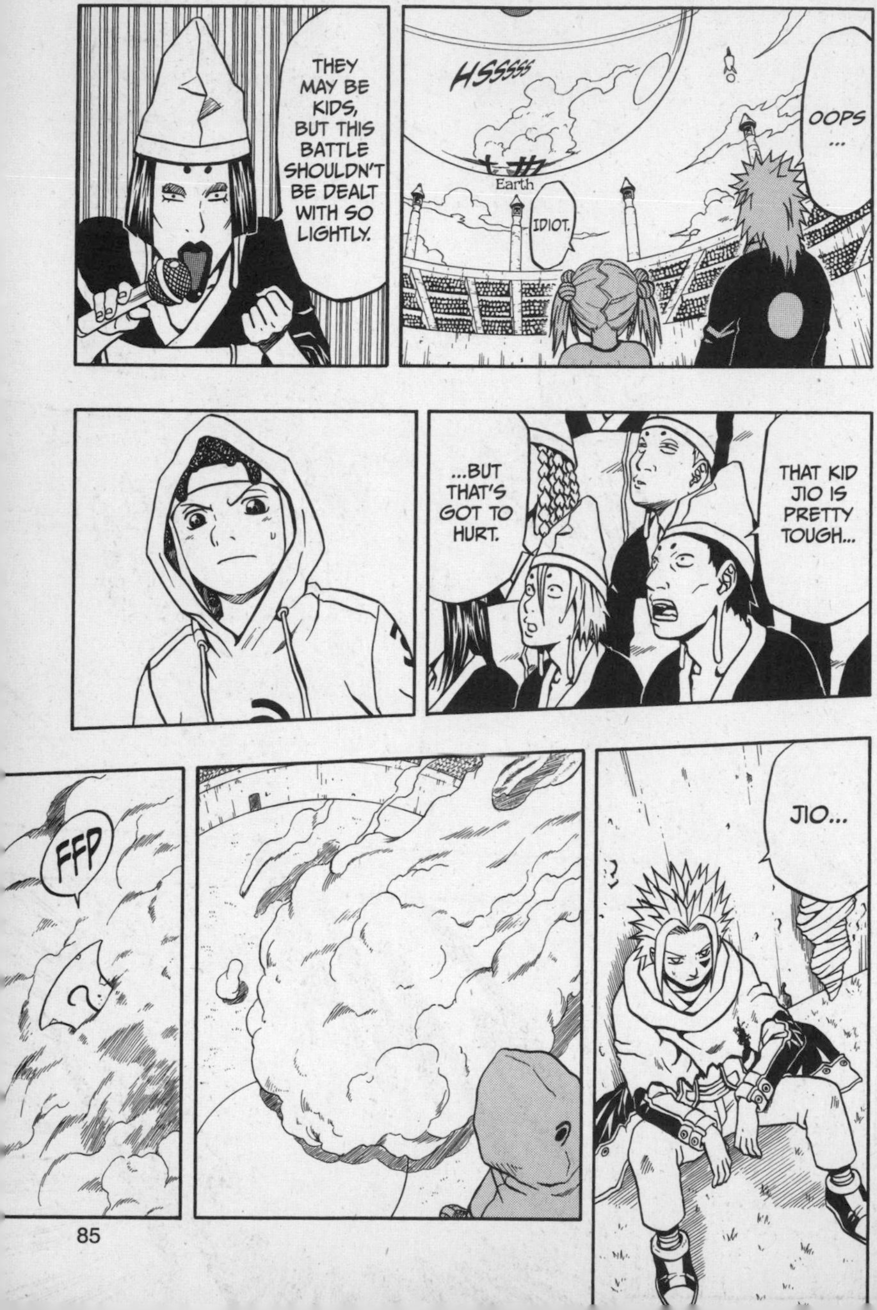
OOPS ...
HSSSSS
Earth
IDIOT.
THEY MAY BE KIDS, BUT THIS BATTLE SHOULDN'T BE DEALT WITH SO LIGHTLY.
THAT KID JIO IS PRETTY TOUGH...
...BUT THAT'S GOT TO HURT.
JIO...
FFP
?

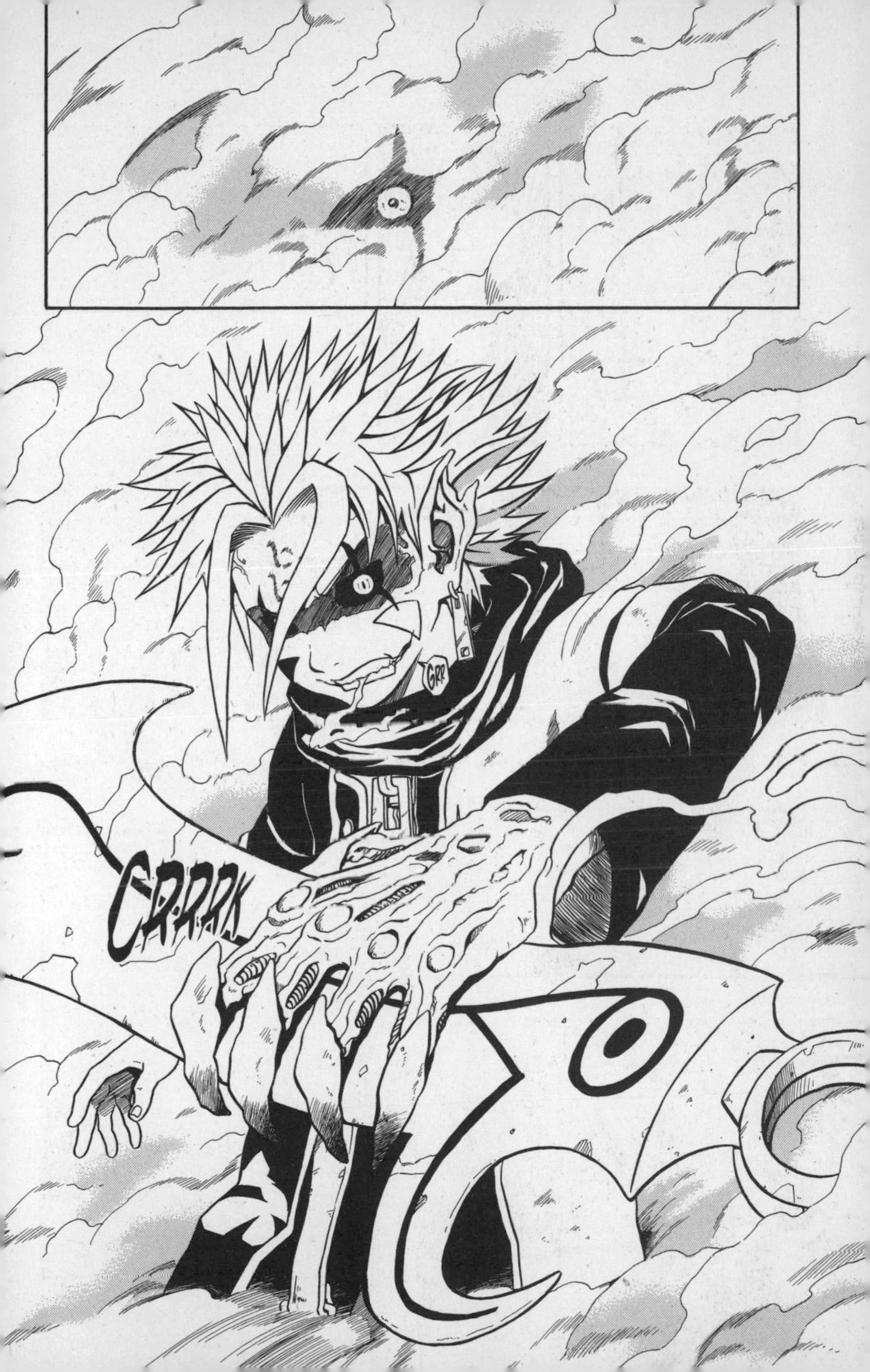
GRR
C-R-R-K

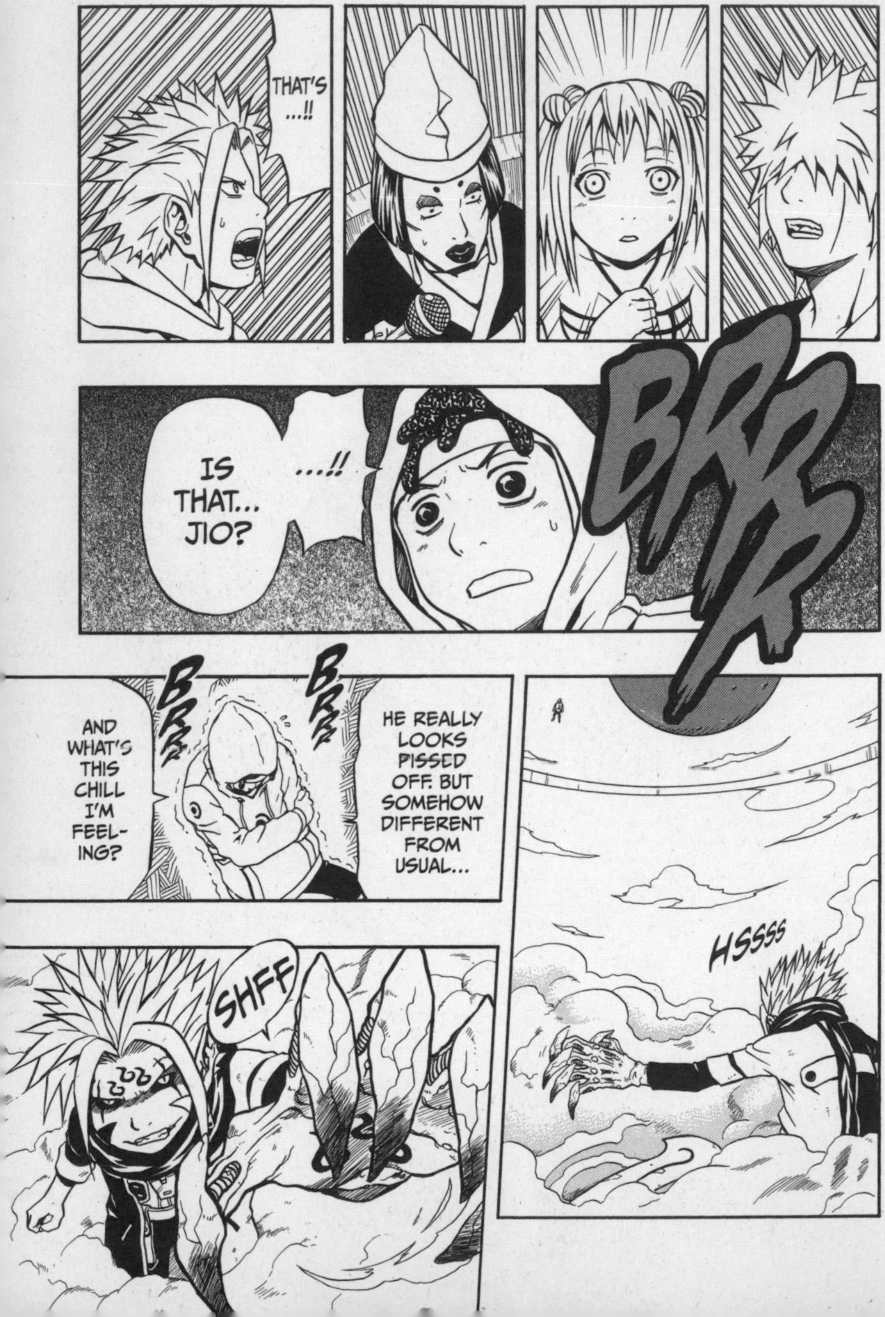
THAT'S ...!!
BRR
...!!
IS THAT... JIO?
HSSSS
BRR
HE REALLY LOOKS PISSED OFF. BUT SOMEHOW DIFFERENT FROM USUAL...
BRR
AND WHAT'S THIS CHILL I'M FEELING?
SHFF

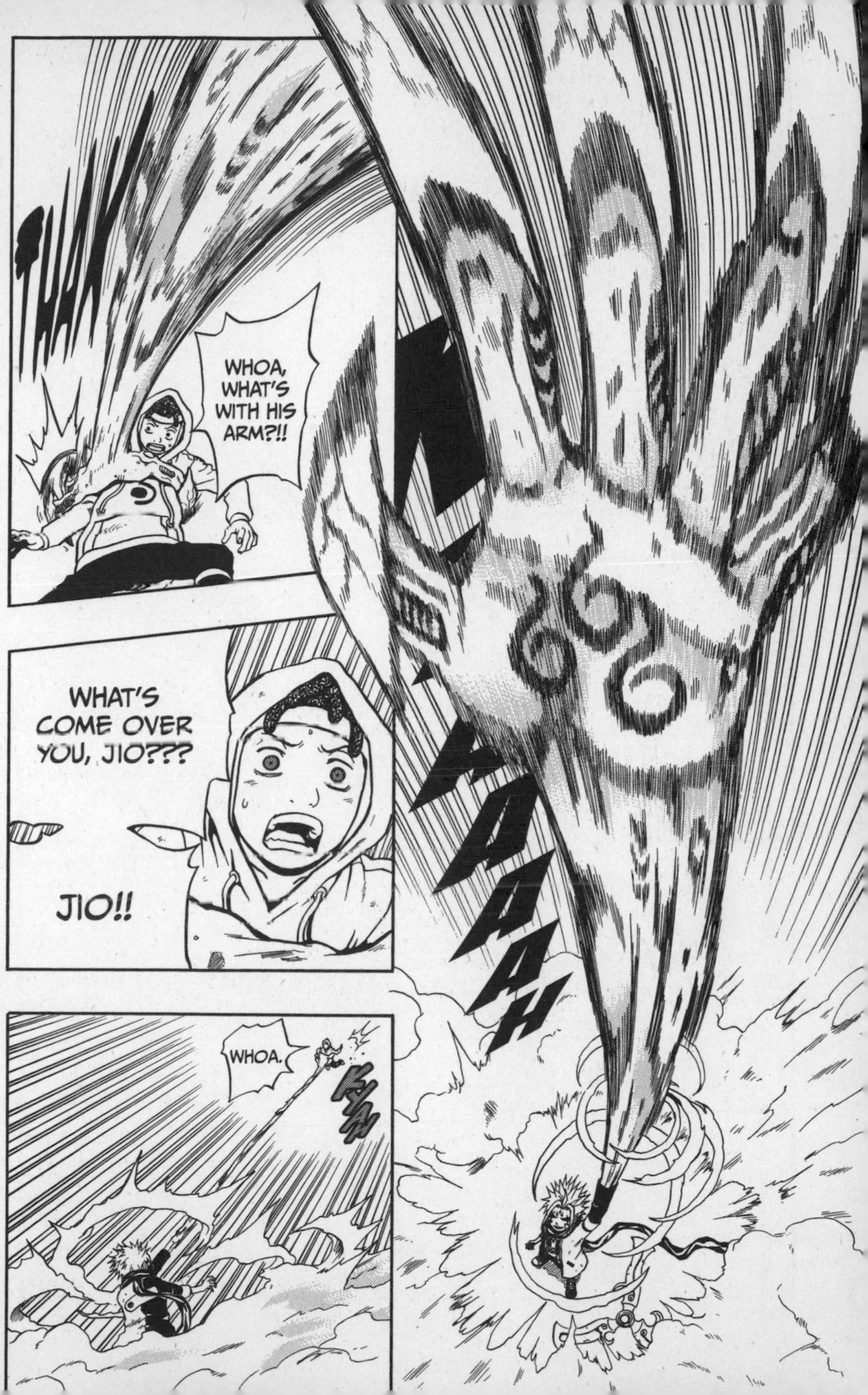
THAK
WHOA, WHAT'S WITH HIS ARM?!!
WHAT'S COME OVER YOU, JIO???
JIO!!
WHOA.

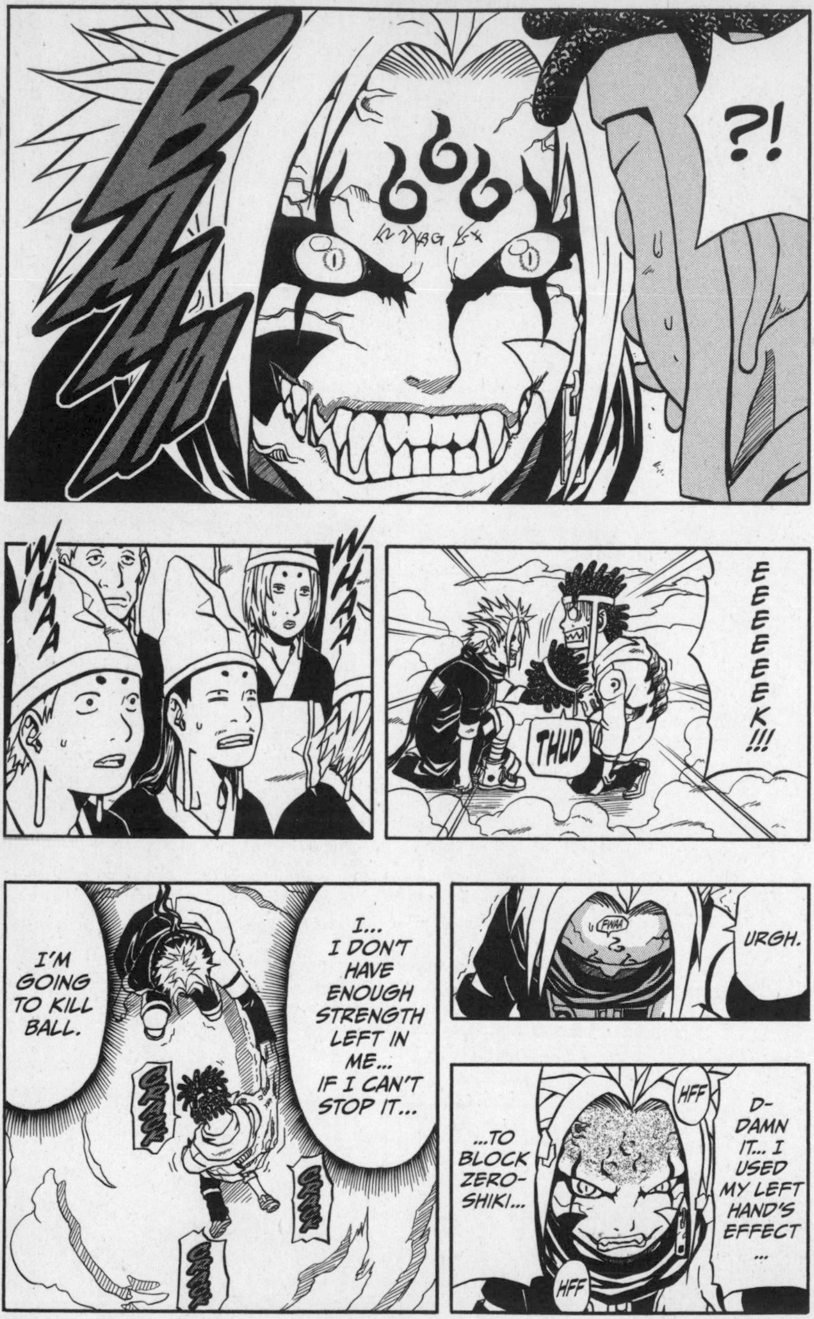

?!
EEEEEEEK!!!
THUD
WHAA
WHAA
URGH.
D-DAMN IT... I USED MY LEFT HAND'S EFFECT ...
HFF
...TO BLOCK ZERO-SHIKI...
HFF
I... I DON'T HAVE ENOUGH STRENGTH LEFT IN ME... IF I CAN'T STOP IT...
I'M GOING TO KILL BALL.

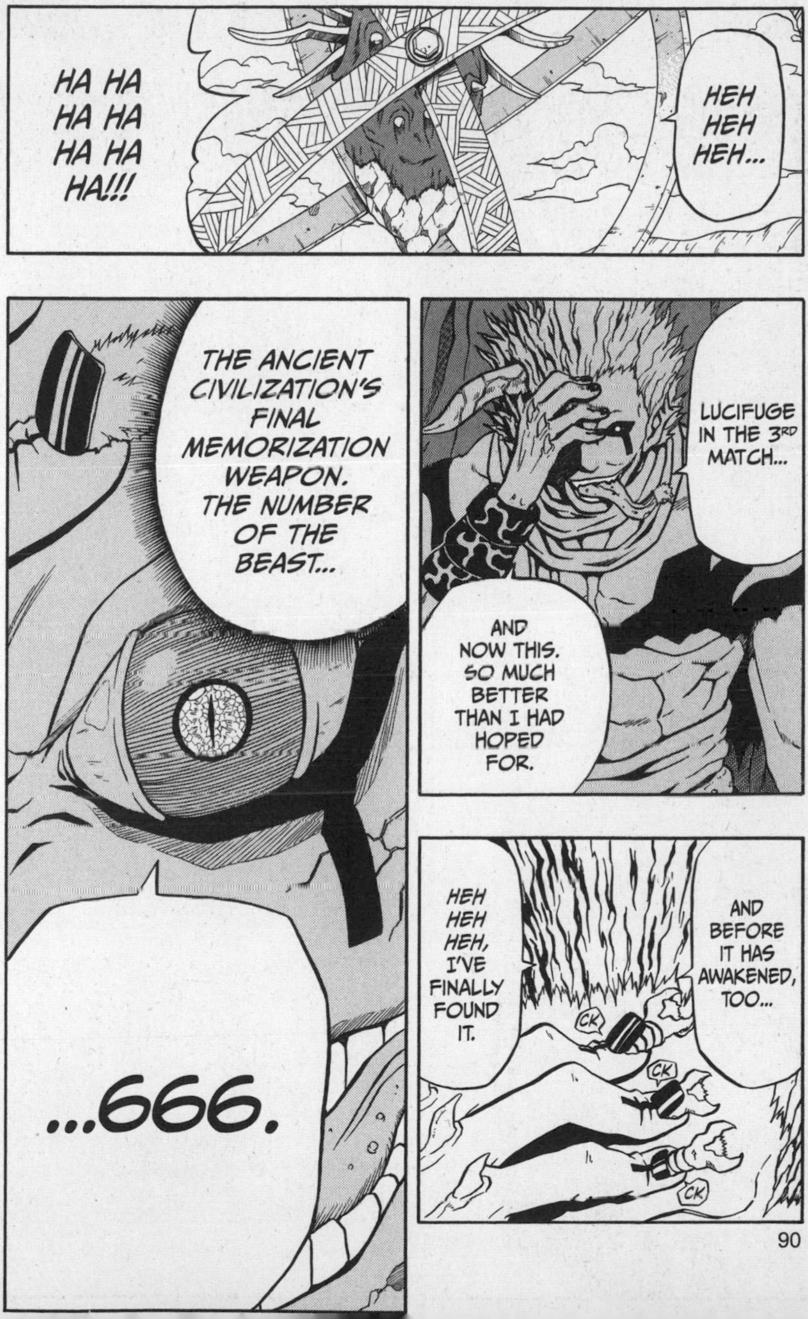
HEH HEH HEH...
HA HA HA HA HA HA HA!!!
LUCIFUGE IN THE 3RD MATCH...
AND NOW THIS. SO MUCH BETTER THAN I HAD HOPED FOR.
AND BEFORE IT HAS AWAKENED, TOO...
HEH HEH HEH, I'VE FINALLY FOUND IT.
CK
CK
CK
THE ANCIENT CIVILIZATION'S FINAL MEMORIZATION WEAPON. THE NUMBER OF THE BEAST...
...666.

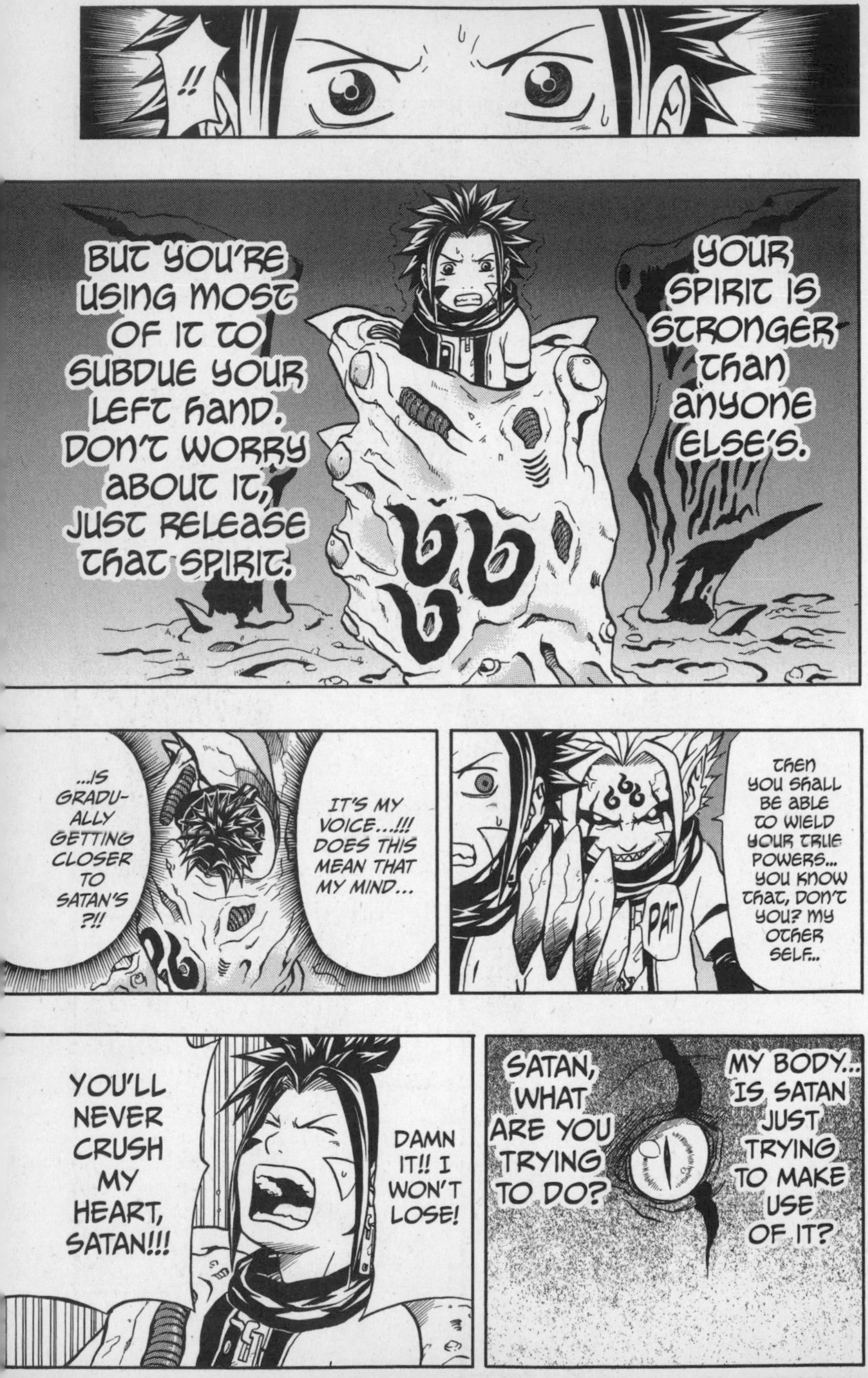
!!
YOUR SPIRIT IS STRONGER THAN ANYONE ELSE'S.
BUT YOU'RE USING MOST OF IT TO SUBDUE YOUR LEFT HAND. DON'T WORRY ABOUT IT, JUST RELEASE THAT SPIRIT.
THEN YOU SHALL BE ABLE TO WIELD YOUR TRUE POWERS... YOU KNOW THAT, DON'T YOU? MY OTHER SELF...
PAT
IT'S MY VOICE...!!! DOES THIS MEAN THAT MY MIND...
...IS GRADUALLY GETTING CLOSER TO SATAN'S ?!!
MY BODY... IS SATAN JUST TRYING TO MAKE USE OF IT?
SATAN, WHAT ARE YOU TRYING TO DO?
DAMN IT!! I WON'T LOSE!
YOU'LL NEVER CRUSH MY HEART, SATAN!!!

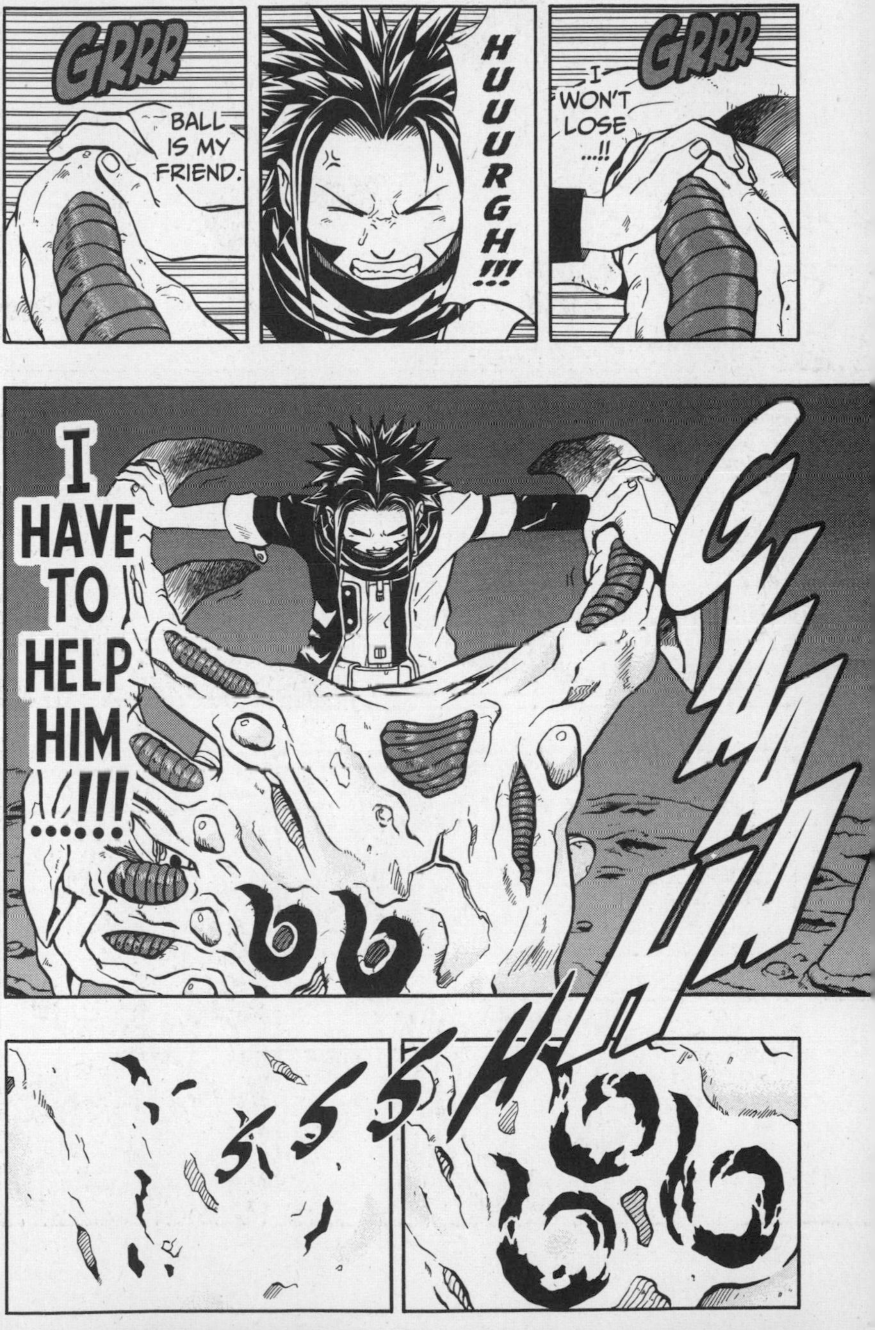
GRRR
I WON'T LOSE ...!!
HUUURGH!!!
GRRR
BALL IS MY FRIEND.
I HAVE TO HELP HIM......!!!

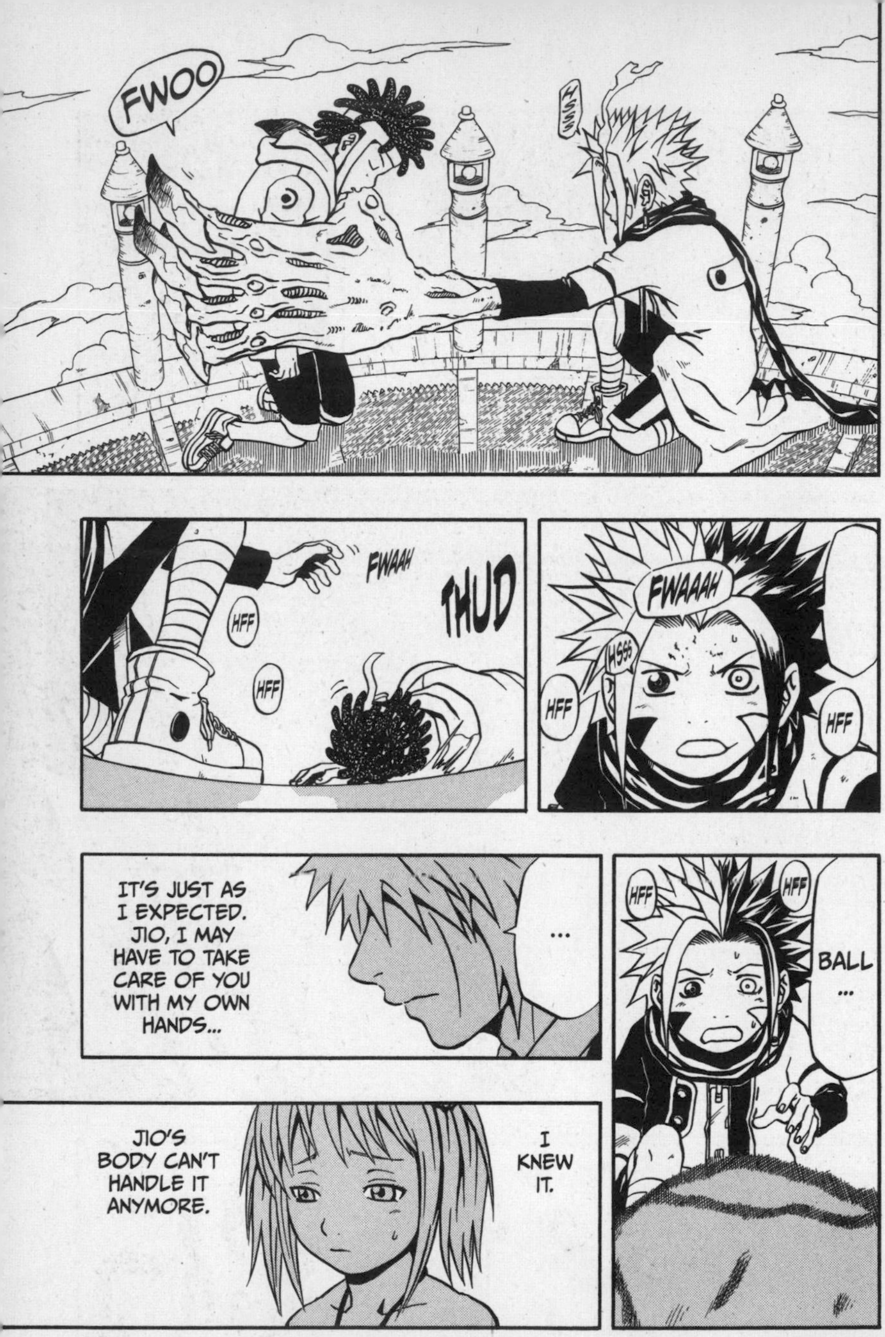
HSSS
FWOO
FWAAAH
HSSS
HFF
HFF
FWAAH
THUD
HFF
HFF
HFF
HFF
BALL ...
...
IT'S JUST AS I EXPECTED. JIO, I MAY HAVE TO TAKE CARE OF YOU WITH MY OWN HANDS...
I KNEW IT.
JIO'S BODY CAN'T HANDLE IT ANYMORE.

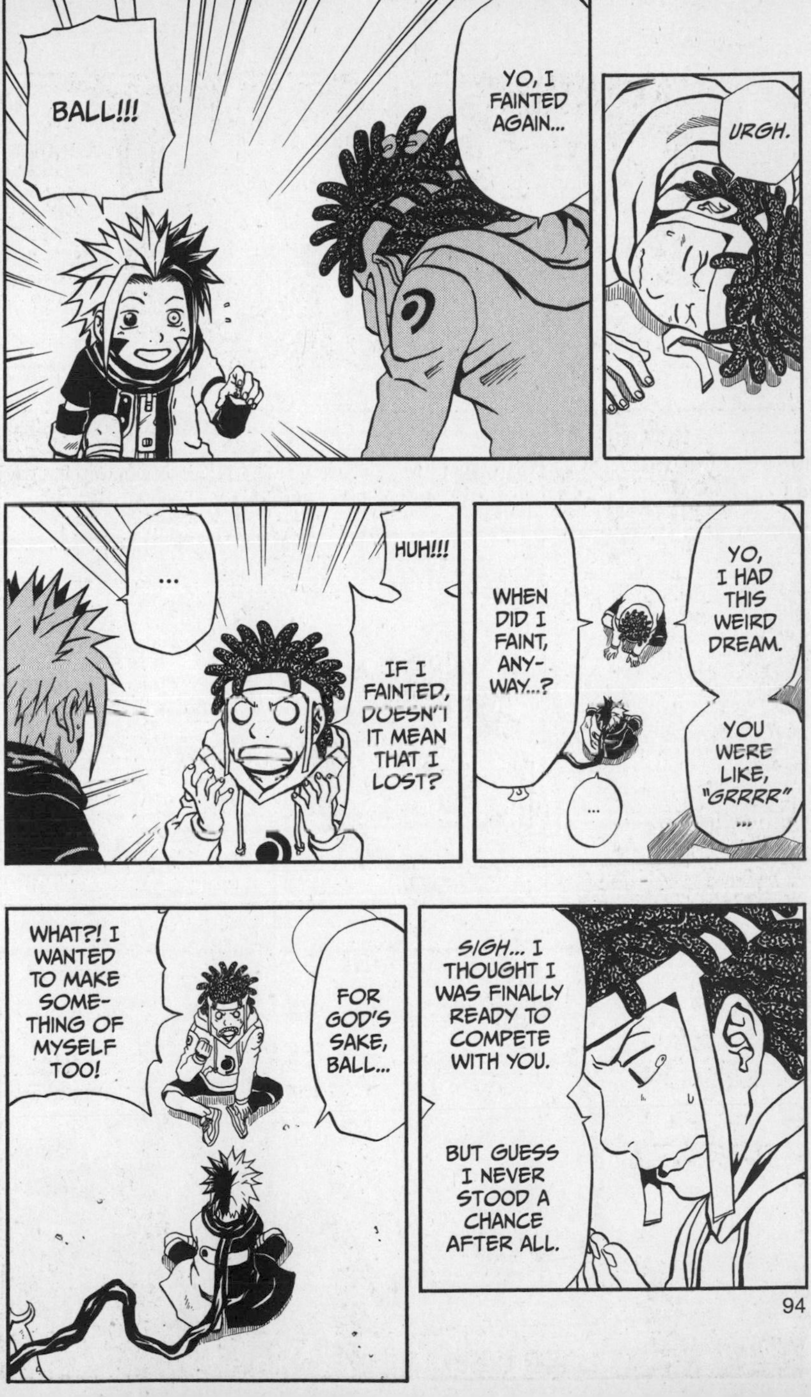
URGH.
YO, I FAINTED AGAIN...
BALL!!!
YO, I HAD THIS WEIRD DREAM.
YOU WERE LIKE, "GRRRR"...
WHEN DID I FAINT, ANYWAY...?
...
HUH!!!
IF I FAINTED, DOESN'T IT MEAN THAT I LOST?
...
SIGH... I THOUGHT I WAS FINALLY READY TO COMPETE WITH YOU.
BUT GUESS I NEVER STOOD A CHANCE AFTER ALL.
FOR GOD'S SAKE, BALL...
WHAT?! I WANTED TO MAKE SOMETHING OF MYSELF TOO!

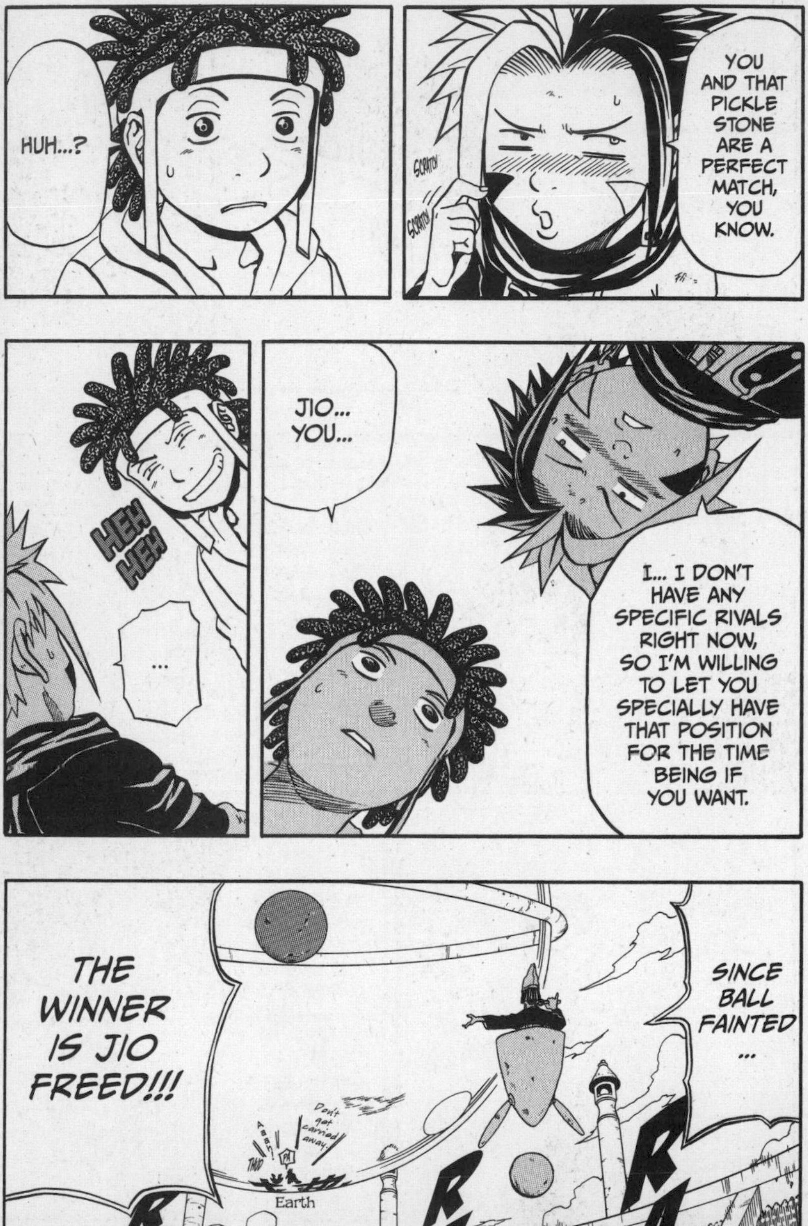
YOU AND THAT PICKLE STONE ARE A PERFECT MATCH, YOU KNOW.
SCRATCH
SCRATCH
HUH...?
JIO... YOU...
I... I DON'T HAVE ANY SPECIFIC RIVALS RIGHT NOW, SO I'M WILLING TO LET YOU SPECIALLY HAVE THAT POSITION FOR THE TIME BEING IF YOU WANT.
HEH HEH
...
SINCE BALL FAINTED ...
THE WINNER IS JIO FREED!!!
Don't get carried away.
Earth

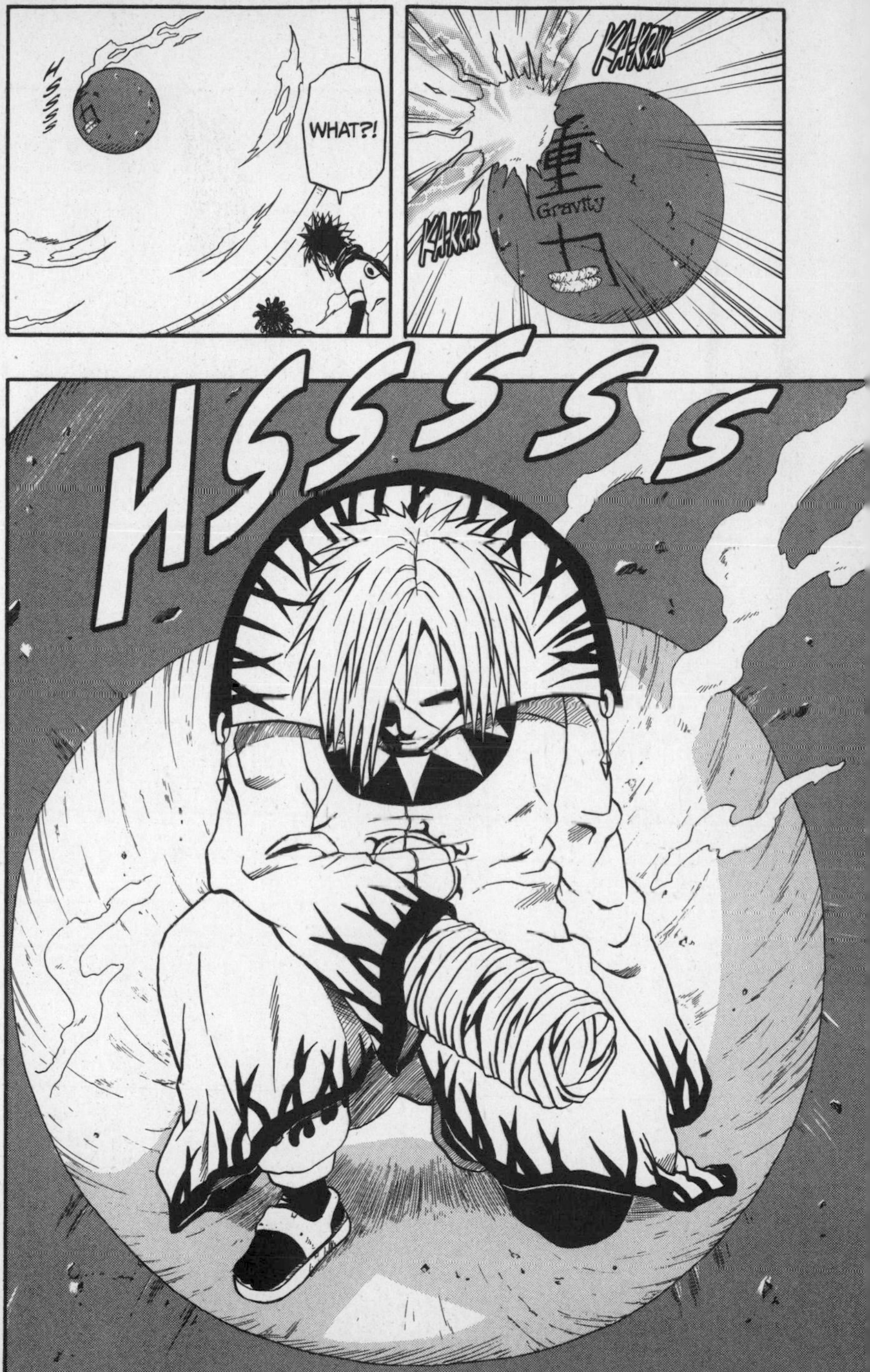
KA-KRAK
重
Gravity
力
KA-KRAK
HSSSS
WHAT?!
HSSSSS

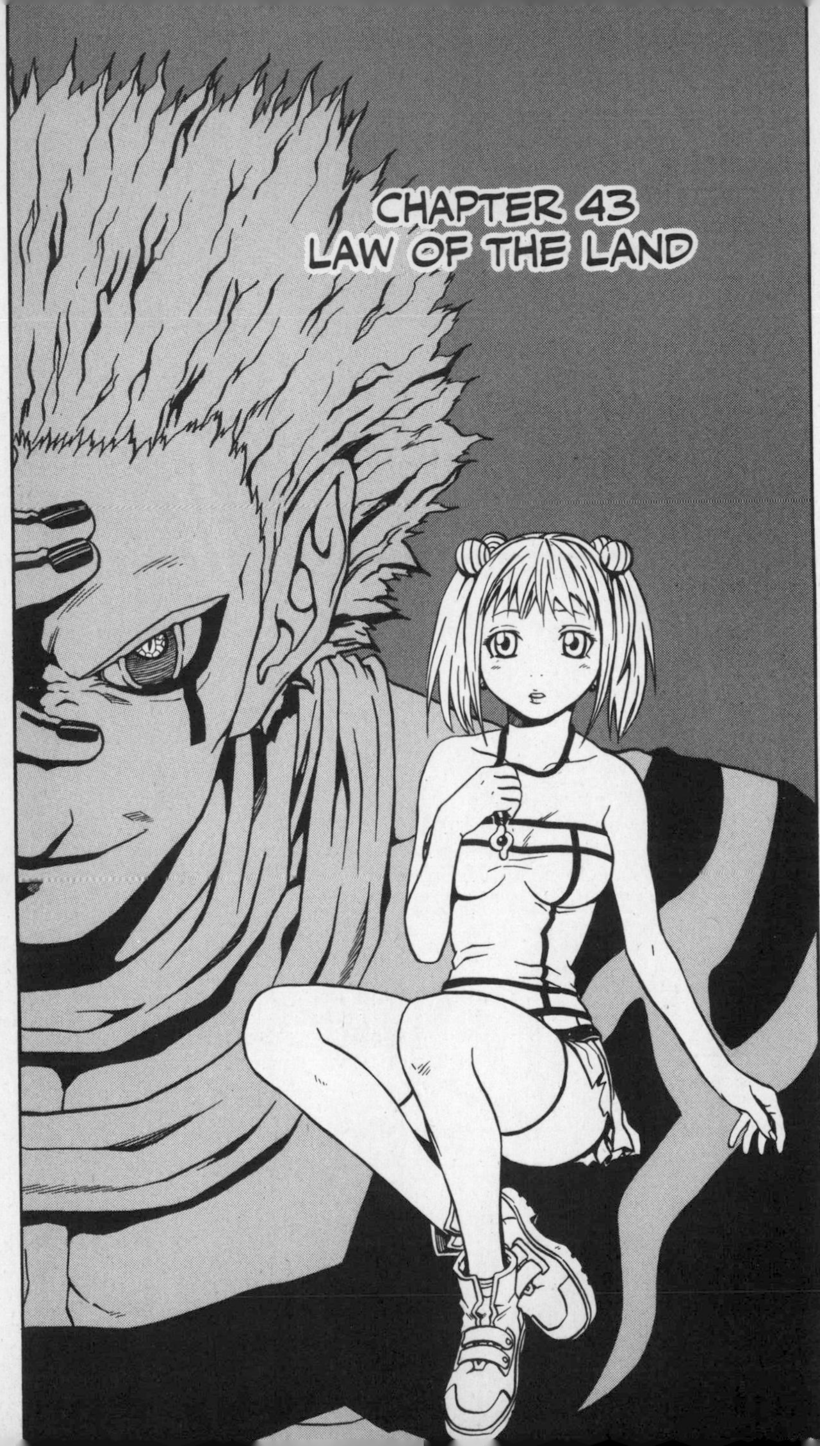
CHAPTER 43
LAW OF THE LAND

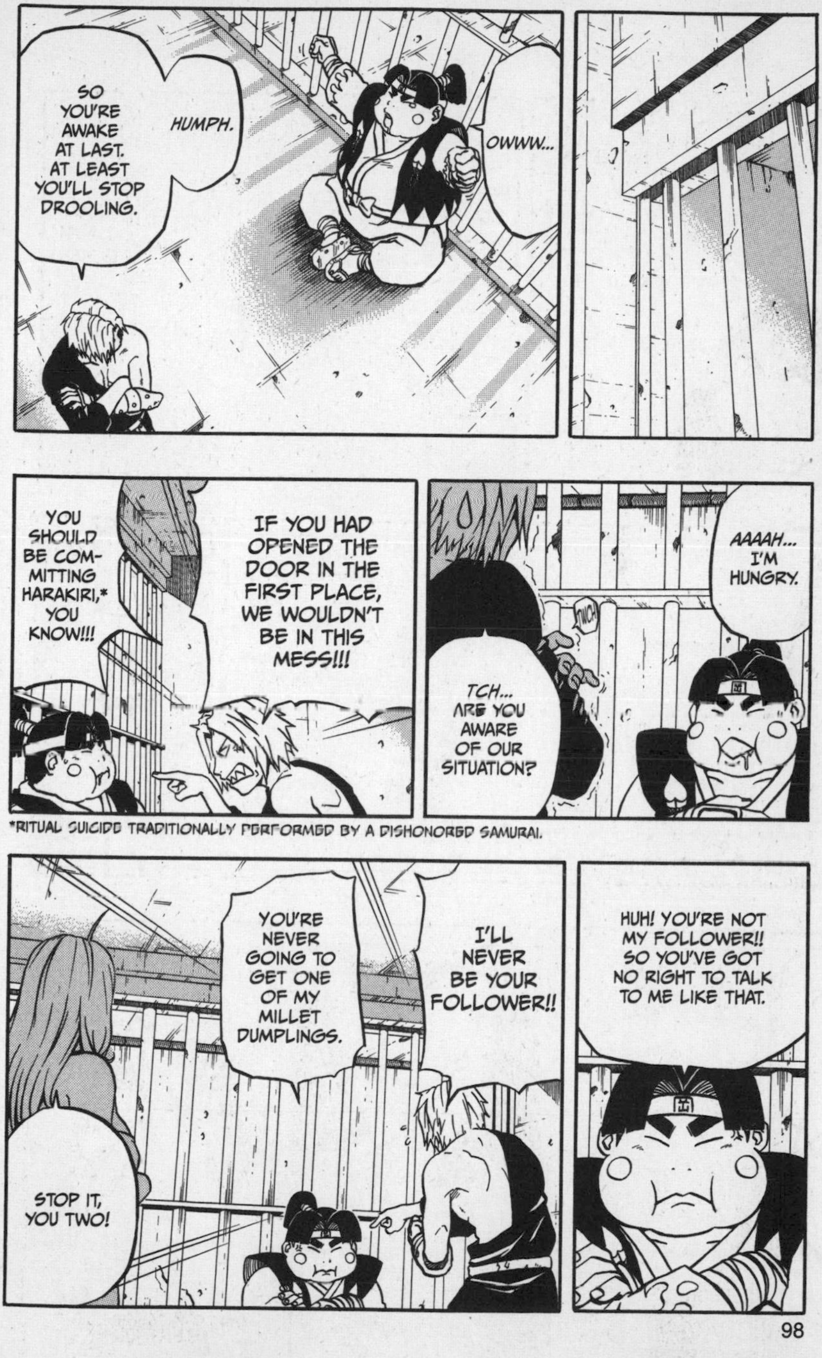
OWWW...
HUMPH.
SO YOU'RE AWAKE AT LAST. AT LEAST YOU'LL STOP DROOLING.
AAAAH... I'M HUNGRY.
TCH... ARE YOU AWARE OF OUR SITUATION?
IF YOU HAD OPENED THE DOOR IN THE FIRST PLACE, WE WOULDN'T BE IN THIS MESS!!!
YOU SHOULD BE COM-MITTING HARAKIRI,* YOU KNOW!!!
HUH! YOU'RE NOT MY FOLLOWER!! SO YOU'VE GOT NO RIGHT TO TALK TO ME LIKE THAT.
I'LL NEVER BE YOUR FOLLOWER!!
YOU'RE NEVER GOING TO GET ONE OF MY MILLET DUMPLINGS.
STOP IT, YOU TWO!

*RITUAL SUICIDE TRADITIONALLY PERFORMED BY A DISHONORED SAMURAI.

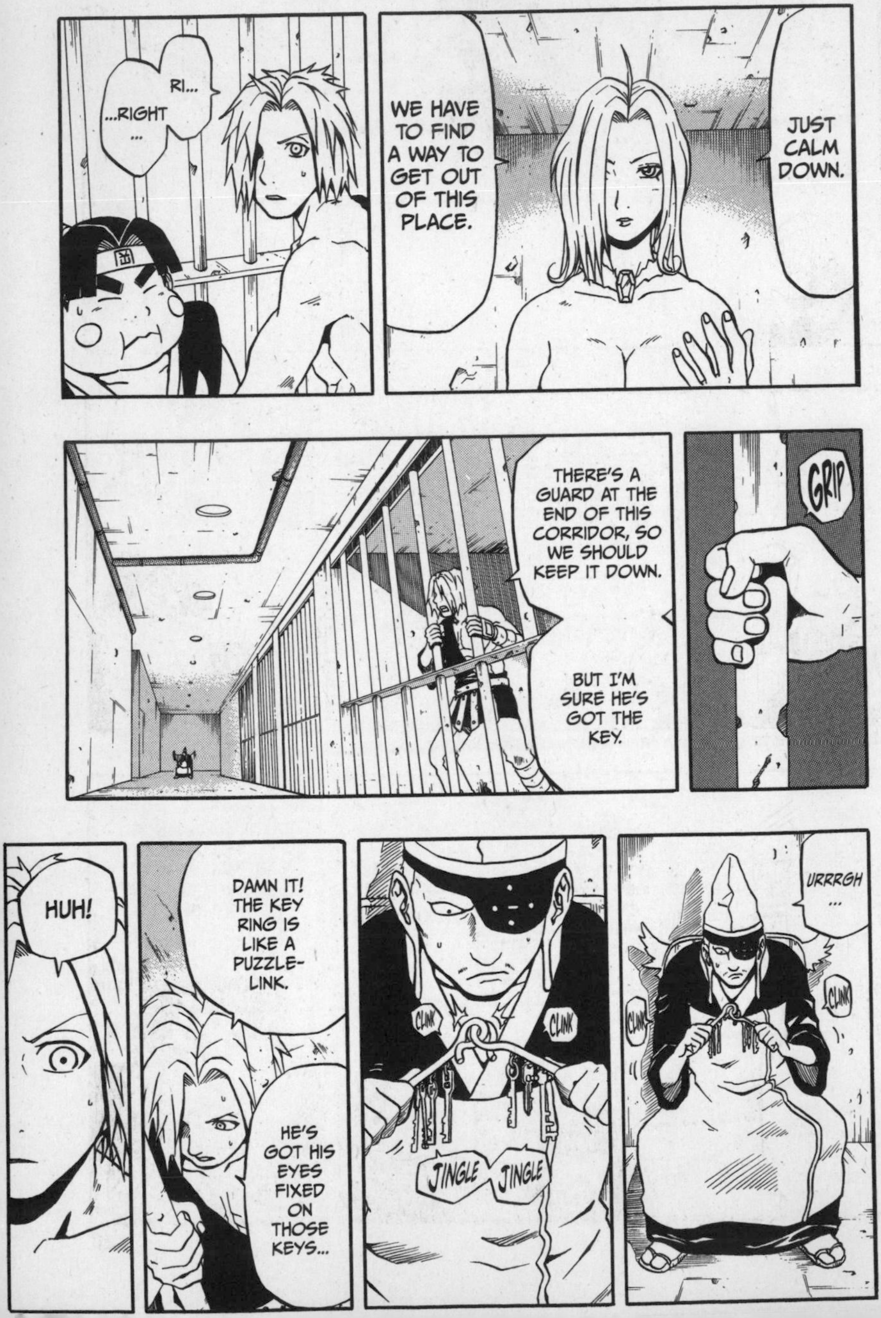
JUST CALM DOWN.
WE HAVE TO FIND A WAY TO GET OUT OF THIS PLACE.
RI...
...RIGHT ...
GRIP
THERE'S A GUARD AT THE END OF THIS CORRIDOR, SO WE SHOULD KEEP IT DOWN.
BUT I'M SURE HE'S GOT THE KEY.
URRRGH ...
CLINK
CLINK
CLINK
CLINK
JINGLE
JINGLE
DAMN IT! THE KEY RING IS LIKE A PUZZLE-LINK.
HE'S GOT HIS EYES FIXED ON THOSE KEYS...
HUH!

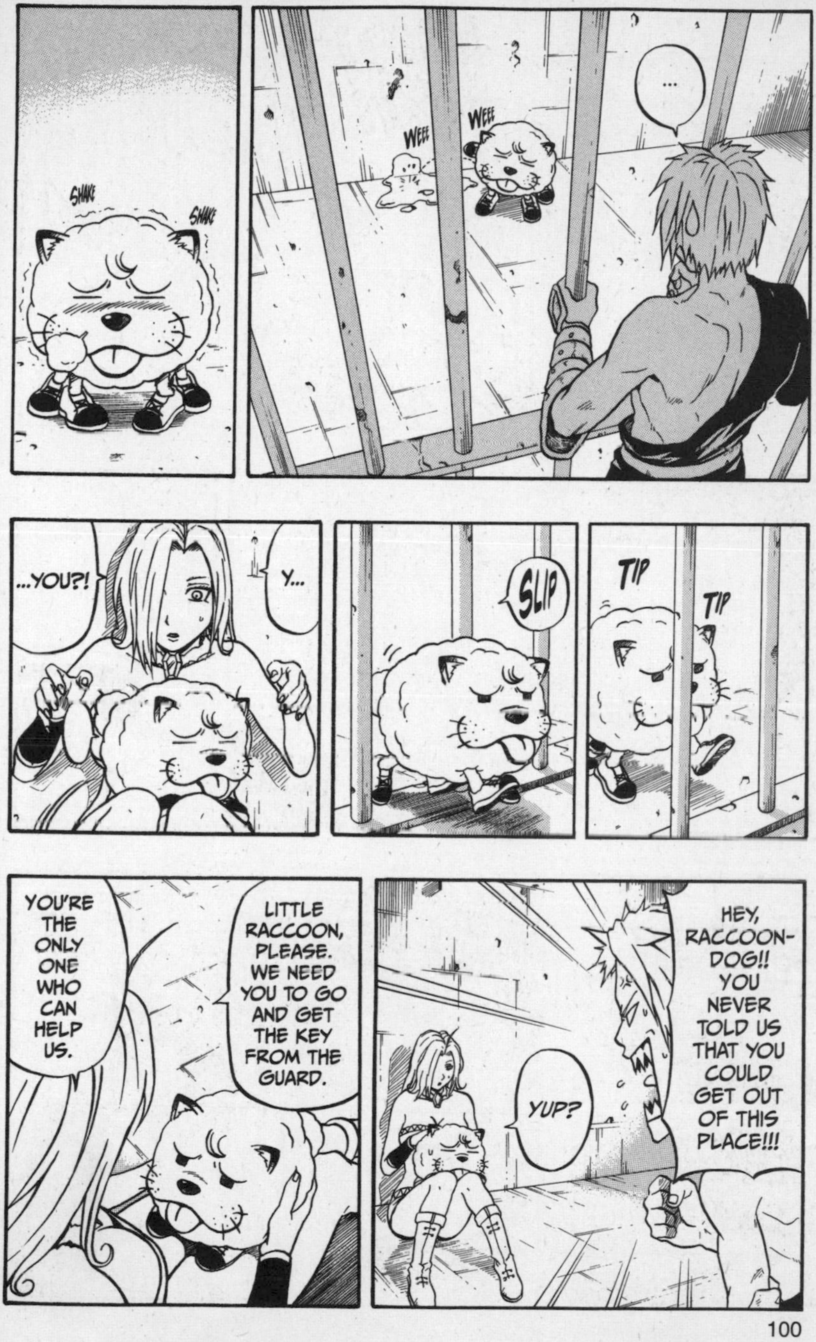
...
WEEE
WEEE
SHAKE
SHAKE
TIP
TIP
SLIP
Y...
...YOU?!
HEY, RACCOON-DOG!! YOU NEVER TOLD US THAT YOU COULD GET OUT OF THIS PLACE!!!
YUP?
LITTLE RACCOON, PLEASE. WE NEED YOU TO GO AND GET THE KEY FROM THE GUARD.
YOU'RE THE ONLY ONE WHO CAN HELP US.

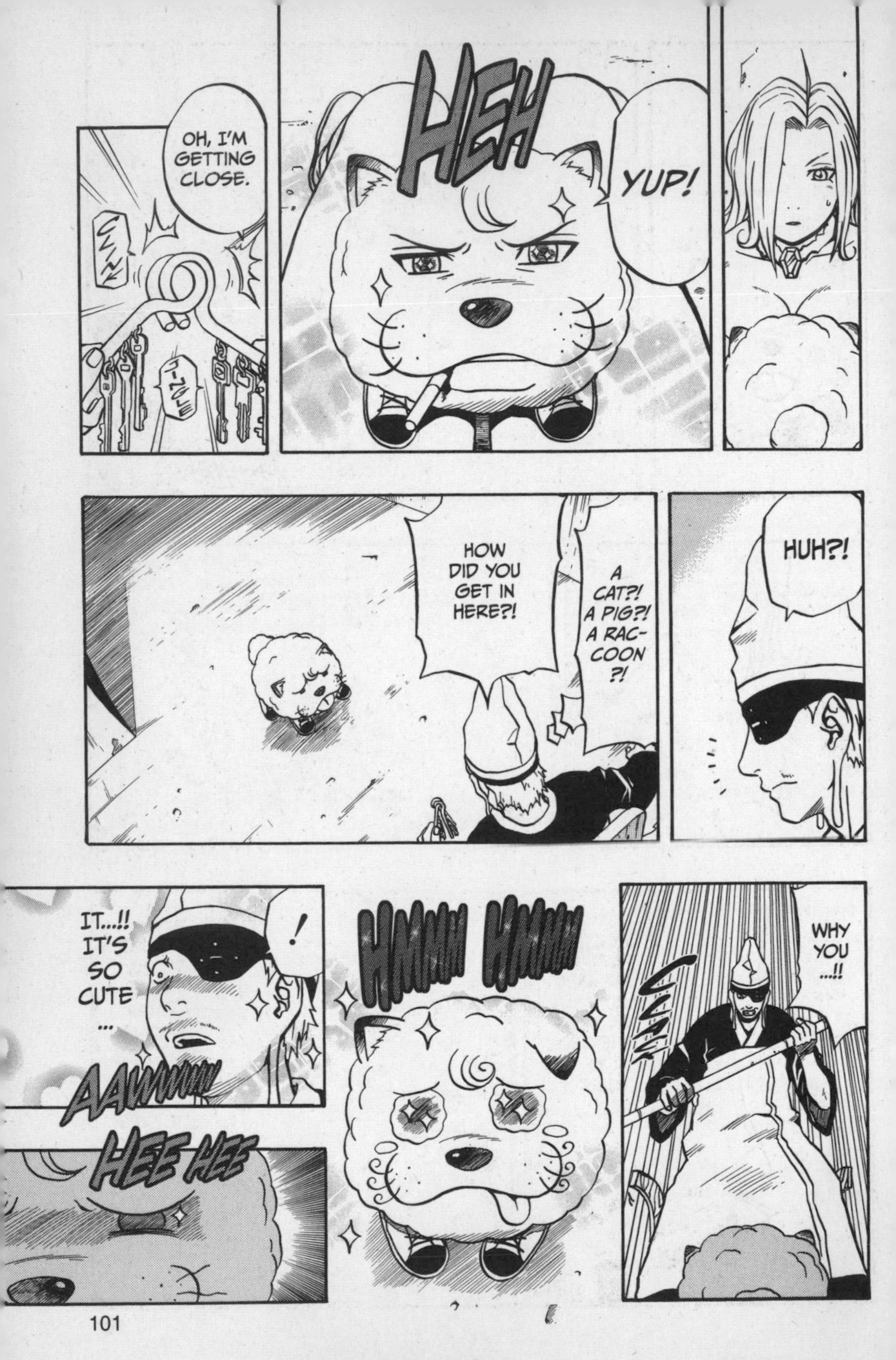
YUP!
HEH
OH, I'M GETTING CLOSE.
JINGLE
HUH?!
A CAT?! A PIG?! A RAC-COON?!
HOW DID YOU GET IN HERE?!
WHY YOU ...!!
!
IT...!! IT'S SO CUTE ...
HEE HEE

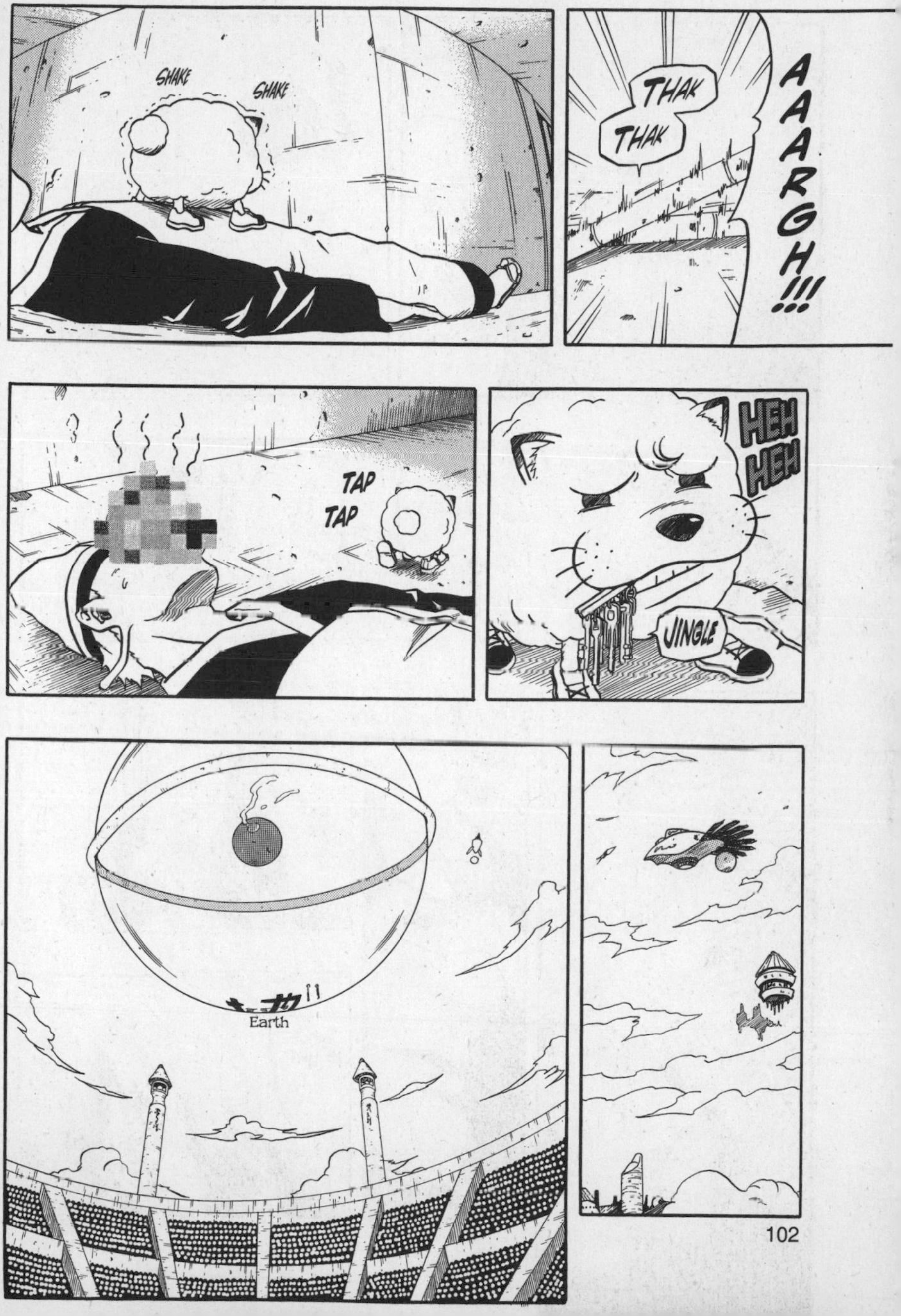
THAK
THAK
AAAARGH!!!
SHAKE
SHAKE
HEH
HEH
JINGLE
TAP
TAP
Earth

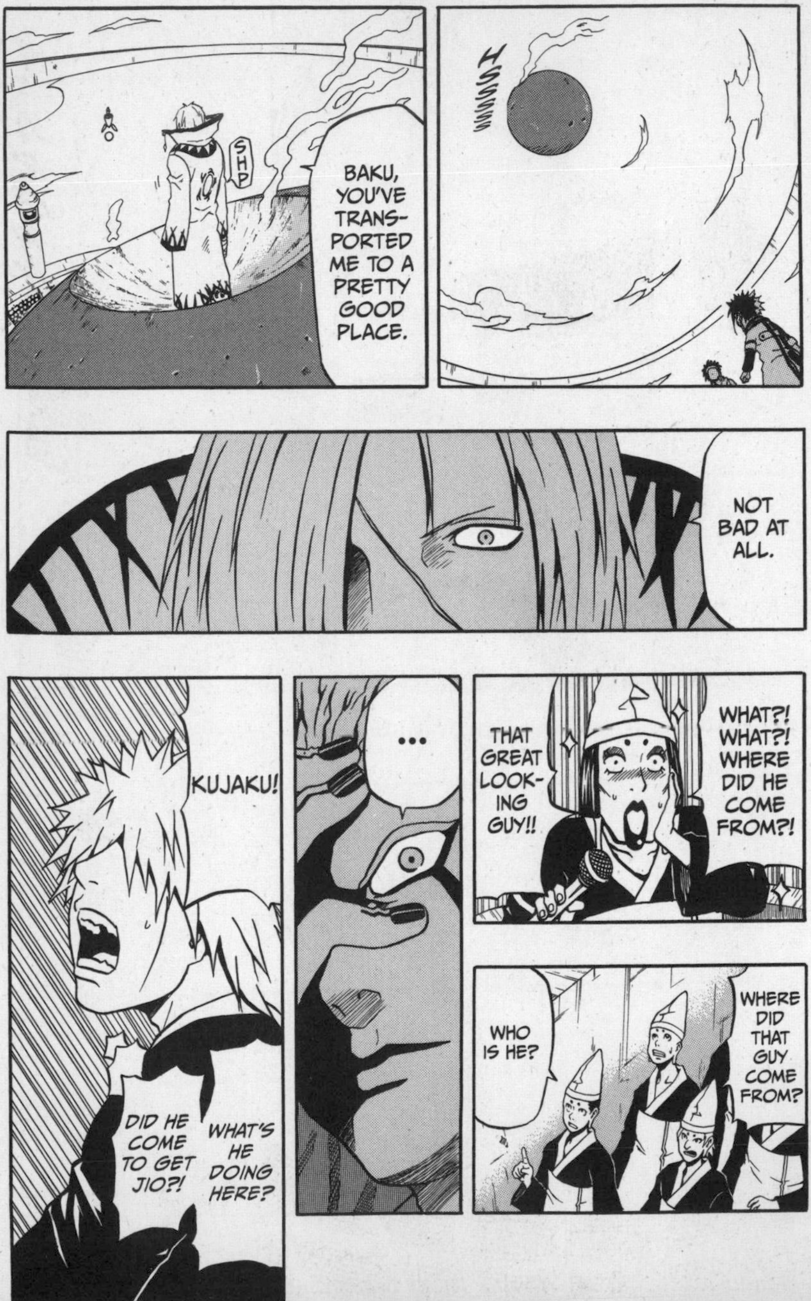
HSSSSS
SHP
BAKU, YOU'VE TRANSPORTED ME TO A PRETTY GOOD PLACE.
NOT BAD AT ALL.
WHAT?! WHAT?! WHERE DID HE COME FROM?!
THAT GREAT LOOKING GUY!!
WHERE DID THAT GUY COME FROM?
WHO IS HE?
...
KUJAKU!
WHAT'S HE DOING HERE?
DID HE COME TO GET JIO?!

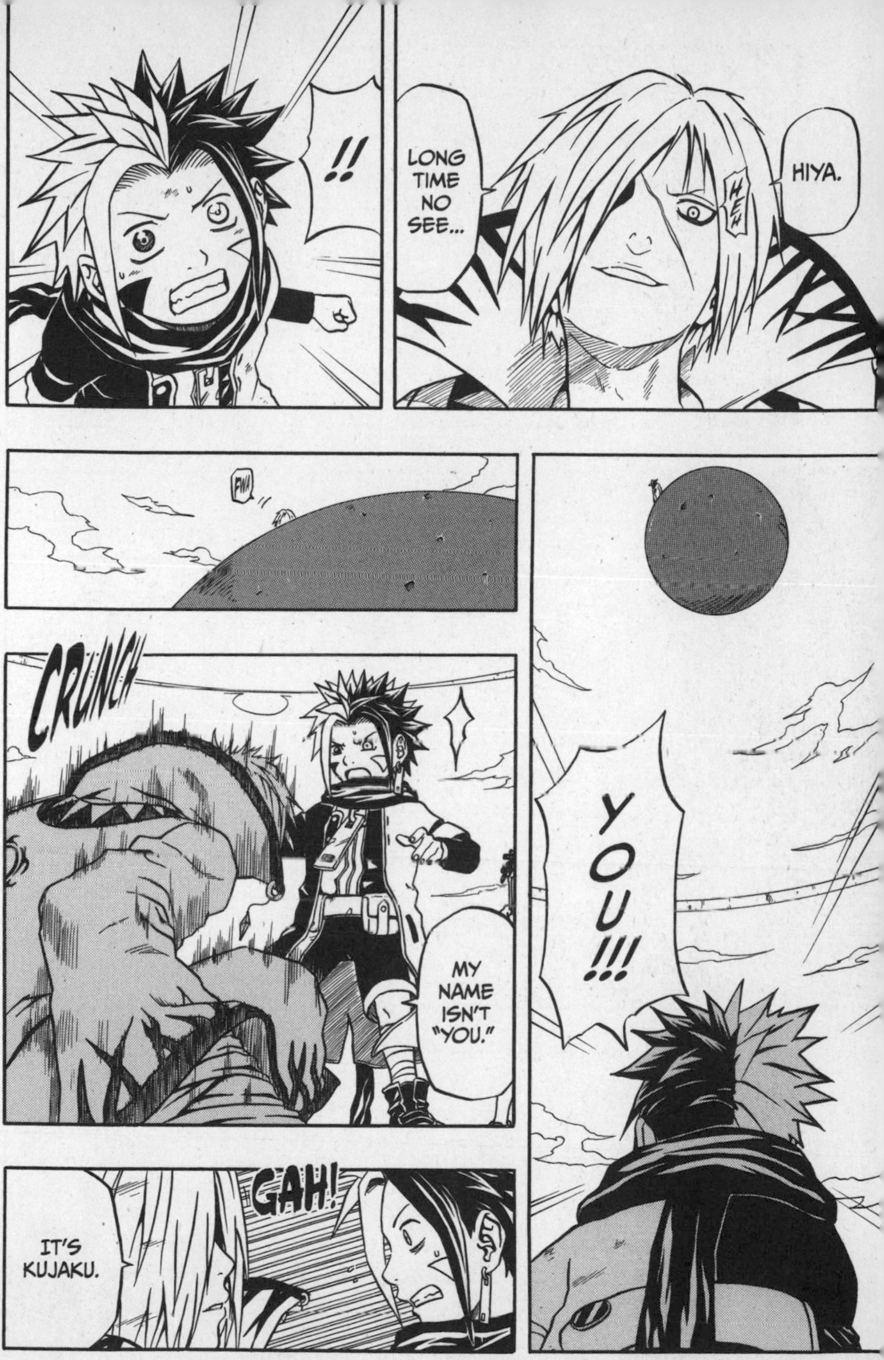
HIYA.
HEH
LONG TIME NO SEE...
!!
YOU!!!
FWA
MY NAME ISN'T "YOU."
CRUNCH
GAH!
IT'S KUJAKU.

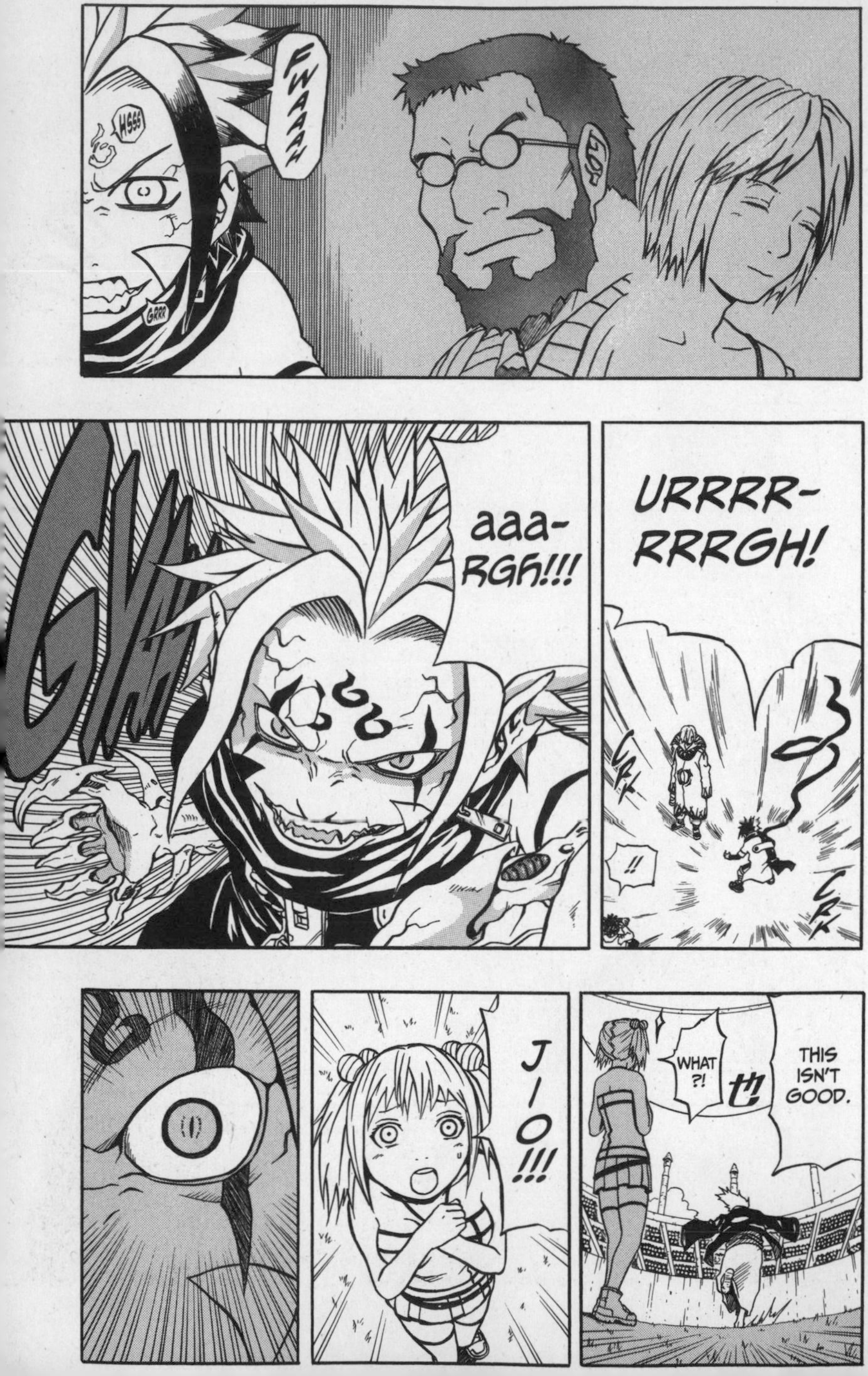

FWAAAAH
HSSS
GRRR
URRRR-RRRGH!
!!
CRK
CRK
aaa-RGH!!!
WHAT?!
THIS ISN'T GOOD.
JIO!!!

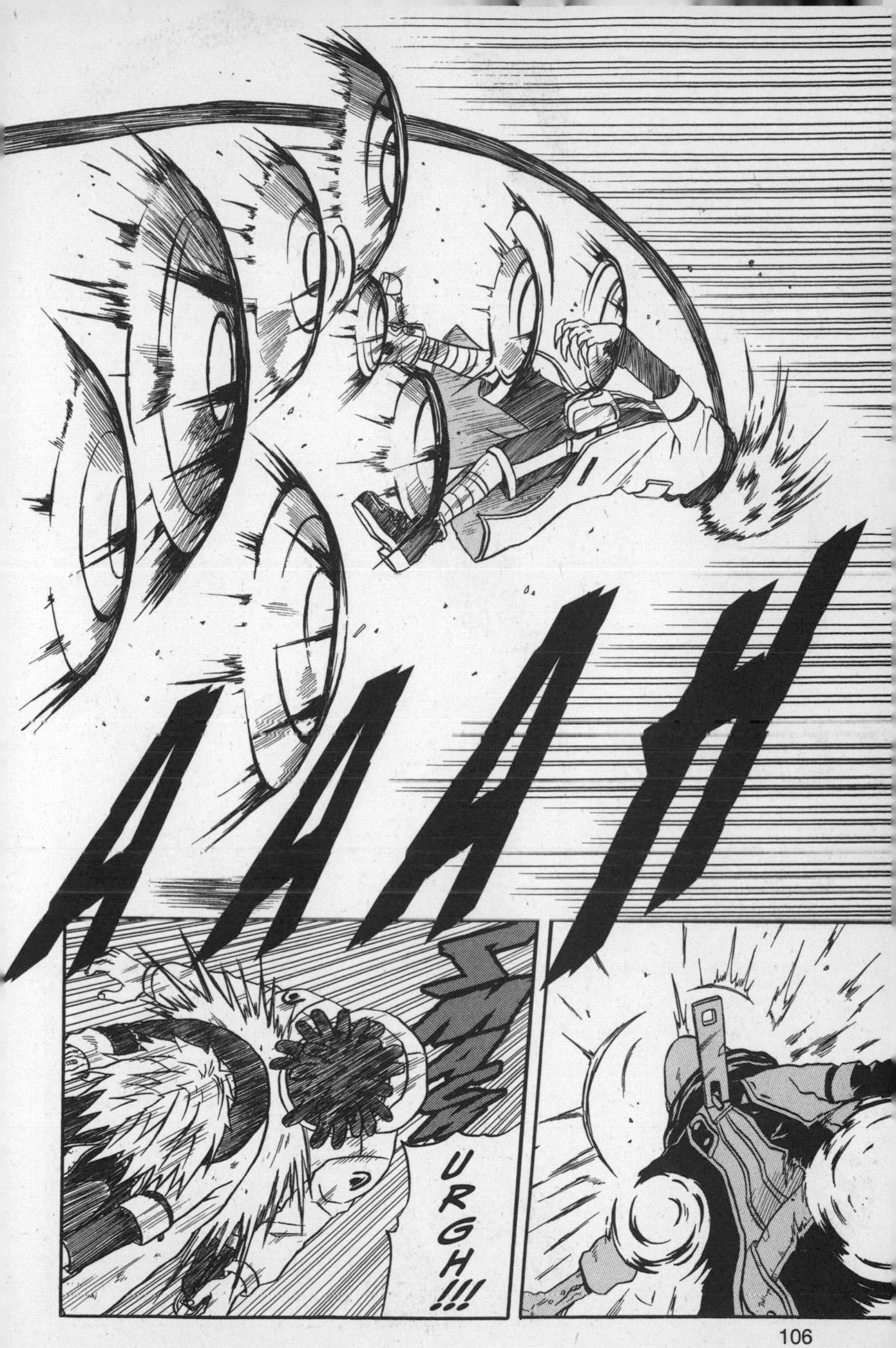
AAAH
URGH!!!

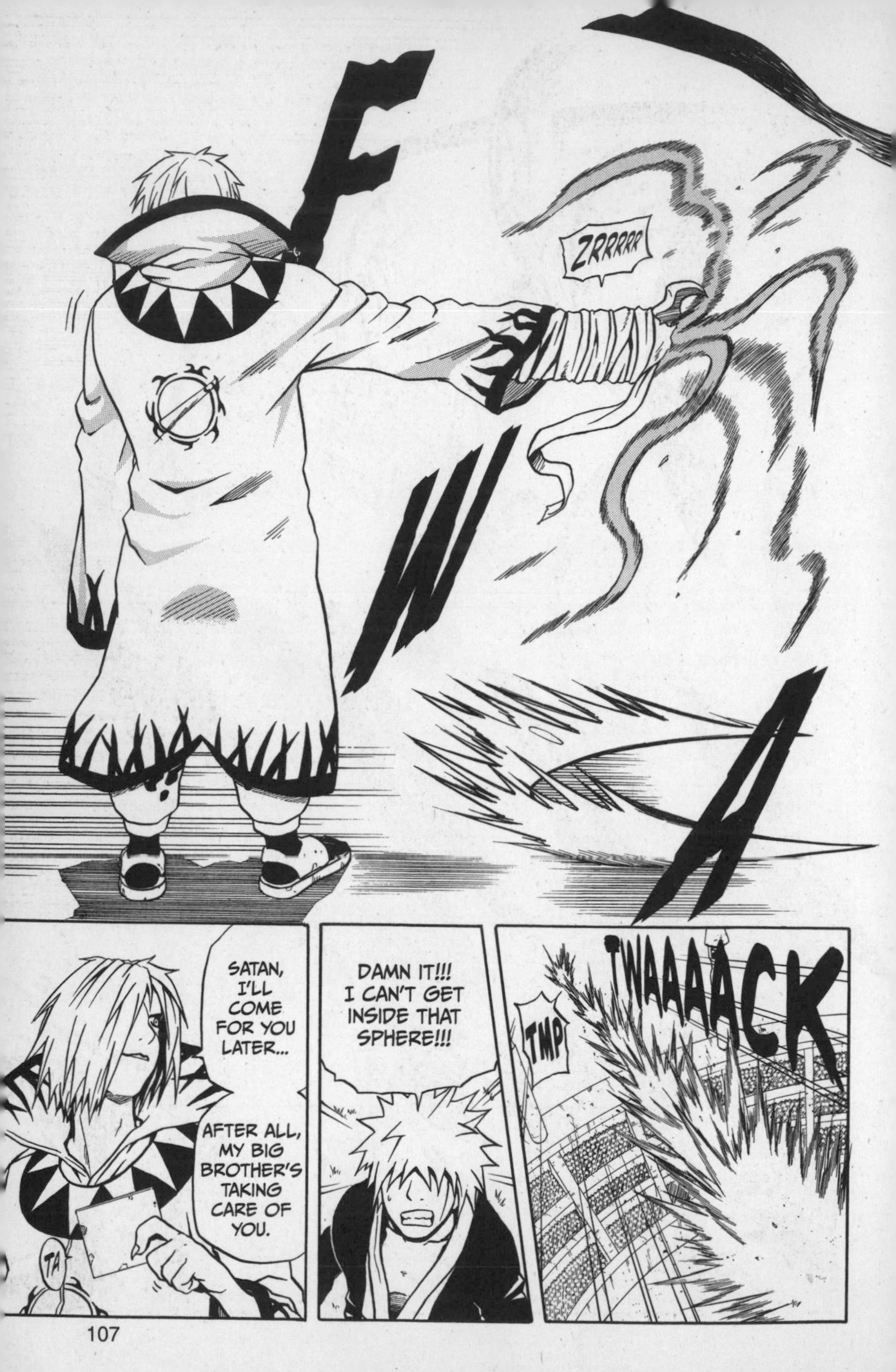
FWA
ZRRRRP
TWAAAACK
TMP
DAMN IT!!! I CAN'T GET INSIDE THAT SPHERE!!!
SATAN, I'LL COME FOR YOU LATER...
AFTER ALL, MY BIG BROTHER'S TAKING CARE OF YOU.
TA

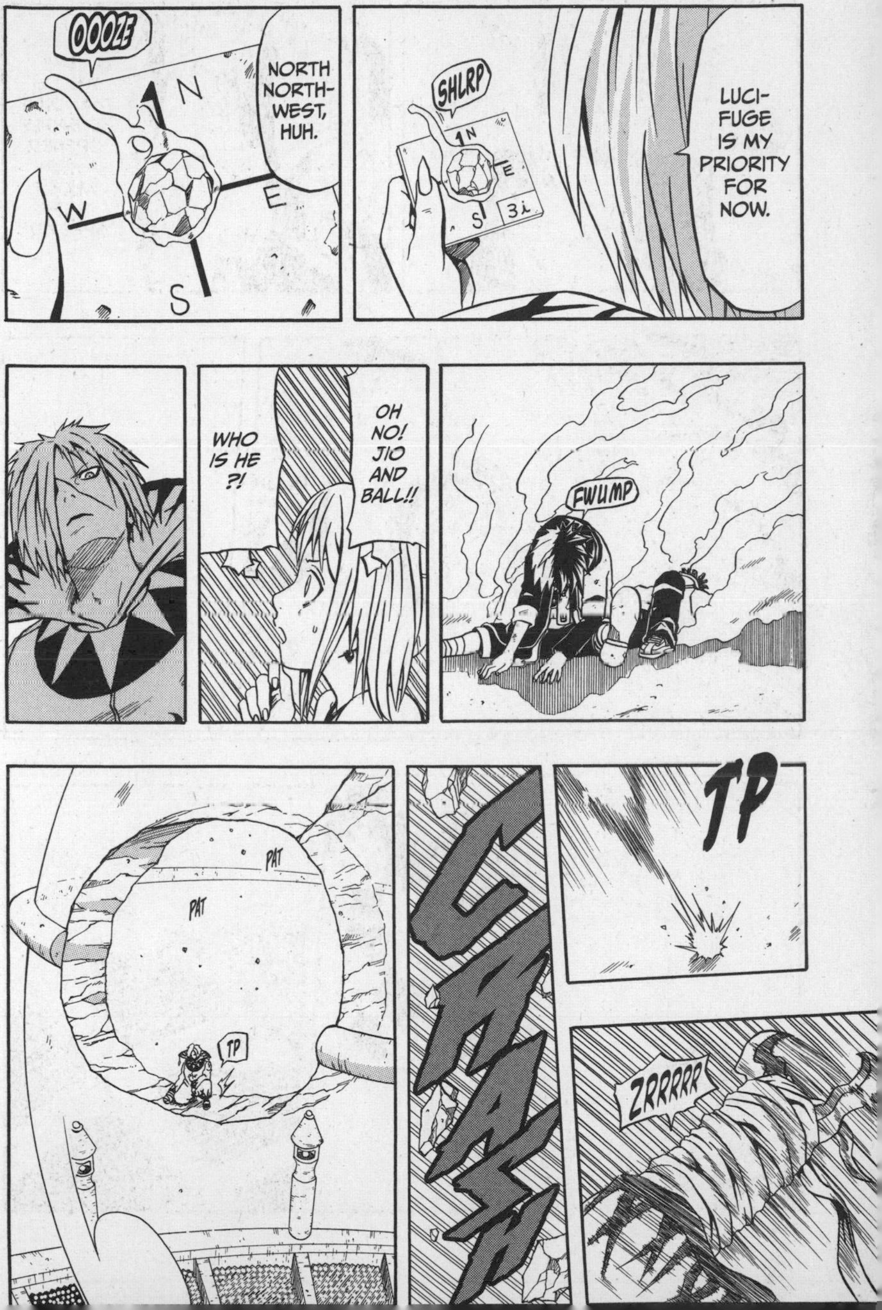
SHLRP
LUCI-FUGE IS MY PRIORITY FOR NOW.
OOOZE
NORTH NORTH-WEST, HUH.
FWUMP
OH NO! JIO AND BALL!!
WHO IS HE ?!
TP
ZRRRRR
PAT
PAT
TP

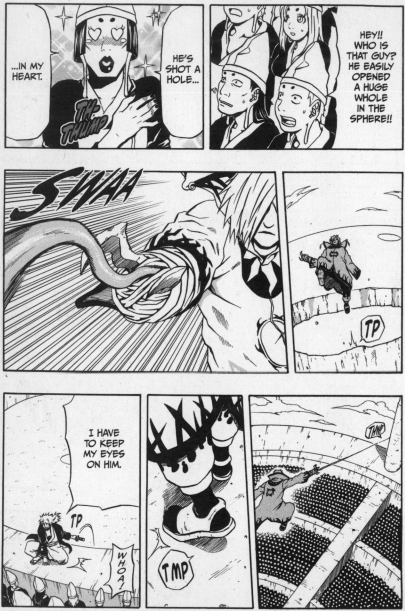

HEY!! WHO IS THAT GUY? HE EASILY OPENED A HUGE WHOLE IN THE SPHERE!!
HE'S SHOT A HOLE...
...IN MY HEART.
TH-THUMP
TP
SWAA
TMP
TMP
I HAVE TO KEEP MY EYES ON HIM.
TP
WHOA!

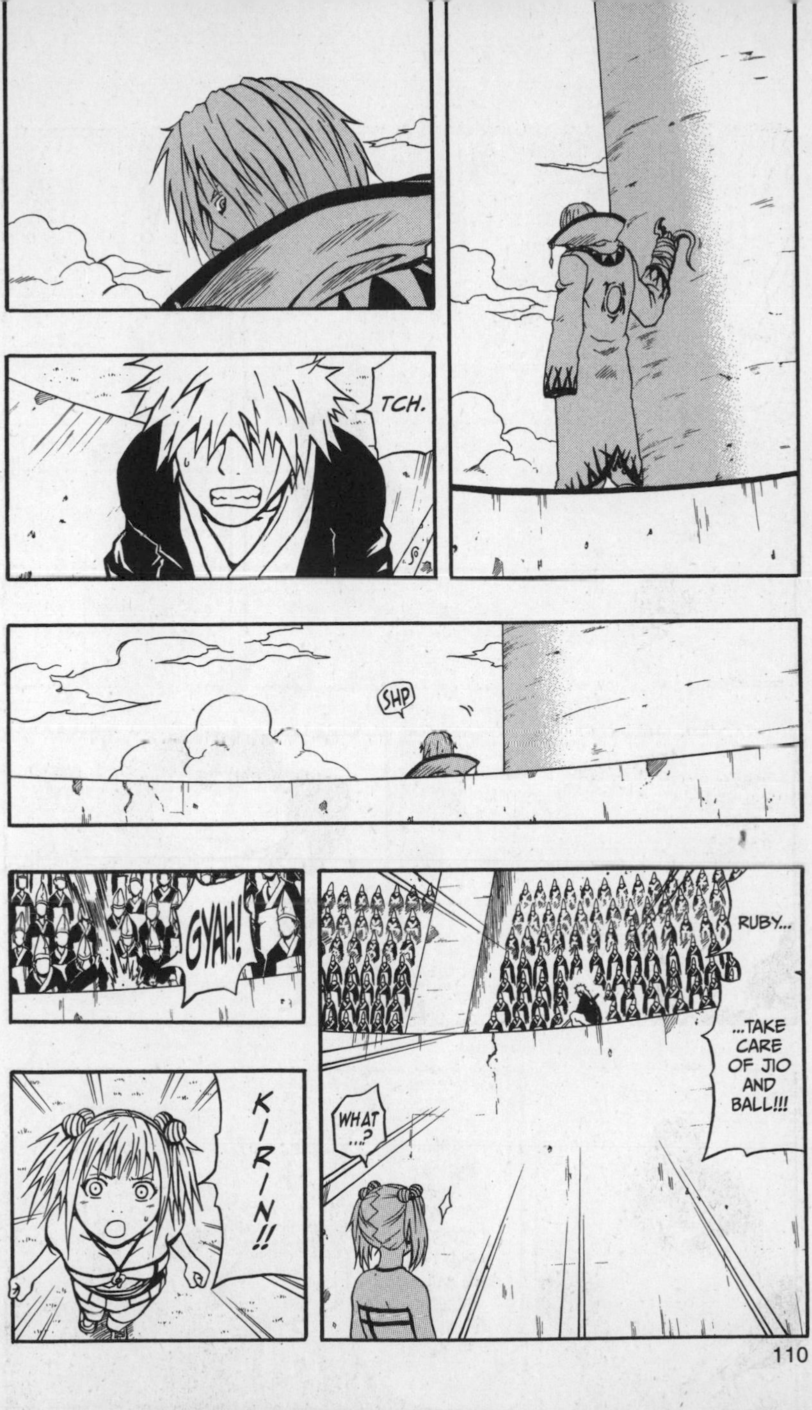
TCH.
SHP
RUBY...
...TAKE CARE OF JIO AND BALL!!!
WHAT ...?
GYAH!
KIRIN!!

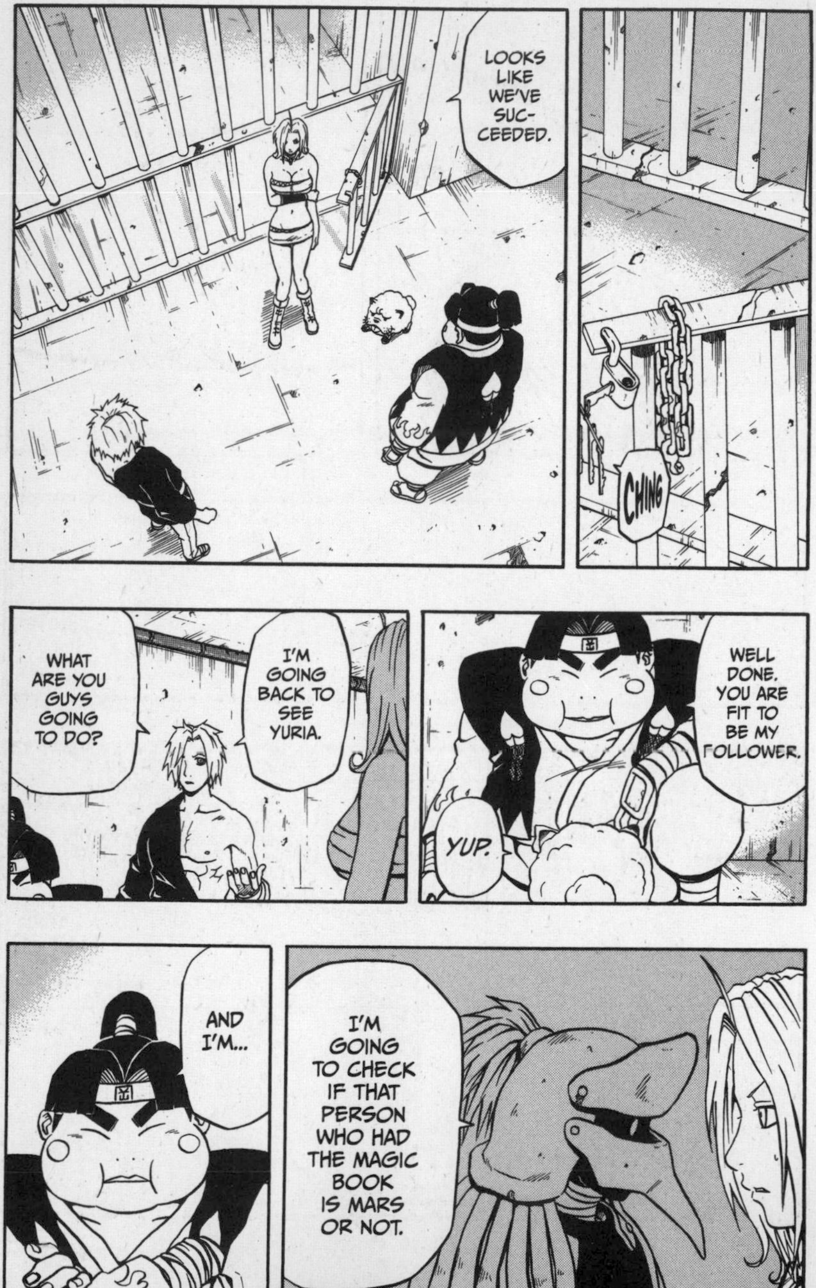
LOOKS LIKE WE'VE SUC-CEEDED.
CHING
WHAT ARE YOU GUYS GOING TO DO?
I'M GOING BACK TO SEE YURIA.
WELL DONE. YOU ARE FIT TO BE MY FOLLOWER.
YUP.
AND I'M...
I'M GOING TO CHECK IF THAT PERSON WHO HAD THE MAGIC BOOK IS MARS OR NOT.

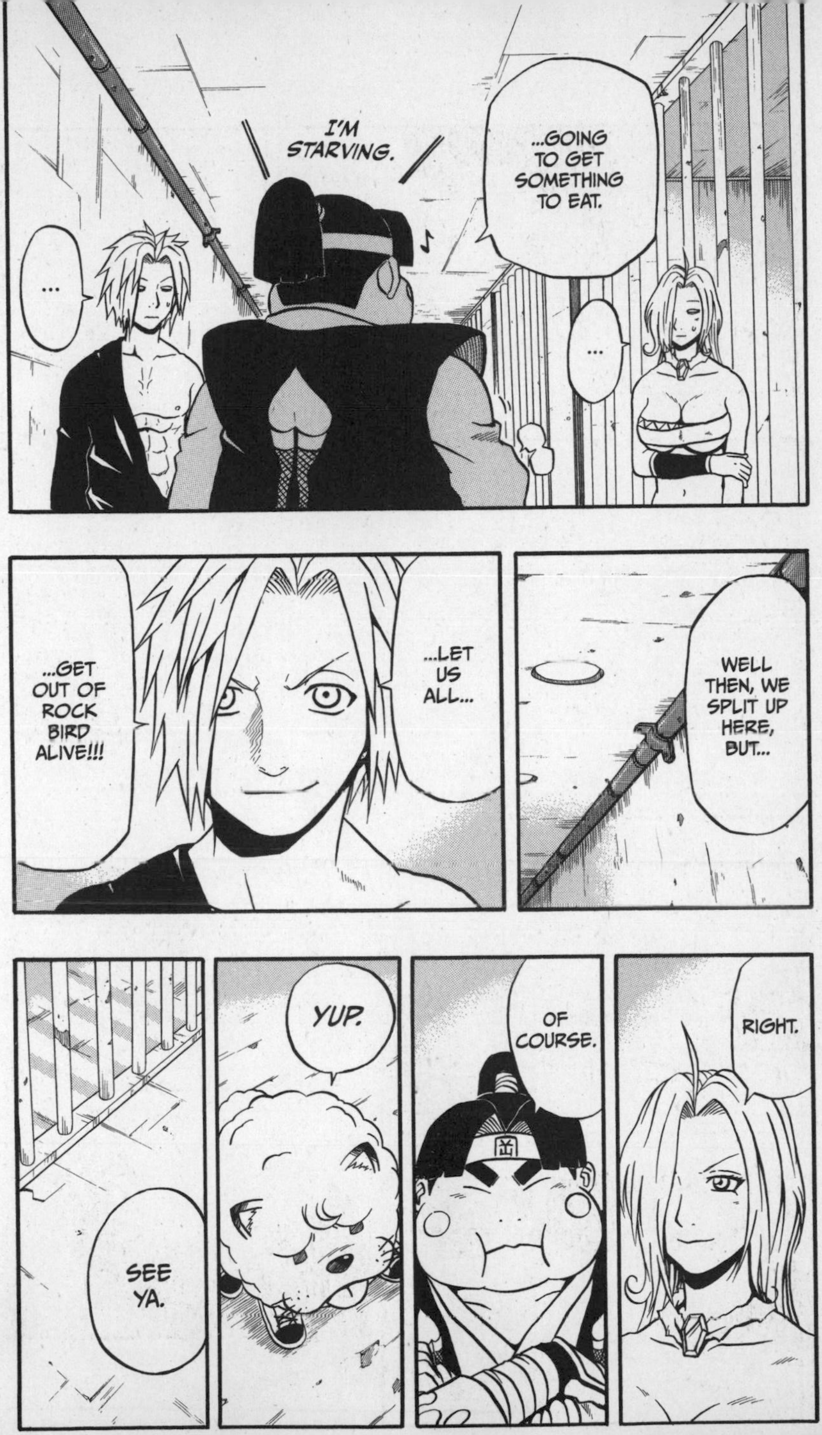
...GOING TO GET SOMETHING TO EAT.
I'M STARVING.
...
...
WELL THEN, WE SPLIT UP HERE, BUT...
...LET US ALL...
...GET OUT OF ROCK BIRD ALIVE!!!
RIGHT.
OF COURSE.
YUP.
SEE YA.

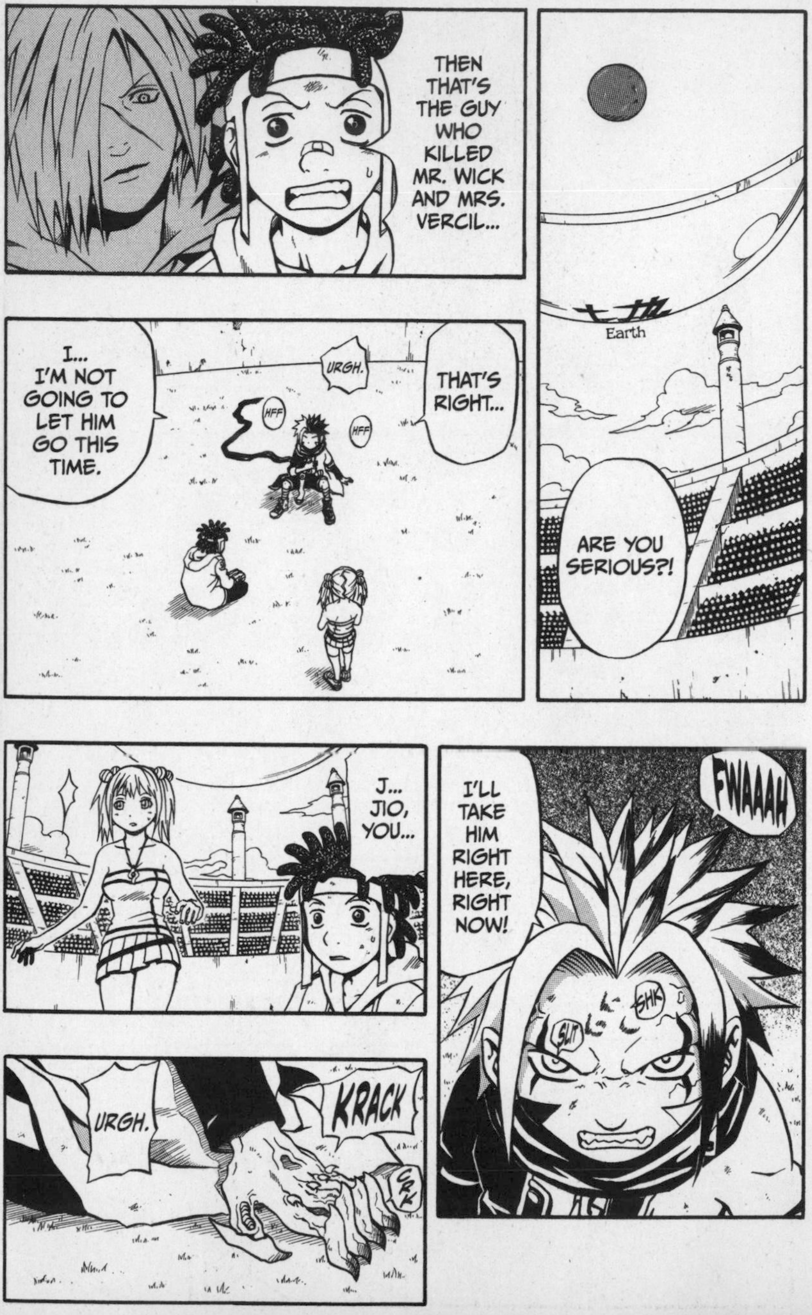
Earth
ARE YOU SERIOUS?!
THEN THAT'S THE GUY WHO KILLED MR. WICK AND MRS. VERCIL...
THAT'S RIGHT...
URGH.
HFF
HFF
I... I'M NOT GOING TO LET HIM GO THIS TIME.
FWAAAH
I'LL TAKE HIM RIGHT HERE, RIGHT NOW!
SHK
SLIT
J... JIO, YOU...
CRK
KRACK
URGH.

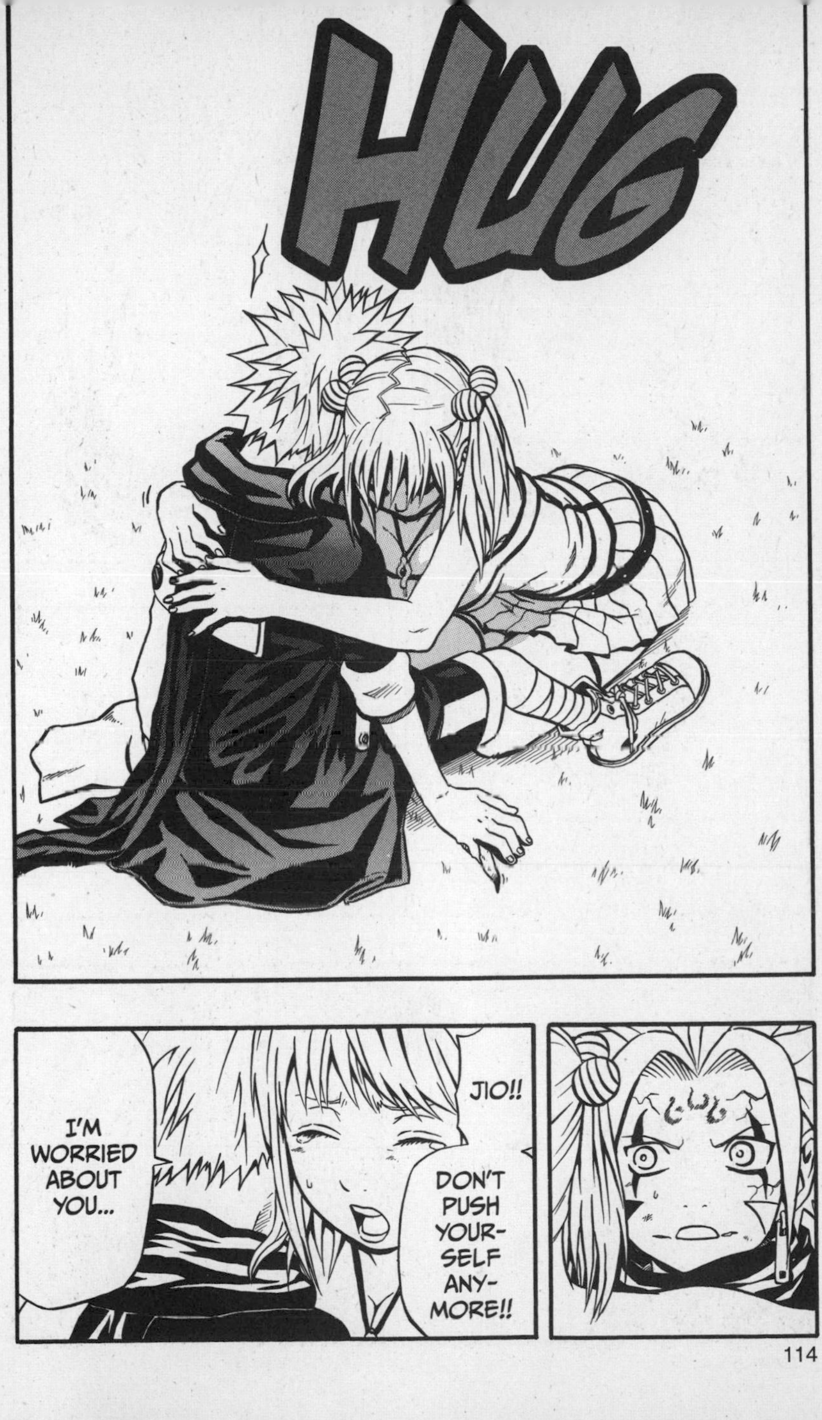
HUG
JIO!!
DON'T PUSH YOUR-SELF ANY-MORE!!
I'M WORRIED ABOUT YOU...

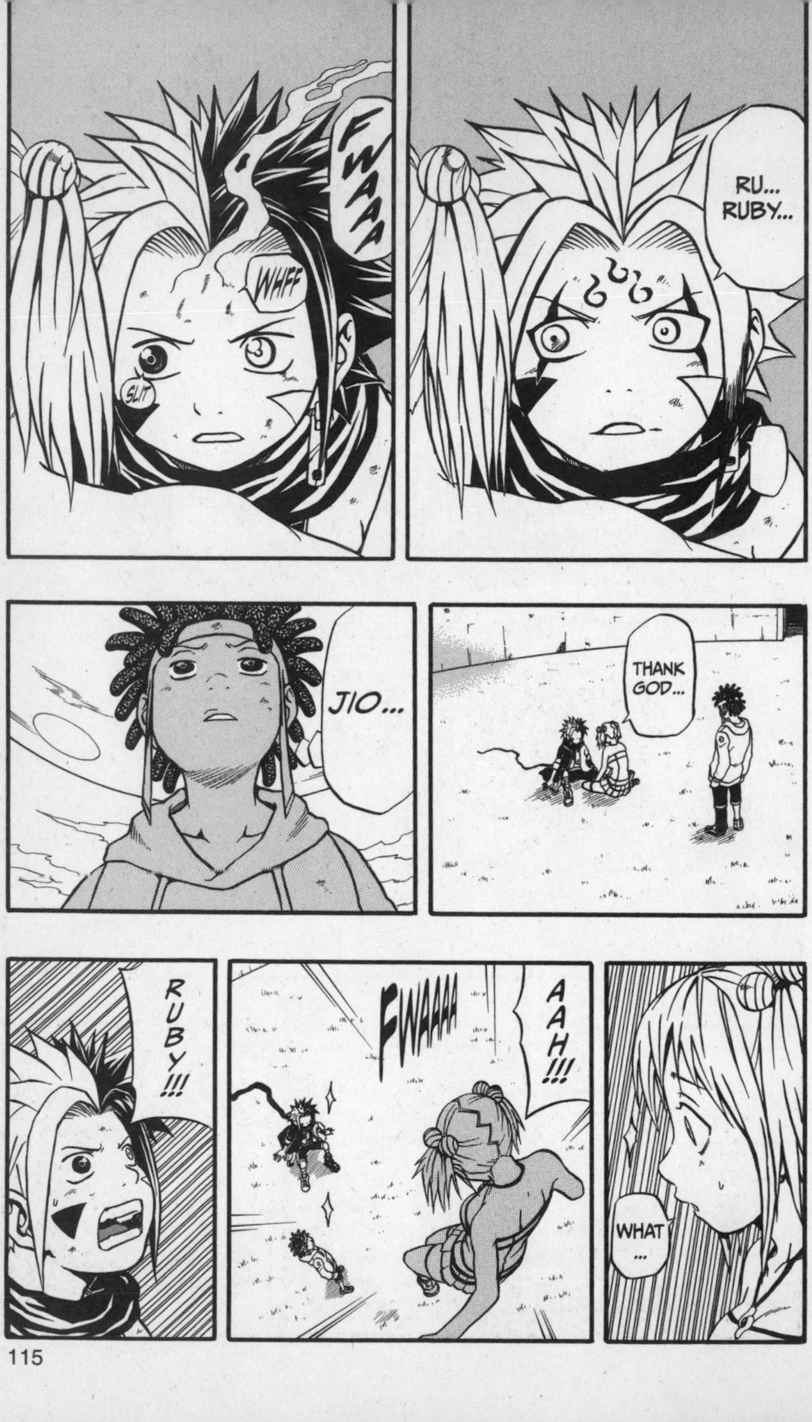
RU... RUBY...
FWAAA
WHFF
SLIT
THANK GOD...
JIO...
WHAT ...
AAH!!!
FWAAA
RUBY!!!

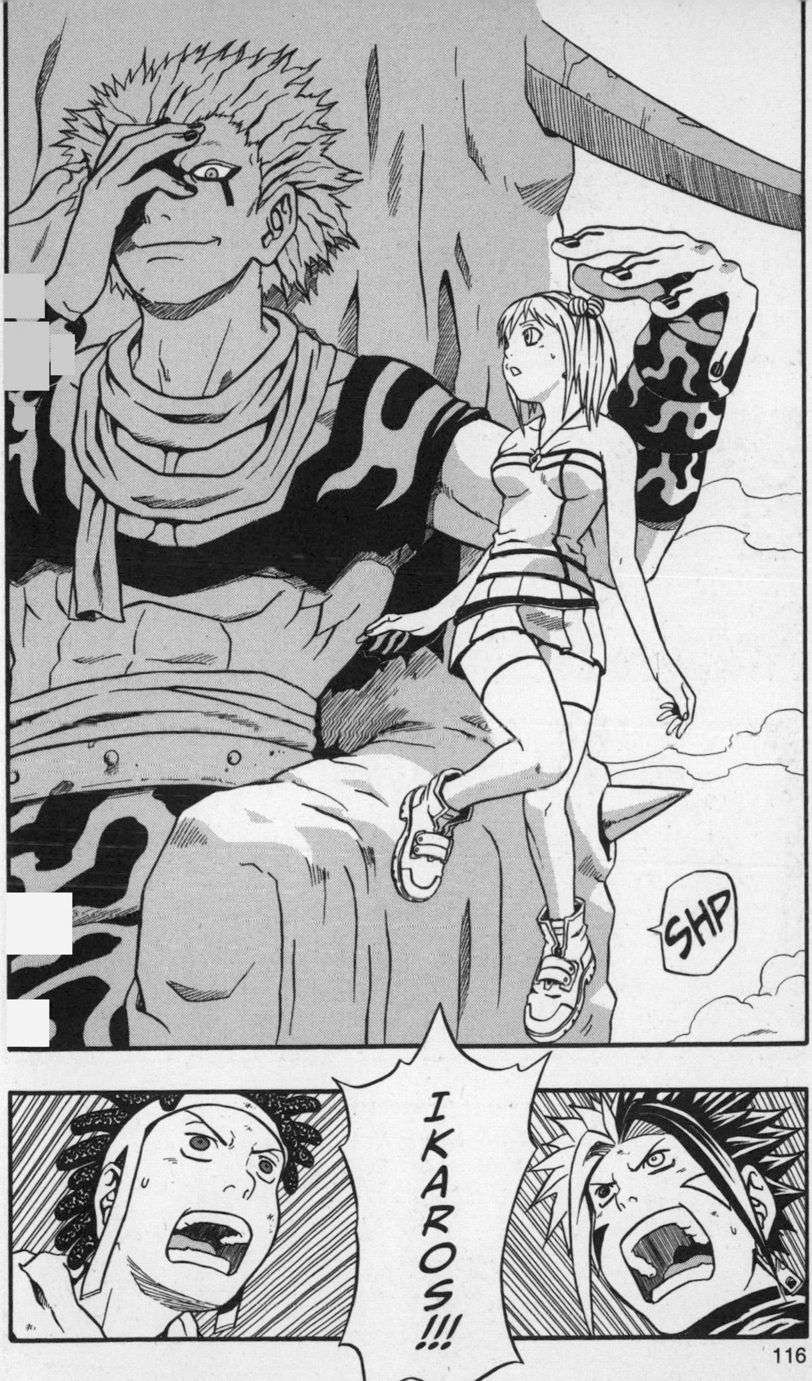
SHP
IKAROS!!!

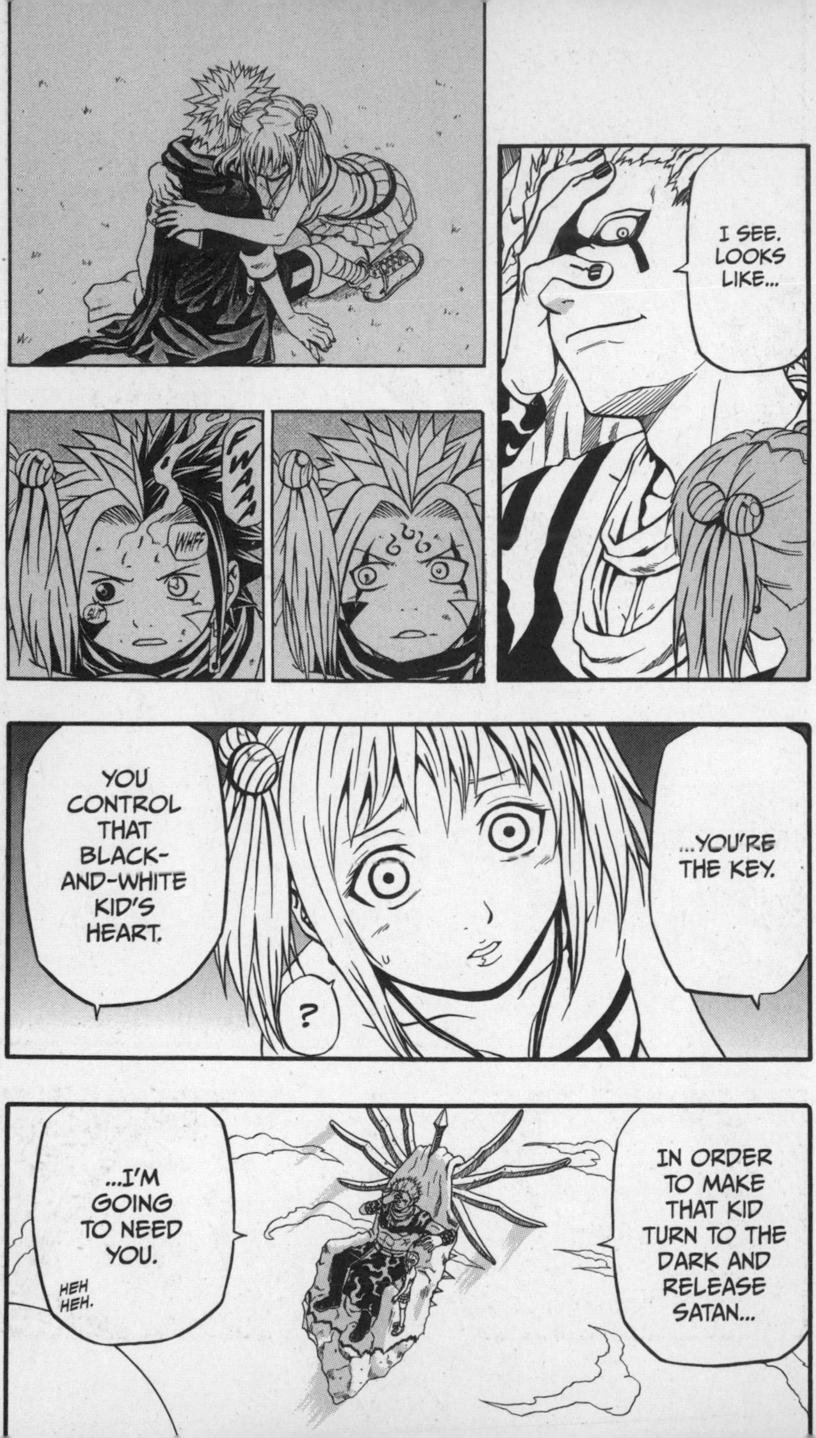
I SEE. LOOKS LIKE...
FWAPP
WHFF
...YOU'RE THE KEY.
YOU CONTROL THAT BLACK-AND-WHITE KID'S HEART.
?
IN ORDER TO MAKE THAT KID TURN TO THE DARK AND RELEASE SATAN...
...I'M GOING TO NEED YOU.
HEH HEH.

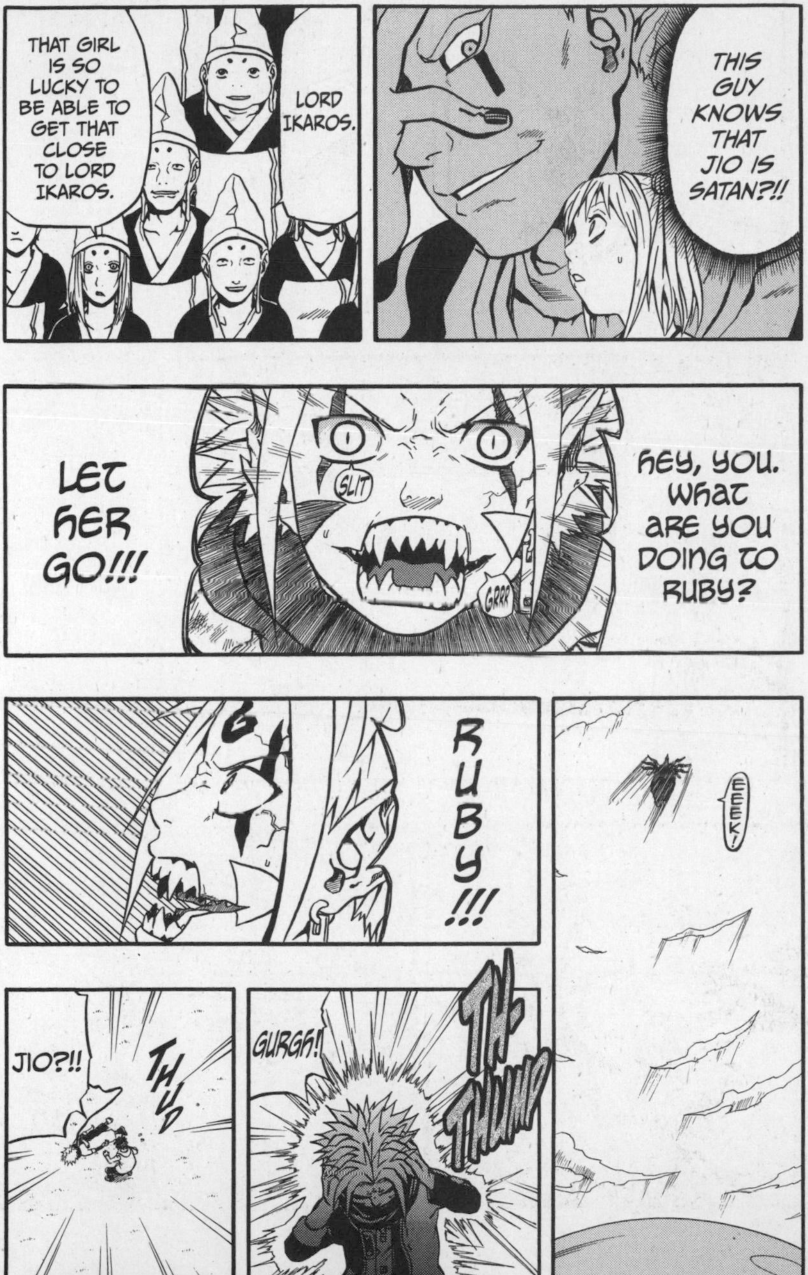
THIS GUY KNOWS THAT JIO IS SATAN?!!
LORD IKAROS.
THAT GIRL IS SO LUCKY TO BE ABLE TO GET THAT CLOSE TO LORD IKAROS.
HEY, YOU. WHAT ARE YOU DOING TO RUBY?
SLIT
GRRR
LET HER GO!!!
EEEK!
RUBY!!!
TH-THUMP
GURGH!
THUD
JIO?!!

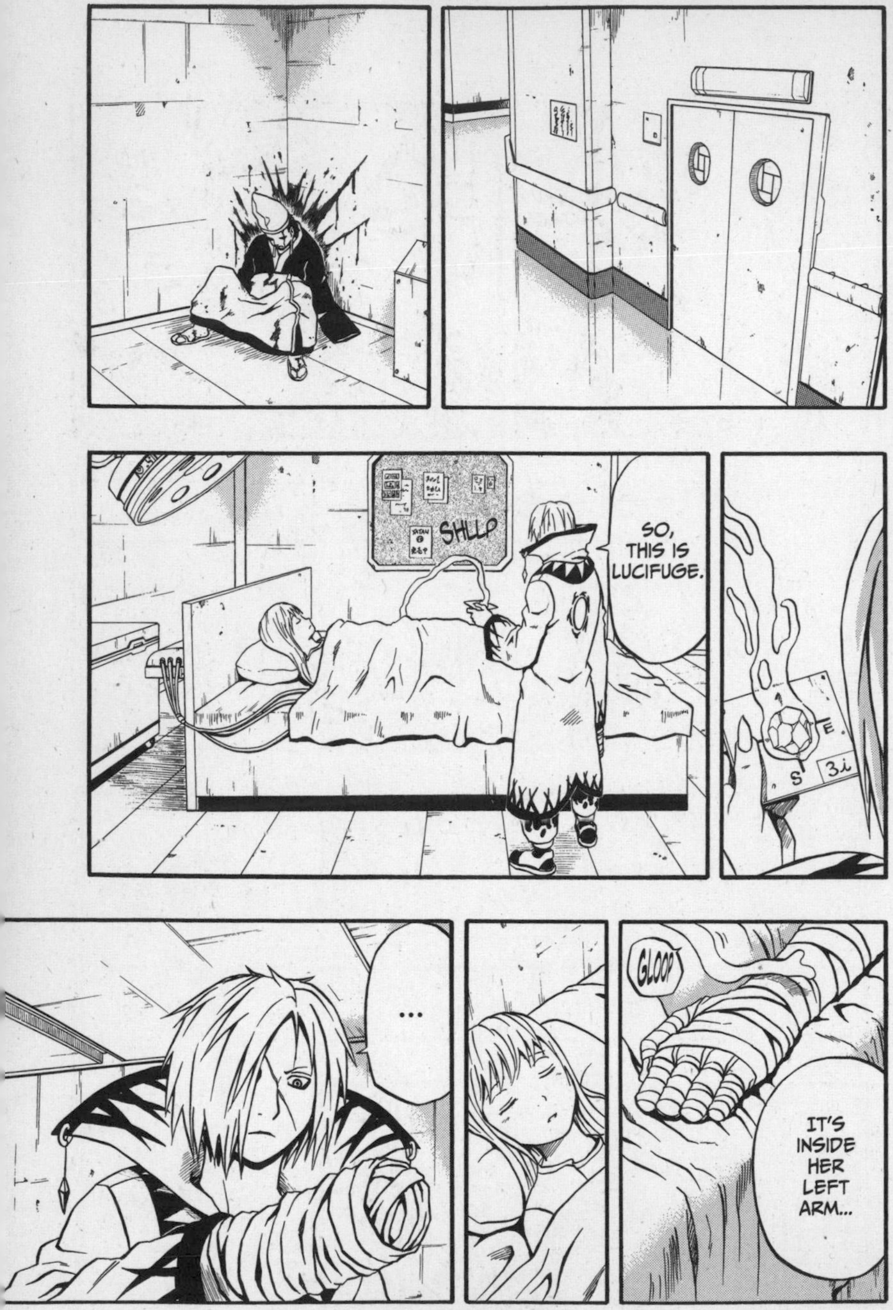
E
S
3i
SHLLP
SO, THIS IS LUCIFUGE.
GLOOP
IT'S INSIDE HER LEFT ARM...
...

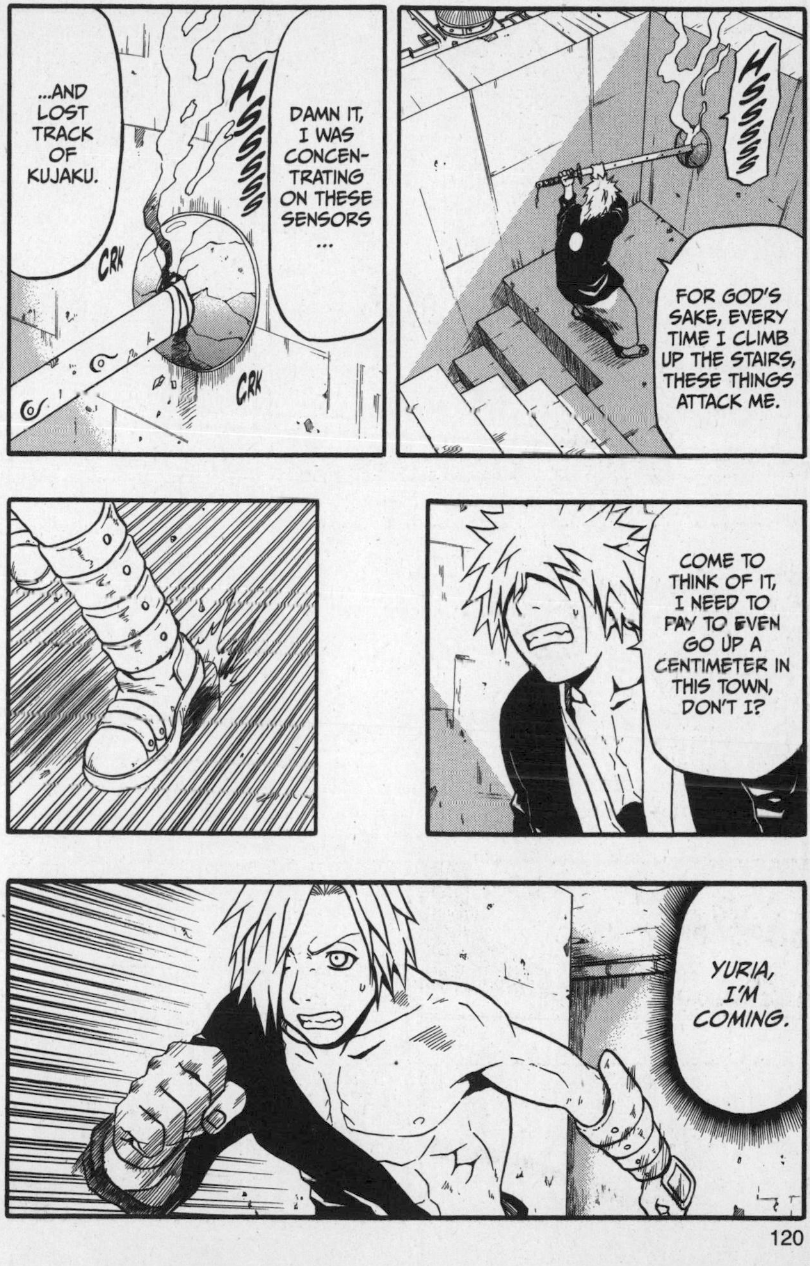
HSSSSS
FOR GOD'S SAKE, EVERY TIME I CLIMB UP THE STAIRS, THESE THINGS ATTACK ME.
DAMN IT, I WAS CONCEN-TRATING ON THESE SENSORS ...
HSSSSS
...AND LOST TRACK OF KUJAKU.
CRK
CRK
COME TO THINK OF IT, I NEED TO PAY TO EVEN GO UP A CENTIMETER IN THIS TOWN, DON'T I?
YURIA, I'M COMING.

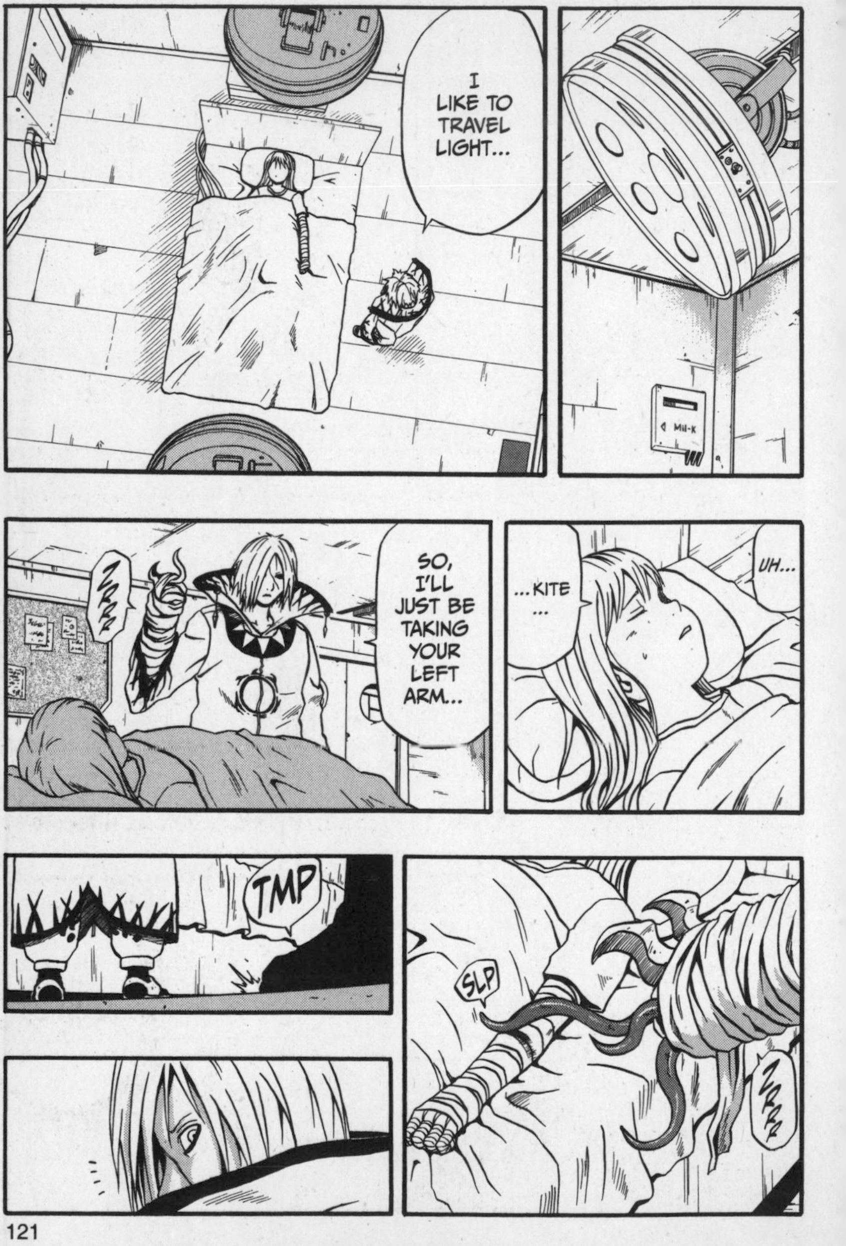
I LIKE TO TRAVEL LIGHT...
UH...
...KITE ...
SO, I'LL JUST BE TAKING YOUR LEFT ARM...
ZRRR
SLP
ZRRR
TMP

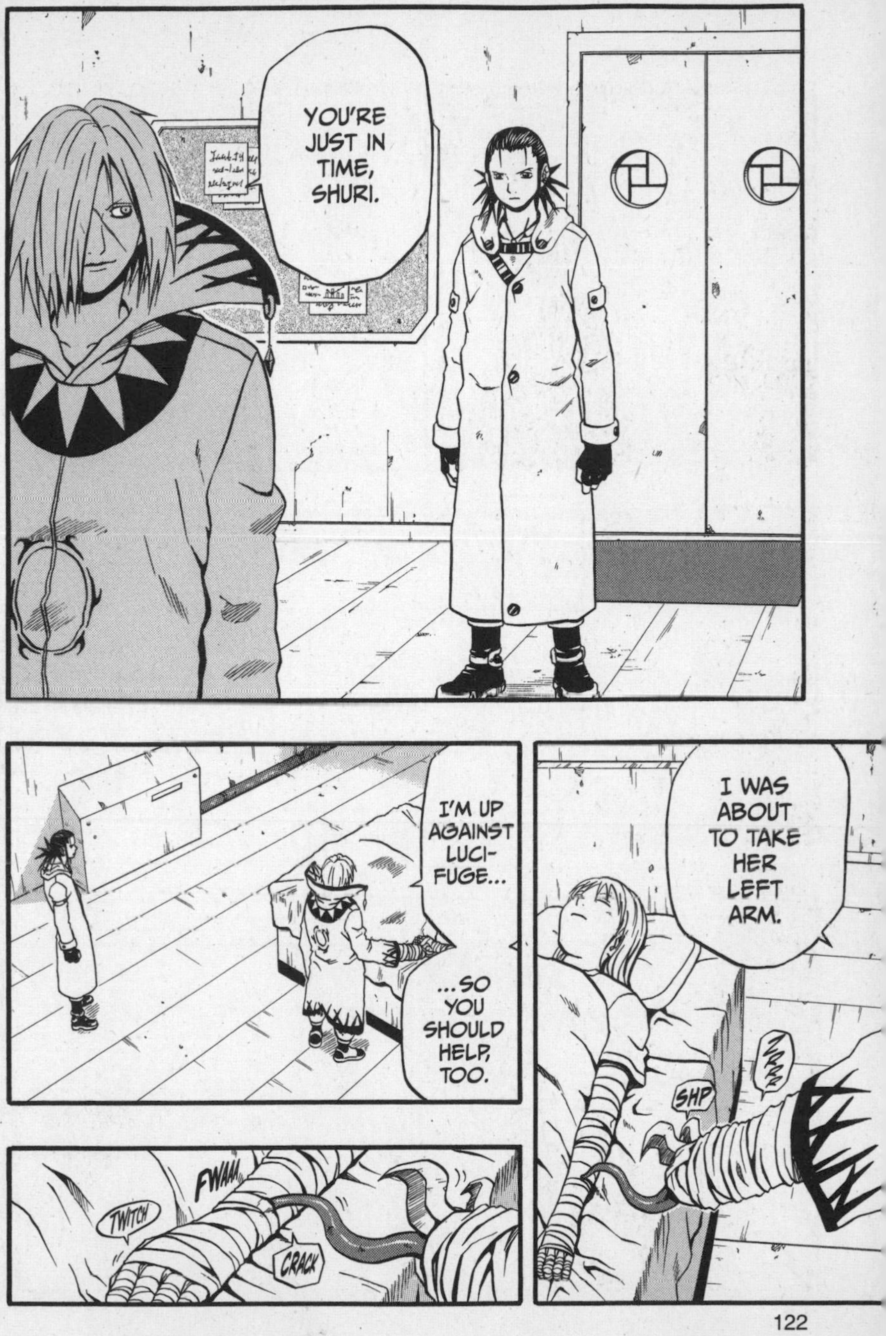
YOU'RE JUST IN TIME, SHURI.
I WAS ABOUT TO TAKE HER LEFT ARM.
ZZZZ
SHP
I'M UP AGAINST LUCI-FUGE...
...SO YOU SHOULD HELP, TOO.
FWAAA
TWITCH
CRACK

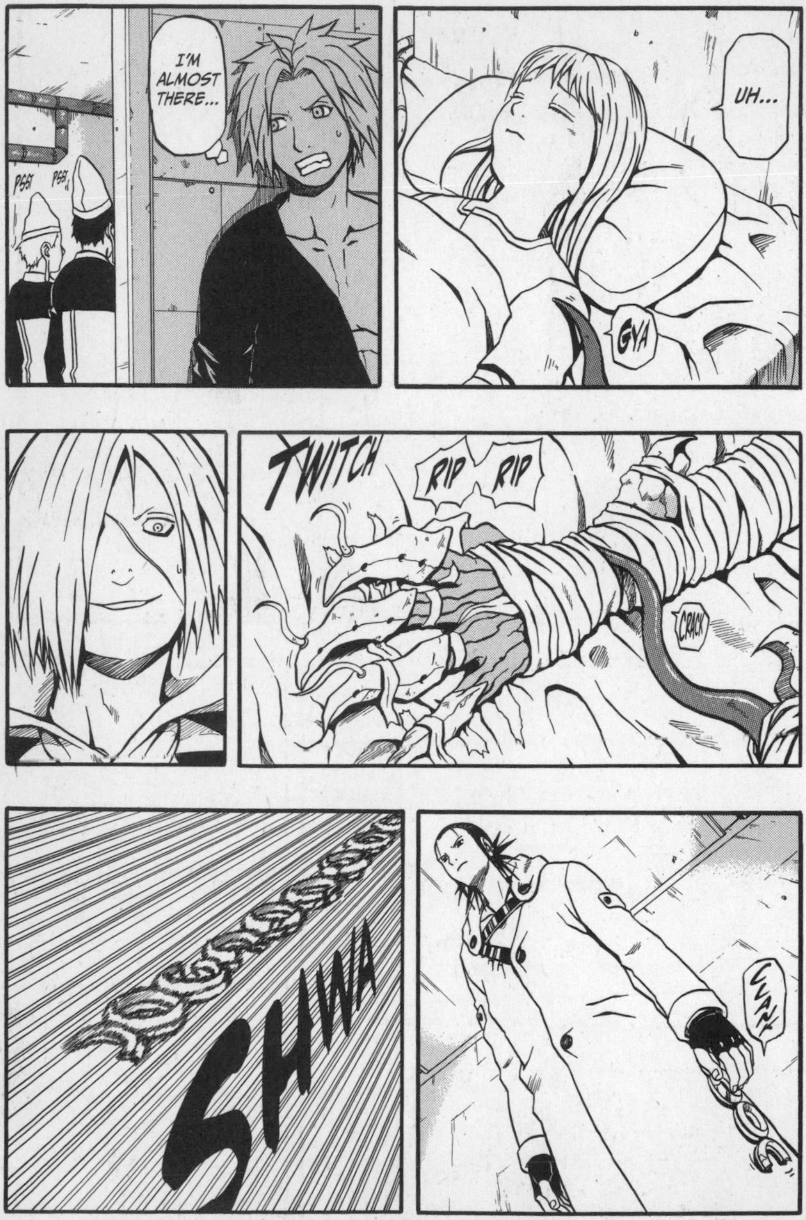
UH...
GYA
I'M ALMOST THERE...
PSST
PSST
TWITCH
RIP
RIP
CRACK
CLANK
SHWA

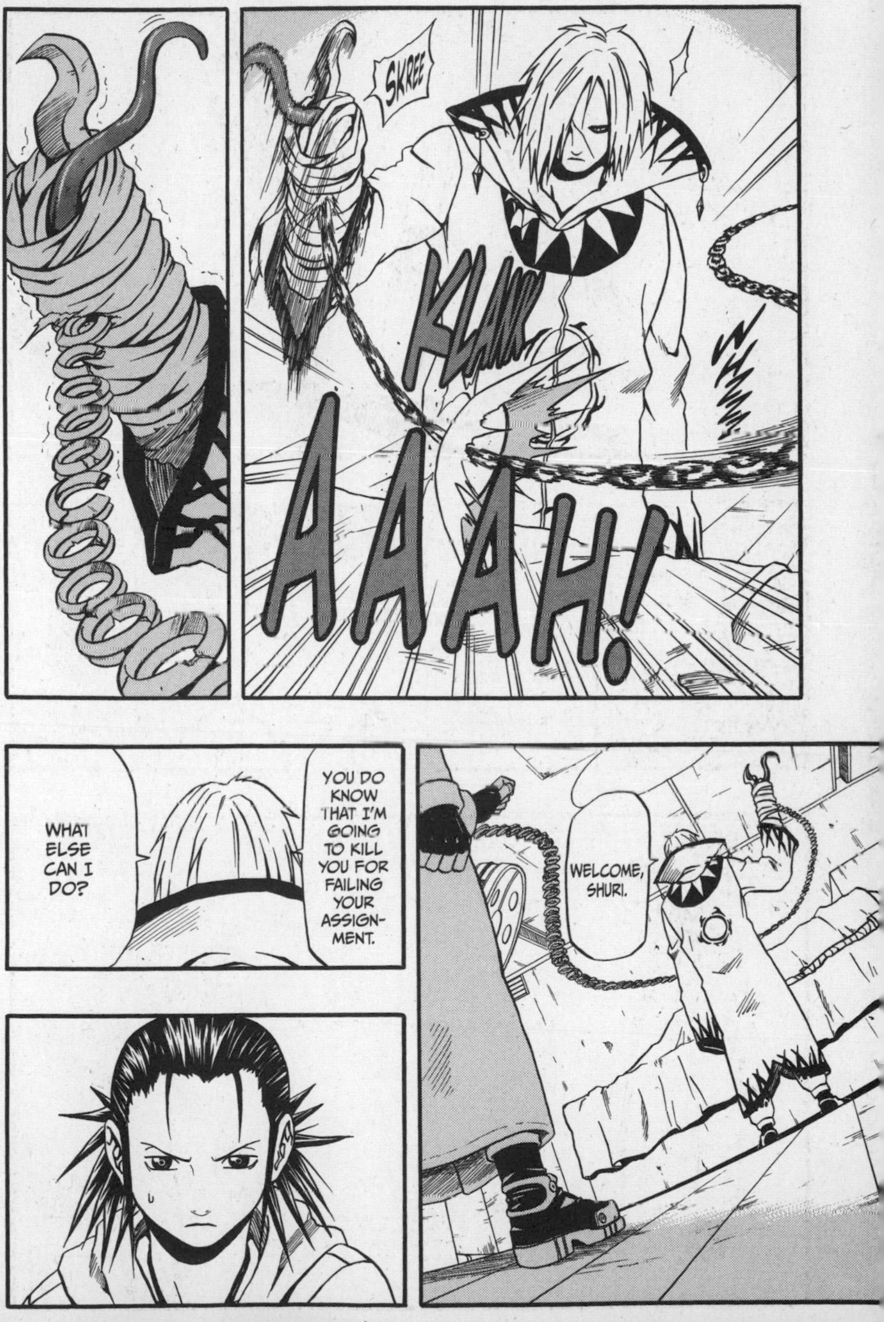
SKREE
KLANK
AAAH!
WELCOME, SHURI.
YOU DO KNOW THAT I'M GOING TO KILL YOU FOR FAILING YOUR ASSIGNMENT.
WHAT ELSE CAN I DO?

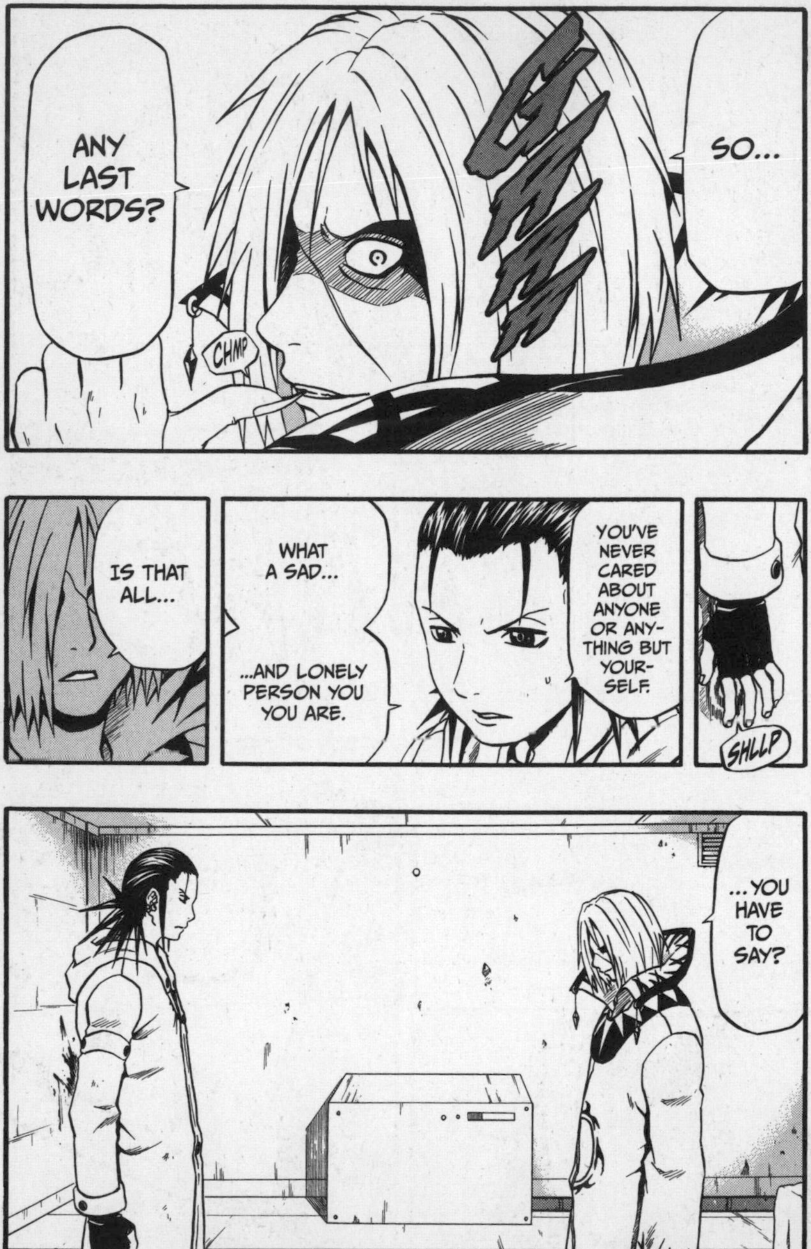
SO...
ANY LAST WORDS?
CHMP
SHLLP
YOU'VE NEVER CARED ABOUT ANYONE OR ANYTHING BUT YOURSELF.
WHAT A SAD...
...AND LONELY PERSON YOU YOU ARE.
IS THAT ALL...
...YOU HAVE TO SAY?

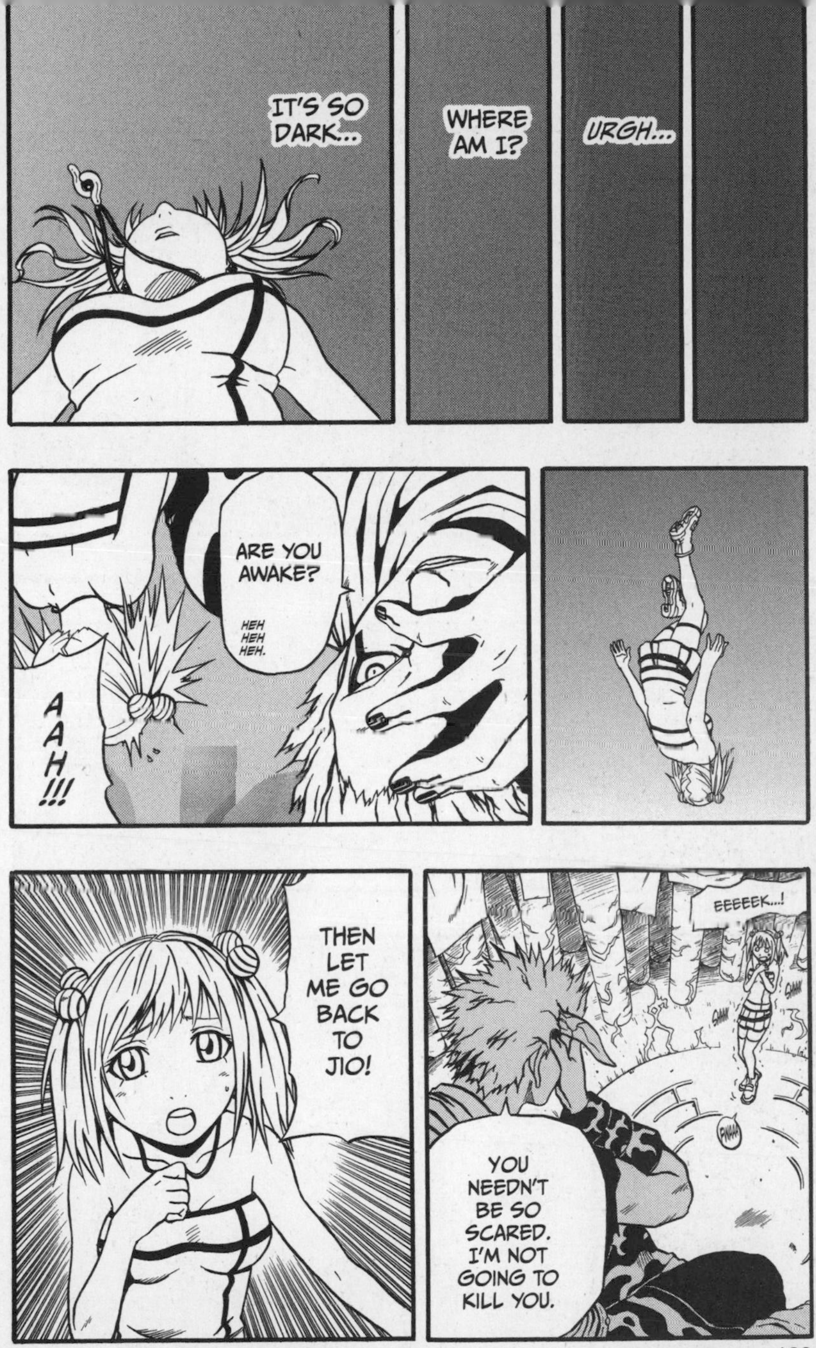
URGH...
WHERE AM I?
IT'S SO DARK...
ARE YOU AWAKE?
HEH HEH HEH.
AAAH!!!
EEEEEK...!
YOU NEEDN'T BE SO SCARED. I'M NOT GOING TO KILL YOU.
THEN LET ME GO BACK TO JIO!

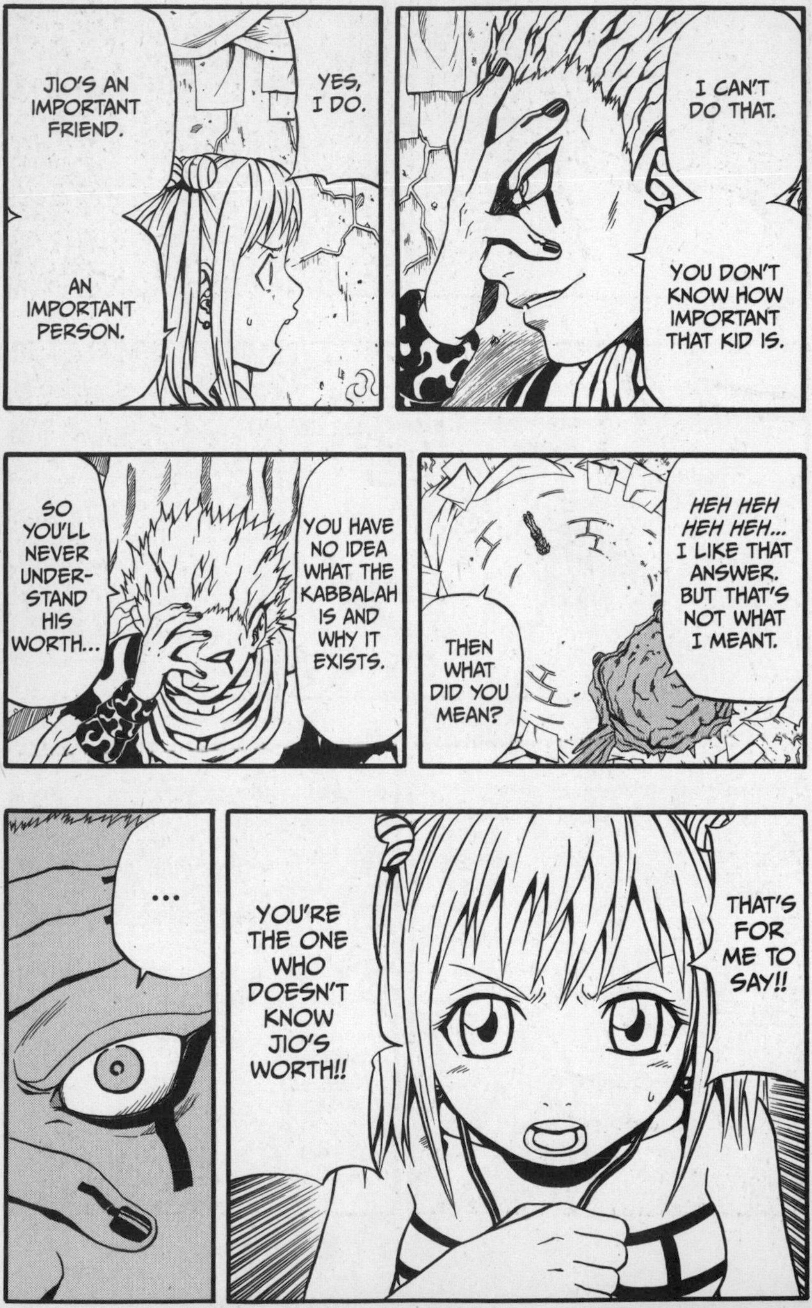
I CAN'T DO THAT.
YOU DON'T KNOW HOW IMPORTANT THAT KID IS.
YES, I DO.
JIO'S AN IMPORTANT FRIEND.
AN IMPORTANT PERSON.
HEH HEH HEH HEH... I LIKE THAT ANSWER. BUT THAT'S NOT WHAT I MEANT.
THEN WHAT DID YOU MEAN?
YOU HAVE NO IDEA WHAT THE KABBALAH IS AND WHY IT EXISTS.
SO YOU'LL NEVER UNDER-STAND HIS WORTH...
THAT'S FOR ME TO SAY!!
YOU'RE THE ONE WHO DOESN'T KNOW JIO'S WORTH!!
...

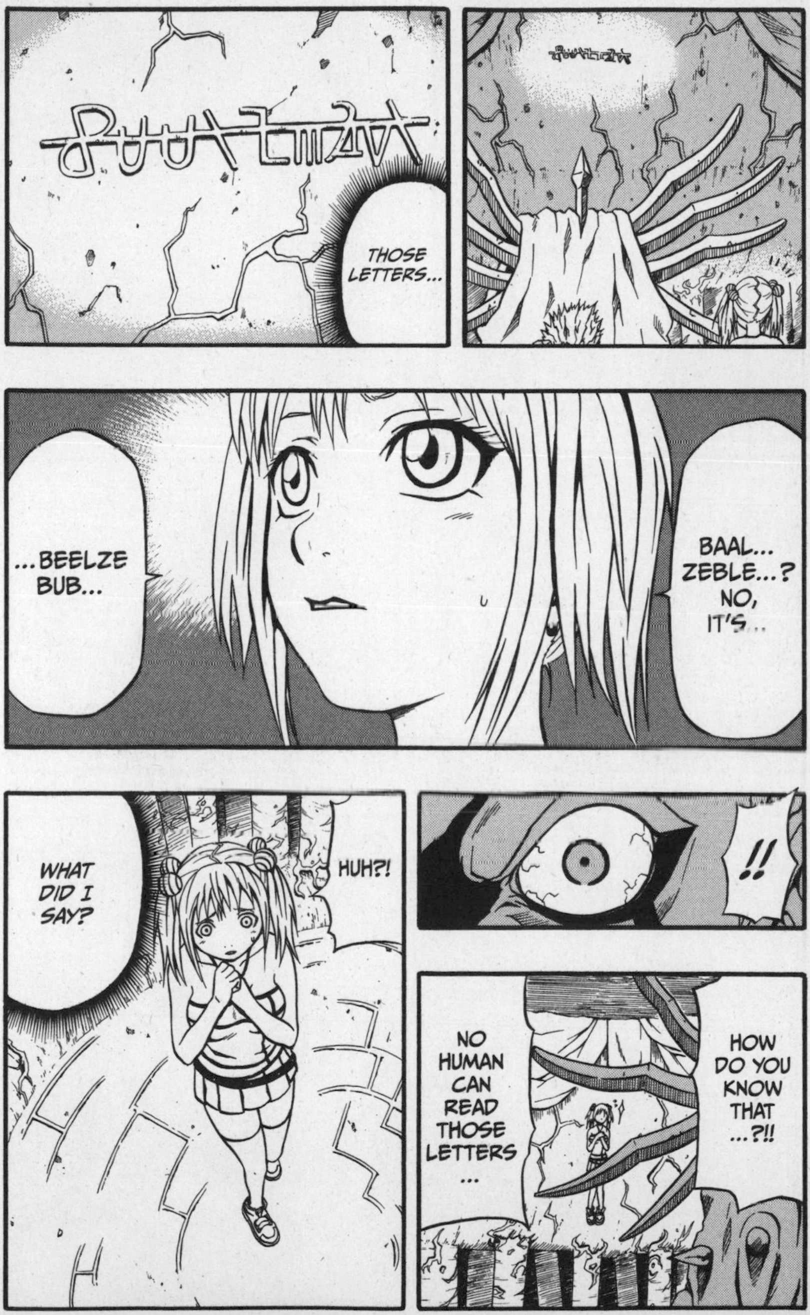
THOSE LETTERS...
BAAL... ZEBLE...? NO, IT'S...
...BEELZE BUB...
!!
HOW DO YOU KNOW THAT ...?!!
NO HUMAN CAN READ THOSE LETTERS ...
HUH?!
WHAT DID I SAY?

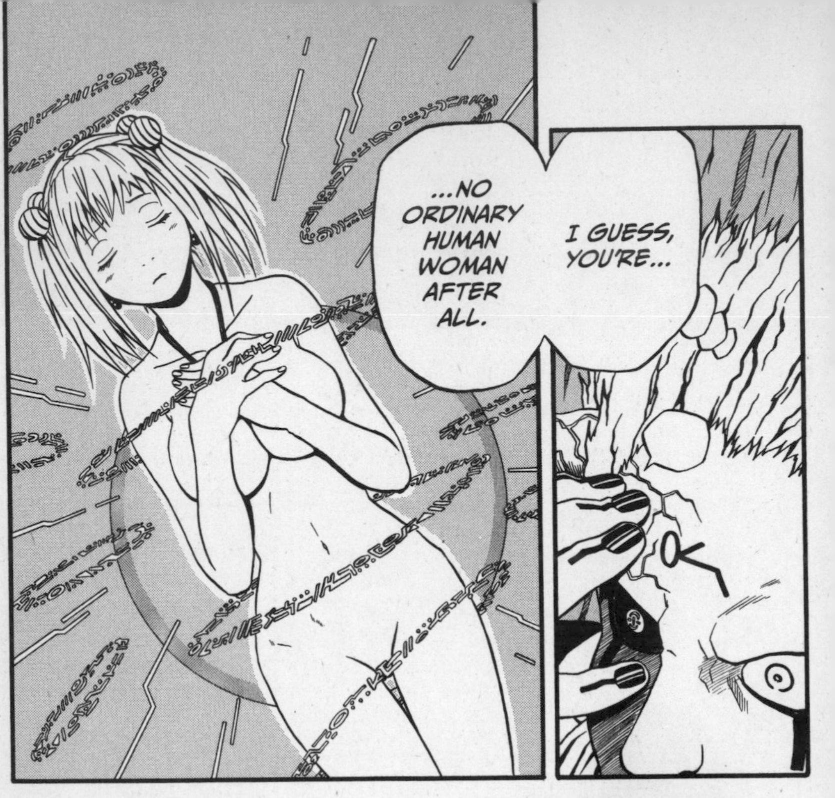
I GUESS, YOU'RE...
...NO ORDINARY HUMAN WOMAN AFTER ALL.

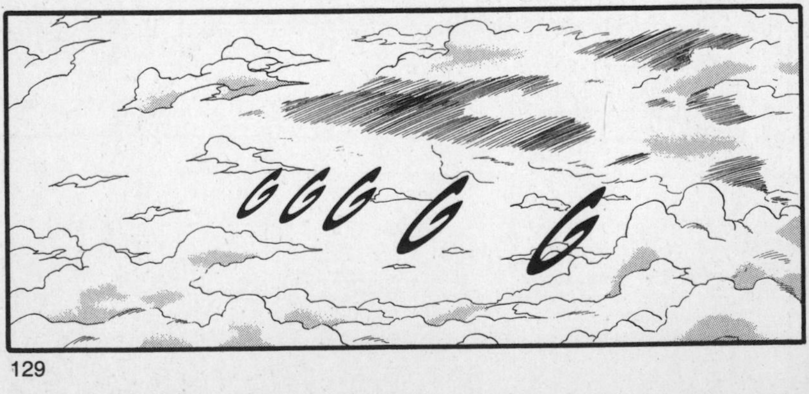
GGGGG

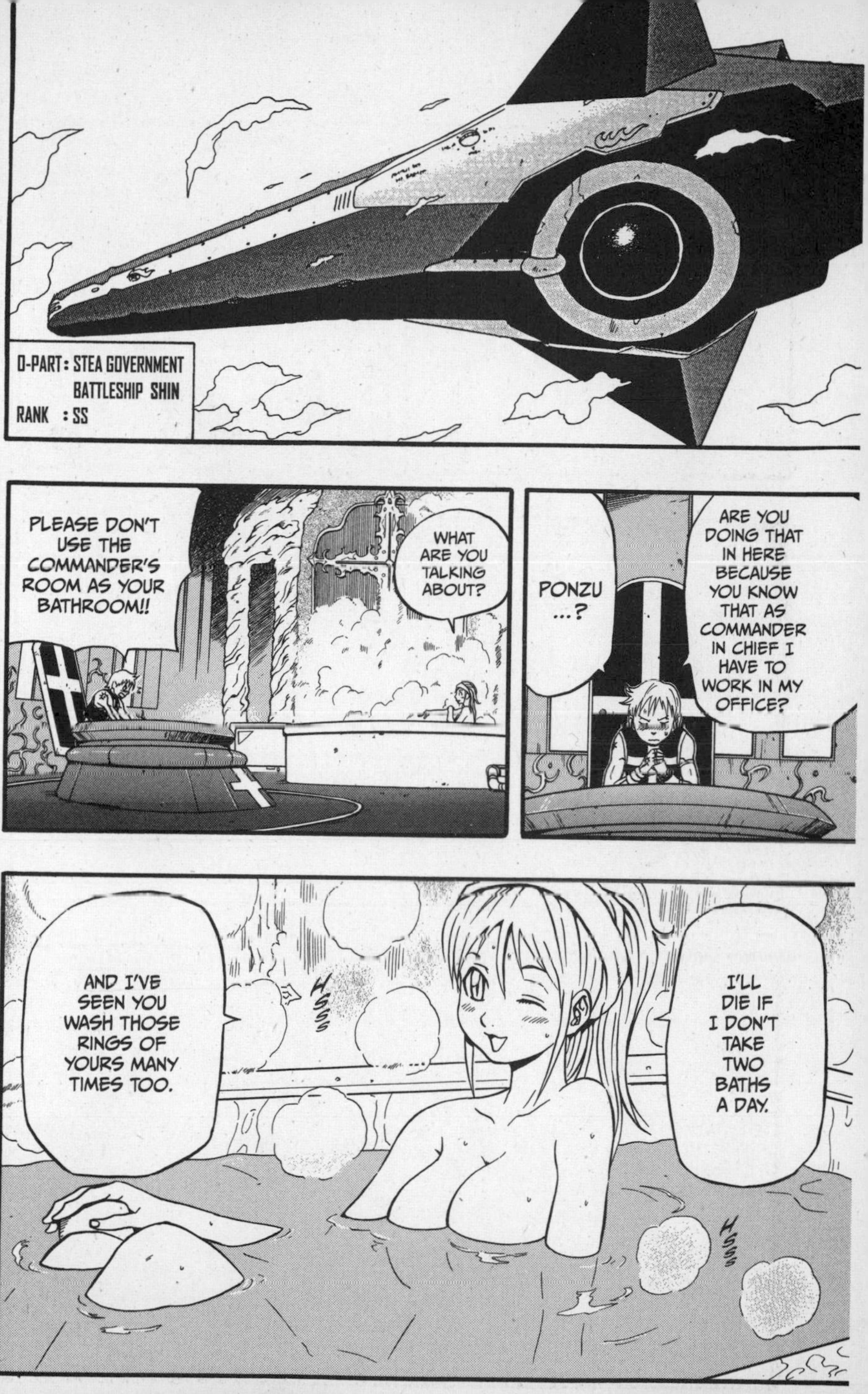
O-PART : STEA GOVERNMENT BATTLESHIP SHIN
RANK : SS
ARE YOU DOING THAT IN HERE BECAUSE YOU KNOW THAT AS COMMANDER IN CHIEF I HAVE TO WORK IN MY OFFICE?
PONZU ...?
WHAT ARE YOU TALKING ABOUT?
PLEASE DON'T USE THE COMMANDER'S ROOM AS YOUR BATHROOM!!
I'LL DIE IF I DON'T TAKE TWO BATHS A DAY.
HSSS
HSSS
AND I'VE SEEN YOU WASH THOSE RINGS OF YOURS MANY TIMES TOO.

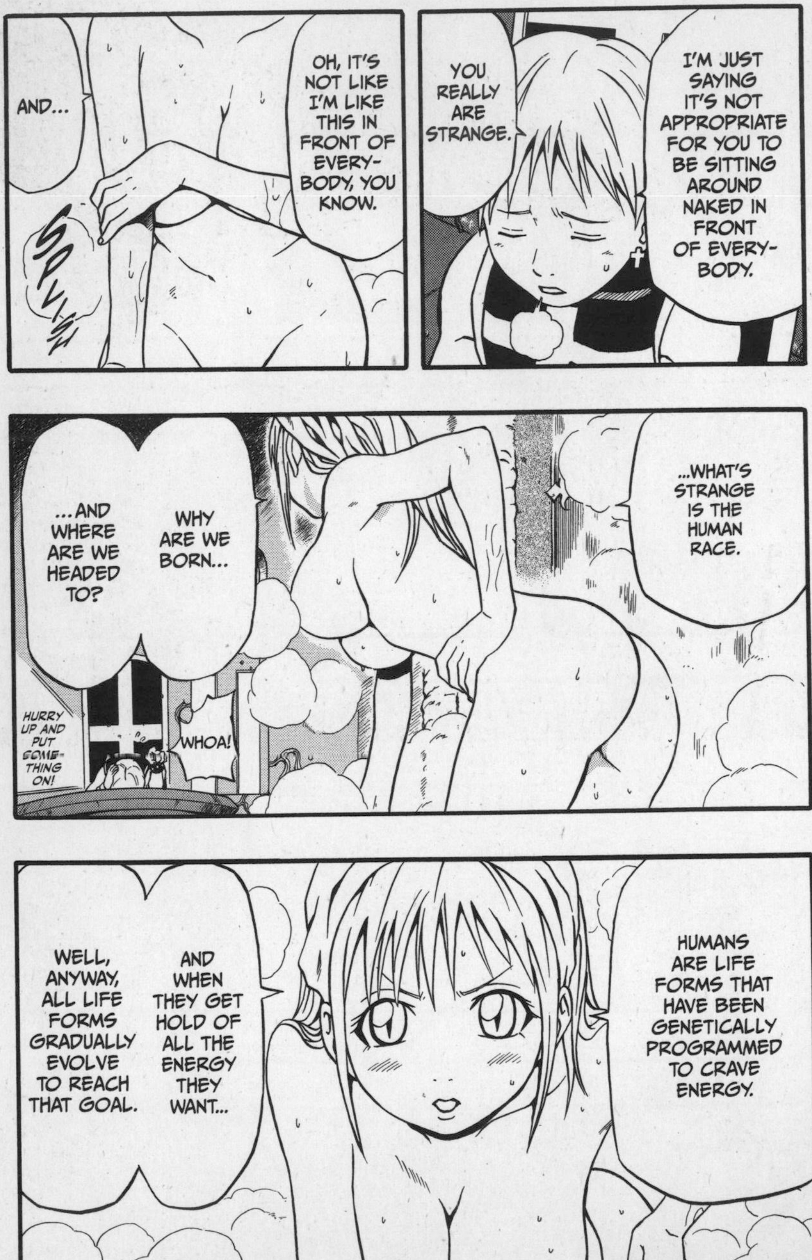
I'M JUST SAYING IT'S NOT APPROPRIATE FOR YOU TO BE SITTING AROUND NAKED IN FRONT OF EVERY-BODY.
YOU REALLY ARE STRANGE.
OH, IT'S NOT LIKE I'M LIKE THIS IN FRONT OF EVERY-BODY, YOU KNOW.
AND...
SPLISH
...WHAT'S STRANGE IS THE HUMAN RACE.
WHY ARE WE BORN...
...AND WHERE ARE WE HEADED TO?
WHOA!
HURRY UP AND PUT SOME-THING ON!
HUMANS ARE LIFE FORMS THAT HAVE BEEN GENETICALLY PROGRAMMED TO CRAVE ENERGY.
AND WHEN THEY GET HOLD OF ALL THE ENERGY THEY WANT...
WELL, ANYWAY, ALL LIFE FORMS GRADUALLY EVOLVE TO REACH THAT GOAL.

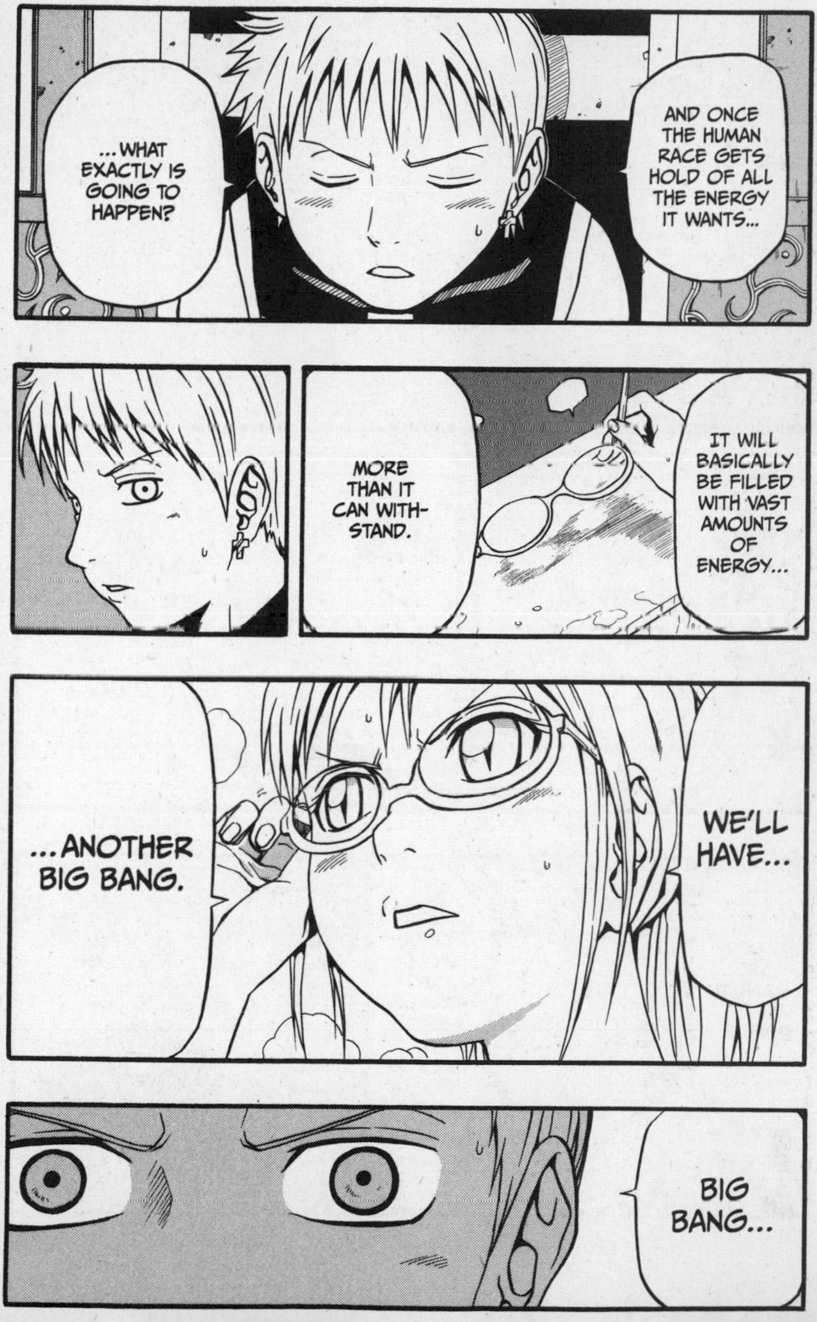
AND ONCE THE HUMAN RACE GETS HOLD OF ALL THE ENERGY IT WANTS...
...WHAT EXACTLY IS GOING TO HAPPEN?
IT WILL BASICALLY BE FILLED WITH VAST AMOUNTS OF ENERGY...
MORE THAN IT CAN WITH-STAND.
WE'LL HAVE...
...ANOTHER BIG BANG.
BIG BANG...

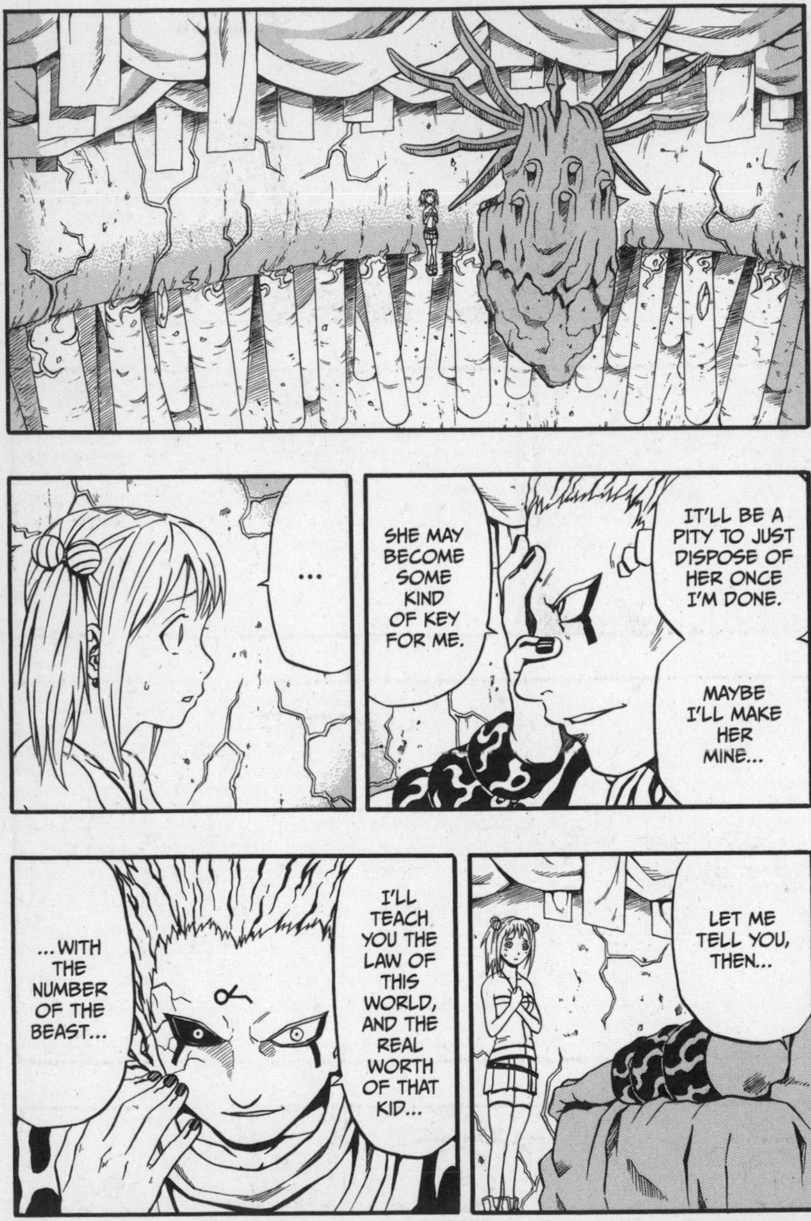
IT'LL BE A PITY TO JUST DISPOSE OF HER ONCE I'M DONE.
MAYBE I'LL MAKE HER MINE...
SHE MAY BECOME SOME KIND OF KEY FOR ME.
...
LET ME TELL YOU, THEN...
I'LL TEACH YOU THE LAW OF THIS WORLD, AND THE REAL WORTH OF THAT KID...
...WITH THE NUMBER OF THE BEAST...

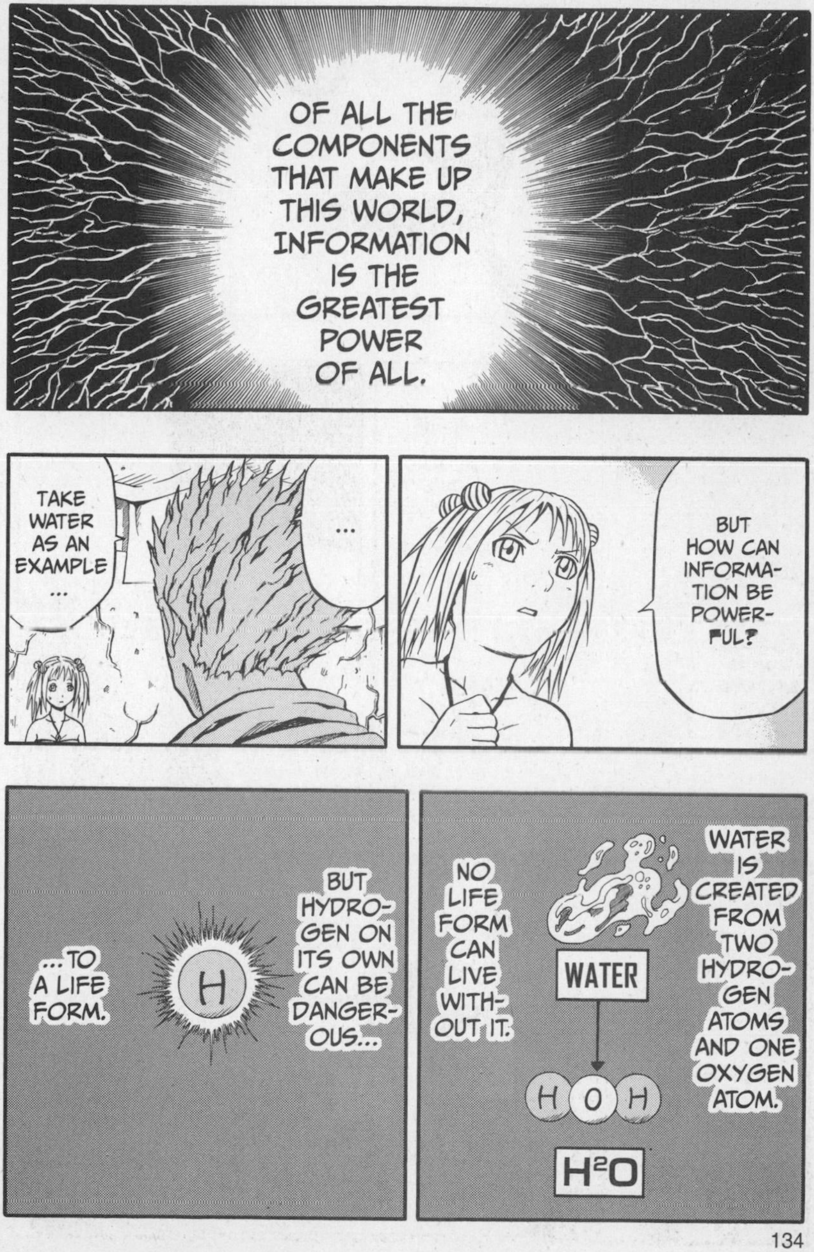
OF ALL THE COMPONENTS THAT MAKE UP THIS WORLD, INFORMATION IS THE GREATEST POWER OF ALL.
BUT HOW CAN INFORMATION BE POWERFUL?
...
TAKE WATER AS AN EXAMPLE ...
WATER IS CREATED FROM TWO HYDROGEN ATOMS AND ONE OXYGEN ATOM.
WATER
H O H
H^2O
NO LIFE FORM CAN LIVE WITHOUT IT.
BUT HYDROGEN ON ITS OWN CAN BE DANGEROUS...
H
...TO A LIFE FORM.

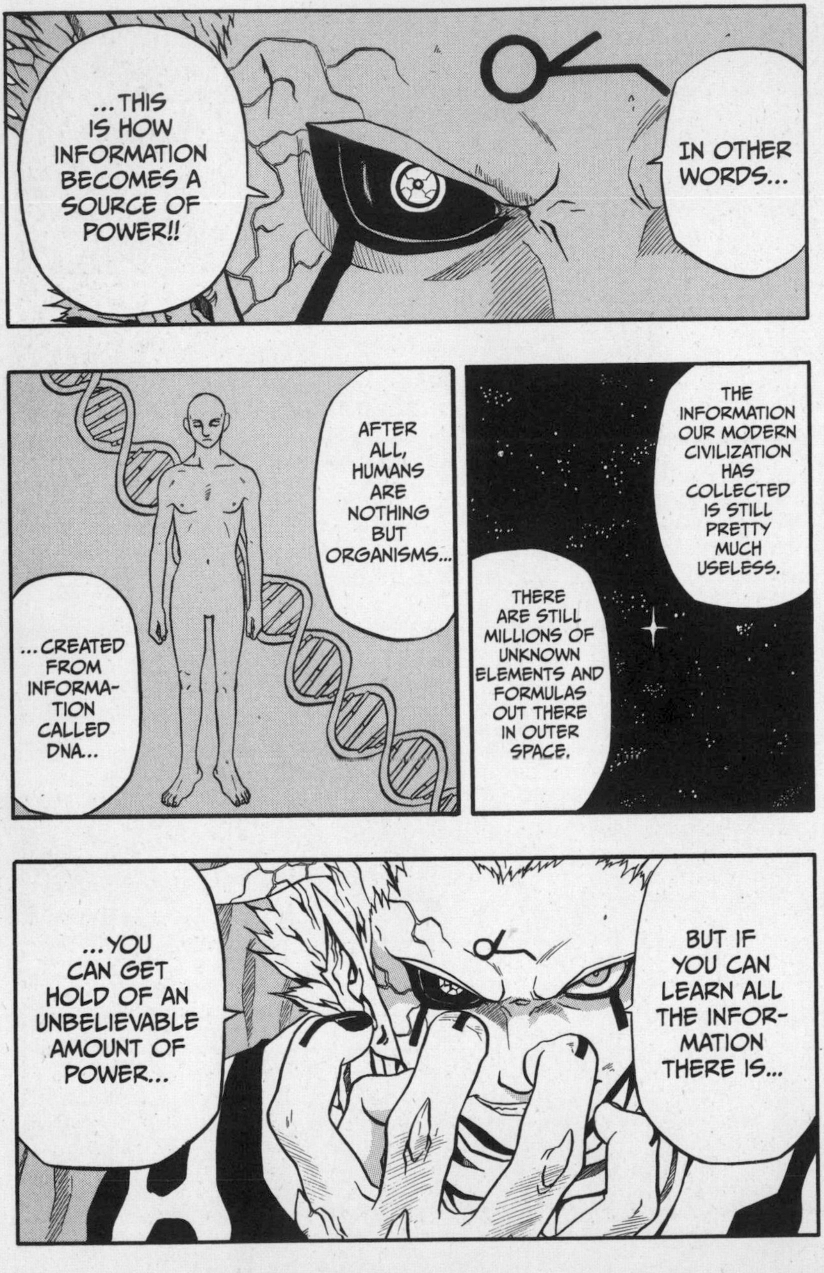
IN OTHER WORDS...
...THIS IS HOW INFORMATION BECOMES A SOURCE OF POWER!!
THE INFORMATION OUR MODERN CIVILIZATION HAS COLLECTED IS STILL PRETTY MUCH USELESS.
THERE ARE STILL MILLIONS OF UNKNOWN ELEMENTS AND FORMULAS OUT THERE IN OUTER SPACE.
AFTER ALL, HUMANS ARE NOTHING BUT ORGANISMS...
...CREATED FROM INFORMATION CALLED DNA...
BUT IF YOU CAN LEARN ALL THE INFORMATION THERE IS...
...YOU CAN GET HOLD OF AN UNBELIEVABLE AMOUNT OF POWER...

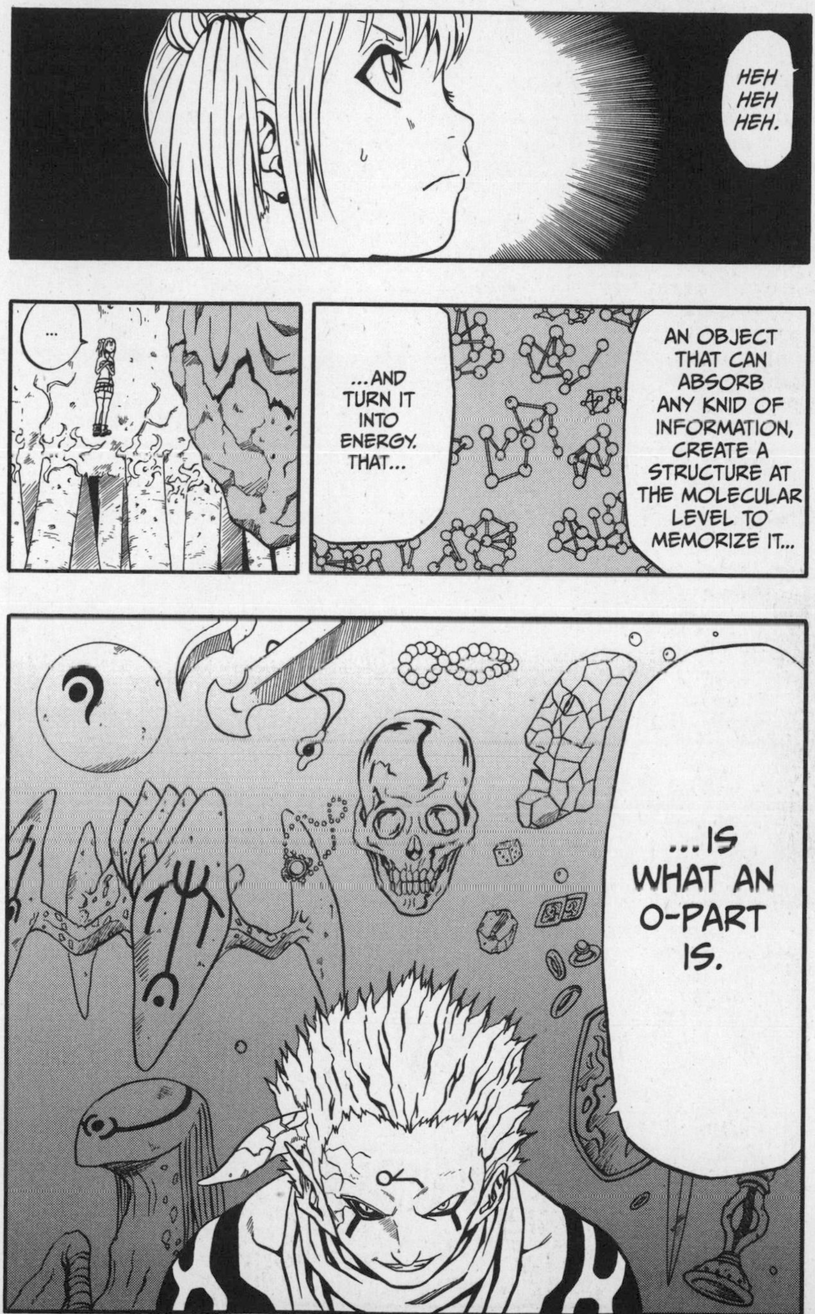
HEH HEH HEH.
AN OBJECT THAT CAN ABSORB ANY KNID OF INFORMATION, CREATE A STRUCTURE AT THE MOLECULAR LEVEL TO MEMORIZE IT...
...AND TURN IT INTO ENERGY. THAT...
...
...IS WHAT AN O-PART IS.

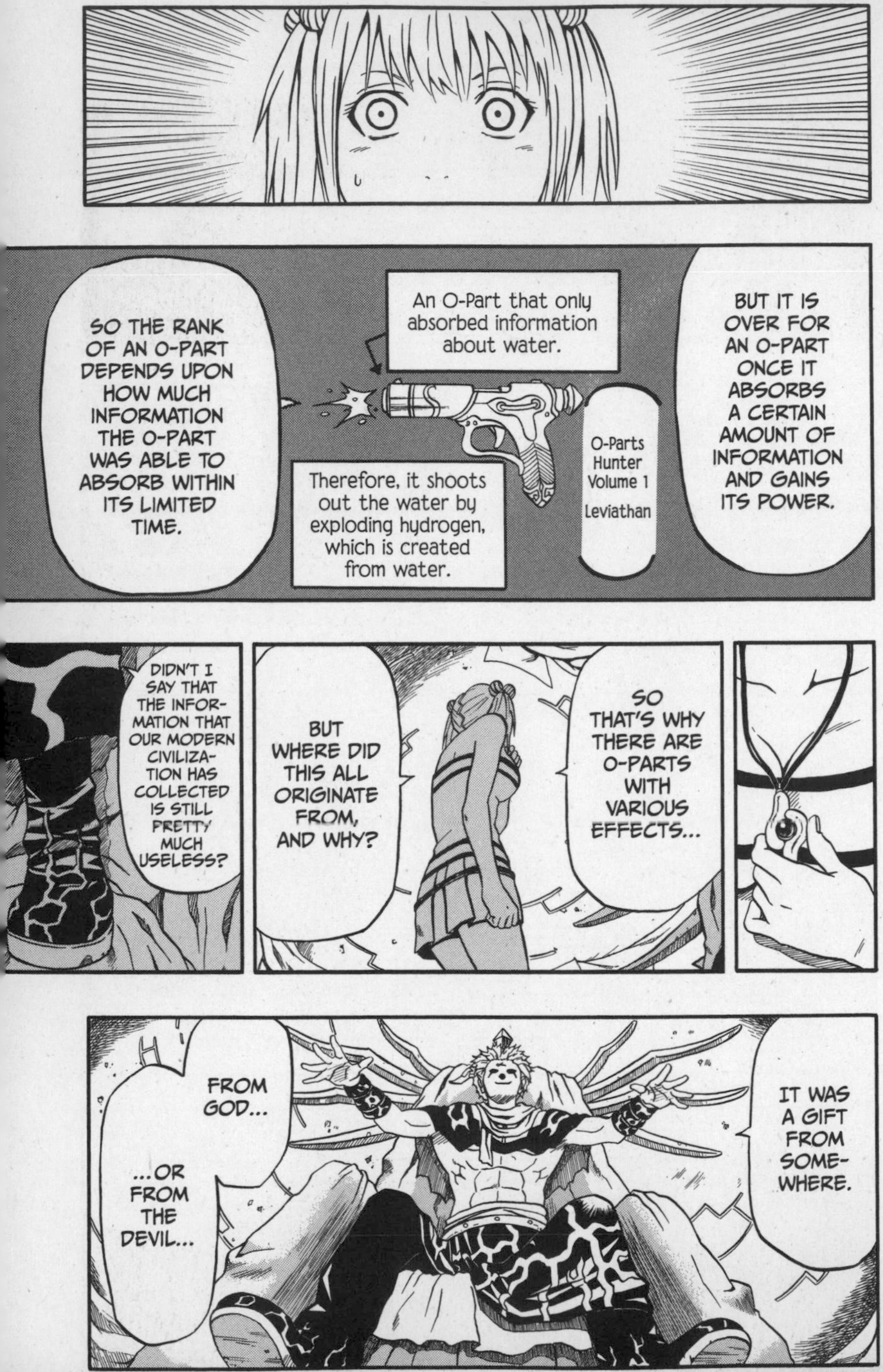
BUT IT IS OVER FOR AN O-PART ONCE IT ABSORBS A CERTAIN AMOUNT OF INFORMATION AND GAINS ITS POWER.
An O-Part that only absorbed information about water.
O-Parts Hunter Volume 1 Leviathan
Therefore, it shoots out the water by exploding hydrogen, which is created from water.
SO THE RANK OF AN O-PART DEPENDS UPON HOW MUCH INFORMATION THE O-PART WAS ABLE TO ABSORB WITHIN ITS LIMITED TIME.
SO THAT'S WHY THERE ARE O-PARTS WITH VARIOUS EFFECTS...
BUT WHERE DID THIS ALL ORIGINATE FROM, AND WHY?
DIDN'T I SAY THAT THE INFORMATION THAT OUR MODERN CIVILIZATION HAS COLLECTED IS STILL PRETTY MUCH USELESS?
IT WAS A GIFT FROM SOMEWHERE.
FROM GOD...
...OR FROM THE DEVIL...

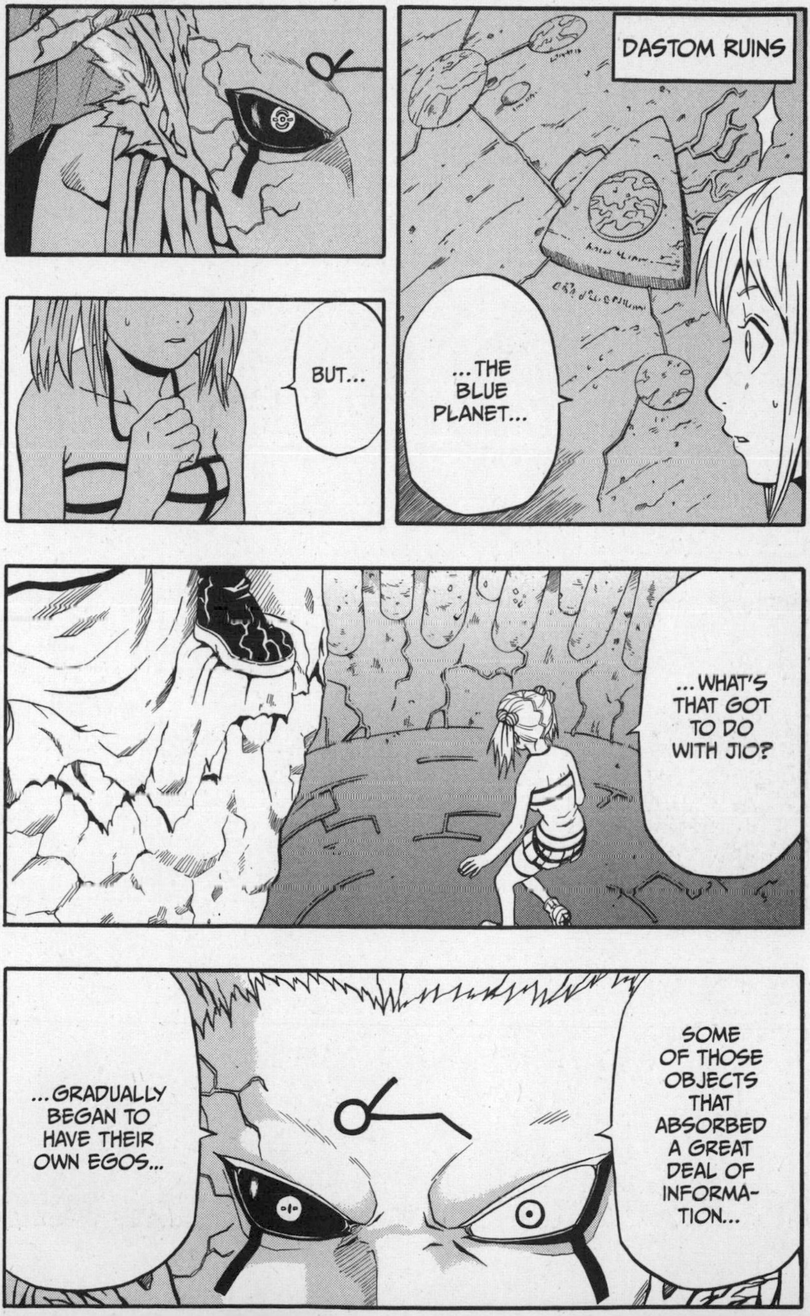
DASTOM RUINS
...THE BLUE PLANET...
BUT...
...WHAT'S THAT GOT TO DO WITH JIO?
SOME OF THOSE OBJECTS THAT ABSORBED A GREAT DEAL OF INFORMA-TION...
...GRADUALLY BEGAN TO HAVE THEIR OWN EGOS...

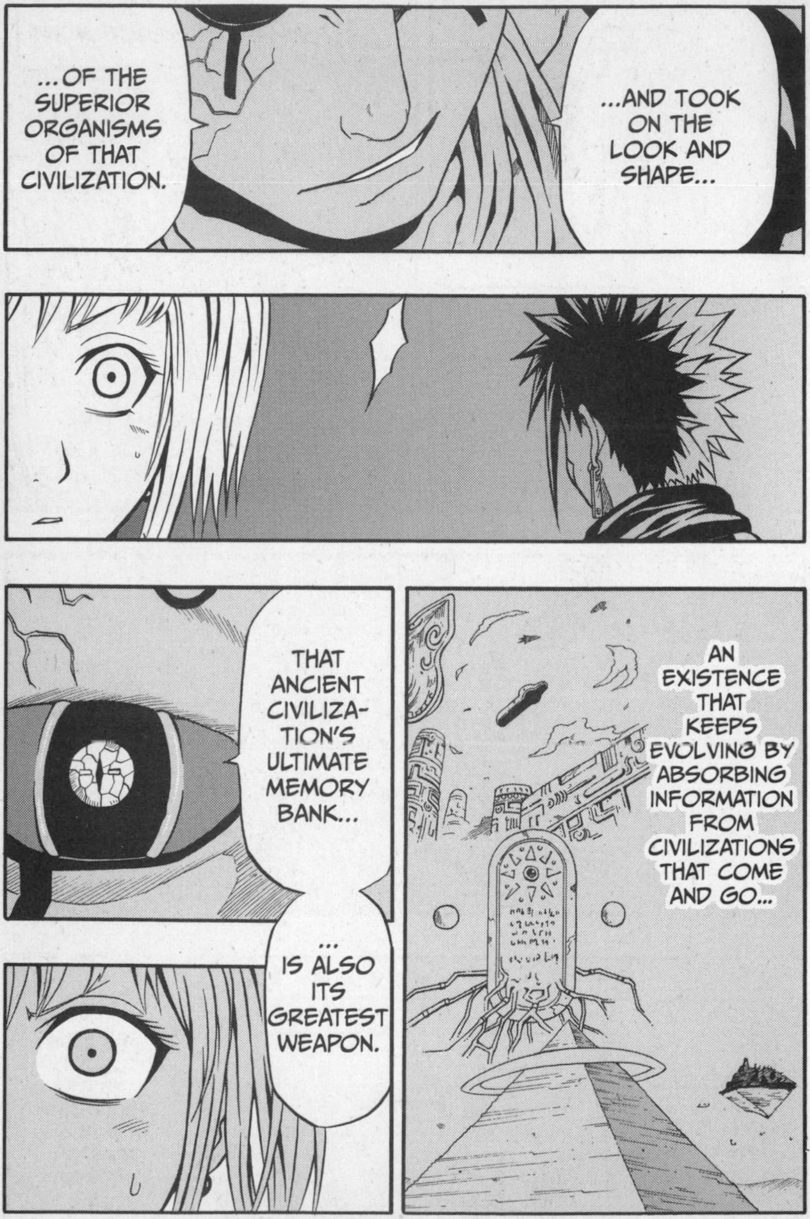
...AND TOOK ON THE LOOK AND SHAPE...
...OF THE SUPERIOR ORGANISMS OF THAT CIVILIZATION.
AN EXISTENCE THAT KEEPS EVOLVING BY ABSORBING INFORMATION FROM CIVILIZATIONS THAT COME AND GO...
THAT ANCIENT CIVILIZA-TION'S ULTIMATE MEMORY BANK...
...IS ALSO ITS GREATEST WEAPON.

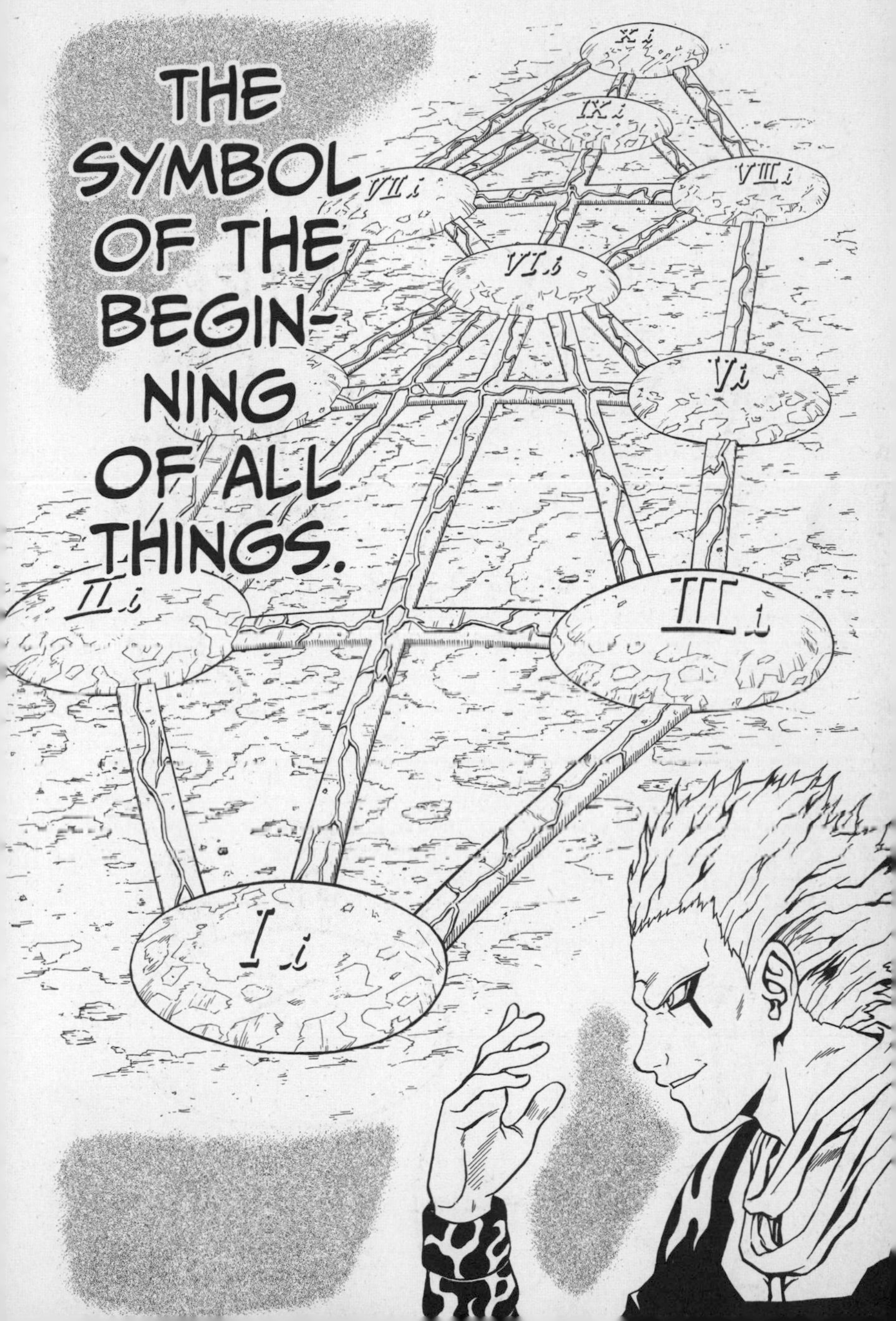
THE SYMBOL OF THE BEGIN-NING OF ALL THINGS.
XI
IXI
VIIi
VIIII
VIi
Vi
IIi
IIIi
Ii

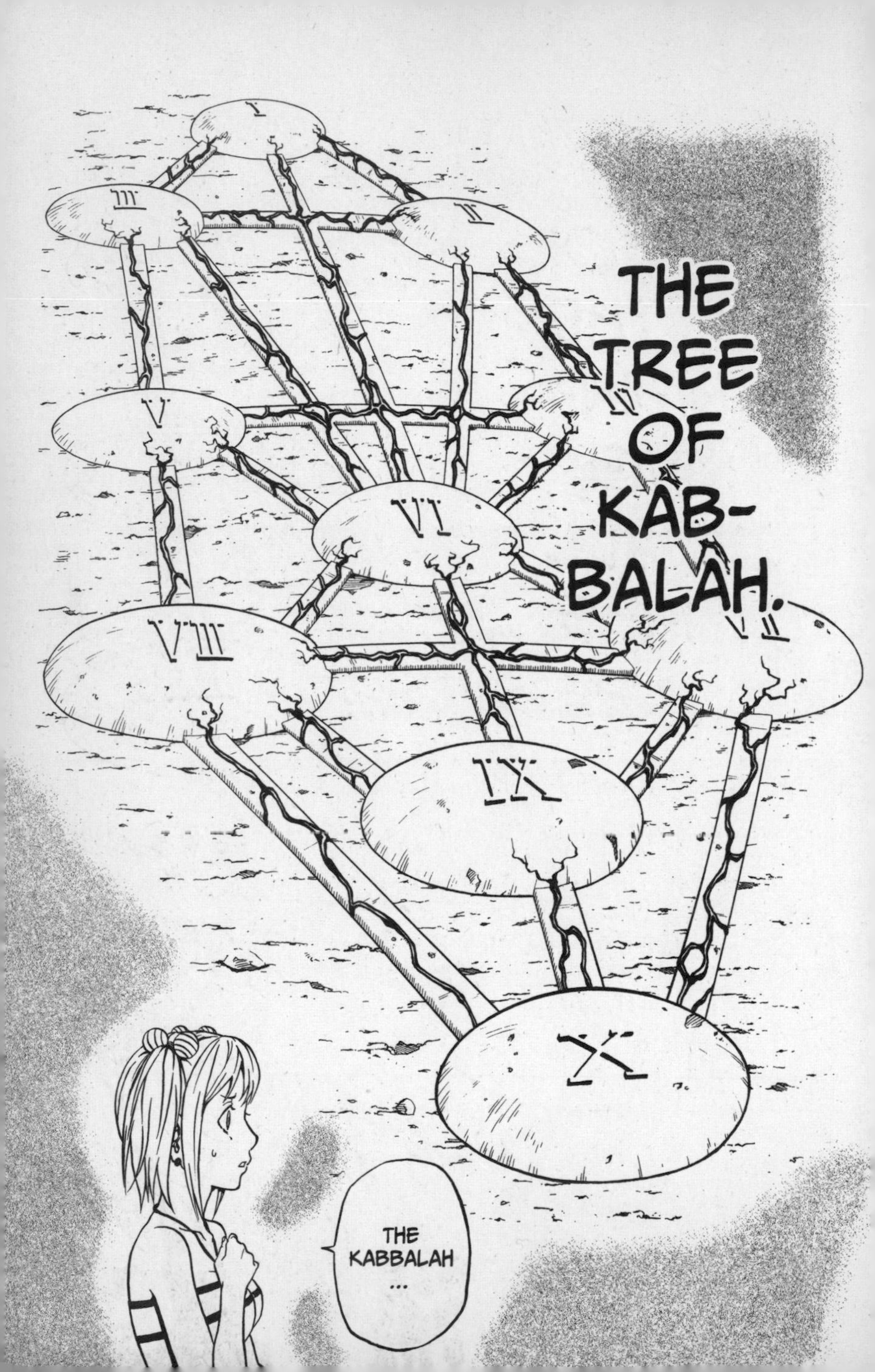
THE TREE OF KAB-BALAH.
THE KABBALAH ...

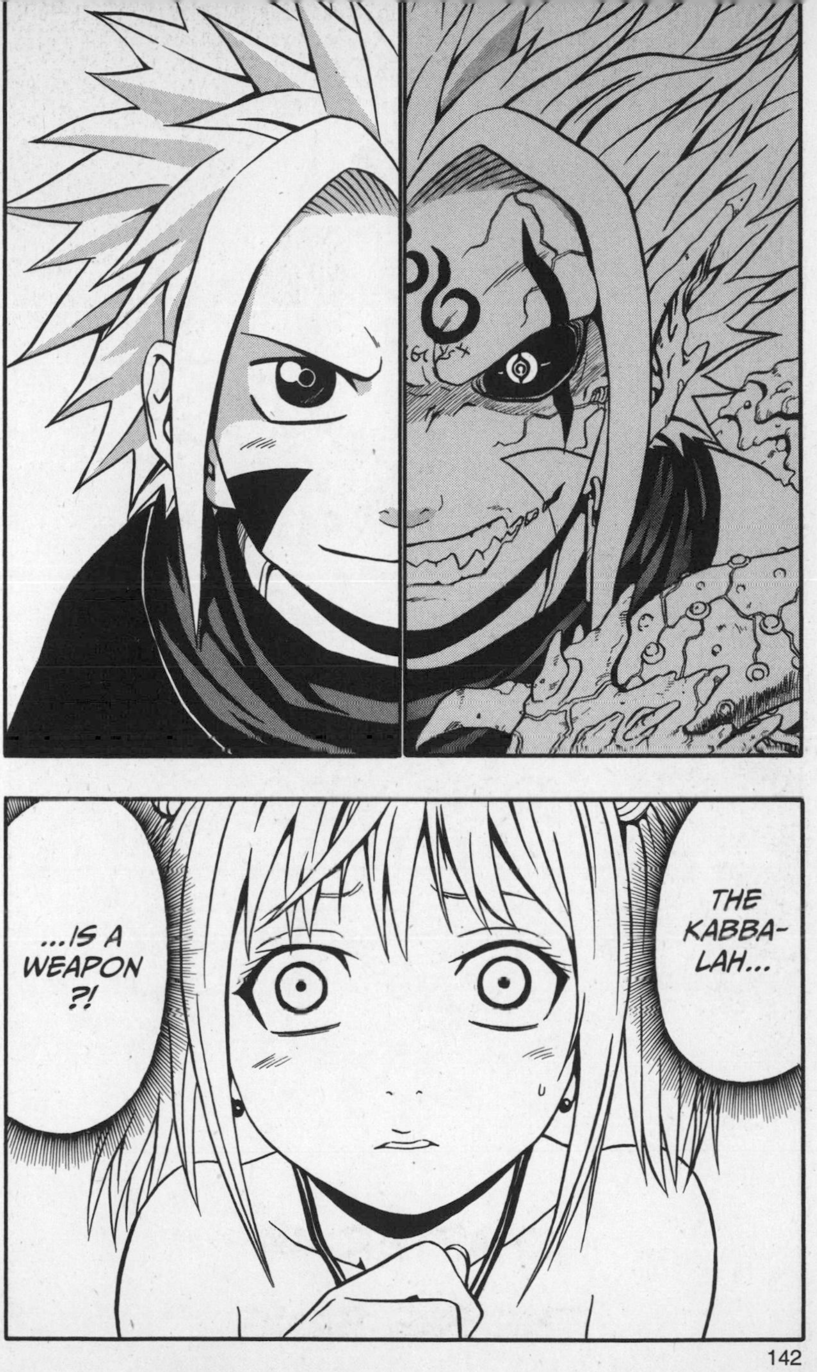
THE KABBA-LAH...
...IS A WEAPON ?!

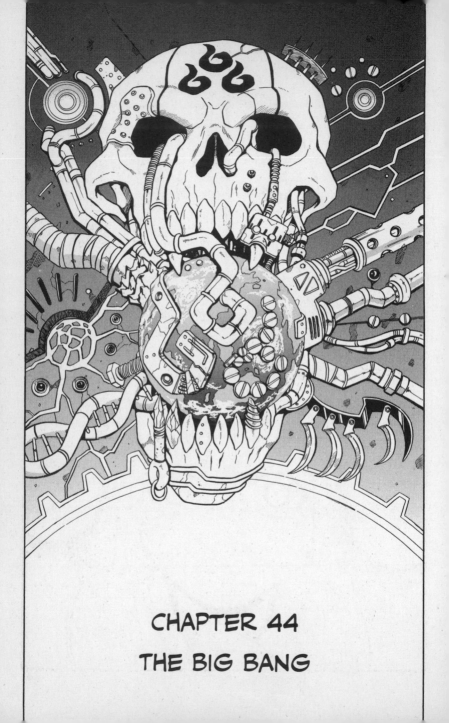

CHAPTER 44
THE BIG BANG

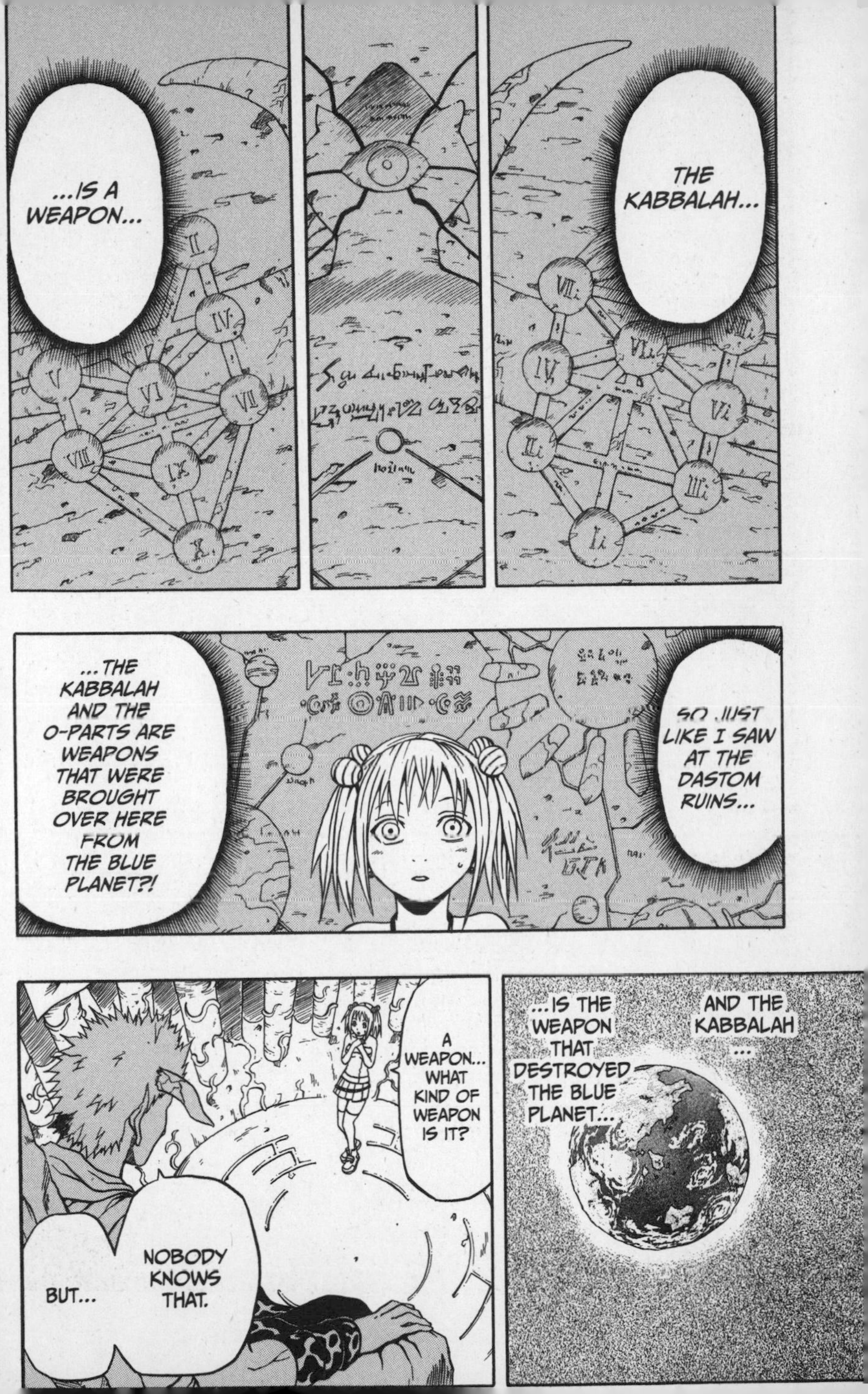
THE KABBALAH...
...IS A WEAPON...
SO JUST LIKE I SAW AT THE DASTOM RUINS...
...THE KABBALAH AND THE O-PARTS ARE WEAPONS THAT WERE BROUGHT OVER HERE FROM THE BLUE PLANET?!
AND THE KABBALAH ...
...IS THE WEAPON THAT DESTROYED THE BLUE PLANET...
A WEAPON... WHAT KIND OF WEAPON IS IT?
NOBODY KNOWS THAT.
BUT...

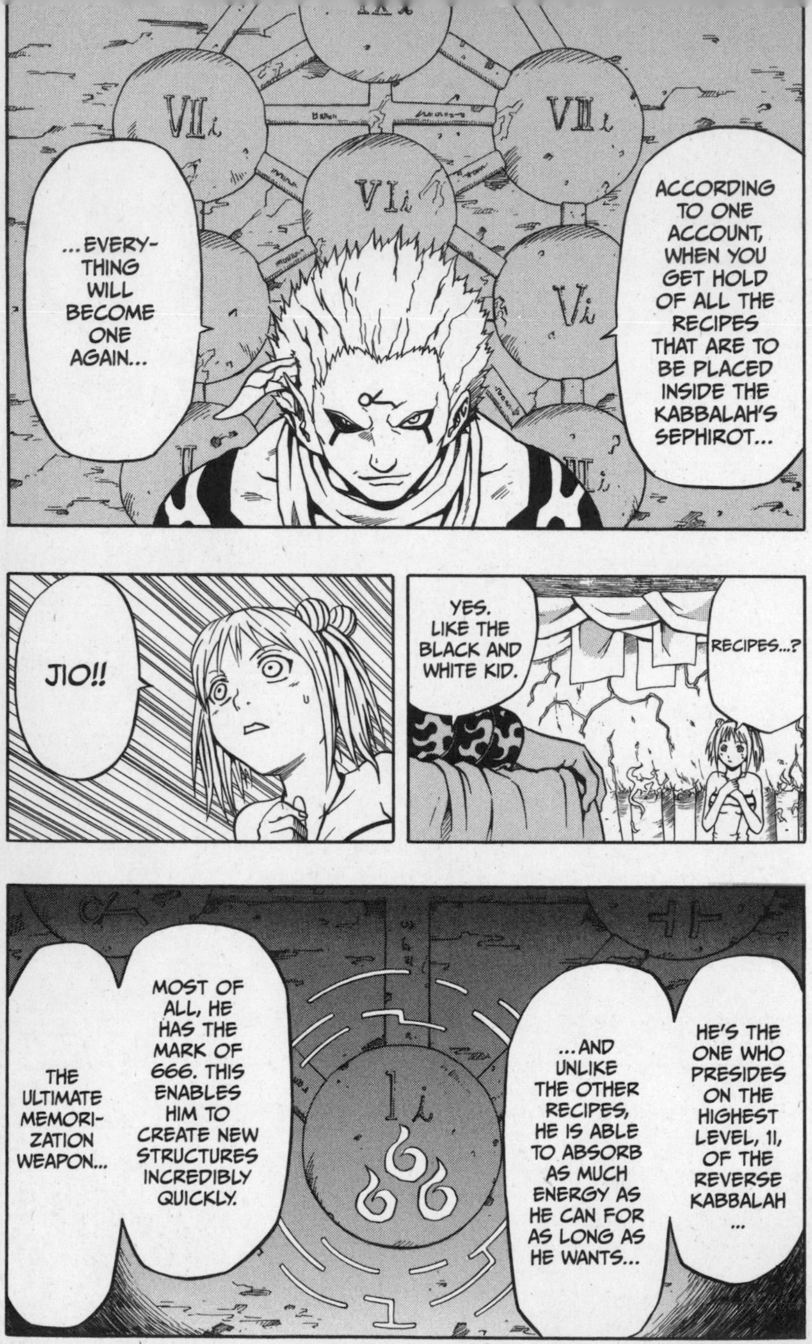
ACCORDING TO ONE ACCOUNT, WHEN YOU GET HOLD OF ALL THE RECIPES THAT ARE TO BE PLACED INSIDE THE KABBALAH'S SEPHIROT...
...EVERY-THING WILL BECOME ONE AGAIN...
RECIPES...?
YES. LIKE THE BLACK AND WHITE KID.
JIO!!
HE'S THE ONE WHO PRESIDES ON THE HIGHEST LEVEL, 11, OF THE REVERSE KABBALAH...
...AND UNLIKE THE OTHER RECIPES, HE IS ABLE TO ABSORB AS MUCH ENERGY AS HE CAN FOR AS LONG AS HE WANTS...
MOST OF ALL, HE HAS THE MARK OF 666. THIS ENABLES HIM TO CREATE NEW STRUCTURES INCREDIBLY QUICKLY.
THE ULTIMATE MEMORI-ZATION WEAPON...

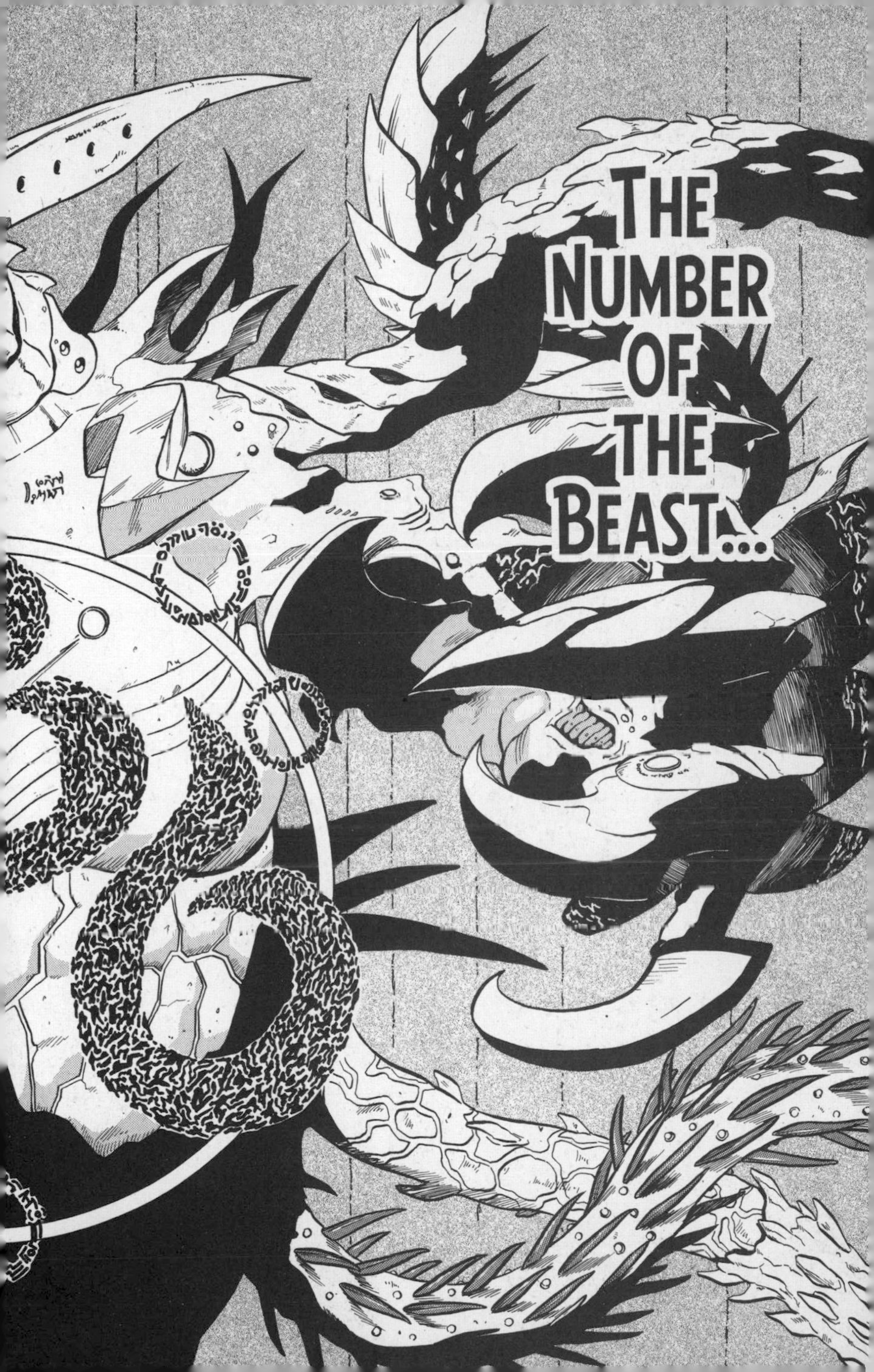
THE NUMBER OF THE BEAST...

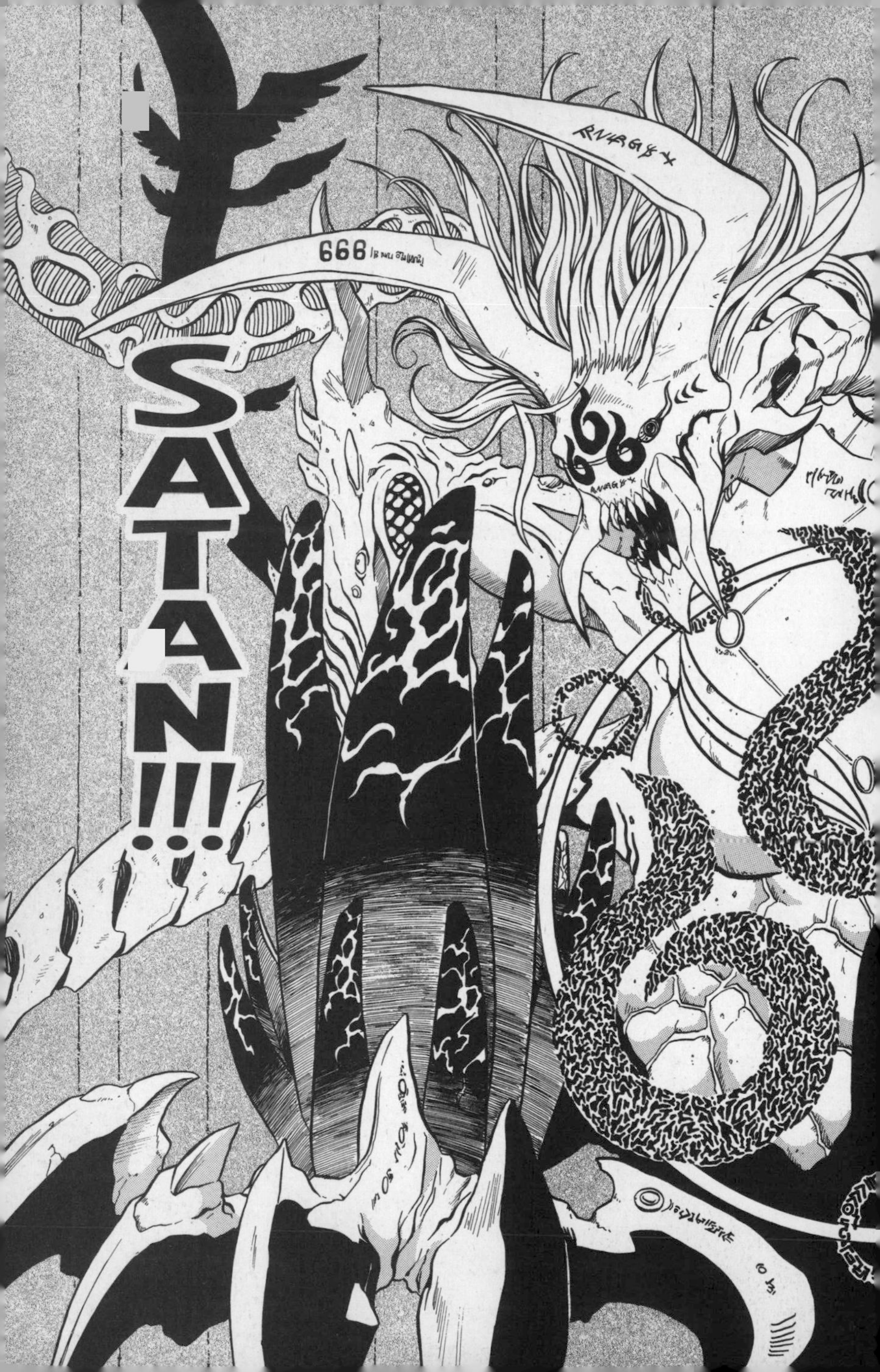
SATAN!!!

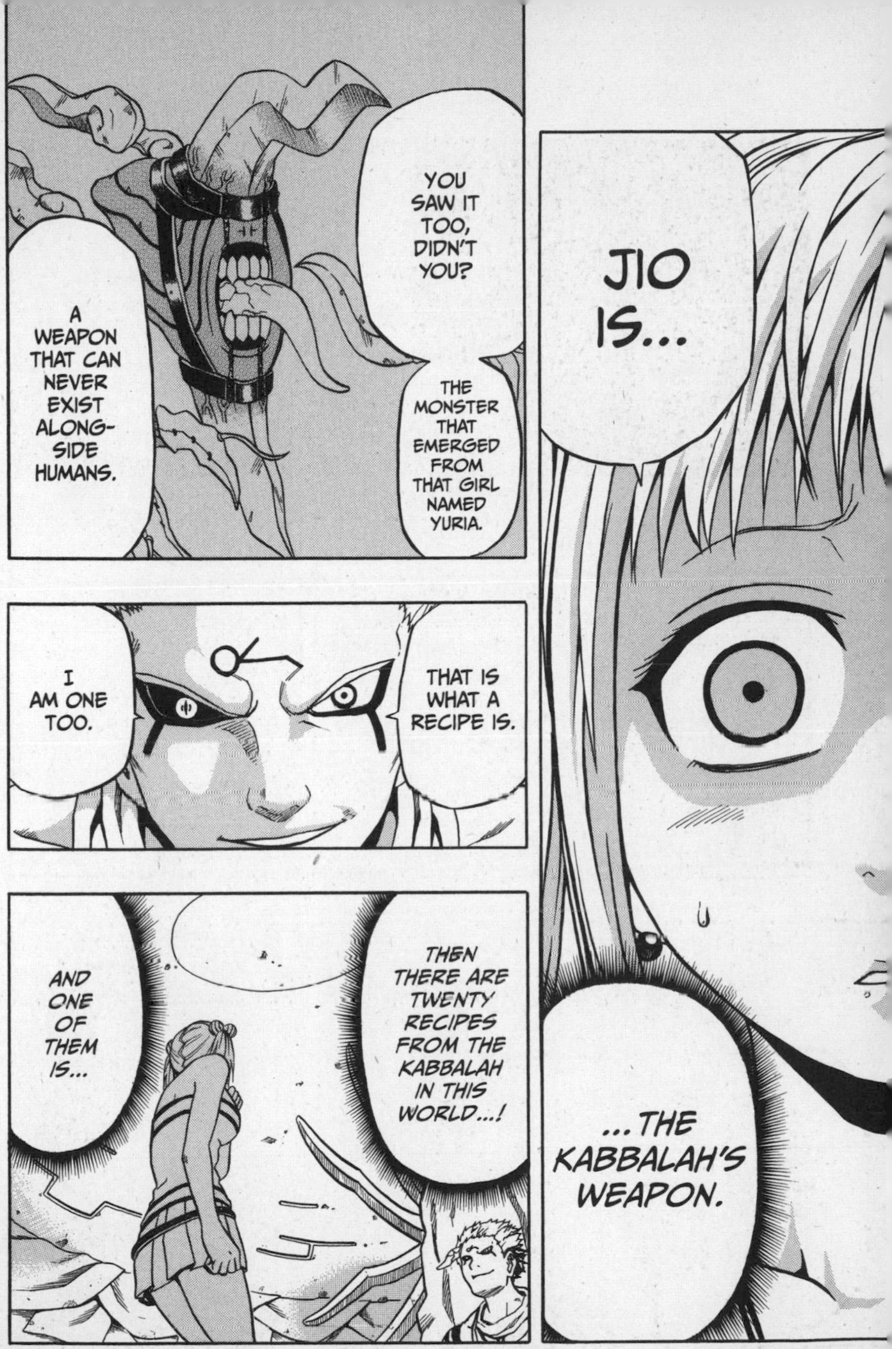
YOU SAW IT TOO, DIDN'T YOU?
THE MONSTER THAT EMERGED FROM THAT GIRL NAMED YURIA.
A WEAPON THAT CAN NEVER EXIST ALONG-SIDE HUMANS.
THAT IS WHAT A RECIPE IS.
I AM ONE TOO.
THEN THERE ARE TWENTY RECIPES FROM THE KABBALAH IN THIS WORLD...!
AND ONE OF THEM IS...
JIO IS...
...THE KABBALAH'S WEAPON.

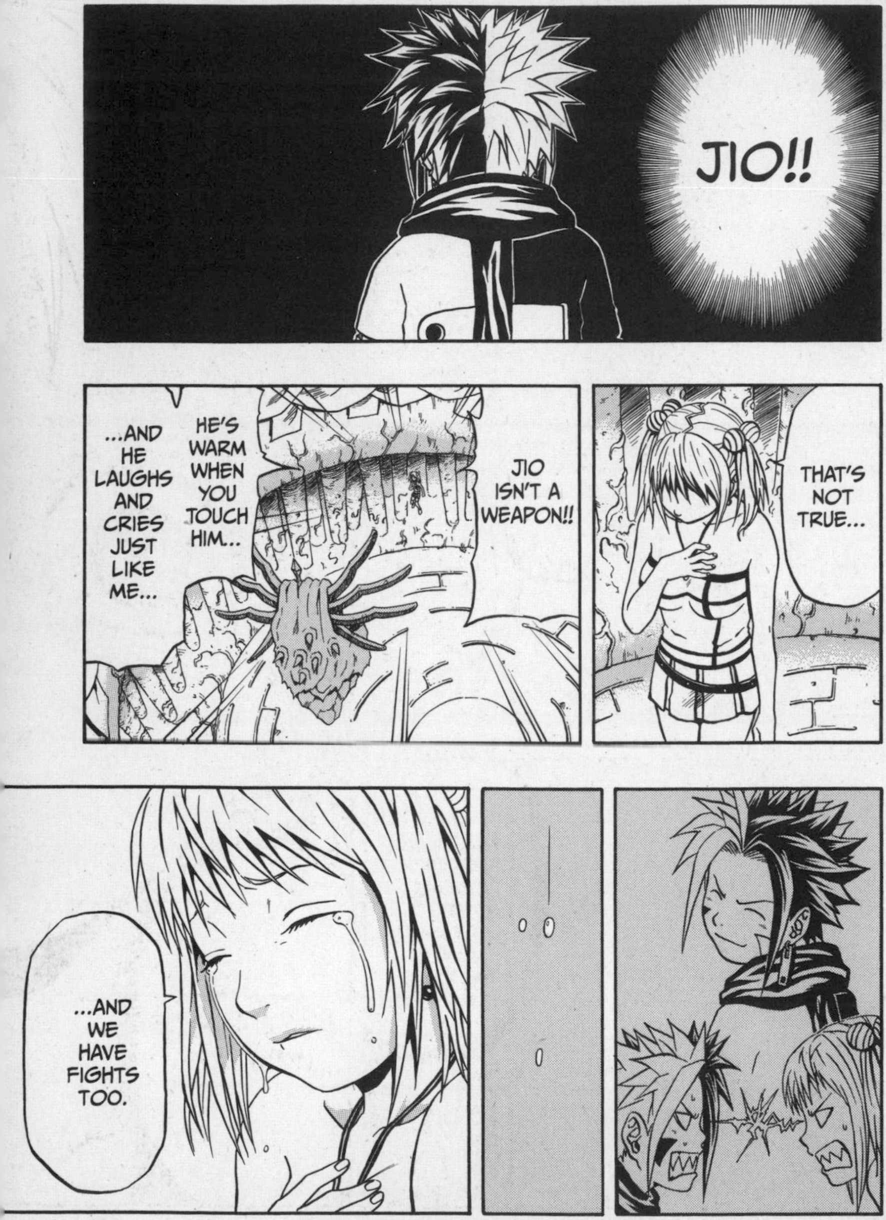
JIO!!
THAT'S NOT TRUE...
JIO ISN'T A WEAPON!!
HE'S WARM WHEN YOU TOUCH HIM...
...AND HE LAUGHS AND CRIES JUST LIKE ME...
...AND WE HAVE FIGHTS TOO.

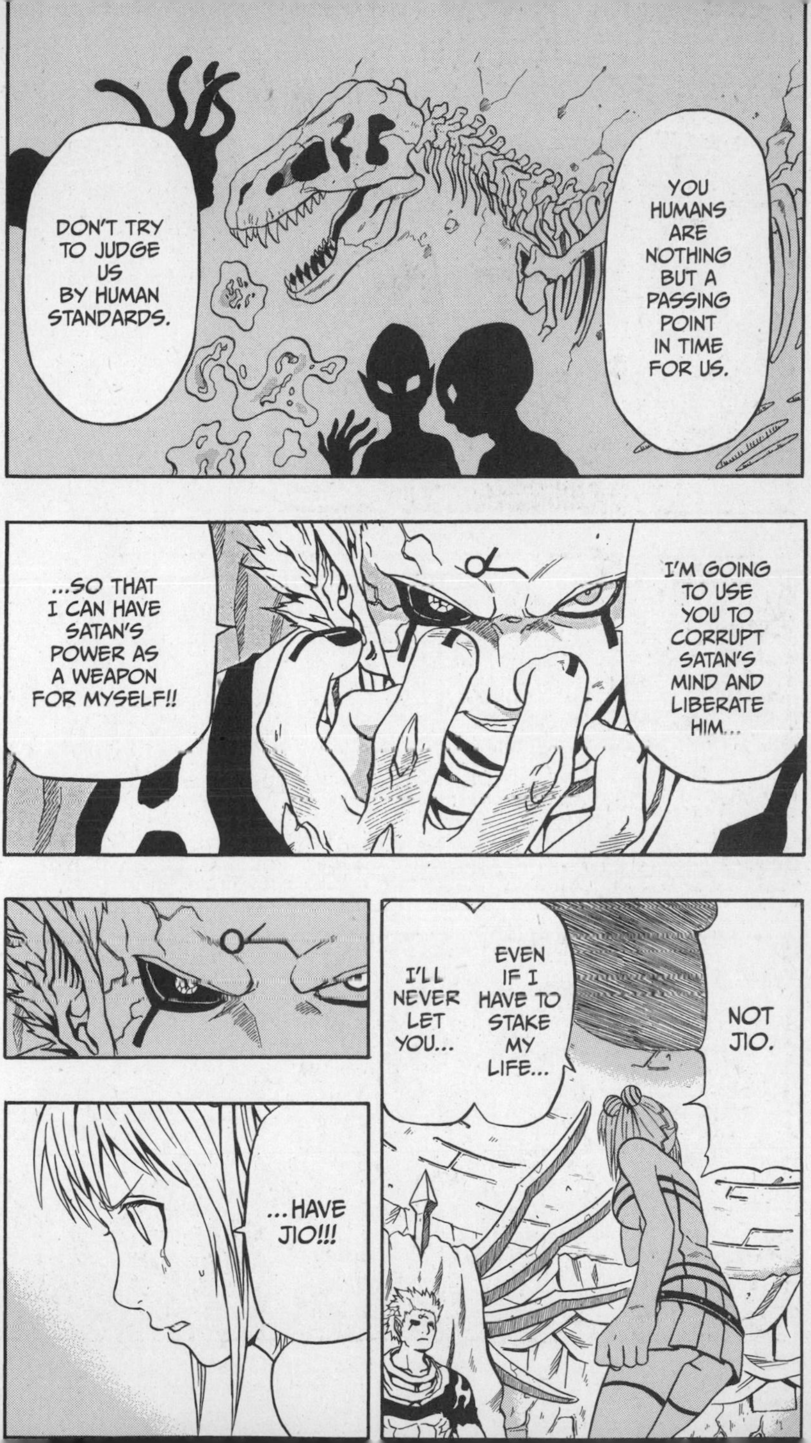
YOU HUMANS ARE NOTHING BUT A PASSING POINT IN TIME FOR US.
DON'T TRY TO JUDGE US BY HUMAN STANDARDS.
I'M GOING TO USE YOU TO CORRUPT SATAN'S MIND AND LIBERATE HIM...
...SO THAT I CAN HAVE SATAN'S POWER AS A WEAPON FOR MYSELF!!
NOT JIO.
EVEN IF I HAVE TO STAKE MY LIFE...
I'LL NEVER LET YOU...
...HAVE JIO!!!

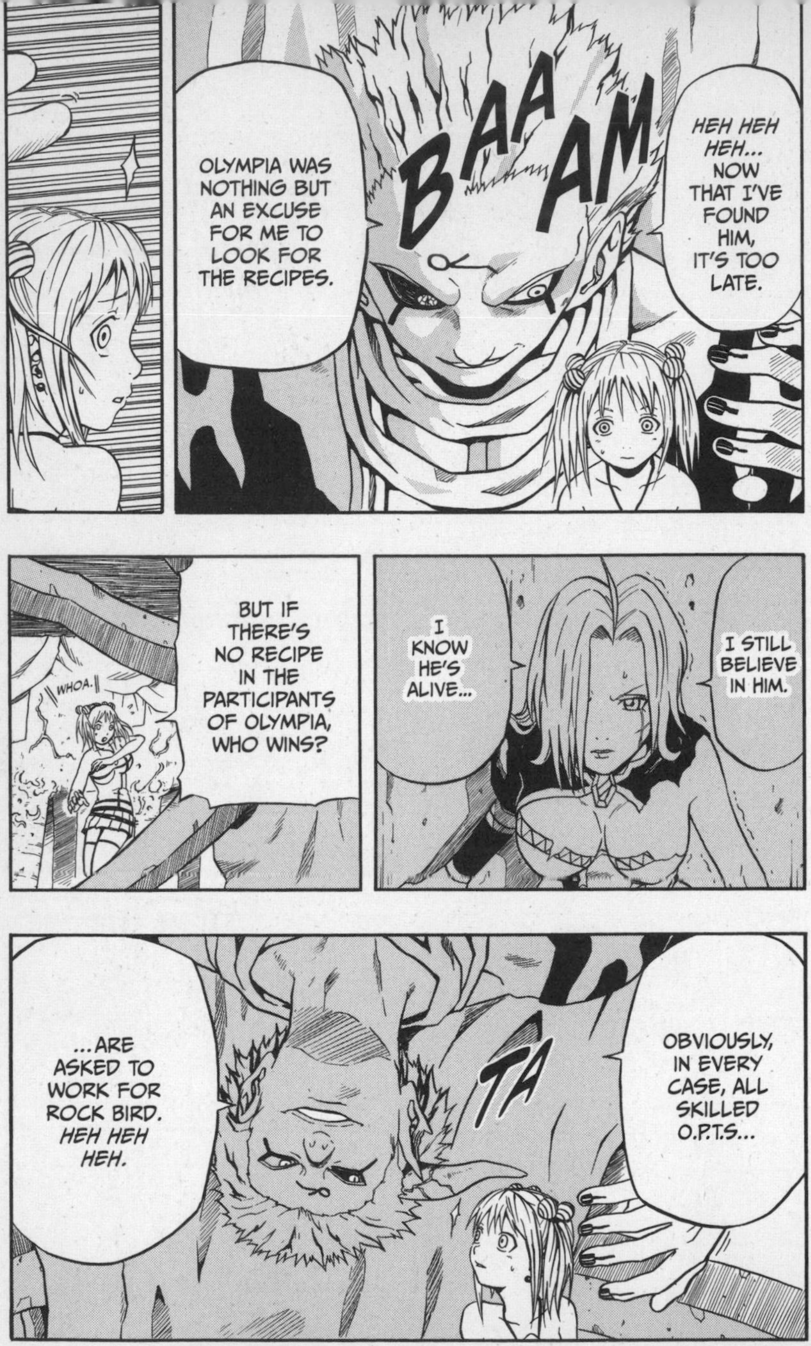
OLYMPIA WAS NOTHING BUT AN EXCUSE FOR ME TO LOOK FOR THE RECIPES.
BAAAM
HEH HEH HEH... NOW THAT I'VE FOUND HIM, IT'S TOO LATE.
BUT IF THERE'S NO RECIPE IN THE PARTICIPANTS OF OLYMPIA, WHO WINS?
WHOA.
I KNOW HE'S ALIVE...
I STILL BELIEVE IN HIM.
...ARE ASKED TO WORK FOR ROCK BIRD. HEH HEH HEH.
TA
OBVIOUSLY, IN EVERY CASE, ALL SKILLED O.P.T.S...

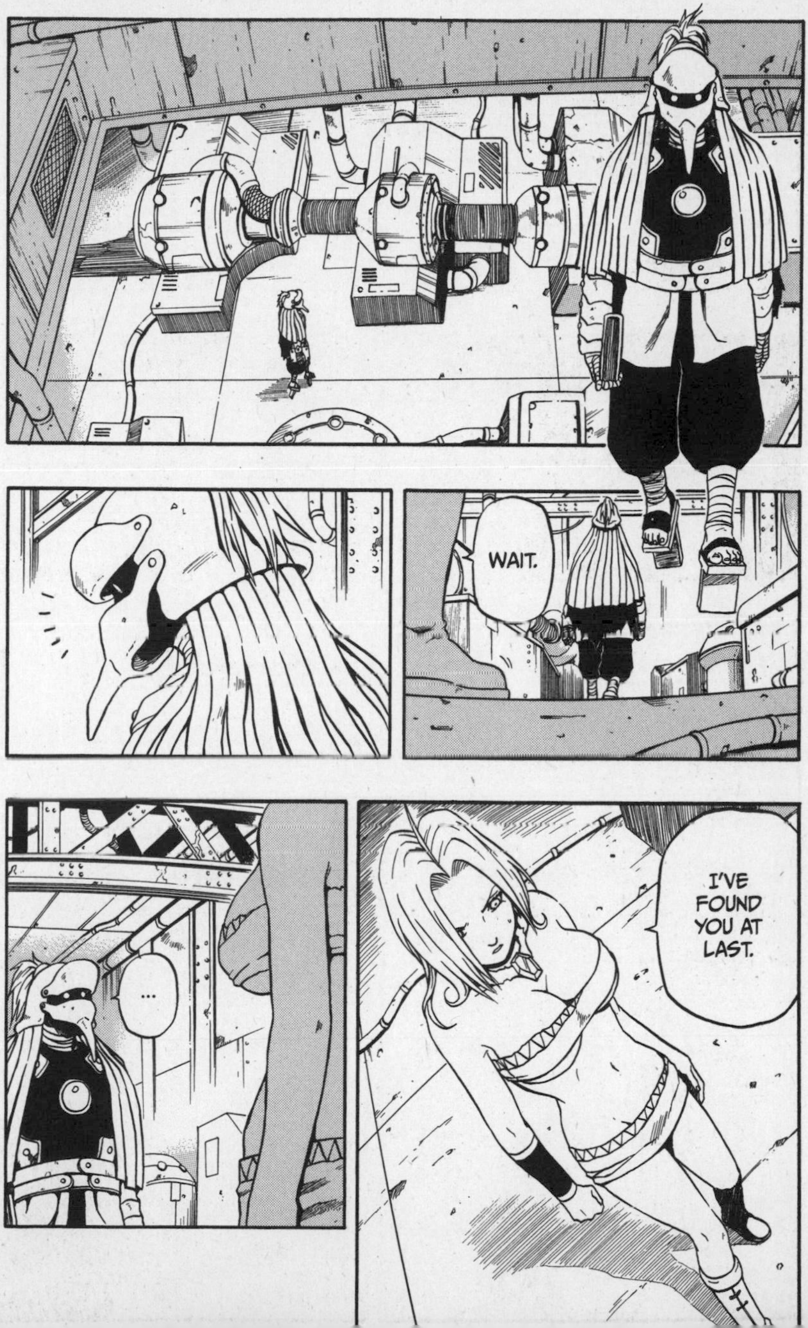
WAIT.
I'VE FOUND YOU AT LAST.
...

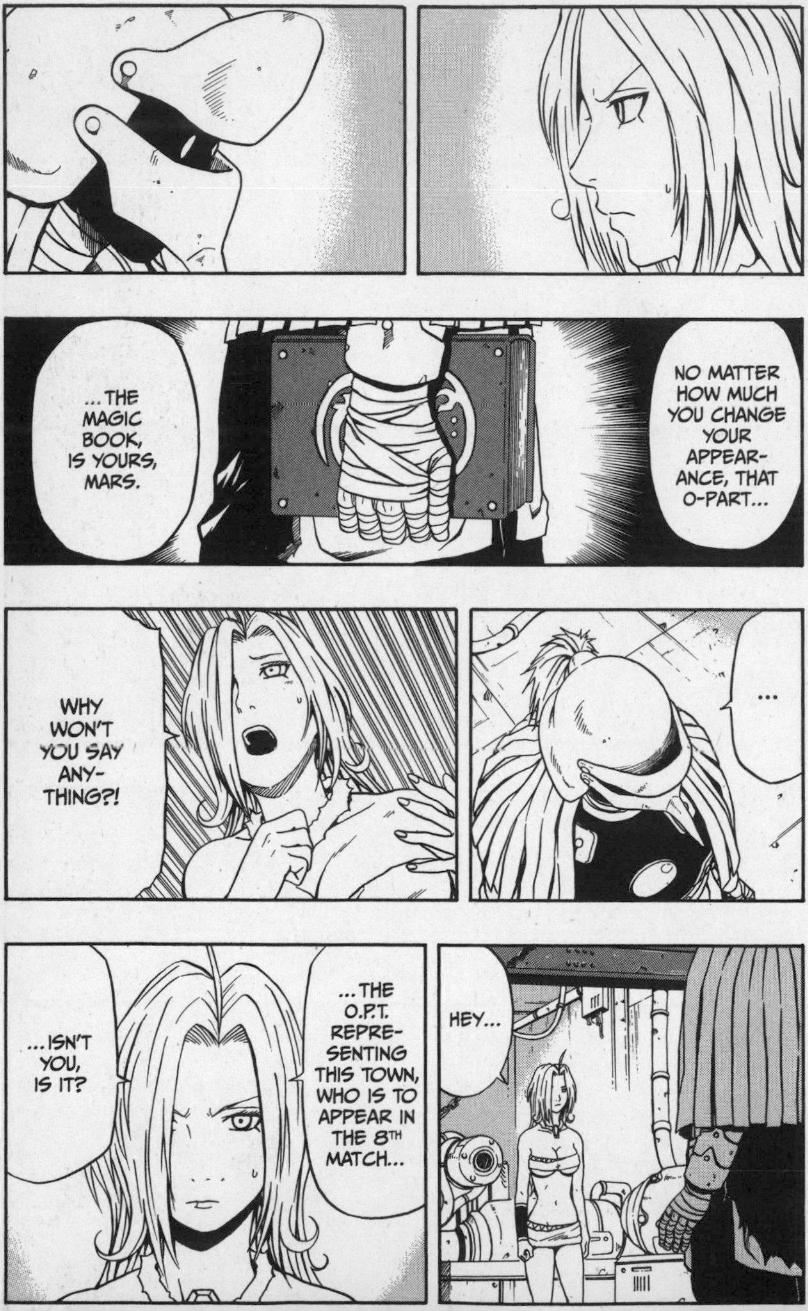
NO MATTER HOW MUCH YOU CHANGE YOUR APPEARANCE, THAT O-PART...
...THE MAGIC BOOK, IS YOURS, MARS.
...
WHY WON'T YOU SAY ANYTHING?!
HEY...
...THE O.P.T. REPRESENTING THIS TOWN, WHO IS TO APPEAR IN THE 8TH MATCH...
...ISN'T YOU, IS IT?

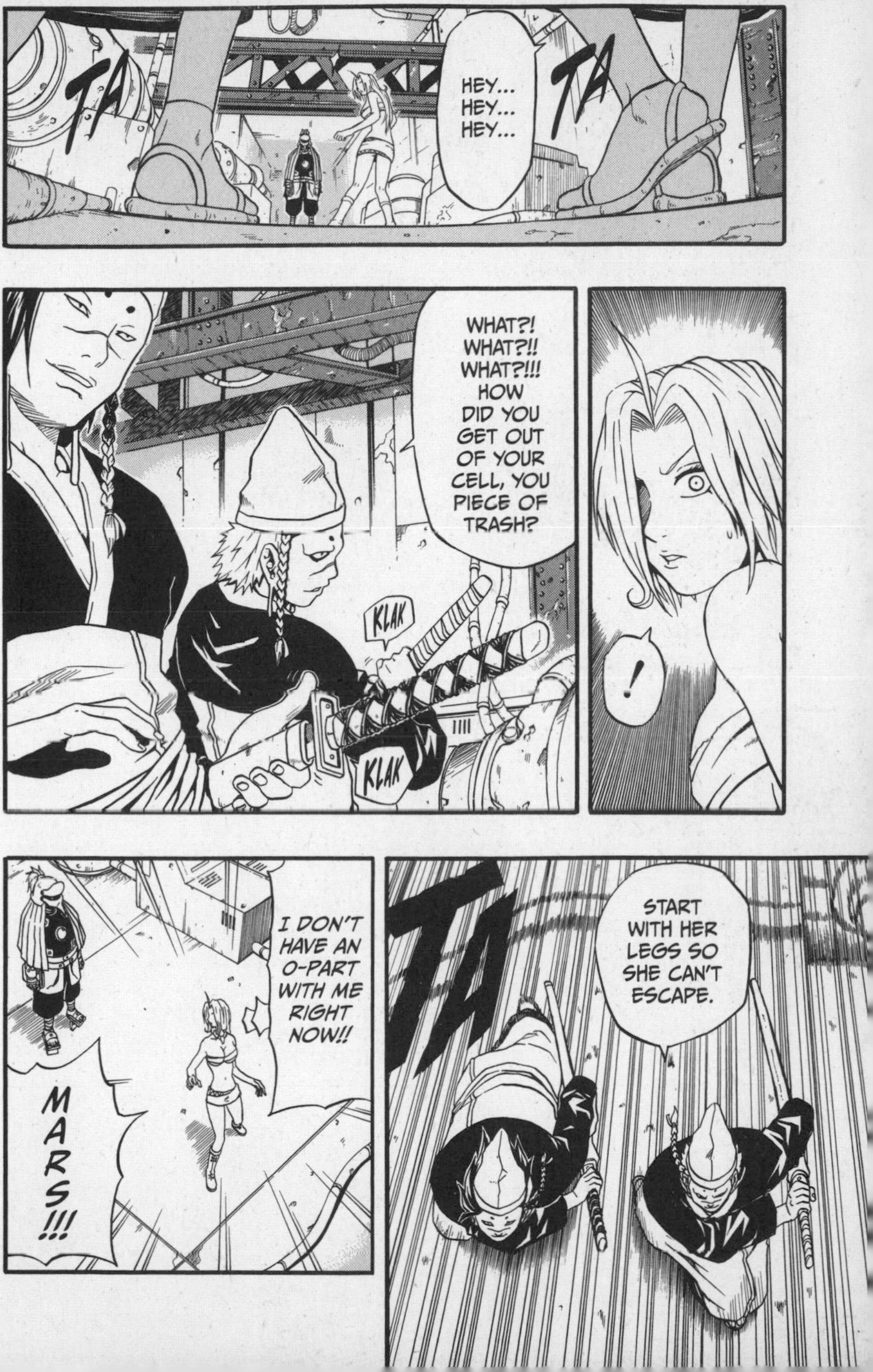
TA
HEY... HEY... HEY...
TA
!
WHAT?! WHAT?!! WHAT?!!! HOW DID YOU GET OUT OF YOUR CELL, YOU PIECE OF TRASH?
KLAK
KLAK
START WITH HER LEGS SO SHE CAN'T ESCAPE.
TA
I DON'T HAVE AN O-PART WITH ME RIGHT NOW!!
MARS!!!

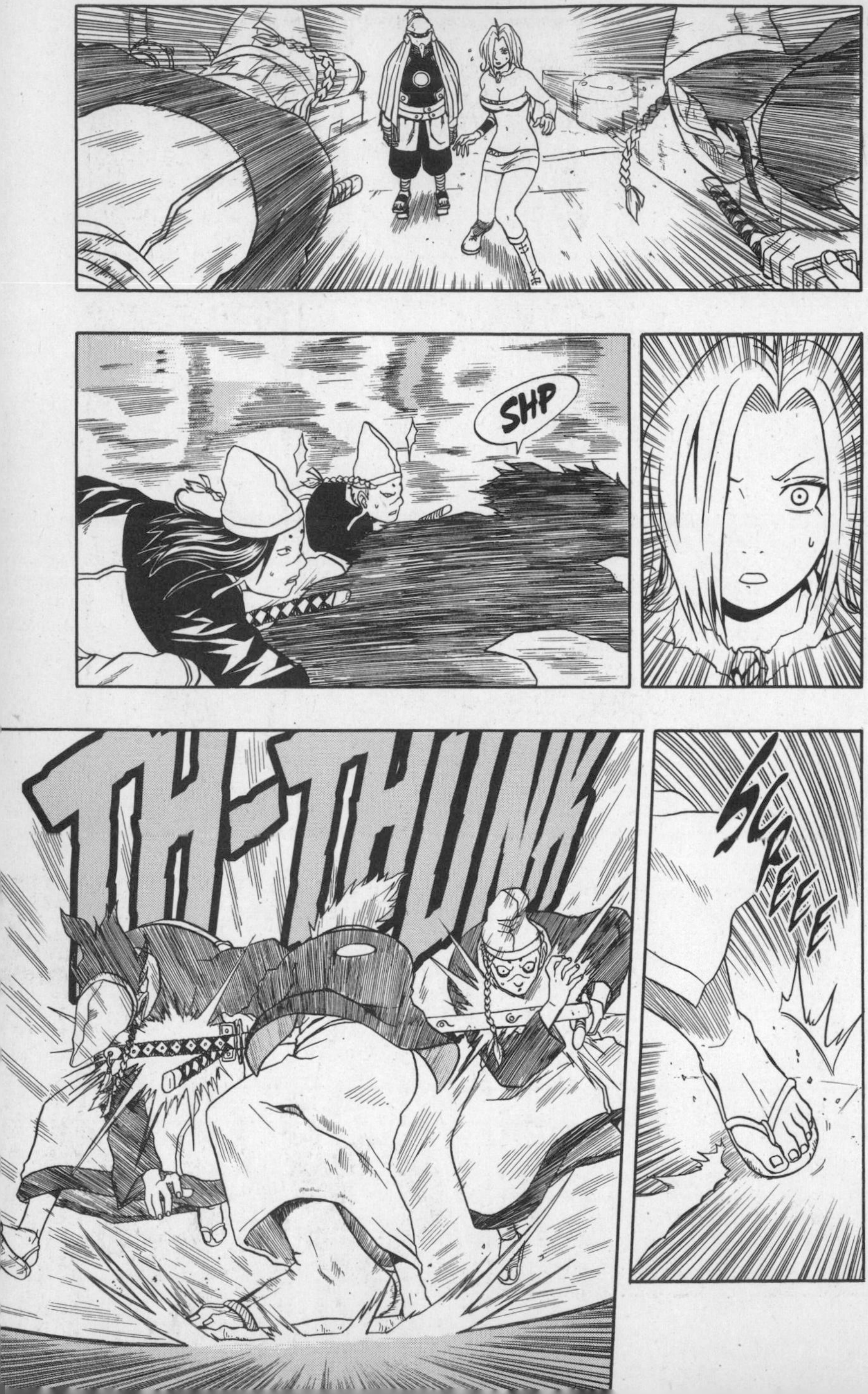
SHP
SCREEE
TH-THUNK

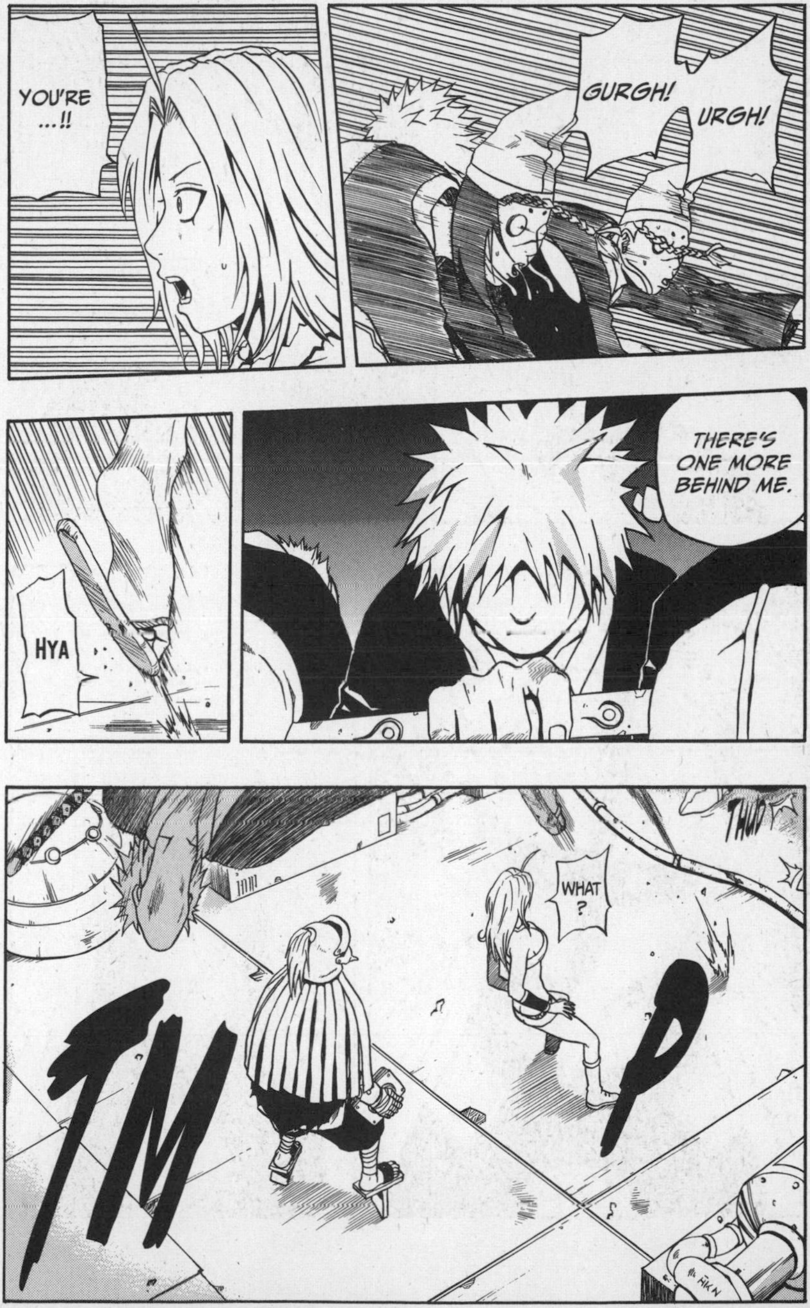
GURGH!
URGH!
YOU'RE ...!!
THERE'S ONE MORE BEHIND ME.
HYA
THUD
WHAT?
TMP

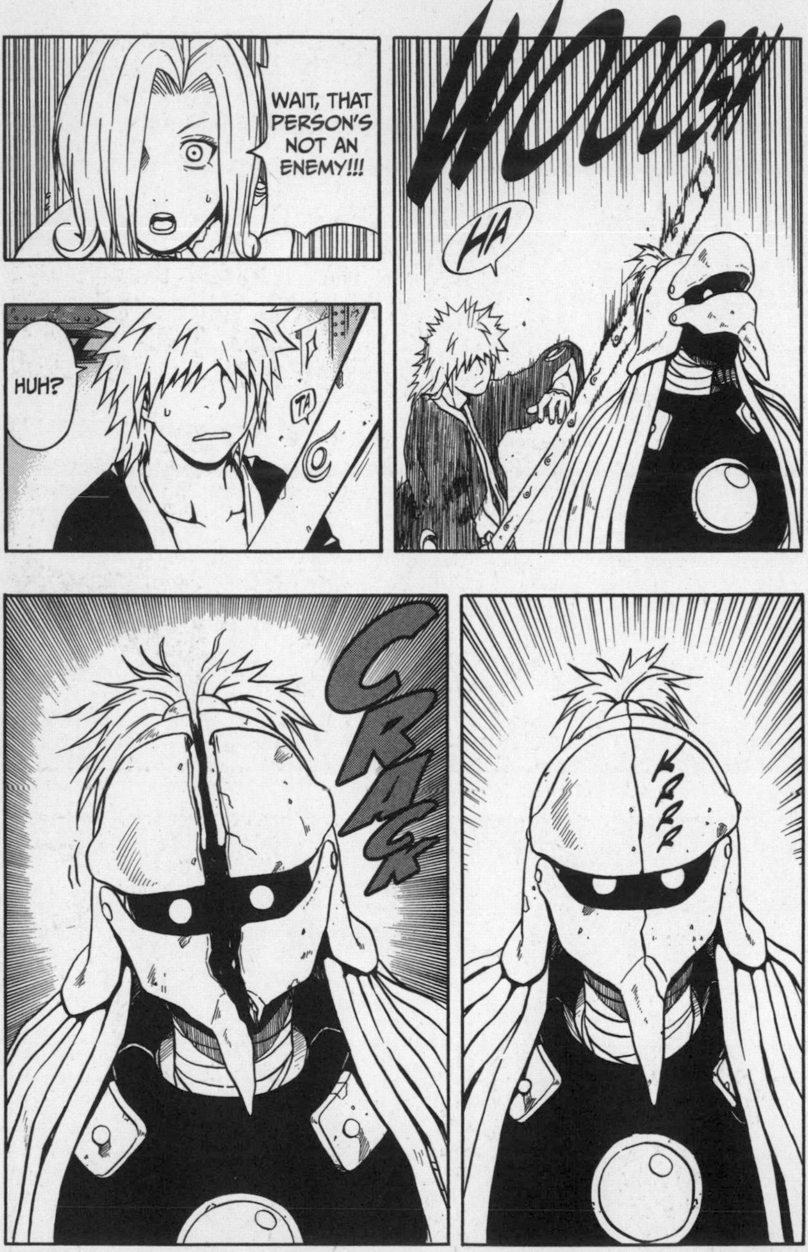
WHOOSH
HA
WAIT, THAT PERSON'S NOT AN ENEMY!!!
HUH?
TA
KRRR
CRACK

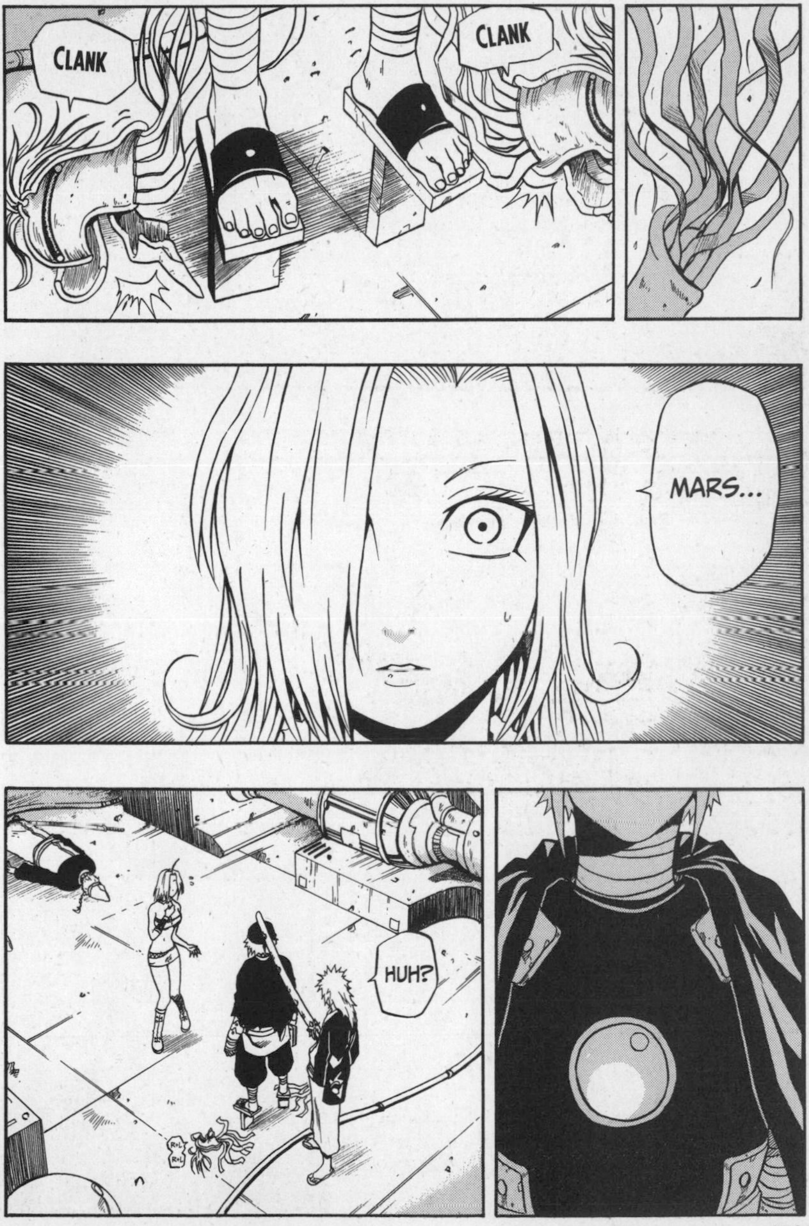
CLANK
CLANK
MARS...
HUH?

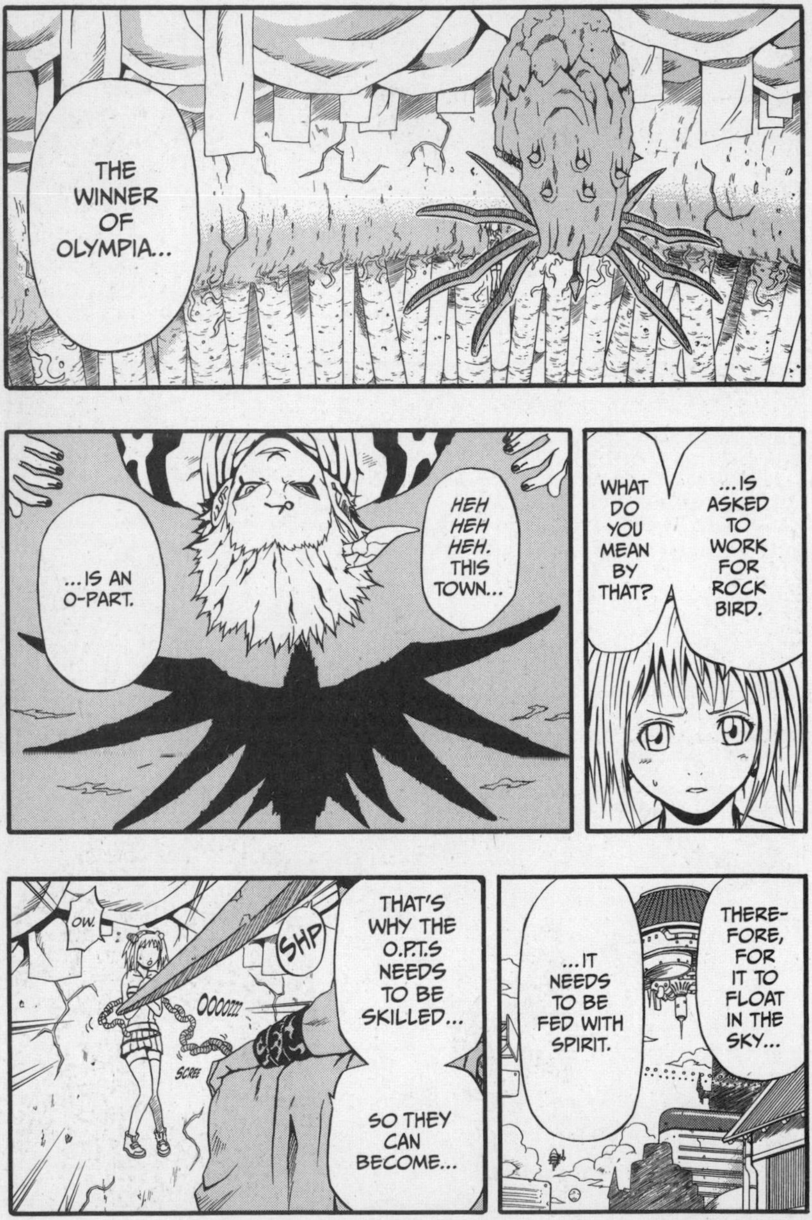
THE WINNER OF OLYMPIA...
...IS ASKED TO WORK FOR ROCK BIRD.
WHAT DO YOU MEAN BY THAT?
HEH HEH HEH. THIS TOWN...
...IS AN O-PART.
THERE-FORE, FOR IT TO FLOAT IN THE SKY...
...IT NEEDS TO BE FED WITH SPIRIT.
THAT'S WHY THE O.P.T.S NEEDS TO BE SKILLED...
SHP
OW.
OOOOZZZ
SO THEY CAN BECOME...
SCREE

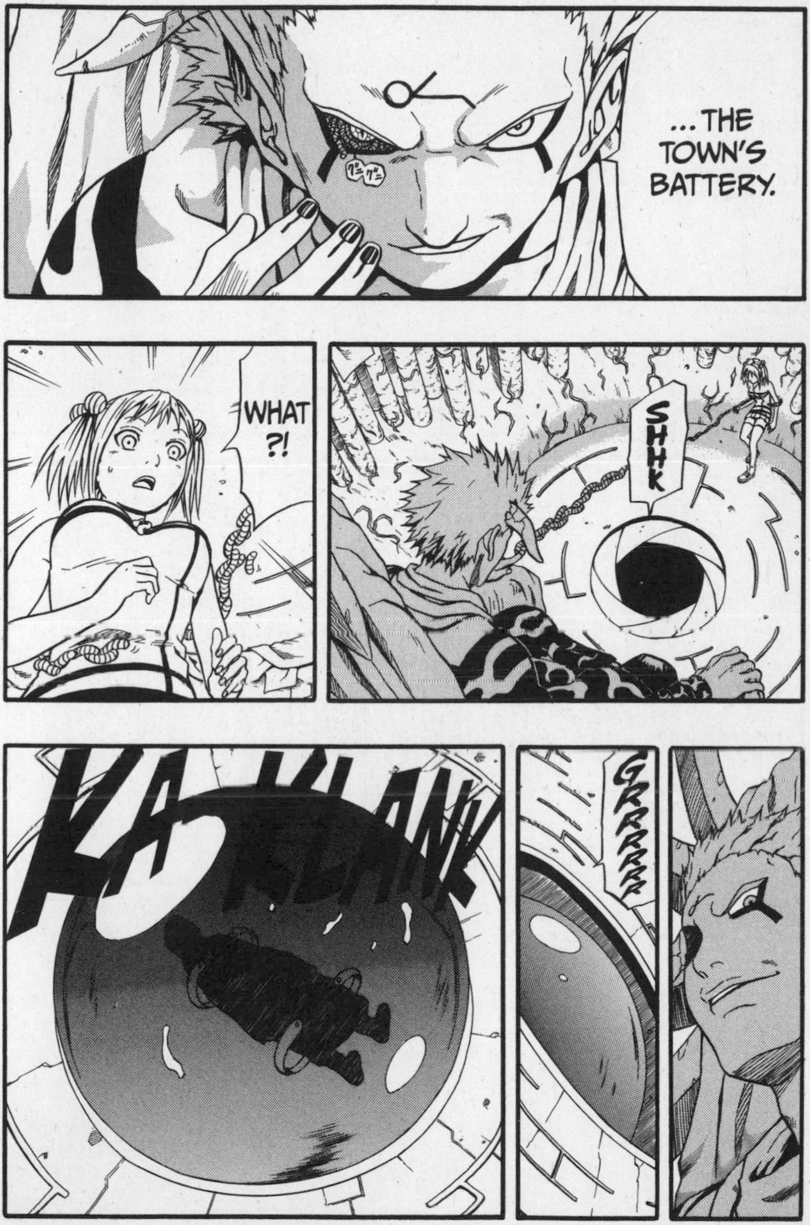
...THE TOWN'S BATTERY.
SHHK
WHAT ?!
GRRRRRRR
KA KLANK

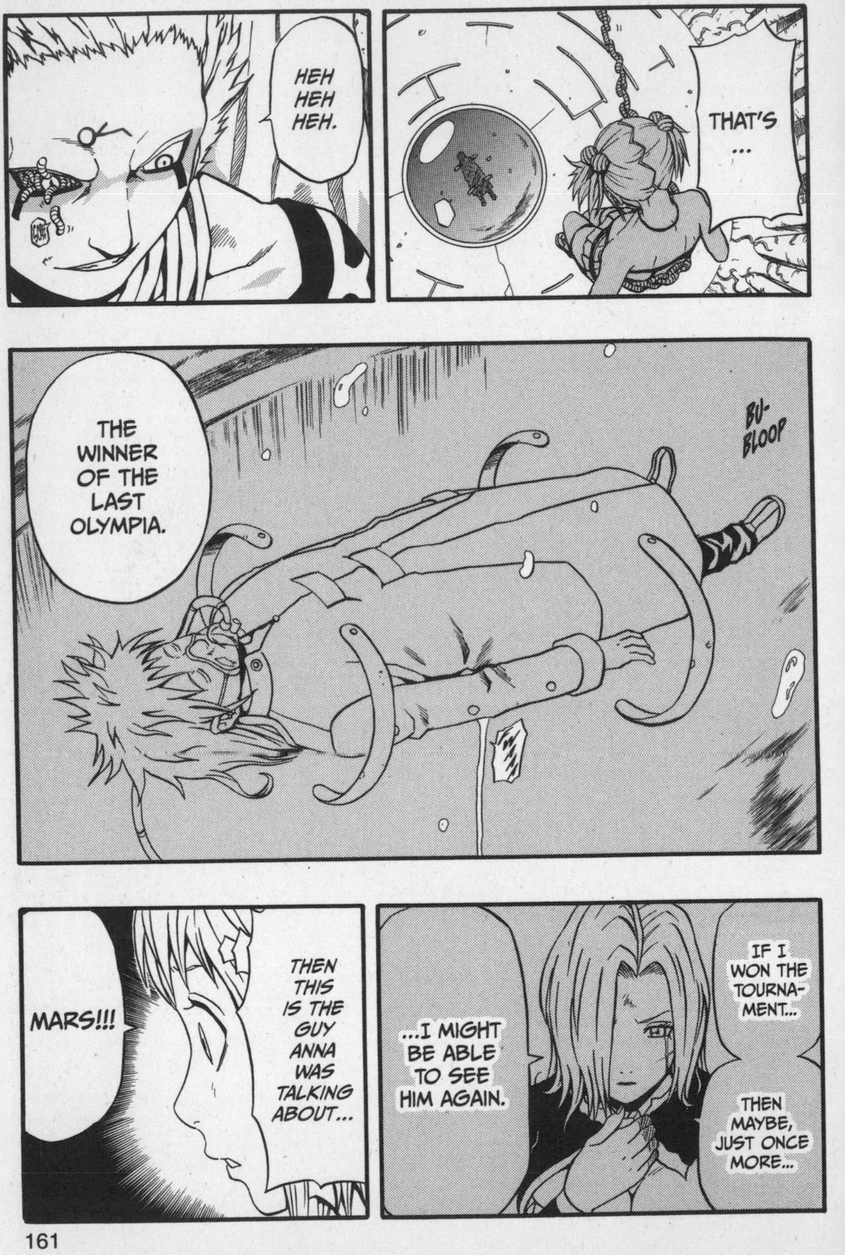
THAT'S ...
HEH HEH HEH.
THE WINNER OF THE LAST OLYMPIA.
BU-BLOOP
IF I WON THE TOURNA-MENT...
THEN MAYBE, JUST ONCE MORE...
...I MIGHT BE ABLE TO SEE HIM AGAIN.
THEN THIS IS THE GUY ANNA WAS TALKING ABOUT...
MARS!!!

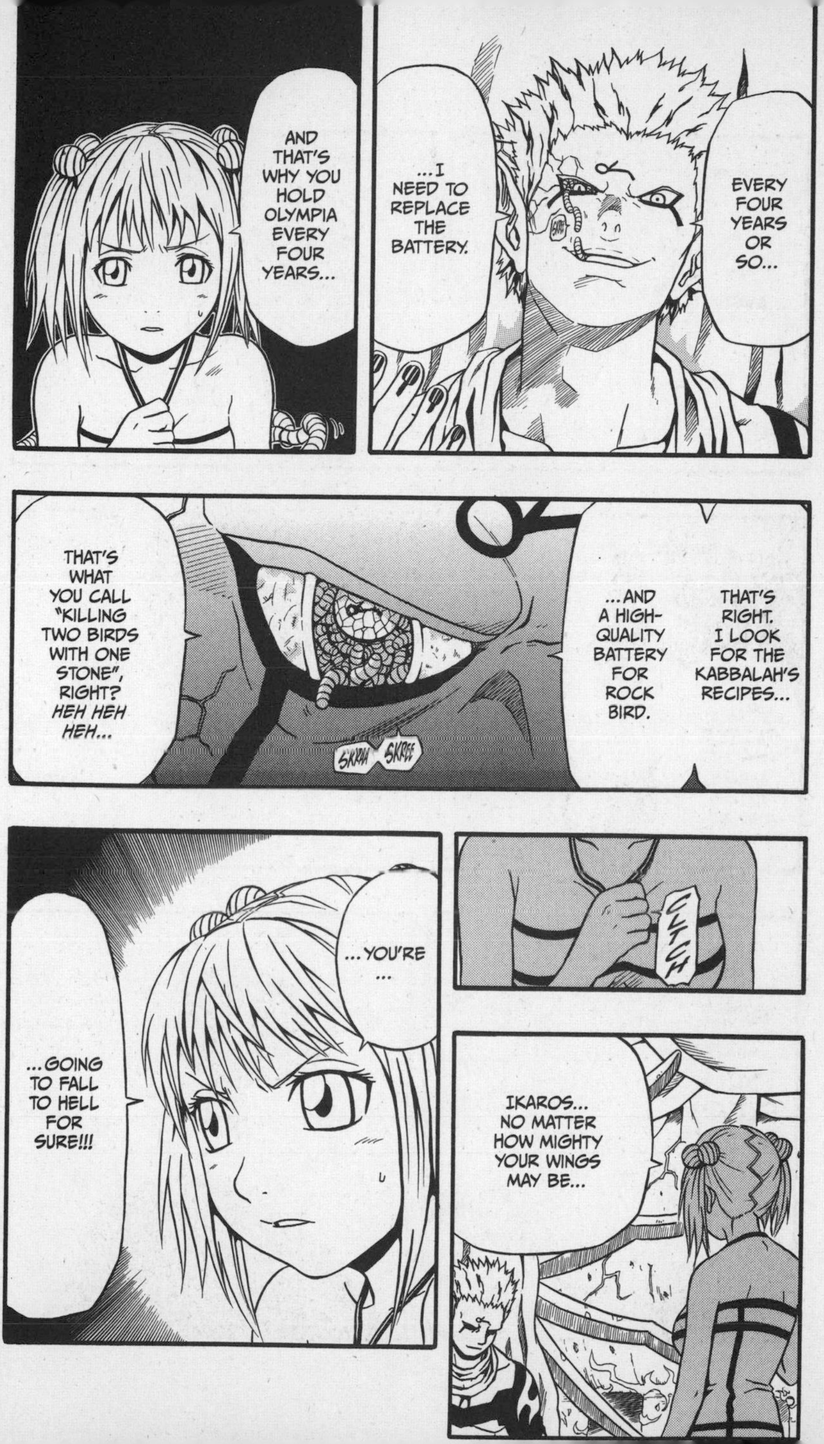
EVERY FOUR YEARS OR SO...
...I NEED TO REPLACE THE BATTERY.
AND THAT'S WHY YOU HOLD OLYMPIA EVERY FOUR YEARS...
THAT'S RIGHT. I LOOK FOR THE KABBALAH'S RECIPES...
...AND A HIGH-QUALITY BATTERY FOR ROCK BIRD.
THAT'S WHAT YOU CALL "KILLING TWO BIRDS WITH ONE STONE", RIGHT? *HEH HEH HEH...*
SKRAA SKREE
CLTCH
IKAROS... NO MATTER HOW MIGHTY YOUR WINGS MAY BE...
...YOU'RE ...
...GOING TO FALL TO HELL FOR SURE!!!

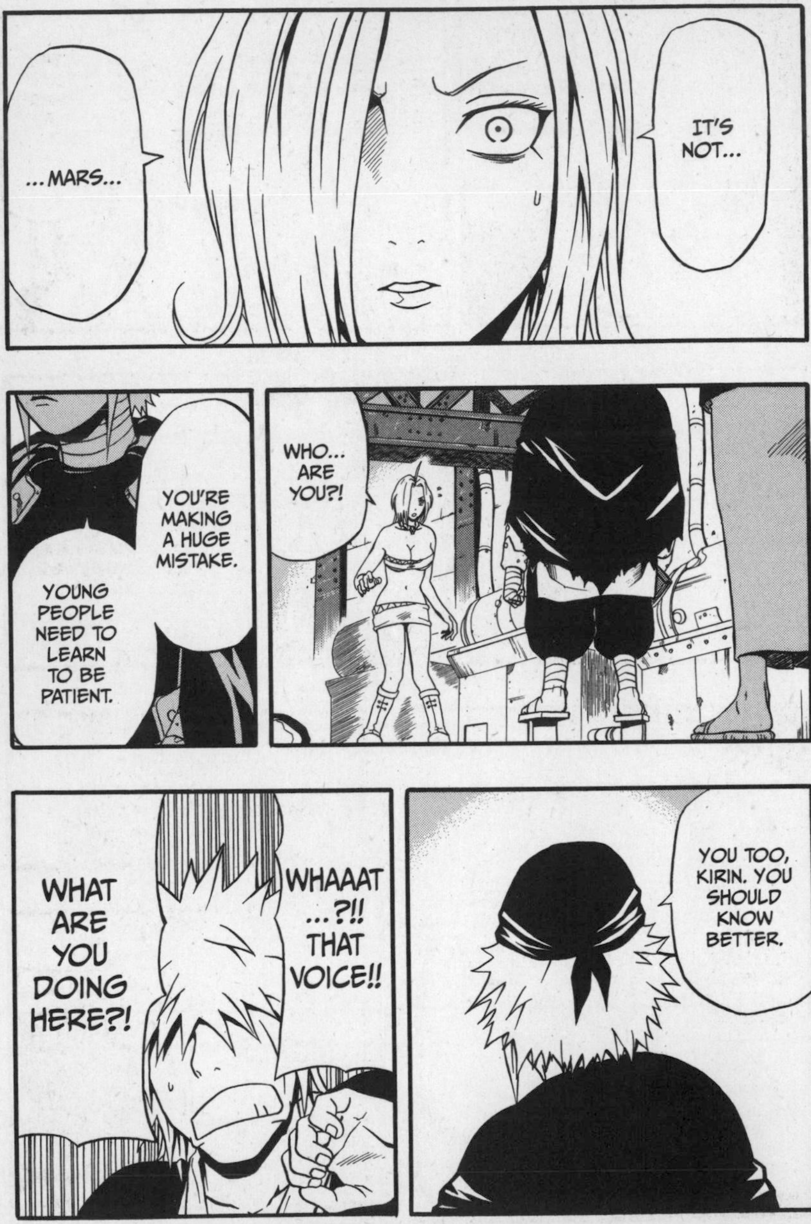
IT'S NOT...
...MARS...
WHO... ARE YOU?!
YOU'RE MAKING A HUGE MISTAKE.
YOUNG PEOPLE NEED TO LEARN TO BE PATIENT.
YOU TOO, KIRIN. YOU SHOULD KNOW BETTER.
WHAAAT ...?!! THAT VOICE!!
WHAT ARE YOU DOING HERE?!

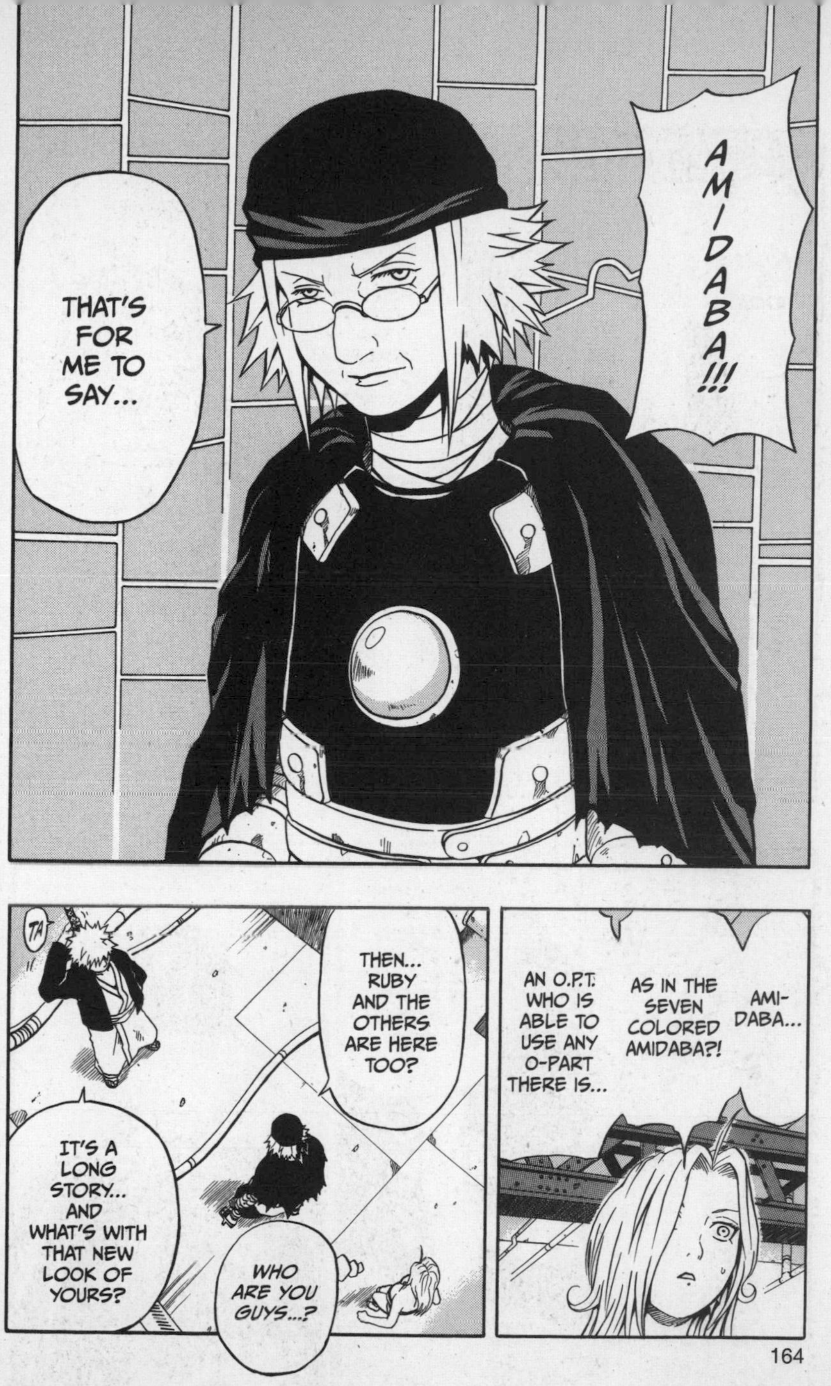
AMIDABA!!!
THAT'S FOR ME TO SAY...
AMI-DABA...
AS IN THE SEVEN COLORED AMIDABA?!
AN O.P.T. WHO IS ABLE TO USE ANY O-PART THERE IS...
THEN... RUBY AND THE OTHERS ARE HERE TOO?
TA
IT'S A LONG STORY... AND WHAT'S WITH THAT NEW LOOK OF YOURS?
WHO ARE YOU GUYS...?

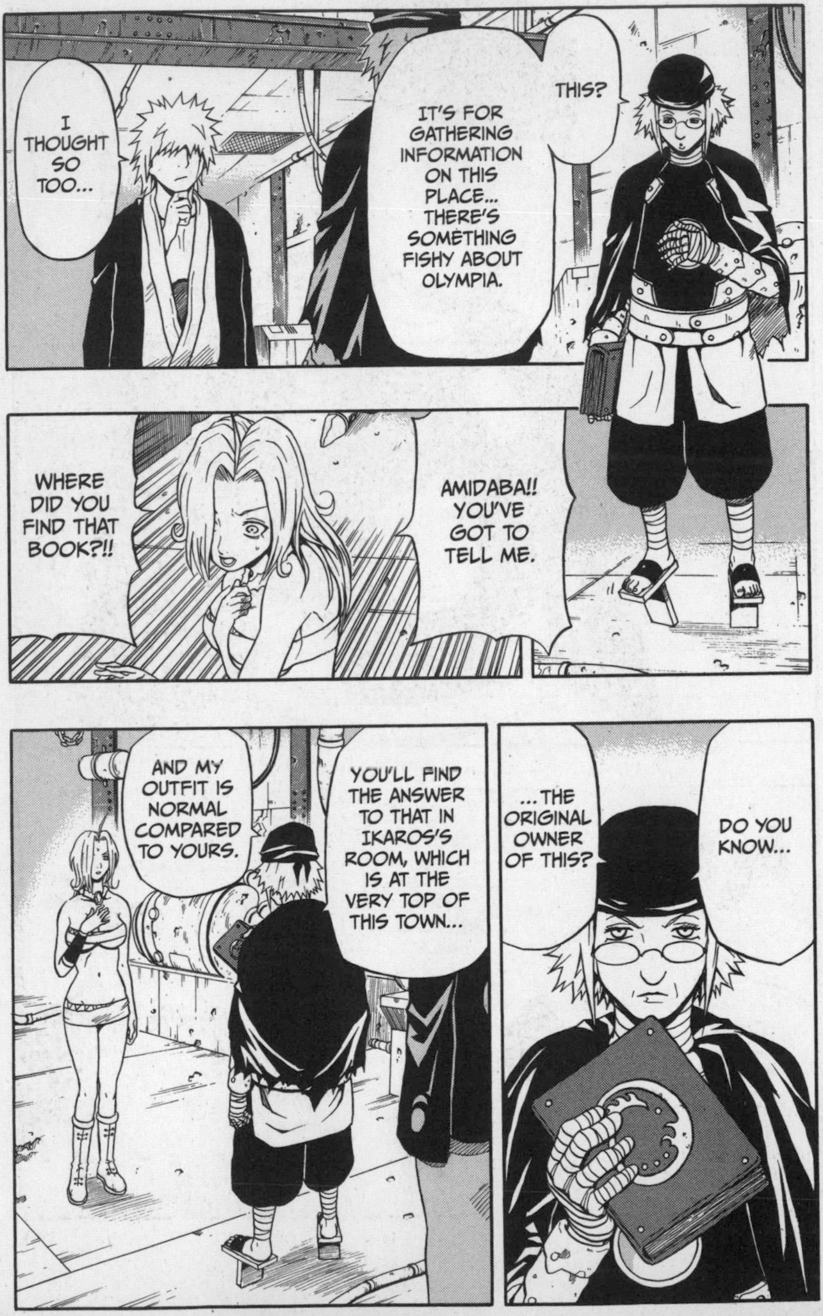
THIS?
IT'S FOR GATHERING INFORMATION ON THIS PLACE... THERE'S SOMETHING FISHY ABOUT OLYMPIA.
I THOUGHT SO TOO...
AMIDABA!! YOU'VE GOT TO TELL ME.
WHERE DID YOU FIND THAT BOOK?!!
DO YOU KNOW...
...THE ORIGINAL OWNER OF THIS?
YOU'LL FIND THE ANSWER TO THAT IN IKAROS'S ROOM, WHICH IS AT THE VERY TOP OF THIS TOWN...
AND MY OUTFIT IS NORMAL COMPARED TO YOURS.

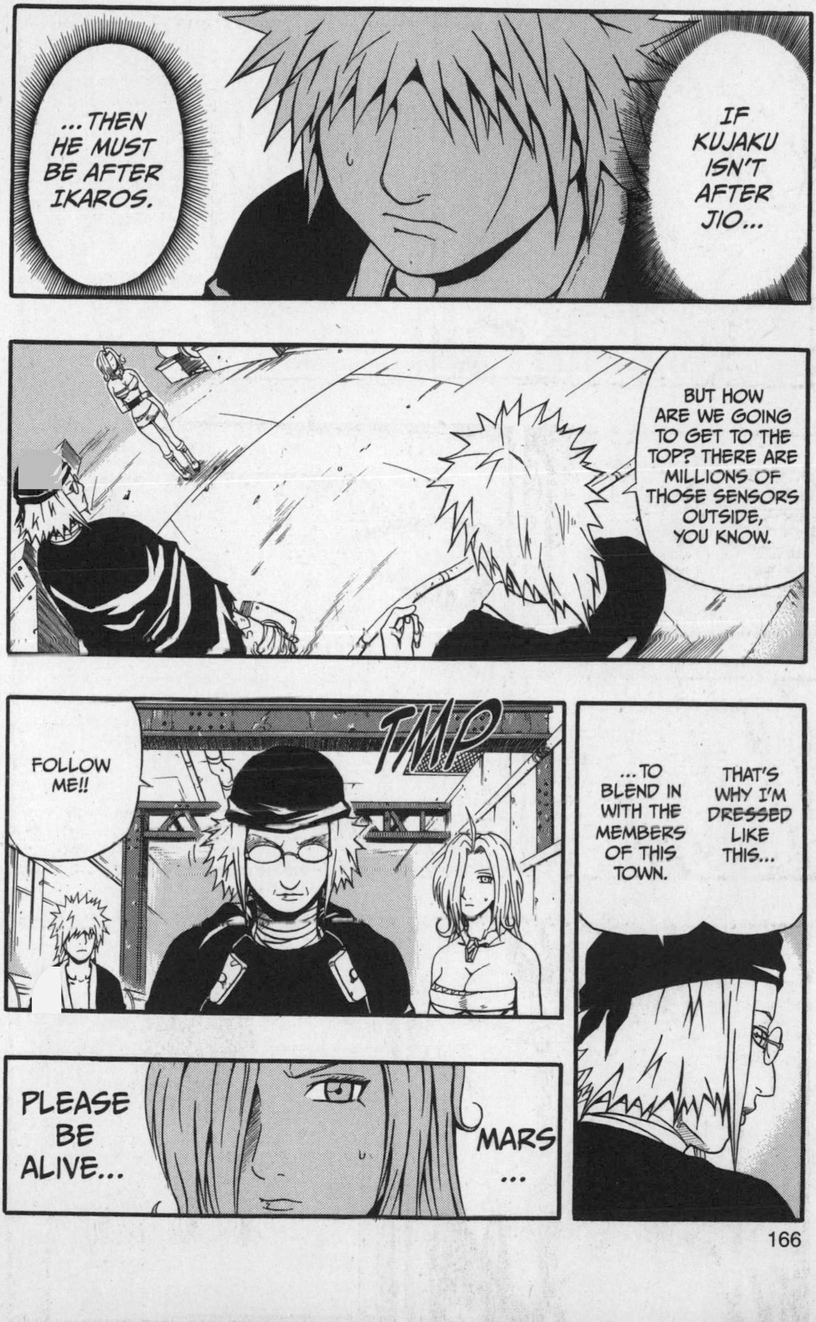
IF KUJAKU ISN'T AFTER JIO...
...THEN HE MUST BE AFTER IKAROS.
BUT HOW ARE WE GOING TO GET TO THE TOP? THERE ARE MILLIONS OF THOSE SENSORS OUTSIDE, YOU KNOW.
THAT'S WHY I'M DRESSED LIKE THIS...
...TO BLEND IN WITH THE MEMBERS OF THIS TOWN.
TMP
FOLLOW ME!!
MARS ...
PLEASE BE ALIVE...

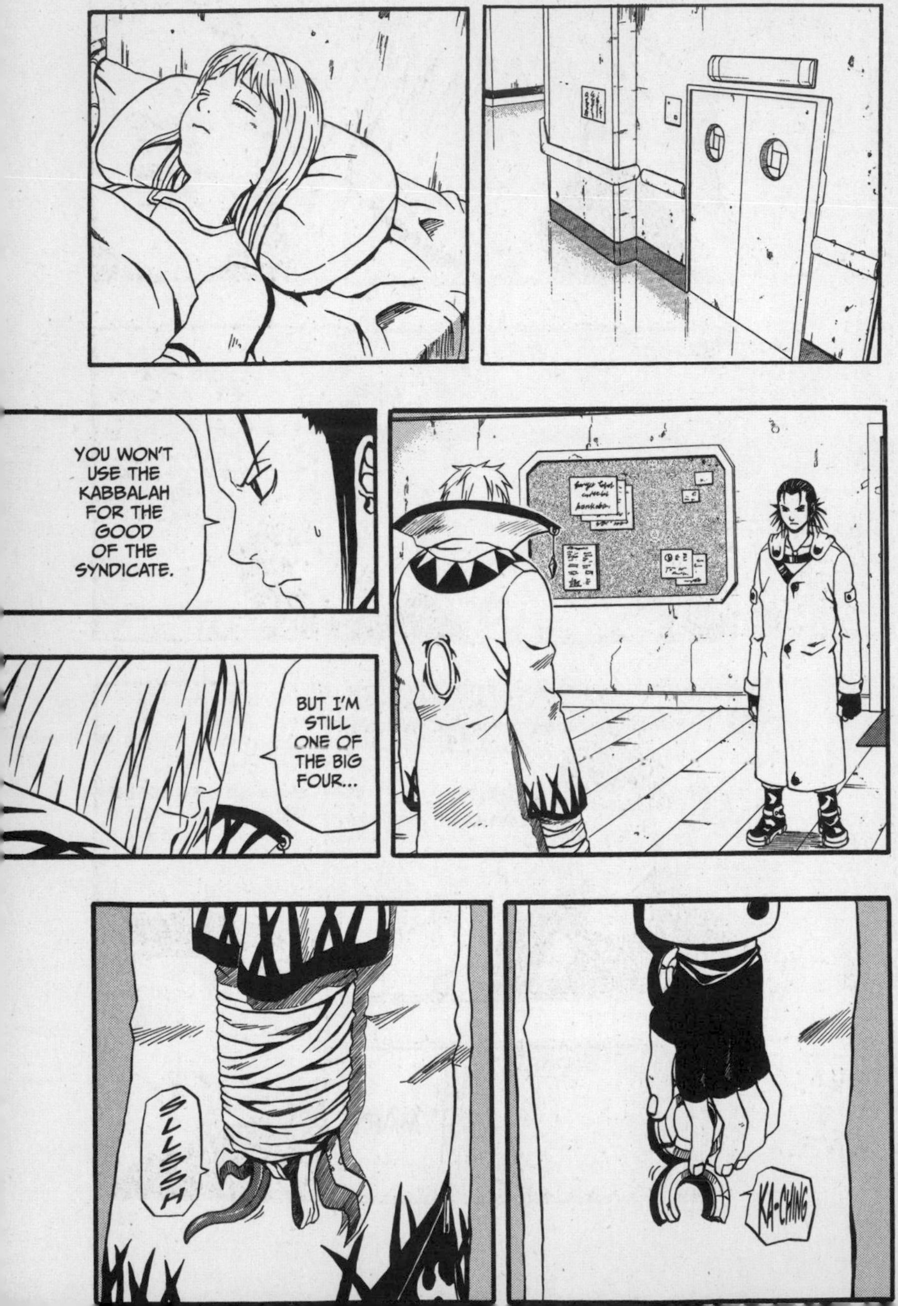
YOU WON'T USE THE KABBALAH FOR THE GOOD OF THE SYNDICATE.
BUT I'M STILL ONE OF THE BIG FOUR...
KA-CHING
SLLSSH

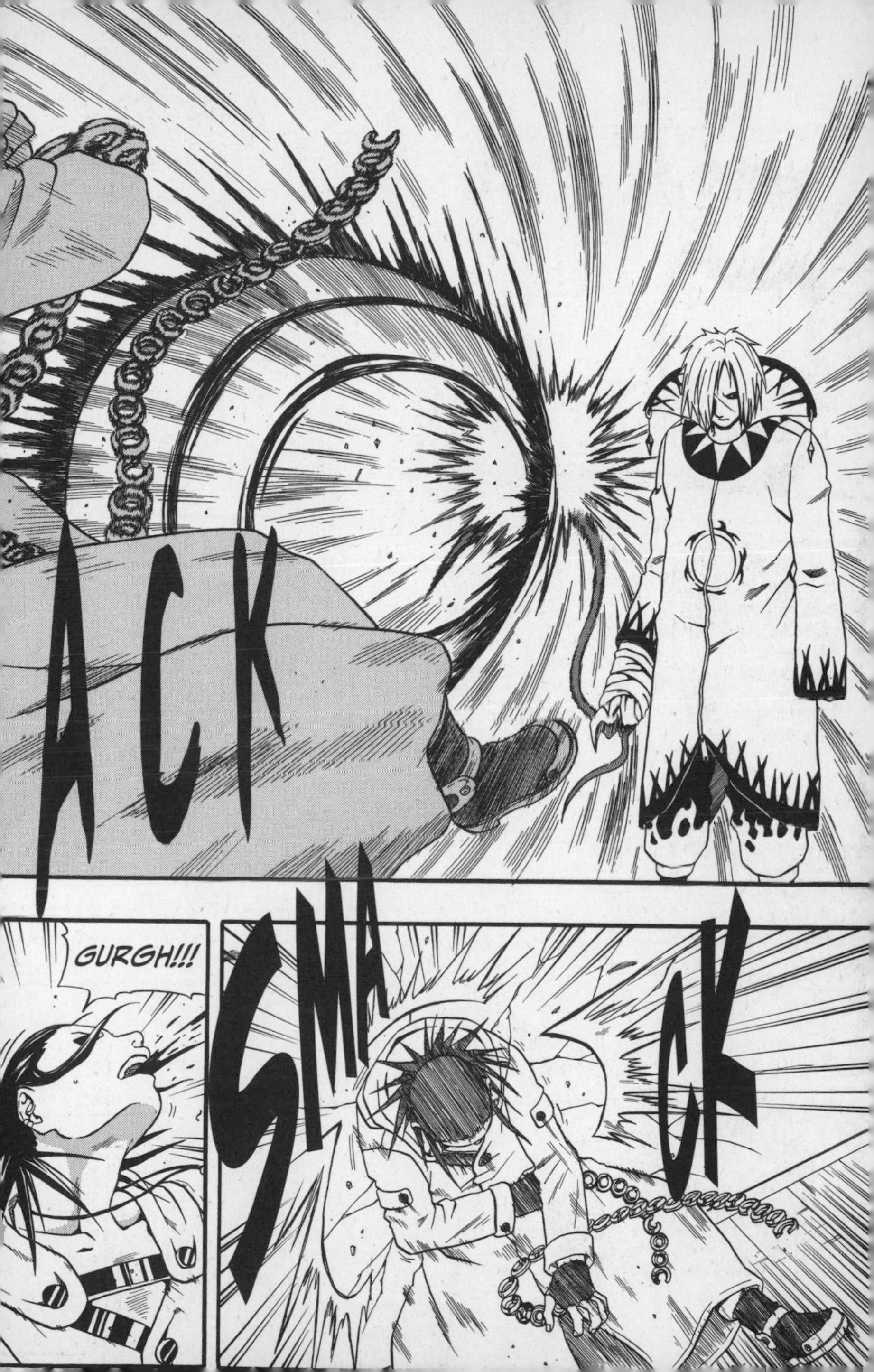
ACK
SMACK
GURGH!!!

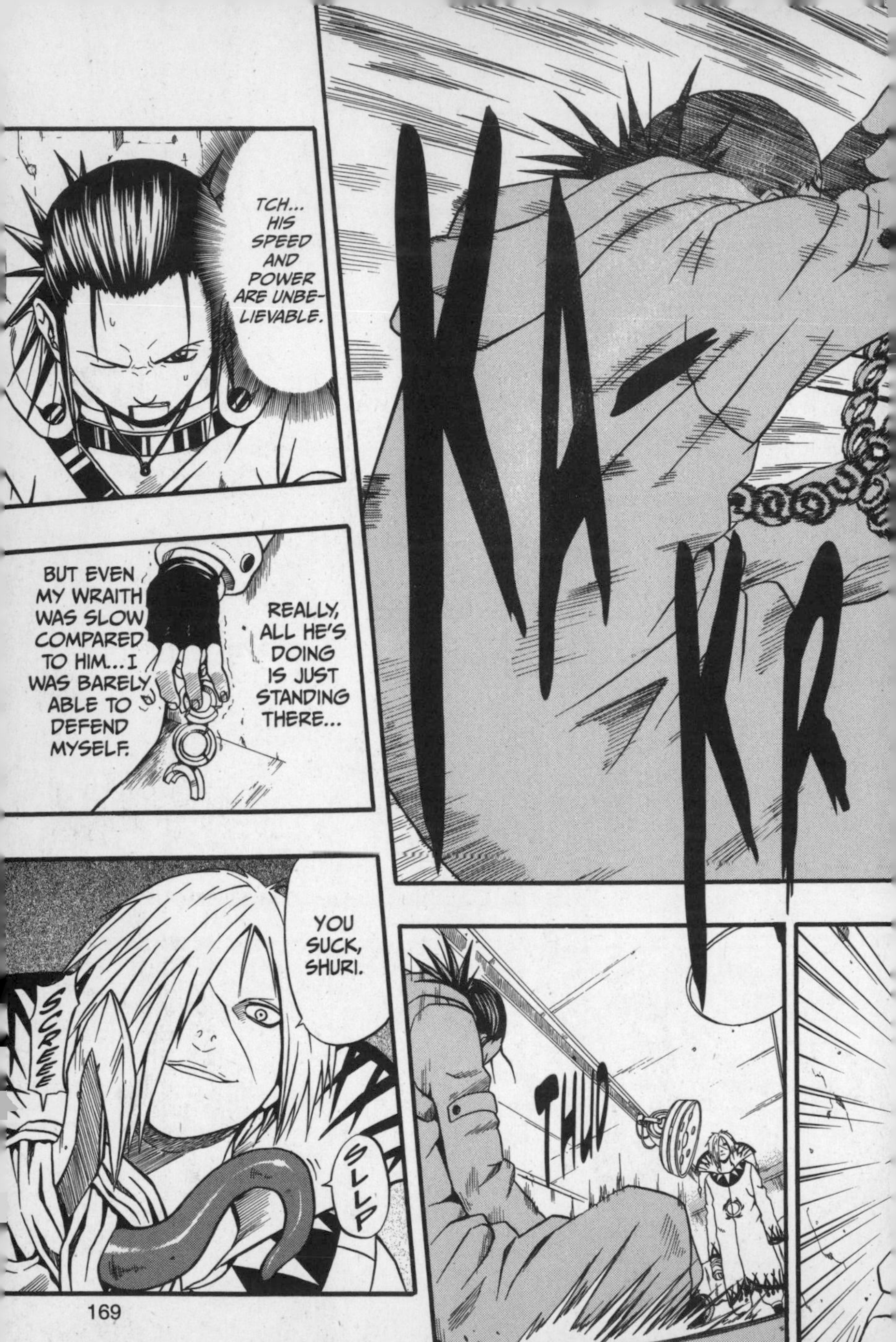
KA-KR
TCH... HIS SPEED AND POWER ARE UNBE-LIEVABLE.
REALLY, ALL HE'S DOING IS JUST STANDING THERE...
BUT EVEN MY WRAITH WAS SLOW COMPARED TO HIM...I WAS BARELY ABLE TO DEFEND MYSELF.
THUD
YOU SUCK, SHURI.
SLLP
SCREEE

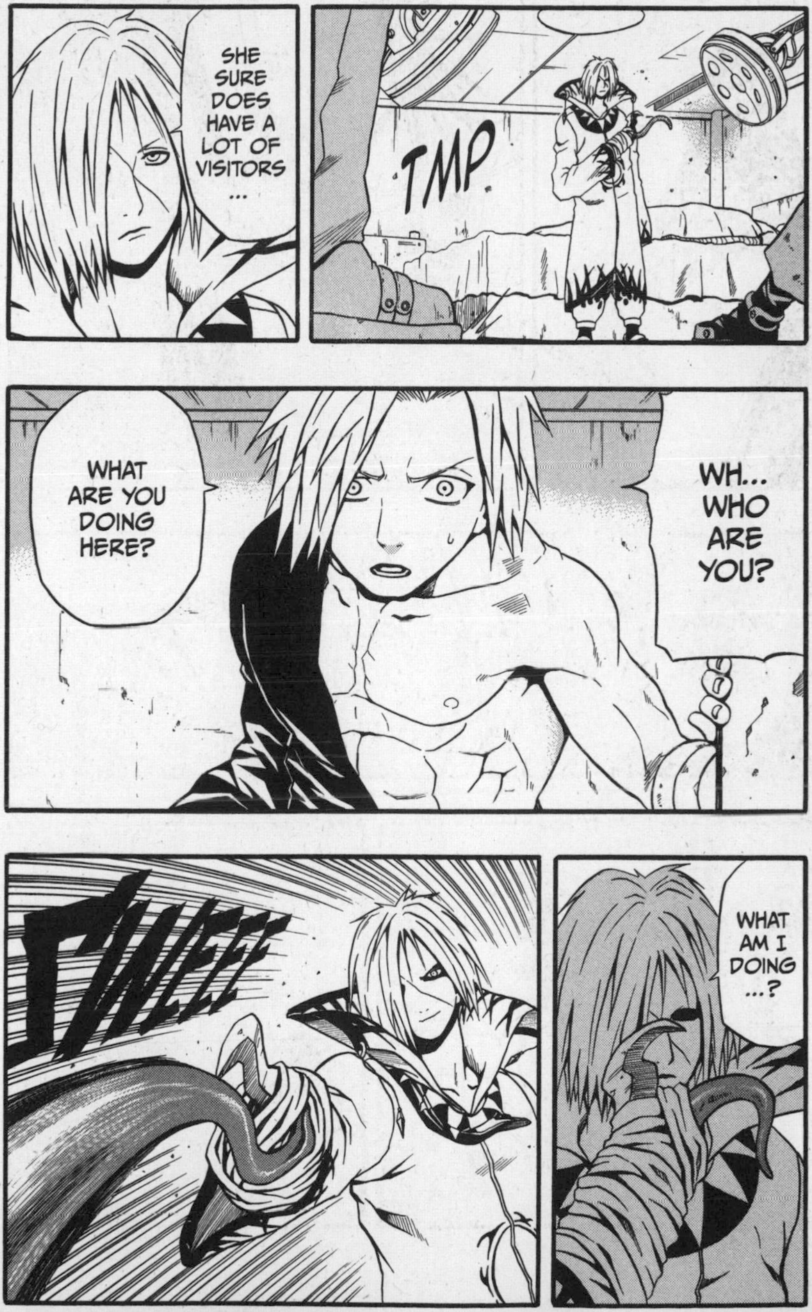
TMP
SHE SURE DOES HAVE A LOT OF VISITORS ...
WH... WHO ARE YOU?
WHAT ARE YOU DOING HERE?
WHAT AM I DOING ...?

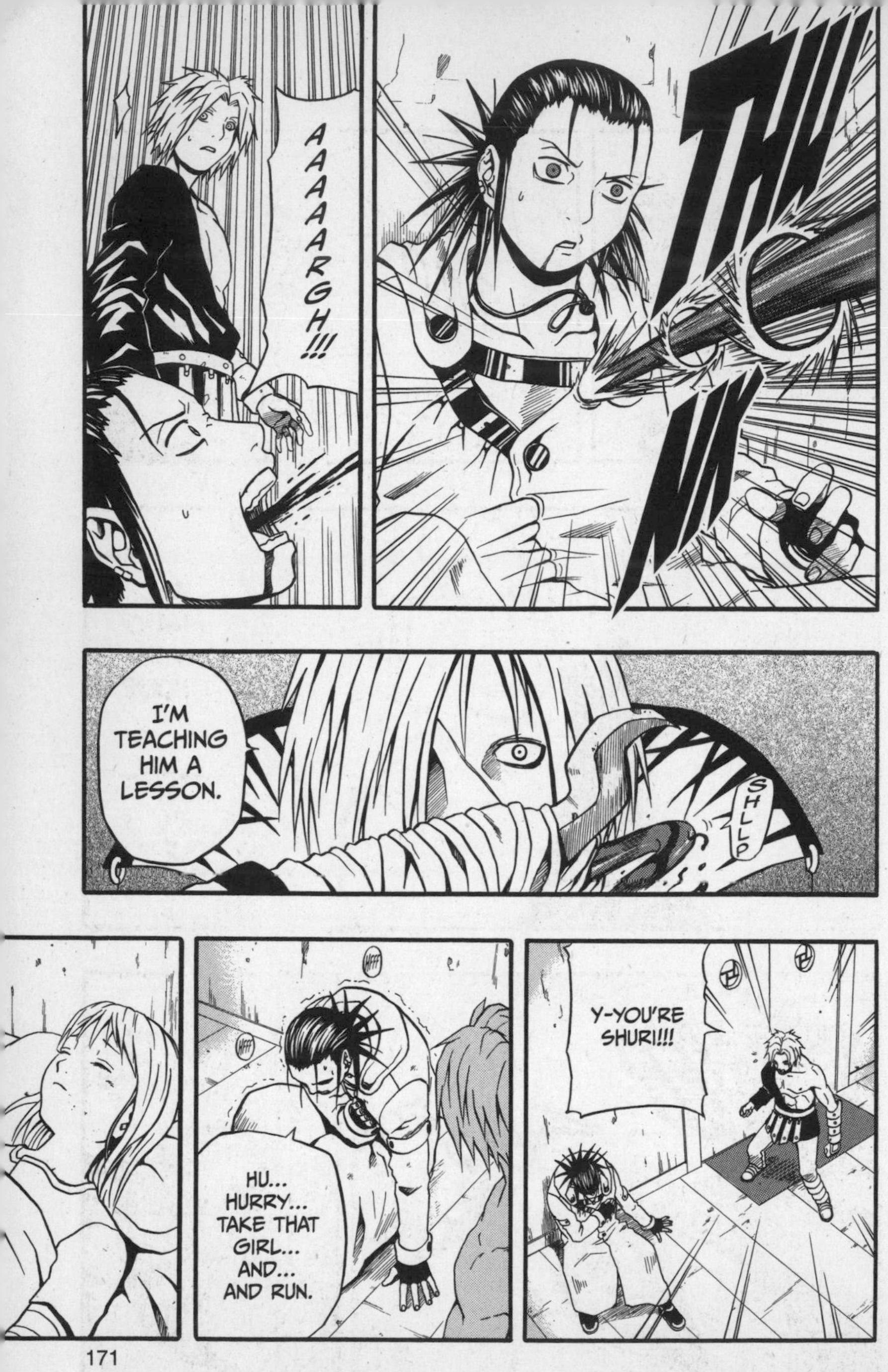
AAAAAARGH!!!
I'M TEACHING HIM A LESSON.
SHLLP
Y-YOU'RE SHURI!!!
HU... HURRY... TAKE THAT GIRL... AND... AND RUN.

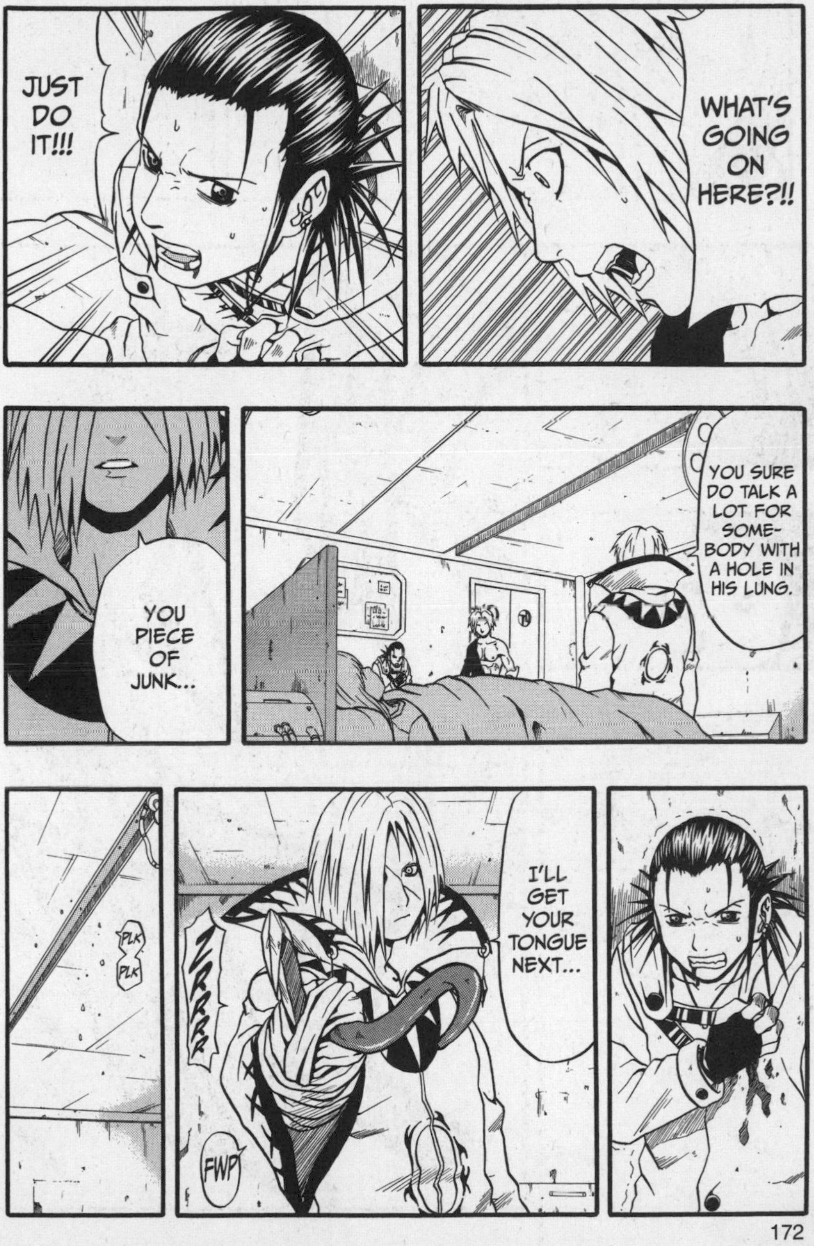
WHAT'S GOING ON HERE?!!
JUST DO IT!!!
YOU SURE DO TALK A LOT FOR SOME-BODY WITH A HOLE IN HIS LUNG.
YOU PIECE OF JUNK...
I'LL GET YOUR TONGUE NEXT...
ZRRRR
FWP
PLK
PLK

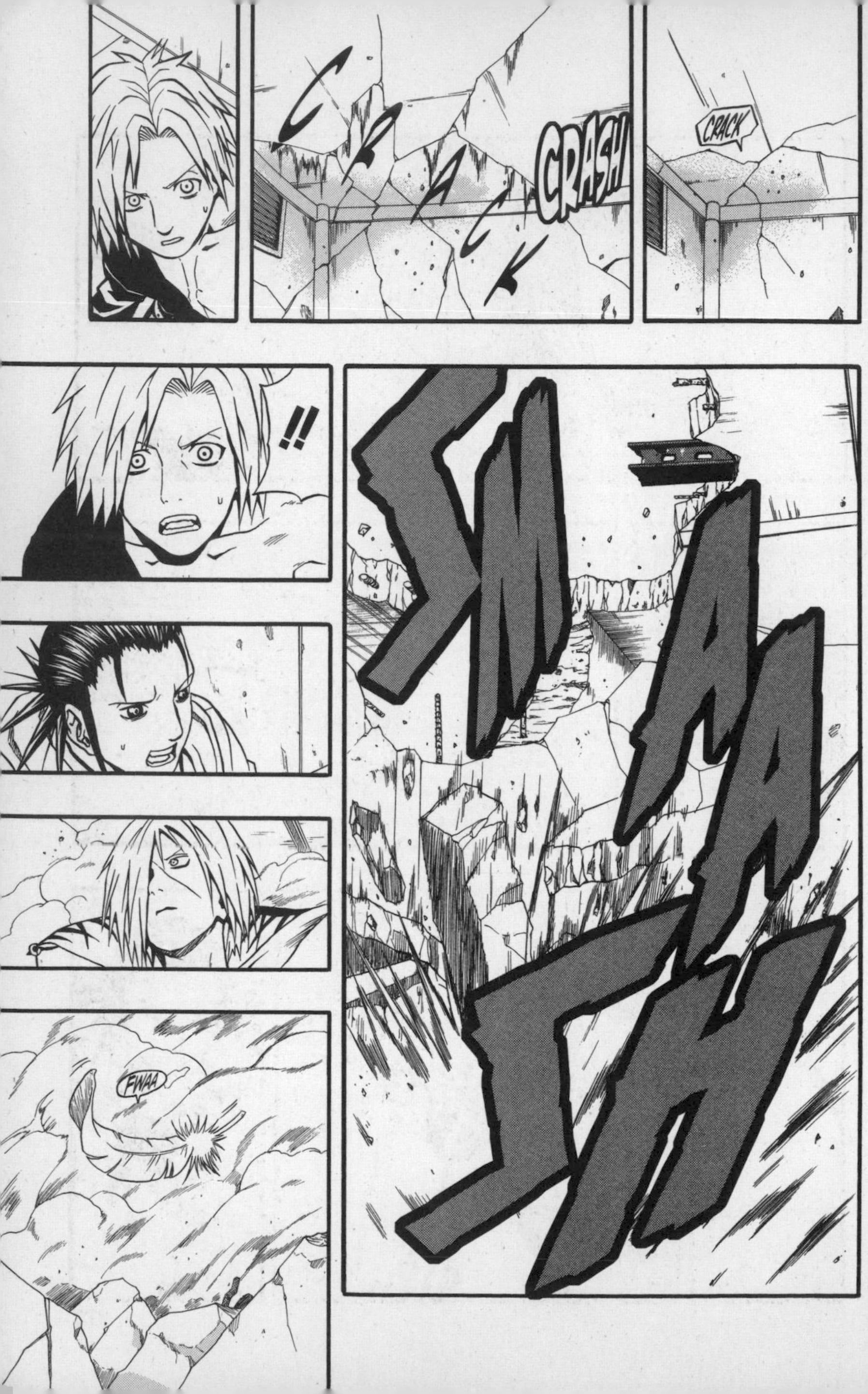
CRACK
CRACK
CRASH
SMAAASH
!!
FWAA

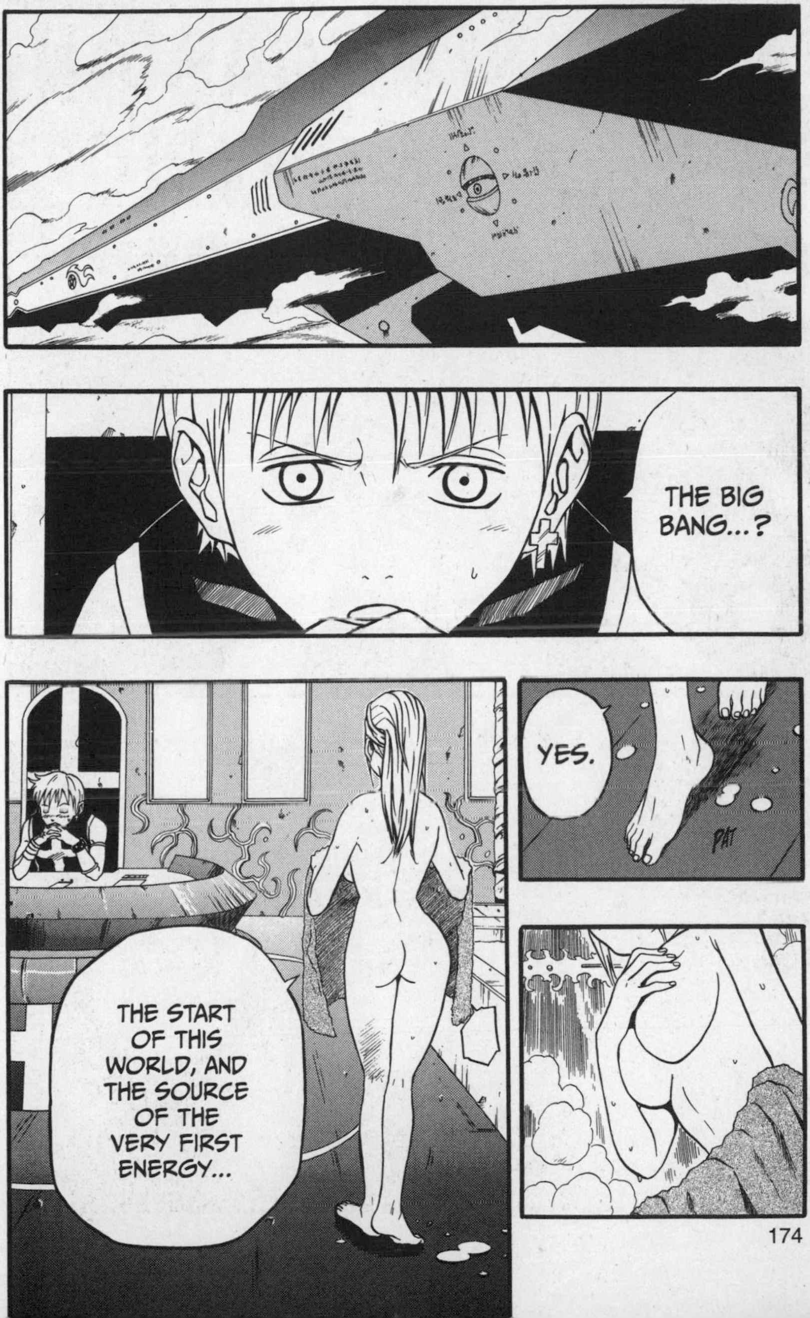
THE BIG BANG...?
YES.
PAT
THE START OF THIS WORLD, AND THE SOURCE OF THE VERY FIRST ENERGY...

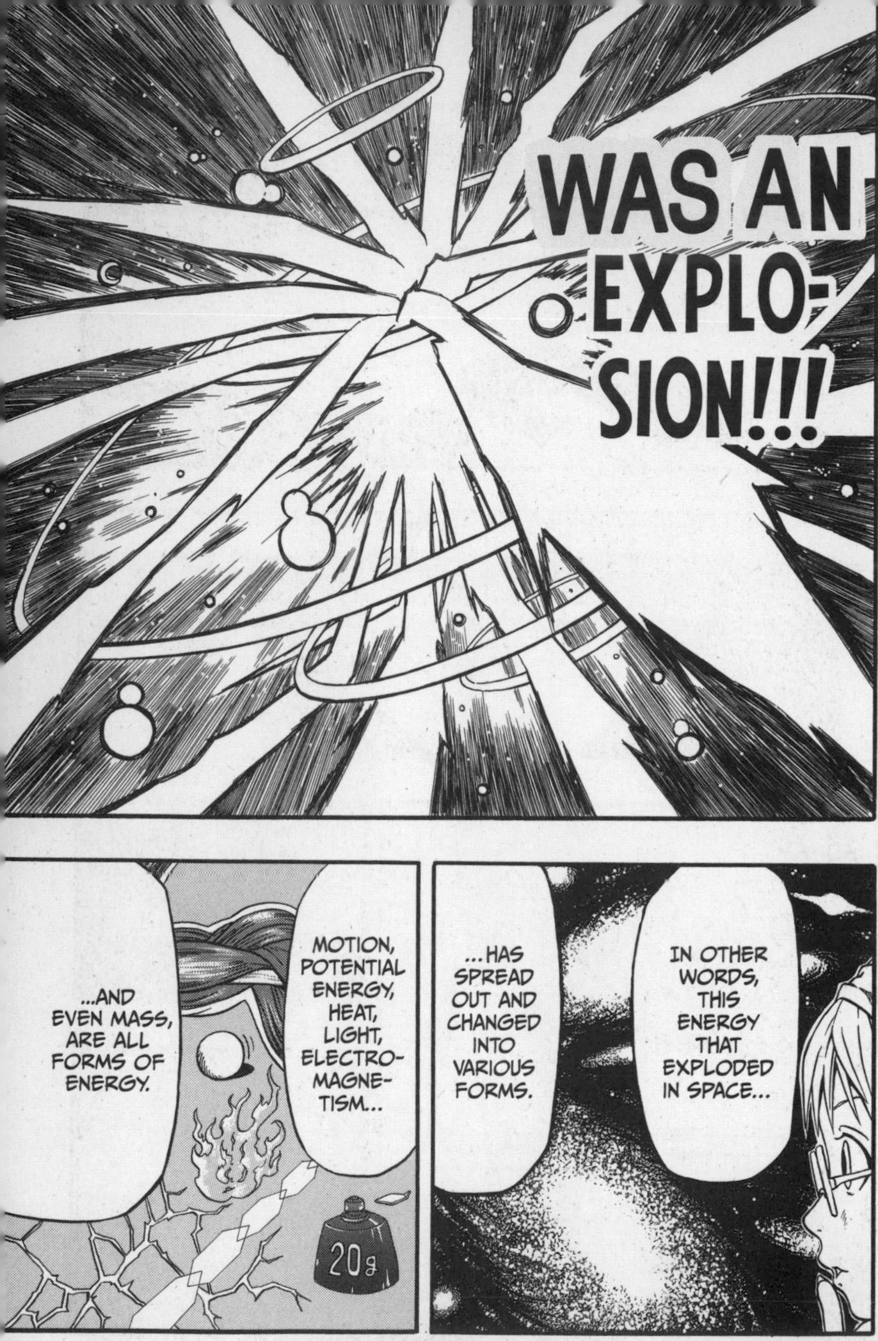
WAS AN EXPLO-SION!!!
IN OTHER WORDS, THIS ENERGY THAT EXPLODED IN SPACE...
...HAS SPREAD OUT AND CHANGED INTO VARIOUS FORMS.
MOTION, POTENTIAL ENERGY, HEAT, LIGHT, ELECTRO-MAGNE-TISM...
...AND EVEN MASS, ARE ALL FORMS OF ENERGY.
20g

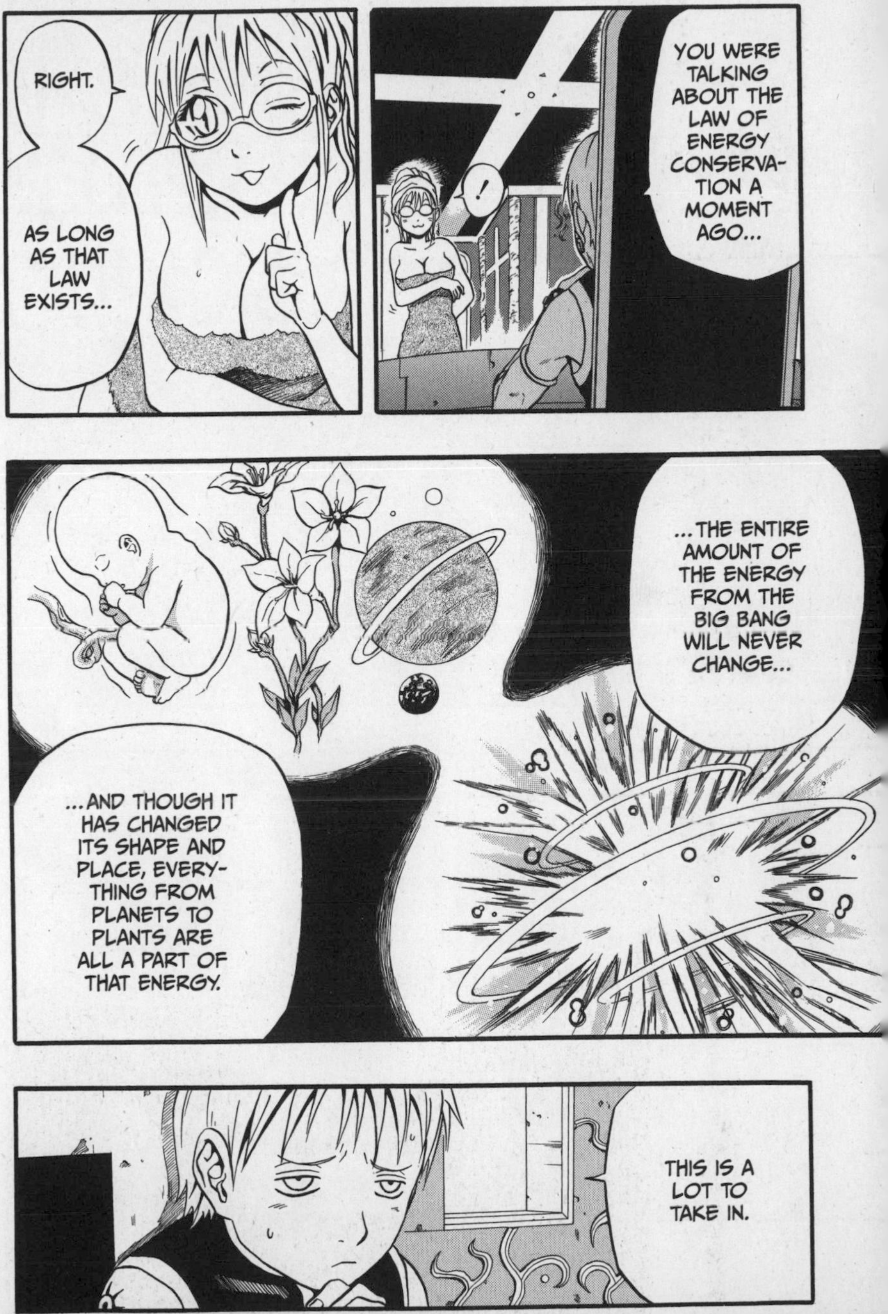
YOU WERE TALKING ABOUT THE LAW OF ENERGY CONSERVATION A MOMENT AGO...
!
RIGHT.
AS LONG AS THAT LAW EXISTS...
...THE ENTIRE AMOUNT OF THE ENERGY FROM THE BIG BANG WILL NEVER CHANGE...
...AND THOUGH IT HAS CHANGED ITS SHAPE AND PLACE, EVERYTHING FROM PLANETS TO PLANTS ARE ALL A PART OF THAT ENERGY.
THIS IS A LOT TO TAKE IN.

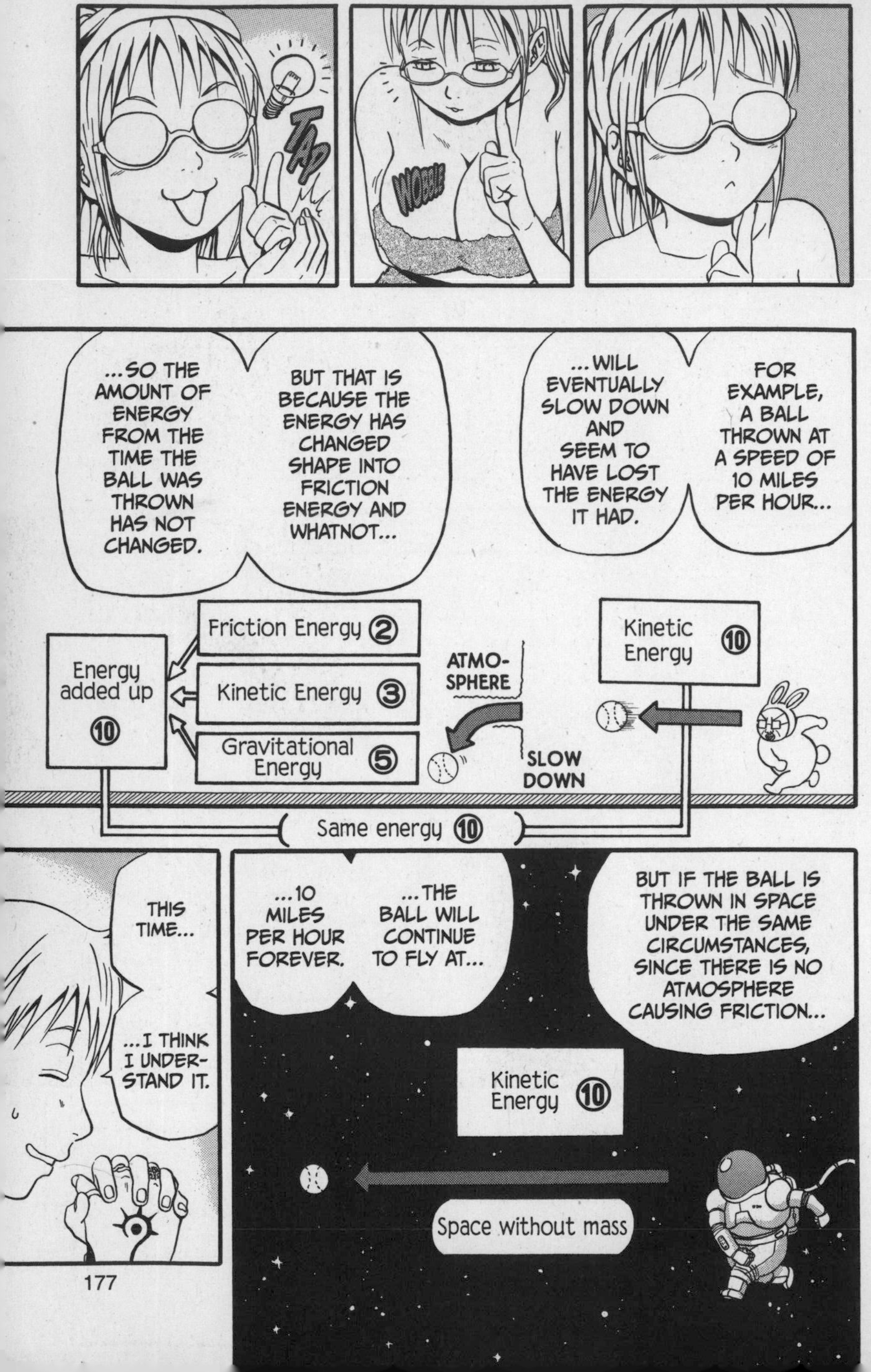
WOBBLE
TAP
FOR EXAMPLE, A BALL THROWN AT A SPEED OF 10 MILES PER HOUR...
...WILL EVENTUALLY SLOW DOWN AND SEEM TO HAVE LOST THE ENERGY IT HAD.
BUT THAT IS BECAUSE THE ENERGY HAS CHANGED SHAPE INTO FRICTION ENERGY AND WHATNOT...
...SO THE AMOUNT OF ENERGY FROM THE TIME THE BALL WAS THROWN HAS NOT CHANGED.
Kinetic Energy 10
ATMO-SPHERE
SLOW DOWN
Friction Energy 2
Kinetic Energy 3
Gravitational Energy 5
Energy added up 10
Same energy 10
BUT IF THE BALL IS THROWN IN SPACE UNDER THE SAME CIRCUMSTANCES, SINCE THERE IS NO ATMOSPHERE CAUSING FRICTION...
...THE BALL WILL CONTINUE TO FLY AT...
...10 MILES PER HOUR FOREVER.
Kinetic Energy 10
Space without mass
THIS TIME...
...I THINK I UNDER-STAND IT.

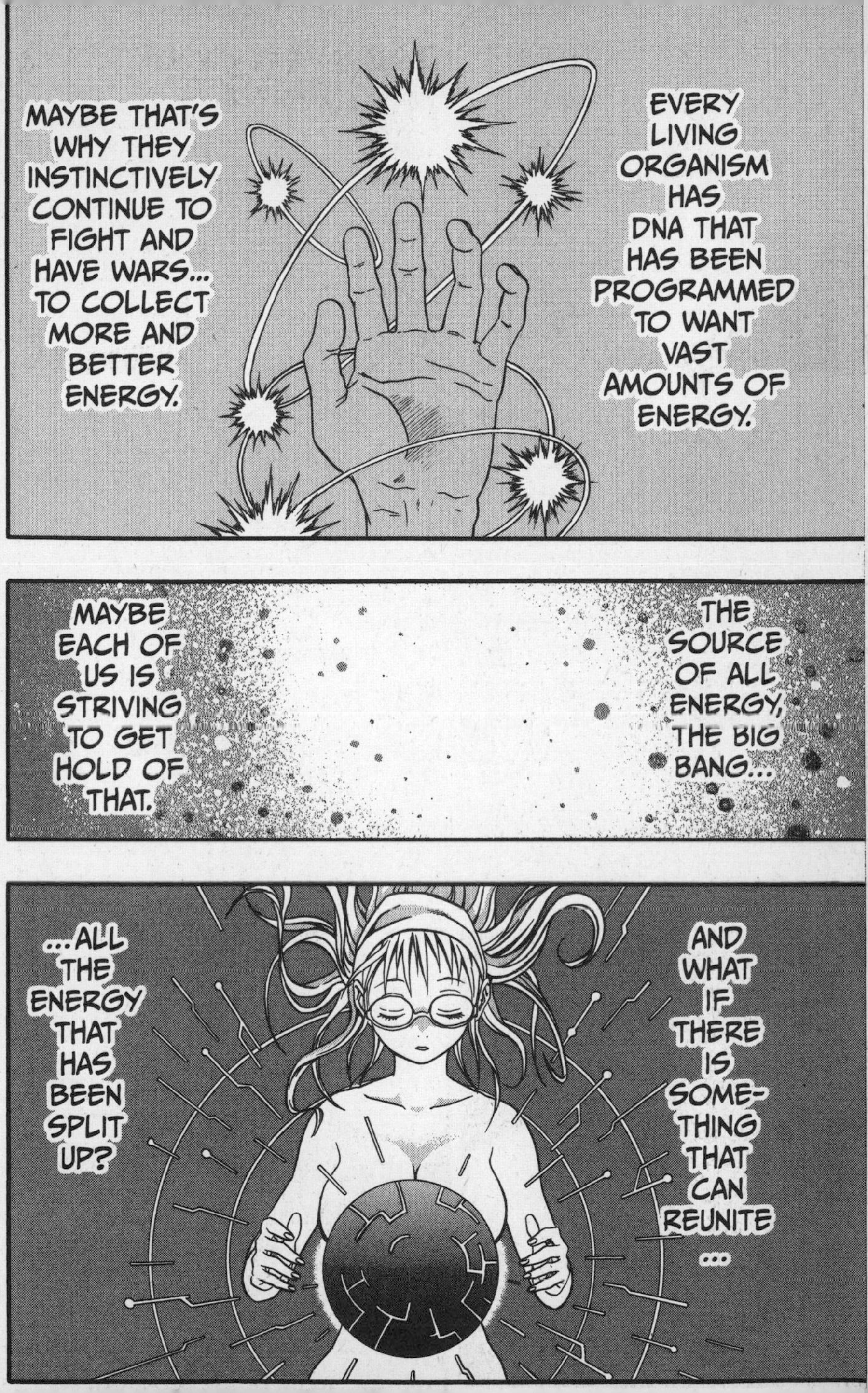
EVERY LIVING ORGANISM HAS DNA THAT HAS BEEN PROGRAMMED TO WANT VAST AMOUNTS OF ENERGY.
MAYBE THAT'S WHY THEY INSTINCTIVELY CONTINUE TO FIGHT AND HAVE WARS... TO COLLECT MORE AND BETTER ENERGY.
THE SOURCE OF ALL ENERGY, THE BIG BANG...
MAYBE EACH OF US IS STRIVING TO GET HOLD OF THAT.
AND WHAT IF THERE IS SOME-THING THAT CAN REUNITE...
...ALL THE ENERGY THAT HAS BEEN SPLIT UP?

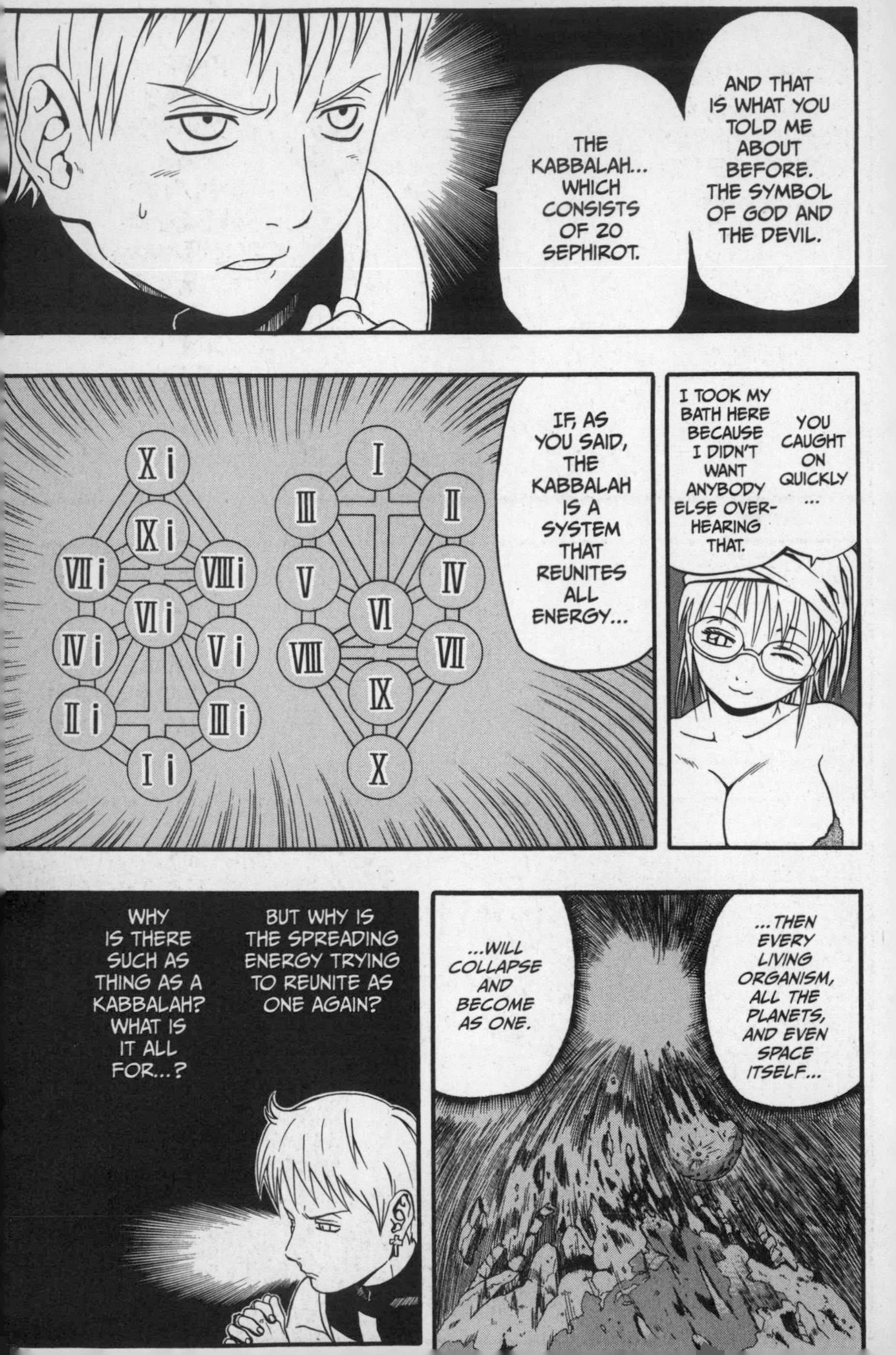
AND THAT IS WHAT YOU TOLD ME ABOUT BEFORE. THE SYMBOL OF GOD AND THE DEVIL.
THE KABBALAH... WHICH CONSISTS OF 20 SEPHIROT.
YOU CAUGHT ON QUICKLY ...
I TOOK MY BATH HERE BECAUSE I DIDN'T WANT ANYBODY ELSE OVER-HEARING THAT.
IF, AS YOU SAID, THE KABBALAH IS A SYSTEM THAT REUNITES ALL ENERGY...
...THEN EVERY LIVING ORGANISM, ALL THE PLANETS, AND EVEN SPACE ITSELF...
...WILL COLLAPSE AND BECOME AS ONE.
BUT WHY IS THE SPREADING ENERGY TRYING TO REUNITE AS ONE AGAIN?
WHY IS THERE SUCH AS THING AS A KABBALAH? WHAT IS IT ALL FOR...?

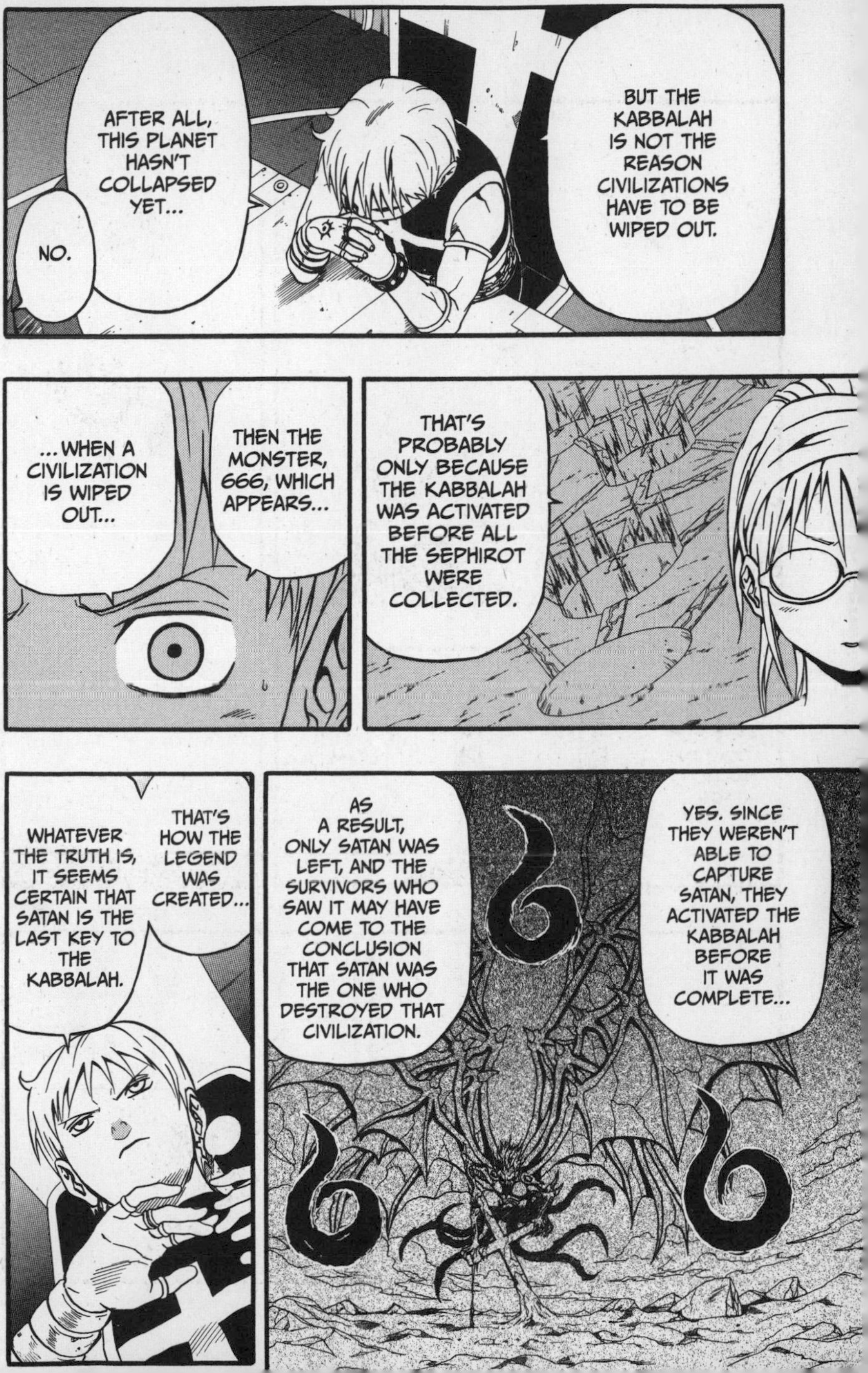
BUT THE KABBALAH IS NOT THE REASON CIVILIZATIONS HAVE TO BE WIPED OUT.
AFTER ALL, THIS PLANET HASN'T COLLAPSED YET...
NO.
THAT'S PROBABLY ONLY BECAUSE THE KABBALAH WAS ACTIVATED BEFORE ALL THE SEPHIROT WERE COLLECTED.
THEN THE MONSTER, 666, WHICH APPEARS...
...WHEN A CIVILIZATION IS WIPED OUT...
YES. SINCE THEY WEREN'T ABLE TO CAPTURE SATAN, THEY ACTIVATED THE KABBALAH BEFORE IT WAS COMPLETE...
AS A RESULT, ONLY SATAN WAS LEFT, AND THE SURVIVORS WHO SAW IT MAY HAVE COME TO THE CONCLUSION THAT SATAN WAS THE ONE WHO DESTROYED THAT CIVILIZATION.
THAT'S HOW THE LEGEND WAS CREATED...
WHATEVER THE TRUTH IS, IT SEEMS CERTAIN THAT SATAN IS THE LAST KEY TO THE KABBALAH.

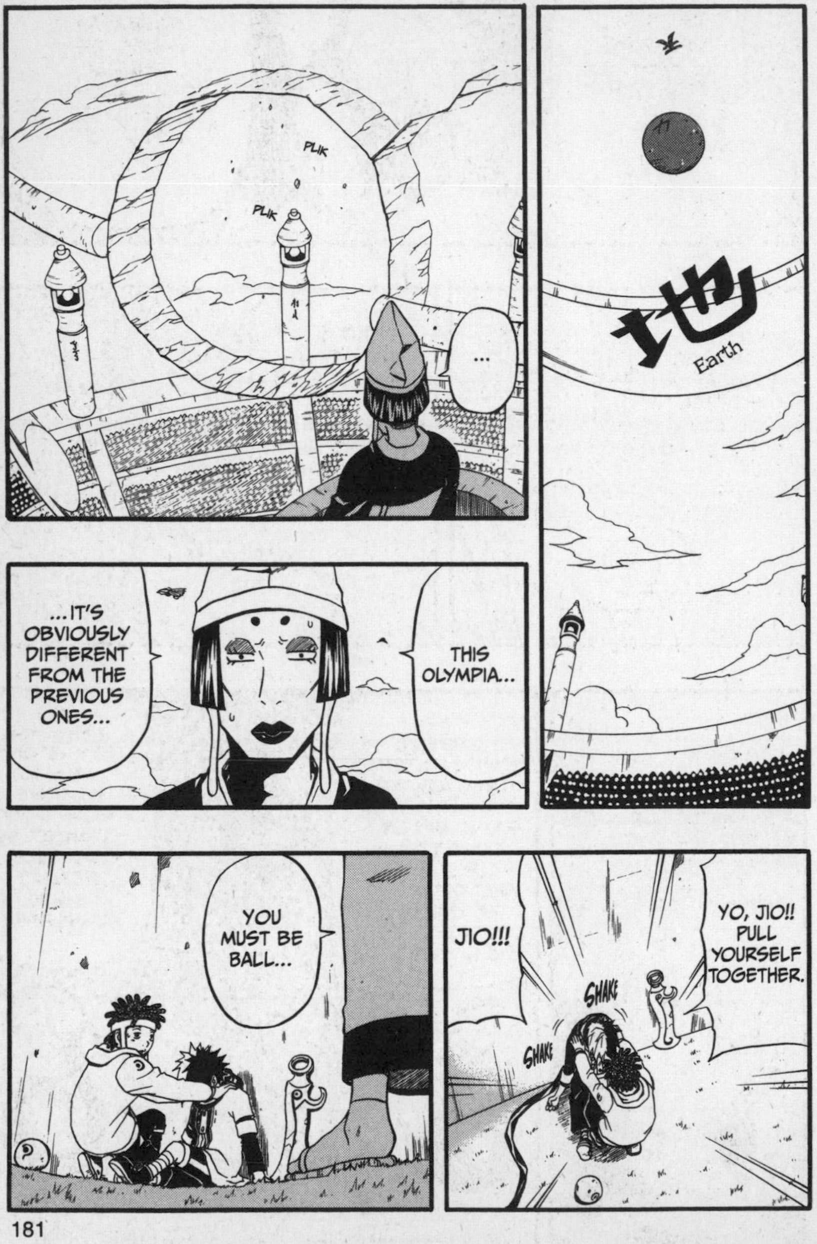
地
Earth
PLIK
PLIK
...
THIS OLYMPIA...
...IT'S OBVIOUSLY DIFFERENT FROM THE PREVIOUS ONES...
YO, JIO!! PULL YOURSELF TOGETHER.
SHAKE
SHAKE
JIO!!!
YOU MUST BE BALL...

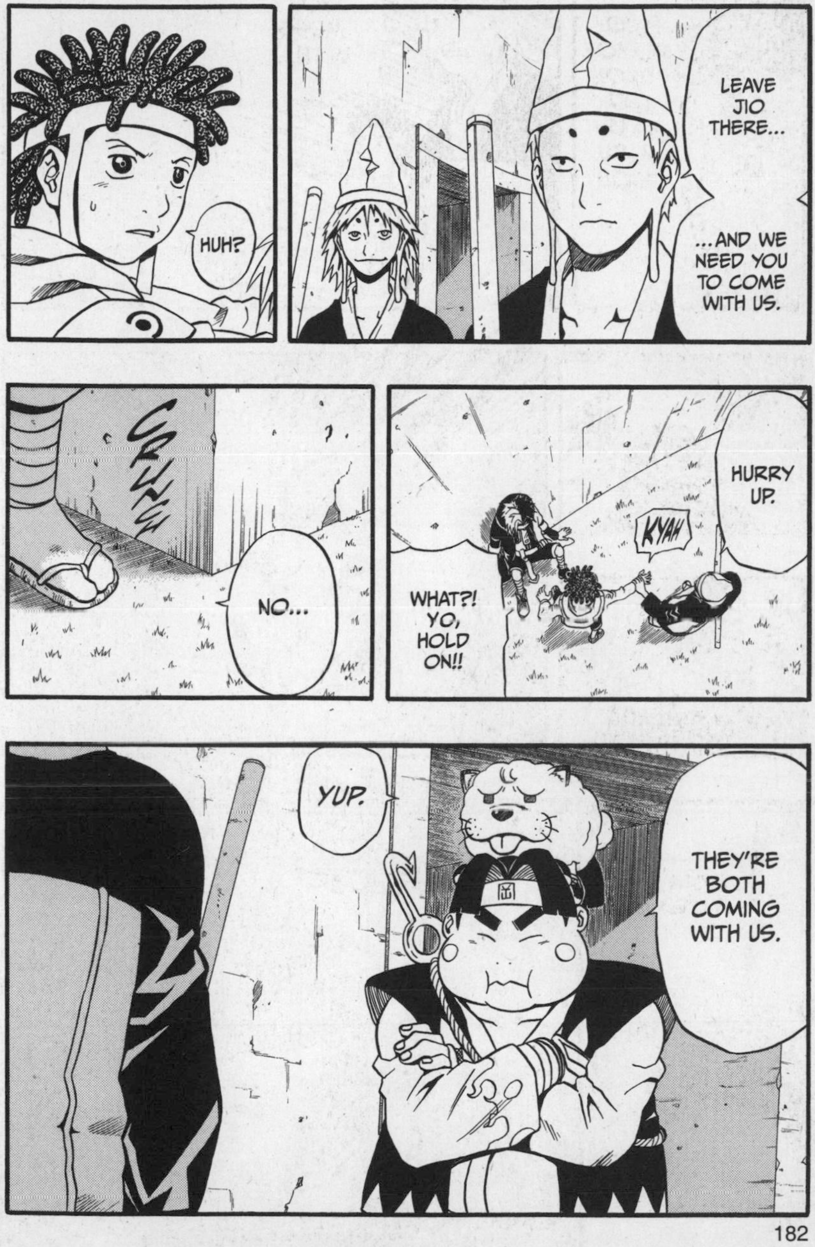
LEAVE JIO THERE...
...AND WE NEED YOU TO COME WITH US.
HUH?
HURRY UP.
KYAH
WHAT?! YO, HOLD ON!!
NO...
THEY'RE BOTH COMING WITH US.
YUP.

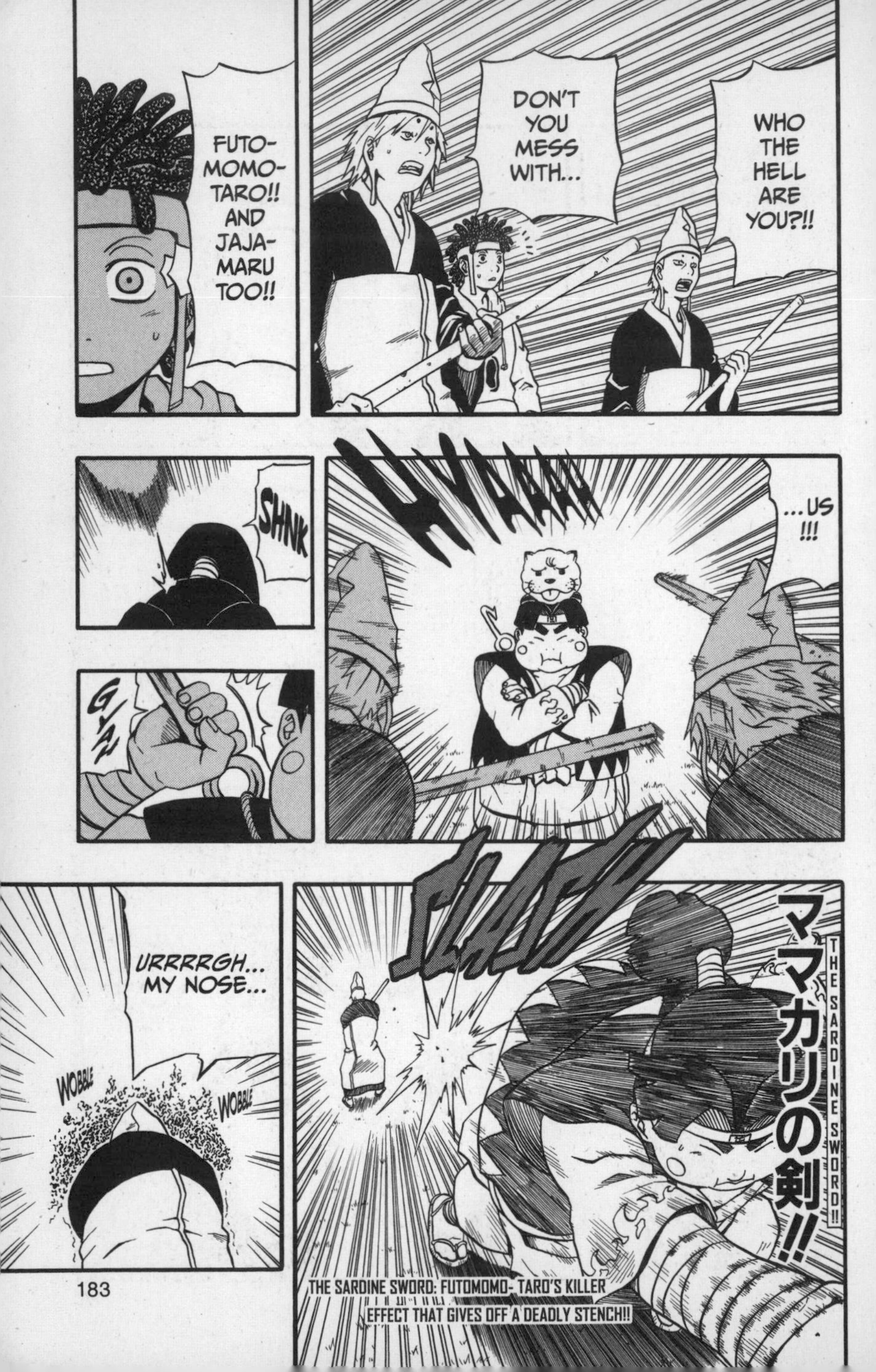
WHO THE HELL ARE YOU?!!
DON'T YOU MESS WITH...
FUTO-MOMO-TARO!! AND JAJA-MARU TOO!!
...US !!!
HYAAAH
SHNK
GYAN
SLASH
ママカリの剣!!
THE SARDINE SWORD!!
THE SARDINE SWORD: FUTOMOMO-TARO'S KILLER EFFECT THAT GIVES OFF A DEADLY STENCH!!
URRRRGH... MY NOSE...
WOBBLE
WOBBLE

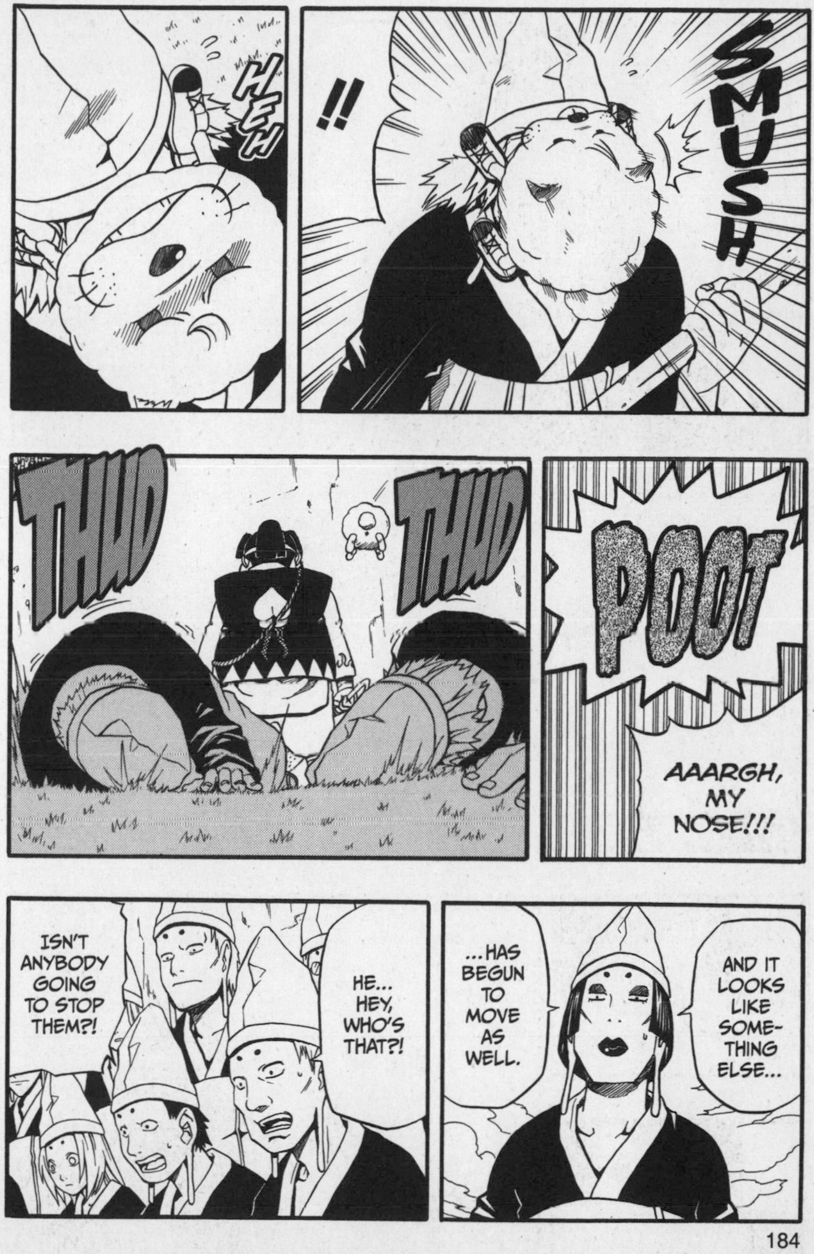
!!
SMUSH
HEH
POOT
AAARGH, MY NOSE!!!
THUD
THUD
AND IT LOOKS LIKE SOMETHING ELSE...
...HAS BEGUN TO MOVE AS WELL.
HE... HEY, WHO'S THAT?!
ISN'T ANYBODY GOING TO STOP THEM?!

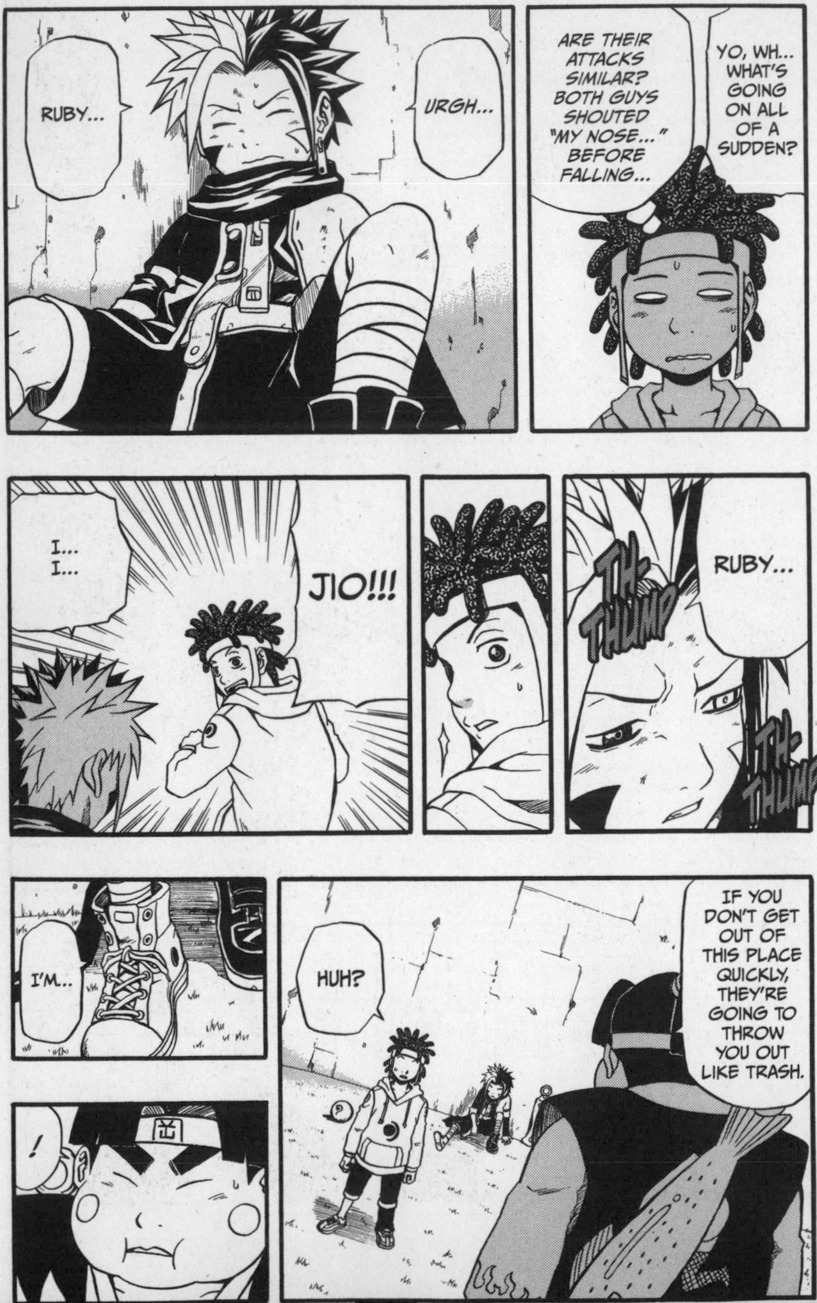
YO, WH... WHAT'S GOING ON ALL OF A SUDDEN?
ARE THEIR ATTACKS SIMILAR? BOTH GUYS SHOUTED "MY NOSE..." BEFORE FALLING...
URGH...
RUBY...
RUBY...
TH-THUMP
TH-THUMP
JIO!!!
I... I...
IF YOU DON'T GET OUT OF THIS PLACE QUICKLY, THEY'RE GOING TO THROW YOU OUT LIKE TRASH.
HUH?
I'M...
!

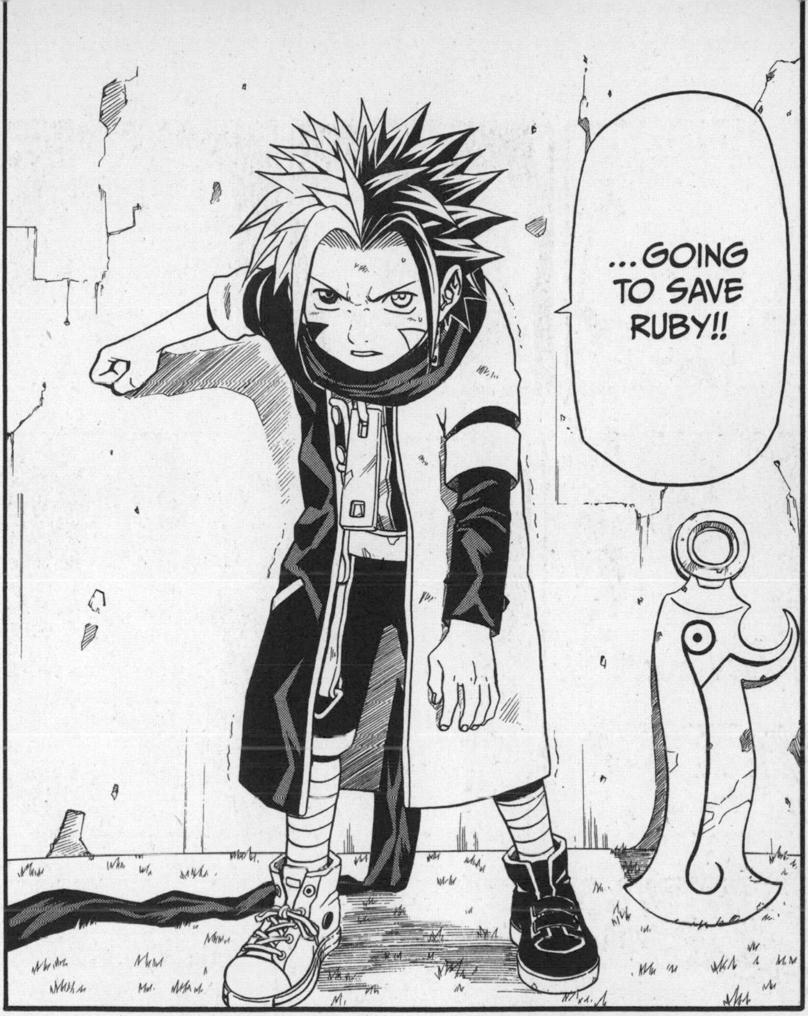
...GOING TO SAVE RUBY!!

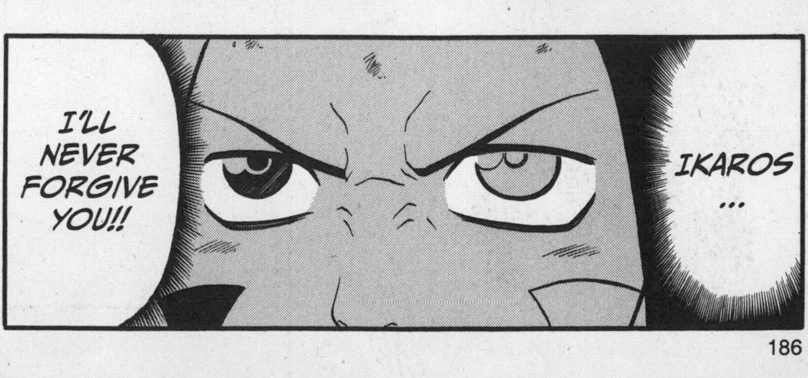
IKAROS ...
I'LL NEVER FORGIVE YOU!!

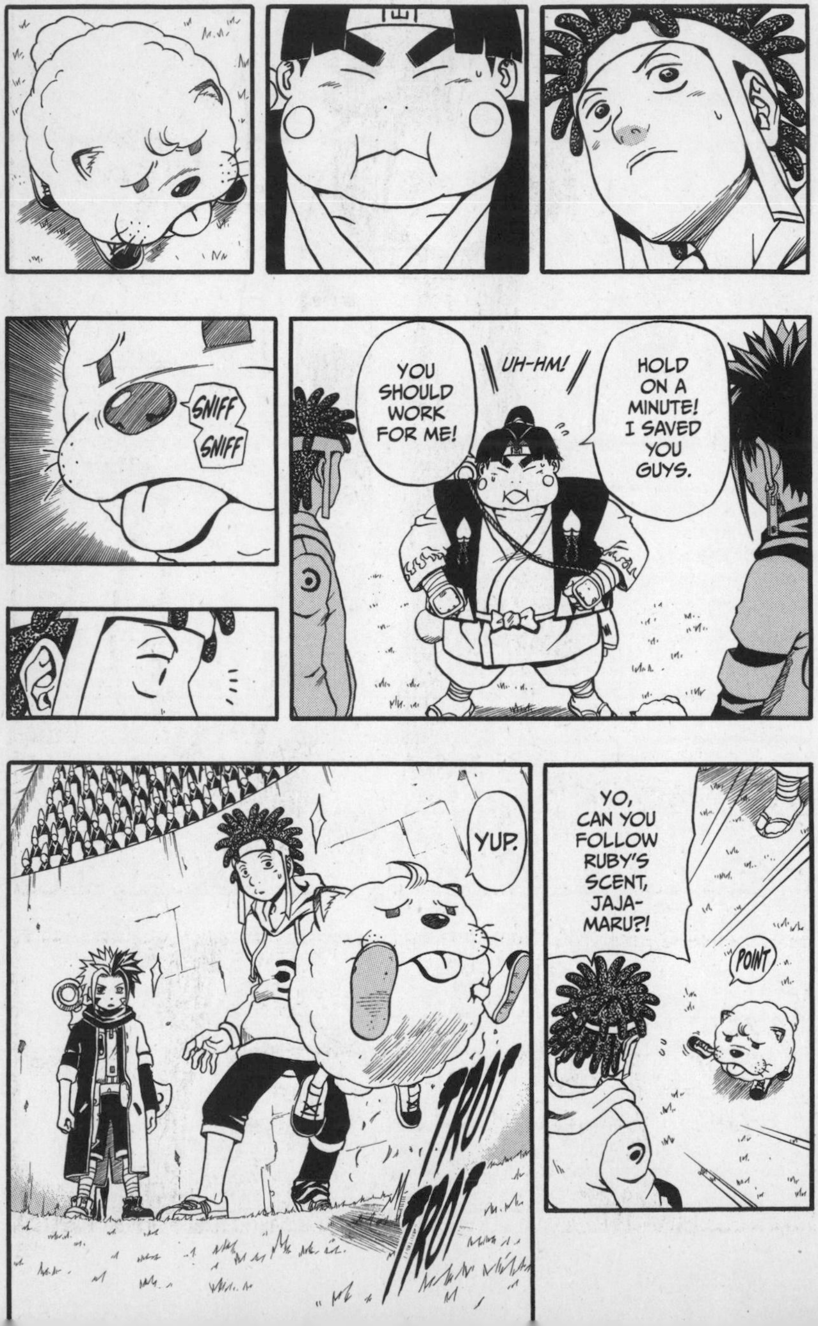
HOLD ON A MINUTE! I SAVED YOU GUYS.
UH-HM!
YOU SHOULD WORK FOR ME!
SNIFF
SNIFF
YO, CAN YOU FOLLOW RUBY'S SCENT, JAJA-MARU?!
POINT
YUP.
TROT
TROT

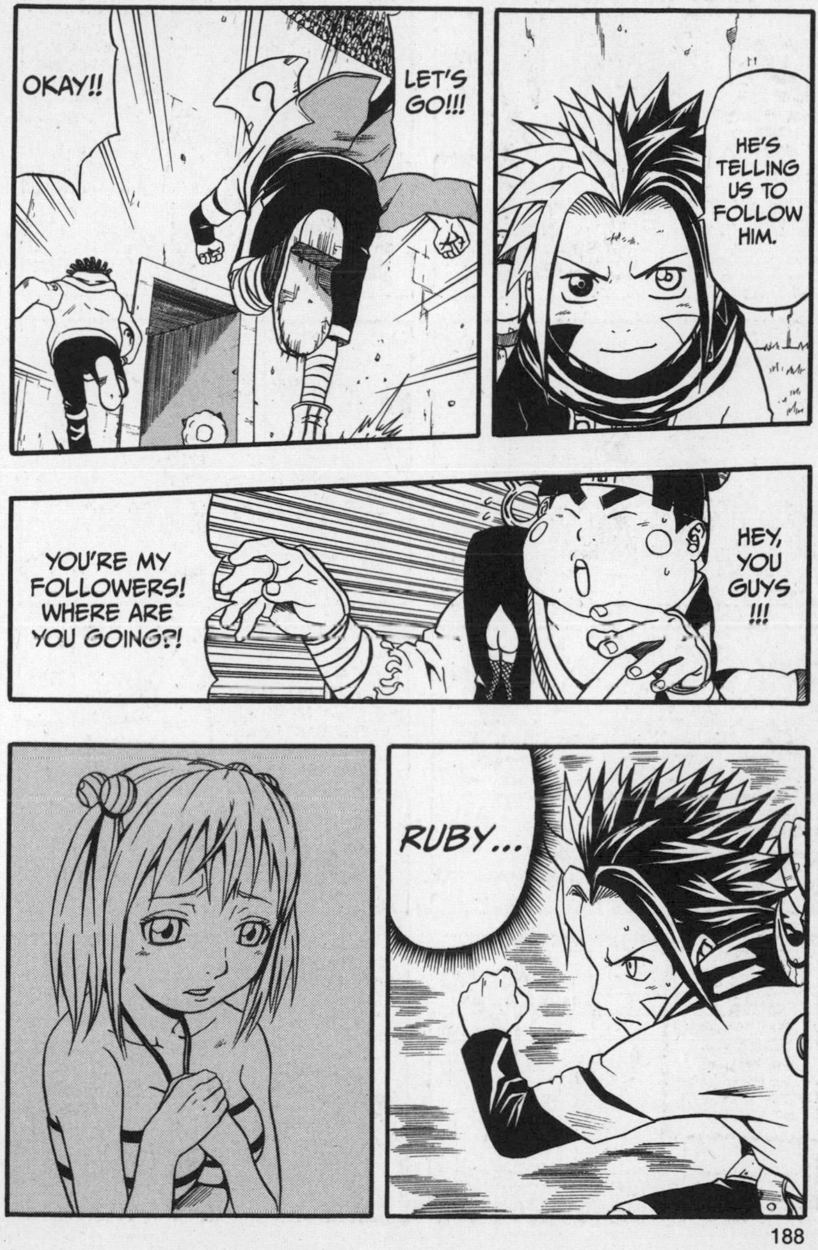
HE'S TELLING US TO FOLLOW HIM.
LET'S GO!!!
OKAY!!
HEY, YOU GUYS !!!
YOU'RE MY FOLLOWERS! WHERE ARE YOU GOING?!
RUBY...

SEISHI, HIS FAMILY, AND SHOPPING

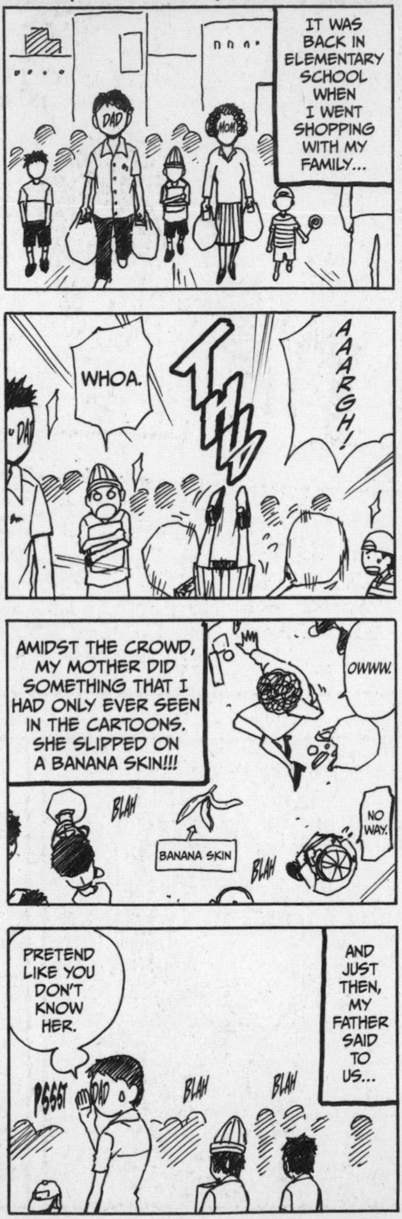
IT WAS BACK IN ELEMENTARY SCHOOL WHEN I WENT SHOPPING WITH MY FAMILY...
DAD
MOM
AAAARGH!
WHOA.
DAD
AMIDST THE CROWD, MY MOTHER DID SOMETHING THAT I HAD ONLY EVER SEEN IN THE CARTOONS. SHE SLIPPED ON A BANANA SKIN!!!
OWWW.
NO WAY.
BLAH
BANANA SKIN
BLAH
AND JUST THEN, MY FATHER SAID TO US...
PRETEND LIKE YOU DON'T KNOW HER.
BLAH
BLAH
PSSST
DAD

SEISHI AND THE TOILET

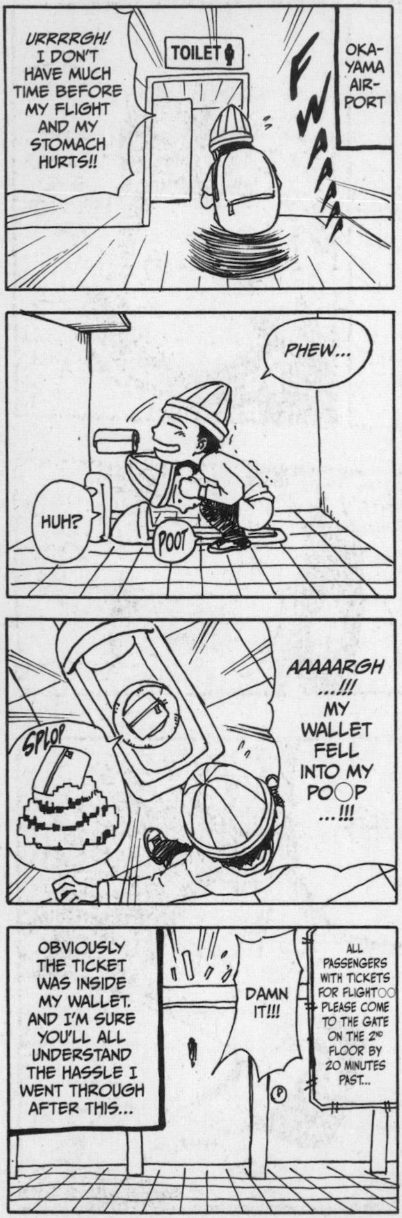
OKA-YAMA AIR-PORT
TOILET
URRRRGH! I DON'T HAVE MUCH TIME BEFORE MY FLIGHT AND MY STOMACH HURTS!!
PHEW...
HUH?
POOT
AAAAARGH ...!!! MY WALLET FELL INTO MY PO◯P ...!!!
SPLOP
ALL PASSENGERS WITH TICKETS FOR FLIGHT◯◯ PLEASE COME TO THE GATE ON THE 2ND FLOOR BY 20 MINUTES PAST...
DAMN IT!!!
OBVIOUSLY THE TICKET WAS INSIDE MY WALLET. AND I'M SURE YOU'LL ALL UNDERSTAND THE HASSLE I WENT THROUGH AFTER THIS...

O-Parts CATALOGUE⑪

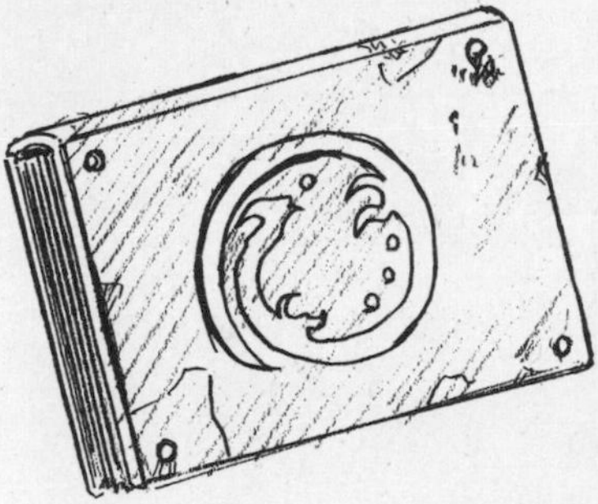

O-PART: THE MAGIC BOOK
O-PART RANK: B
O-PART EFFECT: MATERIALIZATION
THE O-PART OF THE WINNER OF THE LAST OLYMPIA, MARS. THIS BOOK USES A SPECIAL EQUATION TO ANALYZE THE THINGS DRAWN INSIDE IT, AND WILL THE MATERIALIZE THAT OBJECT. A REALLY IMPRESSIVE O-PART.

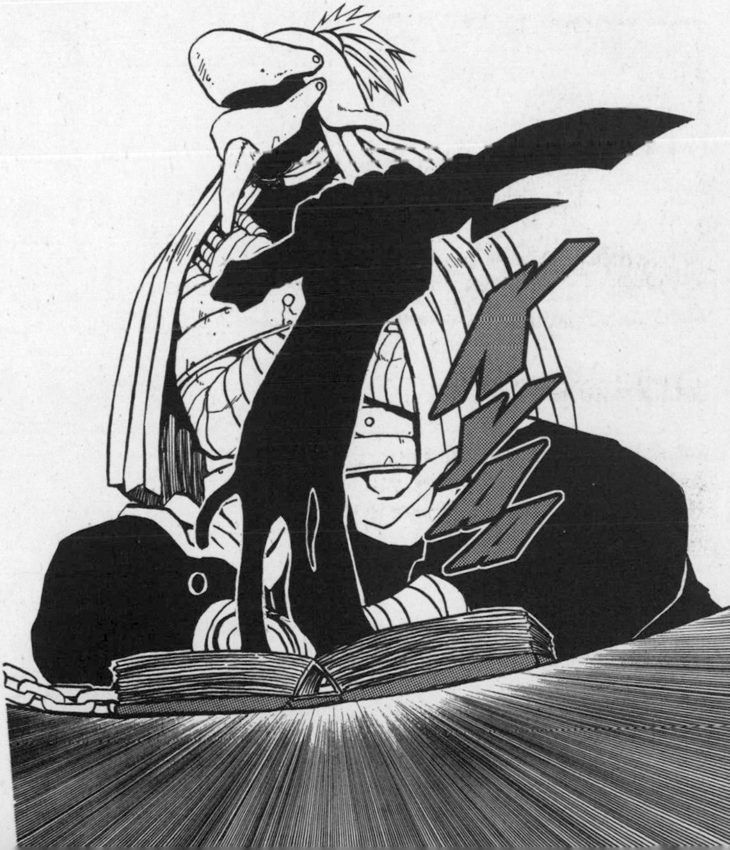

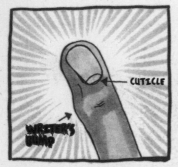

CUTICLE

WRITER'S BUMP

SEISHI KISHIMOTO

I don't know if it's because I use too much pressure when I draw, but the nail on my right middle finger is beginning to change shape...

Wh-what should I do...?

VIZ Media Edition
STORY AND ART BY SEISHI KISHIMOTO

English Adaptation/David R. Valois
Translation/Tetsuichiro Miyaki
Touch-up Art & Lettering/Gia Cam Luc
Design/Andrea Rice
Editor/Carol Fox

Editor in Chief, Books/Alvin Lu
Editor in Chief, Magazines/Marc Weidenbaum
VP, Publishing Licensing/Rika Inouye
VP, Sales & Product Marketing/Gonzalo Ferreyra
VP, Creative/Linda Espinosa
Publisher/Hyoe Narita

Printed in the U.S.A.

Published by VIZ Media, LLC
P.O. Box 77010
San Francisco, CA 94107

10 9 8 7 6 5 4 3 2 1
First printing, August 2008

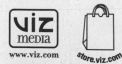

www.viz.com

store.viz.com